BONNIE PRINCE CHARLIE

BONNIE PRINCE CHARLIE

A Biography of Charles Edward Stuart

Susan Maclean Kybett

DODD, MEAD & COMPANY
New York

The picture of Bonnie Prince Charlie on the jacket is reproduced by permission of the Earl of Wemyss and March, K.T., LL.D.

Maps by Christopher R. Smith

Library of Congress Cataloging-in-Publication Data

Kybett, Susan Maclean.
    Bonnie Prince Charlie : a biography of Charles Edward Stuart /
Susan Maclean Kybett.—1st ed.
        p.   cm.
    Bibliography: p.
    Includes index.
    1. Charles Edward, Prince, grandson of James II, King of England,
1720–1788.   2. Great Britain—Princes and princesses—Biography.
3. Jacobite Rebellion, 1745–1746.   4. Scotland—History—18th
century.   I. Title.
DA814.A5K93 1988
941.107'2'0924—dc19
[B]   87-26335
ISBN 0-396-08496-6

*This book is dedicated with love to my mother,
Ann Maclean Jones, of the Isle-of-Lewis in Scotland.*

Contents

viii   *Bonnie Prince Charlie*

Illustrations

x *Bonnie Prince Charlie*

Prince Charles Edward Stuart c. 1785

Charlotte, Duchess of Albany

Henry Stuart, Cardinal York

The author is deeply grateful to

Her Majesty Queen Elizabeth II

for permission to make use of

material from the Stuart Papers.

Acknowledgments

This book would not have progressed very far without the early encouragement and assistance of Dr. Lloyd J. Guth, the subsequent cooperation of the director and staff of the graduate library of the University of Michigan at Ann Arbor, and the Center for Research Libraries in Chicago. To them, I owe much.

I am also grateful to the Earl of Wemyss and March, K.T., LL.D., for sending me photocopies of unpublished pages of the *Journal* written in French by his progenitor, Lord Elcho, who fought alongside Bonnie Prince Charlie. Lord Wemyss was generous enough to provide his own notes to Elcho's manuscript, which helped enormously. Miss Jane Langton, Registrar of the Stuart Papers at Windsor Castle, was unstinting in her support for more than a decade. Mere thanks are not enough for her contributions.

Medical historian, nutritionist, and author Thomas E. Cone, Jr., M.D., is Senior Associate in Clinical Genetics and Medicine at the Children's Hospital Medical Center in Boston, Massachusetts, and is also a member of the medical faculty at Harvard University. He worked tirelessly with me for almost two years while we delved into the many ramifications of nutritional disease as it affected our ancestors. French-born Professor Jean Sareil of New York City's Columbia University, biographer of Cardinal Tencin and author of several books on eighteenth-century France, shared information, dispensed sage advice, and directed me to sources of material in France. I cannot express enough thanks to both gentlemen for their generosity, interest, guidance, and encouragement.

Librarians are always the unsung heroes and heroines of projects of this nature. Without their assistance, we cannot function. Those who assisted me are from the University of Michigan, the Houghton Library at Harvard University, the Library of Congress in Washington, D.C., the British Library, the Public Record Office in London, the Universities of Aberdeen and Edinburgh in Scotland, the Ministère des Affaires Étrangères in Paris, and the Vatican Archives in Rome. There were countless other contributors whose kindness will always be remembered.

My mother, to whom this book is dedicated, was an unfailing source of support, as was my cousin, Mary Broadley-Gomes. My late husband, Harry Kybett, and my children, Elizabeth and Alexander, were very patient and helped enormously. There were also many friends, well wishers, and helpmeets who contributed. They know very well who they are.

Lastly, and by no means as a matter of form, I acknowledge my editor, Cynthia Vartan. Her understanding in the early days of writing, and what I learned from her as the manuscript progressed, will never be forgotten. Cynthia Vartan's thorough professionalism has complemented the efforts of every person who has contributed to this book.

Preface

The late Scottish actor David Niven is the only man ever to have portrayed Bonnie Prince Charlie in a Hollywood-style film production of that name. The company also assembled unsuspecting luminaries such as Jack Hawkins for the role of Lord George Murray and Margaret Leighton for Flora MacDonald. In his popular autobiography, *The Moon's a Balloon*, Niven described how the actors gallantly struggled to infuse some semblance of reality into their parts, but they were beset by lack of information. "*Bonnie Prince Charlie* was one of those huge florid extravaganzas," said Niven, "that reeked of disaster from the start. There was never a completed screenplay, and never at any time during the eight months we were shooting were the writers more than two days ahead of the actors." At the midpoint of the fiasco, the distressed Niven cabled his mentor, Sam Goldwyn, in Hollywood: "NOBODY CAN TELL ME HOW THIS STORY ENDS STOP ADVISE." He never received a response.

The film's ending eventually had Bonnie Prince Charlie sailing off into the horizon while a tearful Flora MacDonald (who was scripted to fall in love with him) waved farewell from a windy clifftop. As the screen credits rolled, the Glasgow Orpheus Choir sang the hauntingly lovely "Will Ye No' Come Back Again" while the audience fished for handkerchiefs. As the meticulous actor suspected, it was not the way things had really happened in history at all.

The scriptwriters were in turmoil on that set. The beginning of Bonnie Prince Charlie's story was even more of a mystery than the ending. In fact, there are still people (admittedly few) who believe that Bonnie Prince Charlie is a mythical figure because his story is so hazy. In novels by Sir Walter Scott and Robert Louis Stevenson, his deeds and actions were unintentionally overromanticized to the extent that he barely survived as believable. Even though we know that Prince Charles Edward Stuart actually existed and was the grandson of the last Stuart king of England, his character escapes us because we lack knowledge about the circumstances that led to his many extraordinary actions. In 1745, fifty-seven years after his grandfather was deposed, Bonnie Prince Charlie tried to win back the throne of his ancestors and caused the last bloody civil war in Scotland. It resulted in many of its people being forcibly scattered all over the world. Today, Scotland still has unhealed wounds from that civil war and many questions remain unanswered as to how it all came about.

It is not generally known that the great Sir Walter Scott was not merely a storyteller; he was an exactingly thorough historian as well. He made a brave attempt to plumb the depths of Bonnie Prince Charlie's life after vast volumes of letters written by members of the fallen Royal House of Stuart were discovered in Italy early in the nineteenth century. They were subsequently purchased in batches by Queen Victoria, who had a fondness for Scotland, between 1804 and 1816. She was instrumental in reversing the laws that had been enacted to punish Highlanders for their support of Bonnie Prince Charlie's rebellion against her great-great-grandfather, King George II. For a hundred years these laws had forbidden Scots from playing the bagpipes or wearing the kilt.

Queen Victoria's desire to understand the Scottish rebellion led her to name Sir Walter Scott a member of the Royal Commission appointed to study the Stuart Papers. However, he and the other members of the commission were unprepared for the enormity of the collection. It contained upward of seventy thousand documents, some several pages long, written in English, French, Italian, Latin, and Spanish. Many were water damaged or had been attacked by termites, and great numbers contained long passages written in numerical ciphers intertwined with strange code names. Thousands of the letters were unsigned and undated so that nobody knew who had written them or to whom they had been sent. It would have taken twenty years of one person's lifetime to uncover all the secrets buried in the Stuart Papers; many remain undiscovered to this day.

The gigantic collection is now in the possession of Her Majesty Queen Elizabeth II and is stored in the Round Tower at Windsor Castle. Access to it is severely restricted and rarely granted because of the fragile condition of the documents. So many researchers have relied on these letters published in James Browne's 1838 history of the Highland clans. They have also borrowed heavily from the now out-of-print biography of the Prince written by Andrew Lang in 1900. A microfilm copy of the Stuart Papers, made during World War II, exists in London, but the photography is frustratingly blurred.

Another problem is that the average researcher usually expects to spend from three to five years on his or her project, but it takes far longer than that to unravel the tangles of Bonnie Prince Charlie, his exiled father (who called himself King James III of Great Britain), and his brother Henry, who became known in Rome as Cardinal York. It was not until the sixth year of my work that I discovered that both Charles and his father were consummate liars and that all the assumptions I and those before me had made based on their letters were wrong. I had to take a new look at old territory, break codes, plunge further into the documents (eighty percent of which have never been published), and seek corroboration of facts from other European archives. This work, over a fifteen-year period, changed the story from what I had supposed it to be when I began. I had embarked on the study with sympathy for the man, but I could sustain very little of that feeling as history unfolded.

One of the major departures in this book is to expose the titular James III as an adept schemer in the European political arena. He has often been depicted as a loving father and a benign, naïve man who would have made a gracious king had he been restored. Contrary to prior assertions that he lived to win back the throne of Great Britain, James had long given up that notion. The aim of his plotting was something else. Clear evidence will also be presented for the first time that Bonnie Prince Charlie was not invited to France, either by the French government or by Louis XV. This alters our notion that the French planned and financially supported the revolution that brought death and destruction to hundreds of Highland Scots at the Battle of Culloden in April 1746. The source of financing will be revealed. The relationship between Charles, his father, and his brother—heretofore described as loving and secure—is also probed and laid bare; the situation was anything but healthy. The Prince's drinking in later life is generally attributed to his painful memories of what happened at Culloden, but it will be shown that Charles was a full-fledged alcoholic long before he arrived in Scotland.

We have been misled on these points by the Stuart Papers at Windsor Castle. Most of the letters penned by the Stuart family were written in Rome and transmitted to Paris. Many were heavily ciphered because they were constantly subject to interception en route to their destination. Almost everyone used ciphers in the eighteenth century; the one used by the Stuarts was not difficult to break. Events bear out that what was said in those letters— ciphered or not—was intended to mislead the robbers of couriers. These letters, taken at face value, have served as the basis of several wrong beliefs still held today.

Probably the major impediment to our understanding of the life and times of Bonnie Prince Charlie has been the erroneous identification of his father's main Paris agent as Lord Francis Sempill, who always wrote letters in English. But it was Colonel Daniel O'Brien (mentioned only twice in a recent biography of Charles claiming to be a "standard") who enjoyed the exiled King's confidence. O'Brien wrote heavily coded letters in atrocious French that are difficult to read and translate; this may be why his writings have been ignored. He would often pen sixty pages a week, a virtual treasure trove of virgin material hitherto overlooked.

Events in Scotland during the years 1745 and 1746 were fully documented by observers at the time, and there is no lack of information on the subject. For this reason most books on Bonnie Prince Charlie concentrate heavily on this period. However, since Charles spent only fifteen months of his sixty-seven-year life in Scotland, I have chosen to dwell on the events prior to 1745 that led to his decision to land in the Outer Hebrides in the first place. The results place the facts of "the Forty-five," the Battle of Culloden, the Prince's flight through the Highlands, and his eventual escape to France in a different light. I have not given a blow-by-blow account of those fifteen months in Scotland but have described the highlights based on newly discovered knowledge of what went on before. There will be a few surprises here, too, including a new estimate of the numbers that joined the Jacobite army and the fact that Flora MacDonald and others who "helped" the Prince to escape harbored a deep resentment of him.

I do not consider my work on the Stuarts entirely finished; perhaps twenty years still would not be enough. But a halt had to be called. Nevertheless, I flatter myself that much more is revealed here than in any book since Andrew Lang's 1900 biography. Anyone who has ever studied Bonnie Prince Charlie stands on Lang's shoulders, and although he and I part company in several major areas, he did open the door and point the way. Another mentor is Marion Hamilton, who undertook the enormous task of cataloging the Stuart Papers in the late 1930s. Some work still needs to be done, and over the past twelve years I have had the honor of updating Hamilton's index. However, her initial labor of identifying, dating, and cross-referencing the Stuart Papers has been of such inestimable value that I could never have hoped to progress far without her contribution.

It remains for me to explain why I chose to write about Prince Charles Edward Stuart, and how I was able to accomplish the task, given the limited access to material. I grew up speaking both Gaelic and English on the Isle-of-Lewis, my mother's birthplace, to which Bonnie Prince Charlie had fled seeking help two hundred years before. The people of Lewis turned him away, although other inhabitants of the Outer Hebrides helped him. I was confused then as to whether he was a good person or a bad person, but my general notion was that he was some sort of folk hero.

This was reinforced when our family went to live in England after World War II. I saw David Niven's "florid extravaganza" (which I thought romantic) when I was about eleven or twelve. But English history lessons plunged me into confusion again. I remember clearly an illustration of valiant, sword-brandishing Redcoats chasing rabble-rousing, rebellious Highlanders in kilts across heather-clad mountains. I was distraught!

In 1968, after I had recently become a transplant to America, I saw a powerful docudrama depicting the Battle of Culloden; it was repeatedly televised all over the world. Produced by the British Broadcasting Corporation, it was based on John Prebble's book *Culloden*, and the old questions came up for me again. Who *was* Bonnie Prince Charlie? Why did this horrible massacre happen to my people? It became even more important to me to find the answers when I discovered that my mother's family—Macleans on the one hand and Campbells on the other—had been on opposite sides at Culloden. Also, in 1968 and 1969, interpretation of the facts was still being highly debated in several quarters, including in academia. Nobody had any answers, and the spate of books published in the 1970s after the docudrama was aired did not shed light on the issue.

Three years into my research, I moved to Ann Arbor to be near the University of Michigan, whose graduate library houses one of the finest collections of rare books on Scottish history in the world. I discovered that the Stuart Papers had been flawlessly microfilmed in 1974 by Micro Methods of Yorkshire and that the microfilmed copy of the entire collection had been purchased by the Center for Research Libraries in Chicago. Through the University of Michigan I was able to have reels of microfilm sent to me in Ann Arbor for study, and eventually I was also able to consult the original documents at Windsor Castle. It is not now necessary to do this if one can gain access to the superb reproductions produced by Micro Methods.

Days and nights of reading in the Microform Reading Room of the University of Michigan brought answers to my questions and then still more questions. Journeys to European libraries were necessary to fill in the gaps. A considerable period was spent on researching scurvy, which afflicted people on land as well as sailors at sea. Its impact on the body and mind permeated eighteenth-century society and deeply affected the central characters in this book. I have already established elsewhere* that Bonnie Prince Charlie almost died from the disease as he was being hunted by Redcoat soldiers.

It is hoped that few still believe that the Jacobite Rebellion of 1745 was a fight between the English and the Scots. It was not. It has been reclassified as a civil disturbance—Scot against Scot. This explanation is painful to entertain and is not entirely accurate, either. When all is said and done, there are many interpretations of what actually happened and why; these vary according to one's information, politics, and prejudices.

As for Charles, a study of his life would not be complete without a study of his times and the problems he faced as an exiled prince. Therefore, his story often shifts from Scotland into the realms of the Pope, to France and Spain, and to the war in Europe. It is there, as well as in the Stuart Papers, that many answers can be found to explain what demons drove the star-crossed Prince.

Susan Maclean Kybett

*The Scots Magazine, August 1976.

BONNIE PRINCE CHARLIE

Chapter 1

The Warming-Pan Baby

Early on Christmas morning in 1688 a fishing boat emerged from the fog-shrouded English Channel and moored at the small French port of Ambleteuse lying between Boulogne sur Mer and Calais. A tall, dark-haired man of regal bearing, wrapped in a hooded cloak against the damp chill, hurried ashore to a coach that waited to take him to Versailles for an audience with his cousin, King Louis XIV of France.

The man was James Stuart, the grandfather of Bonnie Prince Charlie. He is better known as King James VII of Scotland and as James II of England and Ireland. He had just left his three kingdoms behind because his people did not want him anymore. He had been allowed to depart without a hair of his head being harmed; a pension had been arranged for his family; and he carried a small fortune in Crown Jewels concealed underneath his cloak in a leather-bound parcel. The boatmen who ferried James down the River Thames toward the estuary leading to the French Roads saw him throw England's Great Seal into the water, as if to symbolize that no mortal had the right to take away the kingdoms given him by God. The Seal was retrieved later by some surprised Thames fishermen, who found it glistening in the middle of their squirming catch.

Awaiting James near Paris was his beautiful Italian wife, Queen Mary Beatrice d'Este of Modena, who had escaped from London weeks before disguised as a laundress. She had hidden their infant son in a bundle of linen in order to smuggle him out of the country. It was his birth in June 1688 that had been the signal for England to rid themselves of the Stuart dynasty once and for

1

GENEALOGICAL TABLE OF THE HOUSE OF STUART*

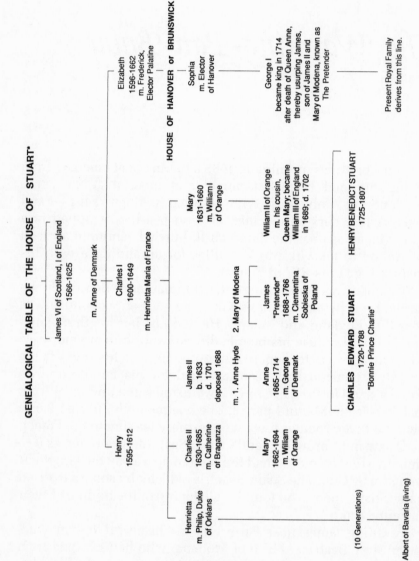

HOUSE OF HANOVER or BRUNSWICK

James VI of Scotland, I of England
1566-1625

m. Anne of Denmark

Charles I
1600-1649

m. Henrietta Maria of France

Elizabeth
1596-1662
m. Frederick,
Elector Palatine

Sophia
m. Elector
of Hanover

George I
became king in 1714
after death of Queen Anne,
thereby usurping James,
son of James II and
Mary of Modena, known as
The Pretender

Present Royal Family
derives from this line.

Henry
1595-1612

Charles II
1630-1685
m. Catherine
of Braganza

James II
b. 1633
d. 1701
deposed 1688

m. 1. Anne Hyde   2. Mary of Modena

Mary
1631-1660
m. William I
of Orange

Anne
1665-1714
m. George
of Denmark

James
"Pretender"
1688-1766
m. Clementina
Sobieska of
Poland

William II of Orange
m. his cousin,
Queen Mary; became
William III of England
in 1689; d. 1702

Mary
1662-1694
m. William
of Orange

CHARLES EDWARD STUART
1720-1788
"Bonnie Prince Charlie"

HENRY BENEDICT STUART
1725-1807

Henrietta
m. Philip, Duke
of Orléans

(10 Generations)

Albert of Bavaria (living)

The table leaves out people not mentioned in this history.

all. This little prince was James Francis Edward Stuart, lawful heir to the throne. His royal parents were literally pushed out of Britain's back door and into the arms of France because they were Catholics.

James II, as he was known in England, had not always been Catholic but had converted during the reign of his brother, Charles II (1660–85). At the time James became King, in 1685, he had been married for eleven years to Mary of Modena, his second wife. She was a devoted Catholic and twenty-five years his junior, but she had never borne him a child. She had conceived several times, but the infants were either stillborn or had not been brought to term. Therefore it was widely believed that she could not be a mother. James himself had demonstrated his fecundity on many occasions with various mistresses and had fathered several illegitimate offspring. He had also sired two legitimate daughters by his first wife, Protestant Anne Hyde. They were Mary, born in April 1662, and Anne, born in February 1665. Mary was now married to her Protestant first cousin, William of Orange, son of James's sister and the Stadtholder of the United Dutch Provinces; Anne was wed to Lutheran Prince George of Denmark.

Because James II was fifty-two years old when he ascended the throne in 1685 and no Stuart had lived beyond the age of sixty, it was anticipated that his daughter Mary and her husband William would soon jointly rule Britain. This was a very comforting thought for the Papist-hating nation; England had pushed out the Church of Rome during the reign of Henry VIII a century and a half before. Henry had established the Church of England, and laws had been enacted that excluded Catholics from any voice in government. Henry outlawed the Catholic Church not only because he wanted a divorce from his first wife, Catherine of Aragon, in order to marry Anne Boleyn; he could easily have dispensed with his first wife as he did his later wives. Rather, it was the political aspects of the Catholic Church that Henry sought to eliminate. The Catholic Church at that time was a highly political party—far different from the institution we know today.

Henry VIII's hatred of Catholics, which has everything to do with our story, was also based on economic considerations. Henry had to ensure England's survival in a highly competitive world. Columbus had charted a route to America when Henry was a year old; since then, Catholic France and Spain had made great strides in conquering and colonizing territories in the New World. Little

England was being left behind. A review of his nation's wealth demonstrated to Henry that most of it was flowing into the coffers of Rome through offertories in English churches; England was in effect financially supporting the explorations of its traditional enemies. Moreover, it was the Pope's plan to keep Britain financially subordinate to Rome.

Henry's main objective in eliminating the Catholic Church was to use the money for an aggressive ship-building program to compete overseas with the Catholic powers. His policy was pursued even more aggressively by his daughter, Elizabeth I, and it put England on the road to greatness. However, the Catholic party had to be totally eliminated in Britain before that came to pass.

James II appeared incapable of grasping the economic reasons for Britain's antipathy toward Catholicism (which had also been outcast in Scotland); he continued to seek out Jesuit priests for advice and counsel on affairs of state. As far as the populace was concerned, as long as William and Mary were in the wings and James II had no male heir to take precedence over them, they were prepared to wait. It was a distinct surprise, therefore, when early in December 1687 Mary of Modena announced that she was once again pregnant and expected to give birth in June.

Princess Anne disliked her stepmother intensely; she was immediately suspicious. She went to St. James's Palace and contrived to be with the Queen as she was disrobing. She inquired if she might feel the Queen's belly, but Mary of Modena would have none of it and withdrew to an anteroom for privacy. Anne wrote several letters to William and Mary in Holland casting doubt on the pregnancy. The Queen added fuel to the fire by frequently predicting that her child would be a son; since males took precedence, this meant that the succession would not pass to Anne's Protestant sister Mary.

Anne was not alone in her suspicions. It was widely known that the Pope and his emissaries had done everything possible since the expulsion of Catholicism to regain a foothold in England; some suspected that a feigned pregnancy and spurious male child would be foisted on the nation to perpetuate a Catholic succession. As Anne reported to her sister in March 1688, "Her being so positive it will be a son, and the principles of that religion being such that they will stick at nothing, be it never so wicked if it will promote their interest, give some cause to fear there may be foul play intended." Even though no fewer than twenty-nine

Protestant and Catholic men and women witnessed the birth of James Francis Edward Stuart on June 10, 1688, a story swept London that the child was really the offspring of a chambermaid and had been smuggled into the Queen's lying-in bed in a warming pan. It was several months before depositions to the contrary from those in attendance at the birth reached the public ear, but the fact remained that the English people did not want the royal succession to go to a Catholic.

The little Prince's arrival upset much of the political machinery that had been put into place on the assumption that William and Mary would soon rule Great Britain. William of Orange was already the nominal head of the League of Augsburg, an alliance of Protestant rulers in Europe that was bent on diminishing France's encroachment on their territories. William's domain, Holland, was particularly threatened because of its proximity to France. His country was also bordered by the Spanish Netherlands, whose ruler, the King of Spain, was a member of the French Royal House of Bourbon. Protestant German and even Catholic Italian states, in fear of being swallowed up by the combined efforts of the French and Spanish Bourbons, also belonged to the League.

William of Orange had practically begged his Catholic father-in-law (who was also his uncle) James II, to bring England into the League to squash the two Catholic powers forever, or at least to take active steps to create an equitable balance of power in Europe. William had even been in secret correspondence on the matter with several powerful leaders of the Whig party in England who desired the same thing. But James II refused to join the League on the grounds that he wished to live in harmony with "mon cher cousin," Louis XIV. Other considerations also blocked the King's vision, all of them religious. The members of the League of Augsburg and the English Whigs wondered how a man could be so bereft of vision as to fail to do an action that would be politically expedient for his nation.

Almost from the moment James II ascended to the throne in 1685, he had moved like a man possessed to reverse existing laws that prevented Catholics from holding public office. He dismissed Protestant military and government leaders and appointed Catholics in their place; the number of Jesuit priests and advisers at court swelled alarmingly. James held Mass openly, which had been banned by law, and he imprisoned seven bishops of the Church of England for refusing to order Anglican clergymen to read a Declaration of Indulgence toward Catholics at every service. Crown appointments in Ireland and Scotland effectively placed Catholics in control, and although a law had been passed that communication with the Pope was treason, James sent an ambassador to Rome expressing his obedience to the Holy See. He also attempted to foist Catholic leadership on Oxford and Cambridge universities.

When he increased the ranks of the standing army without the sanction of Parliament, the populace feared that his plan was to use force to restore England to the Catholic fold. As a king, James considered himself the father of his people and responsible for saving them from the heretical path of Protestantism. He was so filled with religious zeal that he could see nothing beyond restoring the nation to the Church of Rome. Even the other Catholic monarchs, Louis XIV included, shook their heads when they realized that James Stuart was under the spell of hierarchical Jesuit wizardry.

Shortly after the birth of James Francis in 1688, a letter was delivered to the King from his ambassador at The Hague stating that William of Orange would soon be arriving in England with an army to investigate the birth's circumstances and legitimacy. In the meantime, James II sensed a distinct coolness from political and military leaders, particularly from the Duke of Marlborough, who commanded his army.

When James heard that William of Orange had landed with troops at Torbay in Devon and was marching northeast to London, gathering recruits along the way, he tried to reach the Duke of Marlborough. But the Duke had been in league with William all the time; he took the army to join up with William at Salisbury. There he set up an encampment and waited while the befuddled James slowly faced the reality that neither he nor his Catholic heir was wanted. He sank into an abysmal stupor laced with confusion and fear. This was hardly surprising; his own father, Charles I, had been executed at Whitehall in 1649 for treasonably bringing military force against Parliament and causing civil war. His great-grandmother, Mary Queen of Scots, had also been executed after thirty years of involvement in Catholic plots against the English crown.

Therefore, James II, anticipating a similar fate, sent Mary of Modena and his son to France, disguised as a laundress and a bundle of dirty linen. The strategy behind the decision that he leave the country was that nobody wanted another Stuart martyr.

James left England grateful for his life, but his pride was deeply wounded. The circumstances of his exit reinforced in himself the belief that the only true religion was Catholicism and that the British nation was made up of Protestant heretics. This lesson he later passed on to his son.

There was wild rejoicing in the streets once it became known James Stuart was gone. His daughter Mary arrived from Holland to join her husband; cheering throngs lined the processional route when they were crowned at Westminster Abbey in April 1689. Parliament announced "That King James II., having endeavoured to subvert the constitution of the kingdom by breaking the original contract between king and people, and having, by the advice of Jesuits and other wicked persons, violated the fundamental laws, and withdrawn himself out of the kingdom, has abdicated the government, and that the throne is thereby vacant." James never did abdicate, nor did he renounce any claim to the throne. Strictly speaking, there was no foundation in law for what had happened—a fact that disturbed Protestants and Catholics alike in England, Ireland, and Scotland.

Scotland was an independent nation at that time. Many Scots refused to swear oaths of allegiance to William because he was not Scotland's King. It was the Stuart James VI, son of Mary Queen of Scots, who had left Edinburgh in 1603 to become James I of England and Ireland when his cousin, Elizabeth I, died childless. Even before that time, it had long been the fond hope in Westminster that Scotland would join with Ireland and England to create a United Kingdom under an English king, but differences in religious philosophy—the Scots were mostly Presbyterian—and an innate desire to control their own policies had prevented a union up to that time.

Many Lowland Scots would have had no objections to a union, but the fiercely proud Highlanders living beyond the northern mountains and in the islands had no taste for government centralized in Westminster. The Highlanders had a patriarchal clan system that had been formed by centuries of inbreeding. Each clan was made up of family members bearing the same name. They were led by chieftains, little kings in their own right, who had the power of life or death over subordinate clan members. The system was feudalistic, creating many headaches for the Scottish government officials in Edinburgh who had struggled for centuries to bring cohesion to their fragmented nation.

So far, that had proved to be impossible because the Highlanders were a law unto themselves. Situated beyond impenetrable mountains and wild seas, they settled internecine feuds locally, with no interference from Edinburgh. Each time a chieftain felt pressure to conform from Edinburgh or London, he resorted to claiming no other Liege Lord but the lately departed James Stuart. It was mere strategy; at heart many had no liking for the man at all. Whatever their motives, they became known as Jacobites, "followers of James," from his Latin name, Jacobus.

Ireland, with its large population of Catholics, was the scene of the first and most vociferous Jacobites. Their outrage at the dethroning of the lawful hereditary king was based on religious rather than political grounds and on extreme resentment of and anger at England's attempts to "pacify" Ireland. Catholic Ireland had been the number-one target for pacification when England expelled Romanism. One reason for this was that her ports could be invaded by the Catholic powers; Ireland thus was the weakest link in England's defenses. She had to be subdued if Protestantism were to survive. It was to Ireland, then, that James looked as a means to restore him to his rightful place on the throne.

A year and a half after James's flight from England, King Louis XIV financed the first Stuart restoration attempt. He provided fourteen ships of the line, weapons, and thirteen hundred officers and soldiers for a landing at Kinsale in Ireland, to be led by James. On the surface the Sun King's interest in the Irish campaign seemed to be support for the Jacobites, but in reality he was planning a naval strike against William of Orange and the Grand Alliance (successor to the League of Augsburg), which now included England as a member. Louis's stratagem was to use James to create a disturbance in Ireland to divert British forces from the area of the intended French attack.

At first, all appeared to go well for James in Ireland. By far the majority of cities declared for him, and he was able to recruit enough Irishmen to bring his army to thirty thousand men. But there were problems: the arms and artillery brought from France were woefully inadequate, and the countryside was practically devoid of weaponry due to earlier pacification attempts. In addition, food and money were scarce. When William arrived in June 1690 with a composite army of English, German, and Dutch troops totaling thirty-six thousand, James's army was quickly demoralized. In the ensuing Battle of the Boyne (July 1), most of the footsoldiers fled without engaging in battle, and the victory went overwhelmingly to William of Orange. Some twelve thousand people took advantage of the offer to leave their native land to relocate in France and Spain at England's expense.

The Stuarts' residence in exile donated by Louis XIV was the Château of Saint-Germain-en-Laye, about twelve miles west of Paris, overlooking the Seine. As if to give the lie to the warming-pan story, Mary of Modena gave birth to a second child in 1693. She was a charming little princess named Louise Marie, but she was unfortunately carried off by smallpox in 1712. Young James Francis was brought up in a solitary fashion by backward-looking tutors who schooled him thoroughly in languages; their view of life favored the King's view that the destiny of the Stuarts was to uphold the aims of the Catholic Church. James himself took a hand in schooling his son in deportment; how to walk like a king, how to posture majestically, and how to arrange his facial features so that the beholder would fall on bended knee in adoration of God's anointed. No one was allowed to speak unless first addressed by the Prince, who was counseled to speak only to his immediate retainers. Later, James Francis schooled his own son in exactly the same way. It was a comedic farce in view of the fact that the Stuarts had no country to rule.

In the meantime, William of Orange and the Grand Alliance waged war against Louis XIV for eight long years, greatly diminishing the once-healthy French treasury and almost bringing France to its knees. Mary of Orange died childless of smallpox in 1694 at the age of thirty-two, and William was left to rule alone. Princess Anne was next in line.

Anne was an unintelligent, mean, and malleable woman greatly addicted to gambling and laudanum, the opium-based drug of the day. But her woeful obstetric history was of greatest concern. Out of at least nineteen attempts at motherhood, most of her pregnancies had ended in miscarriage or stillbirth. Her only living child, a son, was pathetically frail and diseased. Thinking ahead about the succession, William opened up a correspondence with the father-in-law he had usurped, stating that he would be willing to name young James Francis heir to the throne if the boy were reared as a Protestant.

William earned Anne's everlasting hatred when news of the plan reached her ears. And when James II and Mary of Modena received William's proposal at Saint-Germain, they were enraged at his diabolically heretical suggestion. Even if religion had not been involved, James would never agree to relinquish his own rightful title and thereby set a legal precedent that would forever threaten the prerogatives of his descendants. Nor could he stomach such an outrageous offer from the son-in-law who had plotted to take his place.

By 1697, Louis XIV was more than ready to call a halt to the war with England. He signed the Treaty of Ryswick, by which he was required to officially recognize William as the legitimate King of Great Britain, with Anne as his successor. Louis could see no way out of the dilemma; he had to abandon the interests of his cousin for the moment.

Disheartened and broken in spirit, James retreated into religious contemplation, penning many documents on the art of kingship (a subject upon which he was no authority) for the benefit of his son. A king was answerable only to God, ran the thread of his statements, and it was the duty of subjects to obey their king without question, for he was blessed by God with divine wisdom and was the father of his people. He wrote about "the Church of Rome, which is the only true Catholick and Apostolick Church, and let no human consideration of any kind prevaile with you to depart from her; remember always that Kings, Princes and all the great ones of the world, must one day give account of all their actions before the great tribunal where every one will be judged according to his doings." James also went on at length to lecture his son on the fatal vice of "the forbidden love of Women," advice that the boy took to heart and carried throughout his life. Forty years later, James Francis repeated the same warning to his own son, Bonnie Prince Charlie.

In 1701, the historic Act of Settlement was ratified by the English Parliament establishing the future Protestant path of the succession. Anne's last child passed from suffering at the age of eleven. The House of Commons took advantage of the heirless situation to insert a very important seal on the English Constitution; that henceforward no English monarch could be of the Catholic faith, and that Anne would be succeeded by the branch of the Stuart bloodline that was farthest from Catholicism. James I's daughter, Elizabeth, had married a Palatine prince, Frederick. They were now the Brunswick family, Electors of Hanover in Germany. Although at least fifty other Stuarts were closer in line to the throne, none was Protestant, and so it was decreed that the

Hanoverians would rule Britain after Anne. Their most able scion was a fat prince named George. Three months after the Act of Settlement, James II slipped from life after obtaining a solemn promise from his thirteen-year-old son never to abjure the Catholic faith.

In 1700, France and England were on the verge of war once more. After the death of King Charles II of Spain, Louis XIV was interested in acquiring the Spanish crown. The French King publicly and defiantly proclaimed young James Francis Edward King James III of England, Ireland, and Scotland, rationalizing his previous recognition of William's right to the throne by saying he regarded him merely as *de facto* not *de jure* ruler of Britain. William did not live long enough to take action against Louis. In March 1702 he fell from a horse and died of his injuries, outliving his father-in-law by a mere six months. Anne, now widowed, became Queen of England.

While England and France were fighting over the Spanish Succession, a conflict that was to last twelve years, the union between England and Scotland finally came about in 1707. This deeply angered the many Scots who had fought against it for so long. In 1708, Louis XIV sent twenty-year-old James to Scotland with five thousand soldiers, seven man o' war ships, and twenty-one privateers to test the waters, to see if the Scots were incensed enough to support a rebellion aimed at restoring James as King. The forces sent with James were insufficient by themselves for a full-scale attempt, but France's strength was buoyed by many disgruntled Scottish clan chieftains who had been corresponding with James after the hated union took place. James sailed from Dunkirk at the end of March 1708. A comedy of errors ensued when he arrived in Scottish waters. The French fleet overshot the Firth of the Forth because there were no experienced pilots on board, and when they did manage to find the mouth of the Forth, they lacked pilots to dock at Leith, near Edinburgh. This was just as well, for news of their coming had leaked, and twenty-eight British warships were lying in wait at Leith to engage the intruders. With the open sea behind them, the French fleet turned tail and scattered. James begged to no avail to be put ashore among his people.

When Queen Anne learned of the attempt by her half-brother, she was enraged and placed a price on the head of the "Pretender," a name that stuck with James all his life. It now became a treasonable offense for any of her subjects to communicate with him. London public opinion was easily inflamed against James by the widely circulated broadsheets and cartoons linking his name with the Pope and the devil. Like his father, James Francis Edward had used hated French power against the British nation, and for this he would never be forgiven. A saying of the day was, "God Bless Queen Anne, the Nation's Defender,/ Keep out the French, the Pope and the Pretender."

Three years later, James was desperate enough to directly appeal to the half-sister he had never met, even though the succession was out of Anne's control and in Parliament's hands. James could neither absorb nor understand this fact. In May 1711, he begged her to consider that "the last male Heir of our line" should take his rightful place; he added that "The voice of God and nature calls you to it." But she ignored the pleas from the boy she had hated even before he was born. Anne's ineffectual reign was brought to an end by her death at the age of forty-nine three years later.

The German-speaking Prince George, Elector of Hanover, was not ushered in as King of Great Britain without a great deal of argument between the two main political parties. Taxes had risen steeply in England as a result of foreign wars undertaken by foreign-born rulers, such as William of Orange, and it was well known that George's main objective was to increase the prosperity of the electorate of Hanover by acquiring the Swedish possessions of Bremen and Verden to gain access to the ocean. The Whig party supported English expansionism on a global scale, while the Tories of Anne's administration were far more conservative, suggesting that James Stuart be brought back to rule. The loudest Tory voices on the matter were those of Henry Saint-John, Viscount Bolingbroke, Anne's chief minister, and the Duke of Ormonde. To bring James back would go against the Act of Settlement, so the suggestion was not universally popular. Many believed that Bolingbroke, Ormonde, and other Tories championed James merely because they were fighting a losing battle for supremacy to the Whig party, which favored the incoming German King.

Before his arrival in London to accept the crowns of three kingdoms, George ordered those who opposed him to be removed from office. Bolingbroke joined the court-in-exile of the titular James III, who now was living at Bar-de-Luc in Lorraine. By the terms of the Treaty of Utrecht, which ended the War of the Spanish

Succession in 1713, Louis was required to officially recognize George I's authority as Britain's ruler and to forbid James residence in France. Bolingbroke was appointed secretary of state by James and took up residence in Paris to act as a link between the exile and the French Court, but he was soon to regret that he had ever left England.

Already in the wind was the most ambitious Jacobite undertaking yet planned: a French descent on Scotland, to be assisted from within by ten thousand disgruntled clansmen under the leadership of John Erskine, Earl of Mar. During Anne's reign, Mar had been secretary of state for Scotland, and he had actually supported the Union with England. But upon George's accession he was snubbed by the new king and dismissed from office. He left for Scotland and busied himself drumming up support for the Jacobite cause, telling the Scots that he had seen the error of his ways and that now his only wish was to make them a free people by establishing James on the throne. The Duke of Ormonde, also unwanted by George I, began to organize Jacobite support in England, but his plans were discovered, and he narrowly escaped imprisonment in the Tower of London before fleeing to France.

Bolstered by the defections of Bolingbroke and Ormonde, and by Mar's successful efforts to raise an army of Scotsmen who were poised and ready to strike as soon as they could be assured of French reinforcements, James's spirits soared. He felt that the time had at long last come when he would be restored to the throne of his ancestors.

Bolingbroke, however, was greatly concerned about the situation. He was not alone in believing that his new master's only value to Louis XIV was as a political pawn, to be used as a threat against England whenever the need arose. But James was so anxious to win back the kingdoms lost by his father—and so politically inexperienced at the age of twenty-six—that he was unable to see this clearly.

Bolingbroke found he could not reason with James's mindset, particularly since it was being fed by a gaggle of Jesuit priests. James would heed no advice from the experienced statesmen who had defected; his training had led him to believe he was the divinely inspired authority on every subject. No innovative thought or concept was valid for James unless it emanated from his own brain.

But what bothered Bolingbroke most were James's views on

religion. From past experience, Bolingbroke knew that James would have to guarantee the security of the Church of England, in declarations to be printed and distributed upon his arrival in Scotland, projected for September 1715. With this in mind, the secretary of state prepared a draft for James's signature with a passage reading, "We promise to support, maintain and protect the Church of England." James took the draft to several French Catholic bishops and doctors of theology for examination. Their opinion was that the drafted Declaration fatefully promised "to support and maintain heresy, which no Catholick King can promise." The draft was returned to Bolingbroke amended to read, "We promise to support, maintain and protect *our subjects of* the Church of England," which was hardly the same thing.

Bolingbroke was appalled that the most material passages in his draft had been "turned with all the Jesuitical prevarication imaginable." Sick at heart that he had left England to enlist in so chimerical a cause, he withdrew his support from James and did his best to warn the Scots. In a letter to Mar, Bolingbroke stated that the French had no intention of assisting the effort in Scotland, adding that "the whole coast from Scotland to Spain is against us . . . the attempt can probably end in nothing but the ruin of our cause forever." Bolingbroke drily observed that if the French lifted a finger in the matter, it would be to achieve Bourbon domination of England—not to restore James Stuart.

Unfortunately, the Earl of Mar believed what James had told him, that the French were willing to back his restoration attempt to the hilt. Mar went ahead, assembled leaders from many respected noble families of Scotland, and raised the royal blue and gold standard at Braemar on September 6, 1715, proclaiming James King in full anticipation that he would soon be among them. The city of Perth was captured and held; so was Inverness, while the Scots awaited news of the arrival of James and French reinforcements. Instead came the news from France that Louis XIV was dead.

Although Mar has often been blamed for prematurely beginning the Jacobite uprising known as "the Campaign of the Fifteen," he did so on James's orders and with promises of French help. Even before the death of Louis, James had little guarantee that French help would be forthcoming. He had even less reason to expect assistance from the Regent Orléans, who now ruled France on behalf of the five-year-old Louis XV, great-grandson and heir of the Sun King.

The Regent struck a bargain with George I, agreeing that in the event of the child's death, Orléans would inherit the French crown and not the child's uncle, Philip of Spain, who was legally next in line. As a result of this arrangement, Orléans caused ships lying at Le Havre destined for the Scottish expedition to be unloaded and the weapons confiscated. Furthermore, he forbade all the Irish Jacobites now in French military pay to follow James without permission from the French Court. By this action, Orléans forced the subjects who adhered to James to obey the Court of France rather than their true monarch, thoroughly undermining James. They had little choice because their entire livelihood depended on money from the French.

James had a half-brother in France who was the eldest of four illegitimate children fathered by James II with Arabella Churchill, the Duke of Marlborough's sister. The Duke of Berwick, the half-brother, was eighteen years older than James, and he had already embarked on a distinguished military career in the service of the King of France. He had risen to be one of France's most famous marshals and was then on duty in Spain. Recalling that his father had told him that it was the duty of his subjects to obey his every command, James issued an order to Berwick to follow him and to direct every man under his command to do the same. But Berwick had become a naturalized French citizen; he could hardly go against the orders issued by Orléans without ruining his career, and he said so. The black side of James's unreasonable and dictatorial nature was laid bare to all when he called Berwick "a disobedient subject, and a bastard too," a statement soon repeated in all the coffee houses of Paris. As Berwick wrote to his nineteen-year-old son, the Duke of Liria, "He [James] always speaks of duty, as if he were master to allow people making their fortune, and we are not obliged to abandon all our establishment and leave our children to starve for his projects or fancy."

Blind obedience to his will was exactly what James expected of people, including the Scots, who were still holding out at Perth waiting for him and the promised French reinforcements. Mar had already engaged the forces sent by George I at the Battle of Sheriffmuir in November 1715. Although it was generally considered a drawn battle, soon afterwards the Jacobites were forced to abandon Inverness, captured early in the campaign, because of lack of men. The Highlanders had grown tired of waiting for James and returned to their mountain abodes to secure themselves and their families against the harsh winter. Not until December 22 did James finally arrive at Peterhead, the first time he had set foot on British soil since he was smuggled down the Thames as an infant twenty-seven years before. He came with a retinue of only five men and was dejected to find that only three thousand Highlanders remained with the Earl of Mar.

One wonders why James came to Scotland at all. The Scots were appalled by his stern countenance and his regal hauteur; he walked stiffly, with head held high and eyes cast downward toward his nose. He postured with hand on hip and allowed no one to address him unless he first called them into his presence, which was rarely. He had no words for the men who had risked so much for his cause but supposed that his royal presence and aura were reward enough. His grave, spiritless air of solemnity earned him the name of Old Mr. Melancholy, and it was said that his arrival dampened the Jacobite spirit.

King George I had placed the pro-English Duke of Argyll, chieftain of the largest clan, Clan Campbell, in charge of routing the Jacobites. Argyll commanded an army twice the number that James or Mar could muster, forcing the Jacobites to retreat from Perth to Dundee. Despite what had happened with Berwick and Orléans in France, James continued to lie to his followers about French assistance. He even wrote letters to France, copies of which he liberally distributed for his own ends. One passage in a letter to Orléans read, "We look upon you as our only hope, we earnestly claim your instant help, and we cannot doubt that we will receive it after all the hopes you have given us . . ."! Two days after this classic piece of dissembling was penned, James and Mar parted from their pathetic little army, saying they were going deep into the Highlands to recruit while they waited for the French. Instead they sailed from Montrose back to France, abandoning the Jacobites to their fate. Many could not believe that their king had betrayed them, and they blamed the French; but others swore they would never again draw a broadsword for the Stuarts as long as they lived.

Reprisals against the Jacobite peers who did not escape the country were harsh, as the English government had promised. Viscount Kenmure and the Earl of Derwentwater were beheaded after being found guilty of high treason. William Maxwell, 5th Earl of Nithsdale, who was also scheduled for decapitation, was saved by his courageous wife, Winifred. After vainly pleading for her husband's life at the feet of the coldly dispassionate George I, Lady Nithsdale was at least granted permission to visit him in the Tower of London on the eve of his execution. She brought a change of clothing for herself, then dressed her husband in the robes she had worn. Thus disguised, Lord Nithsdale walked out of the Tower with his wife and escaped.

Other prisoners who were not Peers of the Realm were sentenced to be drawn and quartered: "You must be hanged by the neck, but not until you be dead; for you must be cut down alive, then your bowels must be taken out, and burnt before your faces; then your heads must be severed from your bodies, and your bodies divided into four quarters." It is not known exactly how many suffered this barbarous fate, but enough did to set an example and discourage men from joining the Jacobite cause. One hundred and sixty people were *attainted*, which meant they were banished from the realm and forfeited their estates to the Crown. As for the hundreds of rank-and-file prisoners taken, those who survived the miserable prison conditions were deported to the American colonies to be used as slave labor. Some lucky people with money and connections escaped to France and begged Orléans for pensions or commissions in the army, but the Regent absolutely refused to assist or be implicated in any way with the hapless Scottish refugees James Francis Edward Stuart had misled.

Orléans also refused an audience to James when he demanded an immediate hearing upon his arrival from Scotland. James's treatment of Berwick, his constant quarrels with his possessive mother, and his exaggerated monarchical posturing without a country of his own finally exasperated the patience of all who had tried to show him kindness and sympathy. He was told that he was no longer recognized by France as King James III of Great Britain and was forced to move to the papal territory of Avignon. There he assumed the name Chevalier St. George and shut himself away to undergo primitive surgery to remove thrombosed clots from his anal canal. James's hemorrhoidal distress was not helped by the fact that George I considered his rival's residence in Avignon too close for comfort. George would not rest until the Chevalier was pushed to Rome, where he could be seen to be as "papist as the Pope himself." England at that time controlled Gibraltar and the island of Minorca in the Mediterranean, from which the Royal Navy was eminently capable of dominating Italian ports. The British announced that the port of Cività Vecchia would be mercilessly bombarded by cannon fire unless Pope Clement XI ordered James Stuart to Rome.

Early in 1717, James left Avignon and visited his cousin, the Duchess of Savoy, and also his great-uncle, Duke Rinaldo d'Este of Modena, en route to Rome. There he met the Duke's eldest daughter, Benedetta, who greatly resembled Mary of Modena. James was instantly smitten. He asked Rinaldo for Benedetta's hand in marriage, but the Duke was fearful of offending King George I and gave no immediate commitment to the match. Dissolutely, James and his party traveled on, and in May they reached the Palazzo Gualterio in Rome, a temporary abode until a permanent one was arranged.

James was dissatisfied, bored, and restless after a month. He wrote to Mar in Avignon: "I think my being here a dream, and I wish it were one, but alas, it is not." He was struggling to make sense of what had happened to him and complained of isolation from events happening elsewhere in Europe. He could not reconcile himself to the idea of permanent exile. Furthermore, Duke Rinaldo was still being coy on the matter of Benedetta; twenty-nine-year-old James was growing impatient because he felt it was high time he was married. During the heat of that first Roman summer, Pope Clement put the Gonzaga palace in Urbino at James's disposal, which he liked so much that he stayed there for two years. At Urbino in May 1718, James received the news that his mother had died of cancer in Paris.

Mary of Modena's last letters had been filled with unwanted advice about her son's choice of wife, for by this time Duke Rinaldo had told James that Benedetta could not be his. The old Queen's relationship with her son had never been close, and it had worsened when she criticized the appointment of several Protestants. James had learned from his abortive mission to Scotland that Protestant advisers were necessary additions to his retinue in order to win the confidence of the majority of his subjects. In later years, the sincerity of his apparent tolerance was often questioned, but in the meantime, defying Mary of Modena's insistence upon a Catholic wife, James publicly announced that the religion of his bride-to-be made no matter whatsoever. The statement was politically motivated; he had every intention of marrying a Catholic, and he already had emissaries combing the courts of Europe for a suitable mate.

An ebullient, quick-witted, and highly entertaining young

Irishman named Charles Wogan found Clementina Sobieska in Ohlau, Silesia. At the age of seventeen Clementina was the youngest of three daughters of the Catholic Prince James Sobieski. Her grandfather was the famous King John III of Poland, who had conquered the Turks in 1683 when they threatened to take Vienna by storm. Prince James had not succeeded to his father's exalted title of King because the nobility-dominated Polish Diet elected a new king upon the death of the old. Nevertheless, the Sobieskis were extremely weathly, and Wogan described the petite, flaxen-haired, black-eyed Princess as captivating. The Chevalier sent a Scottish Protestant named James Murray (once Bolingbroke's secretary) to Ohlau to make a formal request for Clementina's hand, and with Murray standing in for James, a proxy marriage was performed in the spring of 1719.

James was in Madrid at the time, engaged in another fanciful scheme to simultaneously invade both Scotland and England. "The Spanish Plot" was financed by King Philip V after meeting with the Duke of Ormonde, who was to command a large force destined for England. Mar was now out of the picture; command of the smaller Scottish expedition was given to the extremely able, sensible, and highly respected George Keith, 10th Earl of Marischal. James himself stayed in Madrid, where he was received with all royal honors, while the two fleets set sail. Soon after they left at the end of March, Ormonde's main force was scattered by a violent storm; he was forced to abandon the mission and return to port. But Marischal's tiny force, made up of 307 Spaniards, got through to Scotland's Western Isles and landed at Stornoway on the Isle-of-Lewis. There they rendezvoused with a small group of Jacobites from France brought over by James Keith, Marischal's brother, and learned that Ormonde had not been able to complete his mission.

The Jacobites were not welcome in Lewis. (This was not the last time these islanders showed hostility toward the Stuarts.) So they sailed southward to Loch Alsh and made their headquarters at Eilean Donan Castle. The end of the rebellion, which came to be known as "the Nineteen," was swift. Eilean Donan Castle was captured and razed by Major General Wightman's men, causing many Highlanders to return to their homes. On June 10, James's thirty-first birthday, approximately fifteen hundred Jacobites met with a similar force of government troops under the command of Wightman at the Battle of Glenshiel. Murderous mortar fire at

Glenshiel did the rest, and the Spanish were forced to surrender. Marischal and his brother escaped to France, but they could never return to their homeland.

There was nothing left for James but to return to Italy and meet his bride. Clementina, Wogan, and Murray awaited James at Montefiascone, where a second marriage ceremony was to be performed at the cathedral. The trio had a story to tell James. En route from Poland, Clementina was arrested and confined at Innsbruck on the order of Emperor Charles VI. This was said to have been done at George I's request because, quite naturally, he had no desire to see James Stuart marry and beget heirs. However, Clementina escaped from Innsbruck disguised as a maid, and the small party dashed over the Alps toward Italy, ever fearful of further arrests by allies of the English King.

James and Clementina held their second marriage ceremony on September 1, 1719. The Pope had secured the Palazzo Muti in the narrow Piazza dei Santa Apostoli, near Rome's Corso, as a permanent residence for them, and James was assured that full royal honors would be accorded him as the legitimate King James III of Great Britain. On December 31, 1720, the Queen (as she was called) gave birth to a male child, who was christened Charles Edward Louis John Sylvester Maria Casimir.

(Scots celebrate this birthday of Bonnie Prince Charlie on December 20 of each year and not on the thirty-first. Up until 1752, Britain was eleven days behind the rest of Europe in dates since it had refused to accept the reformed calendar set up by Pope Gregory in 1582. In 1752, Britain "robbed" the nation of eleven days as it came into line with the rest of her neighbors.*)

In honor of his baptism—the ceremony was presided over by the Pope himself—silver and bronze medals were struck with busts of the King and Queen on one side and a mother and child on the other, framed by the words *Spes Britanniae* ("the hope of Britain").

Congratulatory letters poured in from Irish exiles in Spain and impoverished Scots in France wishing health, wealth, and long life for the "wee bonnie Prince." None of the writers expected that this child would turn Britain upside down in his quest to right the wrongs done to his grandfather thirty-two years before.

---

* This system of dating has led to confusion in chronicling events in England and France between 1582 and 1752. Therefore, England's dating system henceforward will be referred to as "Old Style" (O.S.), while that of the rest of the Continent is "New Style" (N.S.).

Chapter 2

Beyond the Alps

The marriage of James and Clementina was regrettable from the beginning. Their temperaments and expectations of each other were woefully mismatched. James was almost twice the age of his girlish, chattering bride, and he differed greatly from her in character; he was cold and formal in the presence of company. Clementina employed teasing tactics to make him smile, but they only served to irritate James, who was overserious and, as Charles Wogan said, "not always inclined to savour jokes or give himself up to gaiety." For the better part of the day and most evenings, the King could be found in his apartments interminably writing letters with the assistance of his secretary, James Edgar. This did not suit his young wife at all; Clementina was highly spirited. She had anticipated a glittering life as the Queen of England in Rome, but her hopes were dashed soon after the introductory balls and receptions in honor of the newlyweds.

An approximation of the formal etiquette used at the French and English courts was required of those presented to James and Clementina. It entailed bows and curtsies, hand kissing, kneeling, and retreating from royal presentations without turning one's back or tripping over the furniture. James made it plain that although he would lend his presence at important gatherings, he was not obliged as a monarch to host balls or dinners to repay similar invitations, nor was he required to return social visits. Roman society was not used to having royalty in residence, and some of the older noble families resented James's claim to social precedence. They were perfectly willing to welcome the exile to their homeland, but his insistence on royal prerogatives was both anachronistic and foreign to their pomp-free way of life.

The required protocol also hampered international relations. Powerful foreign ambassadors to the Vatican were bound by treaty to make no move that could be construed as sympathy for James Stuart's claims. To bow to him or to kiss his hand would be tantamount to recognition of his claims. So they boycotted functions where he was present. Since the international population greatly influenced Rome's social life, James's presence was requested less and less at functions where pomp and ceremony were expected. The Stuarts were usually avoided by the wealthy English colony who wintered in Rome in a residential area near the Spanish Steps, although some were curious to see the man who called himself their King. He could be observed each day as he walked after Mass. But they called him the Chevalier St. George and snickered when he referred to them as "my subjects."

The sympathetic Pope did his best to arrange certain civilities. He set aside private tribunes (boxes with pews reserved for the highest nobility, royalty, church hierarchy, and their guests) in nearby churches, and a large box at the opera house was furnished with a table and chairs so that the couple could dine while listening to the castrati sing. (In Italy, women were not allowed to appear onstage, so female operatic parts were sung by high-voiced males who had been selected for castration at the age of twelve. This barbaric custom attracted the morbidly curious from far and wide; it also drew discerning music lovers from all over Europe to Rome, where the finest composers, orchestras, and musicians could be heard.)

James and Clementina arrived at the opera house flanked by the liveried palace guard provided by the Pope and made their progression toward the royal box. It was decreed that not one note of music could be played until the King and Queen of England were seated. Whispers coursed through the audience. But over time the whispers gradually became expressions of curiosity rather than of the awesome respect and reverence that James fancied were his due.

The Stuarts, largely friendless, came to spend the majority of their evenings at home. This was of no consequence to the antisocial, suspicious James, who had been able to trust very few people in his life, and the fewer people were about him, the better he liked it.

The lack of social activity stifled Clementina, however, and she quickly became bored, lonely, and homesick. She hated her new surroundings, which were a far cry from her father's opulent estate at Ohlau. The baroque architectural disaster known as the Palazzo Muti was—and still is—a gloomy structure; it occupies a small space in the narrow Piazza dei Santa Apostoli, with the dominating Church of the Apostles at one end and the bustling Corso at the other, rising four floors above street level. Its unknown architect cramped together Doric columns, pedimented windows, balustrades, and rooftop statues of the Twelve Apostles. The ocher stone bays are connected by a frontal wing facing the narrow, arched entrance, barely large enough for a coach to pass through. Most of the windows face inward, overlooking a minuscule courtyard that admits little light or air into the small, high-ceilinged rooms.

There was no space for a garden or trees. The palazzo was suffocatingly hot in summer and miserably cold in winter. The only retreat was the tiny Chapel of La Madonna dell'Archetto, connected to the rear of the Muti by a dark passageway. There the devout Clementina spent much of her time in prayer. Tourists and curiosity seekers could easily have passed unknowingly by the unimposing facade of the Palazzo Muti were it not for the gold and enamel coat of arms of the English Royal Family emblazoned over the arched entryway. A gift from Pope Clement XI, in later years it was mysteriously torn down. Today the Muti has undergone several conversions, to include a barber shop, a tiny restaurant, a travel agency, and various other offices; such is its lowly standing among Rome's important buildings.

The Palazzo Muti was the Stuarts' official residence for the next seventy years. Pope Clement XI also generously donated a summer palace near the shores of Lake Albano: in the eighteenth century it was known as the Palazzo Savelli, but today it is Albano's Palazzo Municipale, or town hall. The building sits on a hill in the heart of town. In James's time the palazzo was on the outskirts of Albano, surrounded by olive groves and chestnut trees. Views from the topmost windows of the two-story building commanded sweeping vistas of the lake, of thickly wooded forests, and of the Mediterranean to the west. The facade of the long, low building had sunny elegance; yellow washed walls and four widely arched porticos dominated the entrance. Its marble stairs, large airy rooms, and vaulted ceilings created a much more cheerful atmosphere than was possible in the Palazzo Muti. In later times, James and his family came to love the bucolic splendor of

Albano, where they hunted boar, pheasant, deer, and wild ducks in the surrounding forests and lakes. But retreats to the Palazzo Savelli were few and far between in the early years because of James's pressing need to improve his situation in life, particularly his financial condition.

James's income derived from several sources, all of them barely adequate. His Holiness had provided the Muti, the palace in Albano, and the many employees necessary to run both households; he also provided a pension of 12,000 Roman écus a year. The expense of a suitable roof over his head was taken care of, but there were many other expenditures. James's other income was applied toward food and clothing, hiring coaches, horses and grooms (the confines of the Muti precluded keeping them at constant beck and call), pensions for those who had followed him and lost everything, salaries for appointed staff—including a hefty sum for couriers—payments to agents and spies, and gratuities to his poorer adherents who had fallen on hard times (and there were many Scottish exiles who frequently needed the King's favor).

Funds received by James were computed by Belloni, his Roman banker, in French livres (which are approximately equal to present-day French francs in purchasing power). The Pope's 12,000 Roman écus converted to 36,000 livres. From France came an annual pension of 72,000 livres, paid to James as long as he observed the terms of the Treaty of Utrecht and stayed away from France. From the Spanish Bourbons came 4,000 pistoles, or 68,000 livres, but this sum was never paid on a regular basis, and between the years 1720 and 1740 James received the pension only eight times. Other funds came from the Stuart family's investment in a building in Paris known as the Hôtel de Ville; shares were paid out in the form of a lifetime annuity (known as *rentes viacre*, or simply *rentes*) amounting to 22,500 livres per year. Clementina also had a lifetime annuity on the Hôtel de Ville, based on an investment made by the Sobieski family, that netted 8,250 livres each year. Thus, in a good year the Stuarts' income was 206,750 livres. But when Spain reneged, as she did twelve times in twenty years, James had only 138,750 livres for essential expenses.

James lived very modestly indeed. By contrast, the cost of moving Louis XV's extravagantly large household to one of his country seats was 100,000 livres each time, and the Prince de Soubise once paid 200,000 livres for a fête in honor of the same

King. James had a few other assets in the form of shares in the French Trading Company in India, which diminished rapidly in value as Britain gained control of Indian commerce; he had jewels of an undetermined number and value passed on by his father. But James, with no subjects to tax for revenues, had to devote a major part of his time to planning ways to increase his income.

Prince James Sobieski had provided his daughter with a magnificent dowry and promises of future riches for children born of the marriage. However, Clementina's wealth never directly benefited James and was hers to do with as she pleased. The main beneficiary was eventually the Catholic Church. The fortune at her disposal contained the fabulous Sobieski Sapphire, now set (ironically) in the crown of the Queen of England. There were also splendid rubies, diamonds, ivory carvings, silver boxes inlaid with enamel, tapestries, hand-carved furniture, and golden crowns taken from Turkish potentates conquered by Clementina's grandfather. Much of this treasure was later taken by Napoleon's soldiers when they held Rome to ransom more than half a century later. For many years it served as a source of bitter feuding between husband and wife. Clementina used it to try to control James in disputes over his chosen advisers and over the upbringing of their children.

One thing James and Clementina did have in common was tenacious, stubborn willfulness. Their battles royal turned the Muti into a "labyrinth of misery," as one retainer described it. Some followers—Charles Wogan for one—were driven away to seek more pleasant situations. Those who stayed disliked Clementina intensely because she was self-centered, argumentative, and thoroughly spoiled. Physically, she was diminutive, pale, and painfully thin. Although portraits depict her as a fragile, sweet-faced, fair-skinned beauty (and in one she appears pious beyond measure dressed in a nun's habit), on her own admission she possessed a "naughty temper," and she was capable of public displays of hysteria to get her own way.

An early demand of hers was that she be allowed to have ladies-in-waiting from her own country; she disliked some of the household members James had brought with him to Rome. But he refused on the grounds that he trusted no one but those hand-picked by himself. In this he was justified. Spies lurked outside in the dusty piazza waiting to carry tidbits of information to their masters, the foreign ambassadors to the Vatican. Spies paid by the English government also kept close watch on James for fear he would try to leave Rome and return to France. James personally scrutinized the backgrounds of his approximately thirty household staff (less than half the number employed by wealthy Roman families), but no matter how careful he was, there were always employees willing to sell information. The Imperial ambassador representing Emperor Charles VI once stated that he had three people within the walls of the Muti in his pay. Although James was aware that information leaked to the outside world, he was rarely able to identify the informants.

Clementina could not fully understand James's secretiveness because she had never lived a life of intrigue, knew nothing of politics, and comprehended little about her husband's unique and complicated position in world events. She cared only that he pay her more attention. She had no idea that a fallen reprobate of a German aristocrat by the name of Baron von Stosch was spying on her for the English government. Operating under the code name "John Walton," he had bribed a chambermaid to check Clementina's bed linen for signs of menstruation, and by this means he hoped to detect early on if the Queen were with child!

Clementina was inexperienced and naïve about the world she now lived in. She was neither educated nor mature enough to become a confidante of her husband, and he was far too preoccupied with business to dance attendance upon Clementina or cater to her whims. Besides, he had a lifelong distrust of women, and Clementina was no exception. Therefore, she was largely ignored and left to her own devices, with the predictable result that she was frequently sullen in her husband's company.

James was greatly preoccupied with setting up a network of agents in Britain and France, now that he was far removed from the hub of political activity. He informed himself about world events via gazettes from Holland and Switzerland, English newspapers, and bulletins from France. He maintained correspondences with Jacobites in Scotland, France, Spain, and Holland.

His energies were drained by dealing with the constant infighting among priests in Ireland. They recognized no monarch but James, and they wrote sycophantic, groveling letters to him seeking ecclesiastic appointments; they spared no venom or vitriol in libeling rival candidates. Their fierce rivalries generated a debilitating stream of volatile correspondence to the Palazzo Muti.

To assist in answering the mountains of correspondence—sometimes as many as thirty or more handwritten pages in a day—

the King relied heavily upon James Edgar. It was in his beautifully clear hand that the majority of the King's letters were written in both French and English. James called Edgar "my faithfull scrivener"; the secretary was liked and respected by everybody. He had the remarkable ability to pour oil on troubled waters and soothe with sensible advice, and he handled requests for pensions or money with great delicacy and kindness. Edgar was highly educated and possessed a cool head, yet he stayed in the background, secure in his only ambition to serve James. His apartments, adjoining his master's, were an oasis of peace, quiet, and common sense, and he refused to involve himself in the bickerings rampant among the inhabitants of the Muti.

For hours into the night, Edgar and the King devised numerical and verbal codes vital for the transmission of letters, which were constantly subject to interception, frequently without the writer or recipient ever knowing. Couriers were often bribed, or they were robbed or even murdered for the dispatches they carried. In the most common practice, a letter was intercepted, the wax seal was carefully melted (after an impression of it was taken with a drop of mercury), and the letter was copied, resealed with the impression, and sent on its way, looking as if it had never been tampered with. Very few sensitive letters could be sent by "a safe and sure hand." James used banker Belloni's messengers for internal communications. But for dispatches leaving the country, trusted travelers often carried them sewn into the lining of their clothes. James and Edgar eventually became satisfied with the cipher system they devised. Because ciphers varied for each correspondent and had to be changed periodically, this, along with decoding incoming letters, became Edgar's most engrossing task.

If the King was not working with Edgar when Clementina sought him out to whine for attention or complain about members of the household, he was with the Scotsmen he had brought from Avignon to serve as his closest advisers. They and their families had followed him since 1715; indeed, they had given up everything for the Stuart cause. Predominant among them was John Hay and his vibrant wife Marjorie. Hay, the second son of the 7th Earl of Kinnoul, was about fifteen years older than the King. His sister was married to the Earl of Mar. When Mar declined to follow James to Rome, Hay took over his position as unofficial secretary of state for overseas affairs.

Marjorie Hay was the accomplished and worldly daughter of the 5th Earl of Stormont. She was about the same age as James and was one of the few women for whom he held genuine respect. He looked to her rather than to Clementina for smooth management of the household. James conducted his court to emulate the British lifestyle as much as possible, so he relied greatly upon the Hays for advice. Marjorie was given several major responsibilities, not the least of which was to school Clementina in the British queenly style of deportment; she was free to make whatever other suggestions she thought fitting. In many respects Marjorie Hay was the lady of the house. The young Queen seethed. Understandably, she came to resent the Hays to the point of hatred, and although her stated reason was that they were Protestant and therefore heretics, the truth of the matter was that James infinitely preferred to be in their mature company and had little patience with his young wife's vacuous prattle.

A third member of the family was Marjorie's bachelor brother, James Murray of Stormont, who had been a lawyer in Scotland. His legal mind proved invaluable to James in the years of planning and plotting that lay ahead of them. Both Hay and Murray were criticized by some Jacobites (those still snugly in possession of their estates) for being of insufficient stature to serve the King, perhaps because they were second sons of noblemen. However, the brothers-in-law were highly educated and were considered to be "gentlemen of fortune" with incomes from their families' estates in Scotland to support them. The fact that they were Protestant was all-important to James.

Now that he had been pushed beyond the Alps and was seen by Britons as "papist as the Pope himself," James countered the damage. Part of his strategy to win back the throne was to make an outward show of religious toleration by appointing Protestants to positions of trust. He went further, even allowing Anglican services, presided over by Anglican ministers, to be held in the Muti, causing astonishment among the British colony in Rome. The cynics who held that his action was an insincere attempt to convince the world that he was tolerant were correct, for in later years James persistently referred to Protestants as "heretics." As for his trust in the Hays and in James Murray, all three had quietly converted to Catholicism, which was unknown to anyone until they left the King's service. It is possible they made this change at the beginning of their attachment to the King, as James Edgar had done, but for political reasons it was not made public.

To the rigidly Catholic Clementina, it was a distasteful sham. She frequented the baths at Lucca and made desultory grace-and-favor visits to convents to remove herself from the confines of the Muti and from company she considered odious. Periodic squabbles broke out among the courtiers when other Protestants resisted Catholic attempts to convert them; the Palazzo Muti became a hotbed of intrigue as men jostled for the King's favor. Hay and Murray were jealously and sneeringly referred to as "the Brethren," and one Anglican minister, Ezekiel Hamilton, quit the Muti in disgust. For years afterward, he wrote malicous letters to the Hays, to Murray, and to James Edgar, accusing them of "selling your Bible for a King." James did his best to rise above these "tracasseries," as he called the bickering, but Clementina added to it by siding with those who resented the Hays and Murray and demanded that they be dismissed. A demand was not the kind of request to make of James, who believed that women should be submissive, respectful, obedient, and seldom heard from. He revealed his thunderous temper even when his decisions were meddled with or challenged by men, let alone by his young wife. Ungallantly, he took to freely discussing Clementina's shortcomings with the Hays and Murray, adding to the "tracasseries" and creating an untenable situation for the proud Sobieski Princess.

To be fair, Clementina did try to please her husband; she once gave him a gift of a puppy and addressed notes to her "Cara mio." But the situation was irreconcilable because her prejudice against Protestants and her jealousy of Marjorie Hay both ran too deep. The atmosphere put a great strain on John Hay, who wanted to take his wife and leave Rome, but James, desperately in need of his services, begged him to stay on. This they did for a few more years, but Hay was unhappy all the time, resolving to put distance between himself and Rome as soon as James released him. In a letter to Mar, Hay described life with the royal couple:

> Their tempers are so different that, tho' in the greatest trifles they are never of the same opinion, the one wont yield one Inch to the other; the dread of being governed and the desire of governing, passion, youth ingrafted by a little mean education, will ever afford matter for supporting their differences, which must end in something very dismall, their healths are equally ruined by it, and it is impossible they can hold out so; . . .

Shortly after this was written, James decided that the only way to end the constant wrangling in his household was to make it clear to his wife that he was master of the house and that he would tolerate no interference from her on the matter of his chosen advisers. For a while Clementina buried her feelings and tried to please him. During this lull in hostilities she conceived a second child. But even before she gave birth to Henry in March 1725, it was obvious that the troubles had not gone away but merely simmered under the surface.

It was in this highly charged atmosphere that Prince Charles, now four years old, was reared. Clementina had always been far too immature and too engrossed in her own resentments to pay him much more than fleeting attention. James sent to Paris for a nurse, known only as Mrs. Sheldon; her family had followed James's father into exile. It was James, not Clementina, who constantly checked with Mrs. Sheldon to see how his son was progressing.

From the beginning Prince Charles was a cause for great concern, for although letters from Rome claimed the heir to the throne was lusty and long-limbed, Charles's legs were actually very weak at birth, and it was feared he would never be able to walk. Rickets may have been the problem, since this was a common ailment in the eighteenth century. Not until well after his third birthday had he gained enough strength to support himself without assistance. James consulted several prominent physicians for remedies and exercises, which he passed on to Mrs. Sheldon. But she did not want to put the child through pain, and she protested that "His Royal Highness should not walk very well for another few months than risk making him ill." She used reins to support the Prince's early walking efforts, explaining that "his knees are still rather weak and as this bothers him somewhat he doesn't like putting his weight on them."

James continued to devise exercises for Charles into puberty. Once the lad was on his feet, he followed a daily regimen of jumping up and down and dancing to music, which he loved. It was claimed that the Prince of Wales (as he was called) was a merrymaking, rambunctious boy who had mastered English, French, Italian, and the bass viol by the age of four. That he was mischievous and energetic there was no doubt, for he was often doing "penances" at the behest of his father. But there was something sadly awry in his capacity to learn. Perhaps because he had had to spend so much time strengthening his body in early childhood, there was little time for lessons, or perhaps the deficiency that caused his weak condition at birth also impaired his ability to study. Whatever the reason, Charles never fully mastered English, his primary language. Nor did he attempt a serious study of French until he was twenty-four years old; on his own admission, he never learned to speak fluent Italian. All his life he had to employ people to read and write for him: he was functionally illiterate. Yet a constant outpouring of sanguine letters from Rome to Jacobites overseas exaggerated the Prince's abilities, masking the truth and creating a false picture of his development.

Most of Charles's childhood letters that were written correctly in his own hand were accomplished with the aid of his beloved tutor, Sir Thomas Sheridan, who was more like a father to Charles than was James. At this time, Sheridan was a spry, fifty-year-old half-cousin to the King. Before James's father, James II, had legally married his first wife, Anne Hyde, and produced legitimate issue in Mary and Anne, the couple had had a daughter out of wedlock named Helene. Sir Thomas was her son. He was a wonderfully patient man who had great sympathy for the little boy in his charge, and he doted on the Prince all his long life, spoiling him shamefully. It was one of the few affectionate relationships Charles ever experienced, but not even Sir Thomas could induce his pupil to apply himself to learning.

The Prince's atrocious spelling in adulthood is legendary: "God nose" instead of *God knows*, "gems" for *James*, and in one letter, the word *country* is spelled four different ways, none of them correct. Being pushed to the foreground as the Prince of Wales, having an overindulgent tutor, and being addressed as "Your Royal Highness" could not have instilled in Charles the discipline required for study; the acquisition of a professional tutor did not improve matters.

James sent to France for Andrew Ramsay, a highly educated Scottish convert to Catholicism and friend of the philosopher Fénelon. Ramsay and Fénelon shared the view that children should be stimulated rather than forced to learn; the Scotsman had earned a reputation for his success in educating spoiled royal children at the Court of France. But not even Ramsay could make headway with Charles, and he gratefully returned to Paris after spending about seven months with his reluctant pupil. It is difficult to keep from drawing the conclusion, particularly in view of the Prince's conduct later on in life, that in intelligence he was less than gifted.

Charles was rarely seen in public in these early years, possibly for reasons of security; but more likely he was kept from view so that his physical infirmities remained hidden. As a result he was often lonely, with only old men for company, and he had no playmates of record. He was four and a quarter years old when his brother was born, but Henry was never a companion to Charles. Henry, too, was dangerously feeble and puny at birth; it was several weeks before James felt confident enough to notify his adherents that he had fathered another son. Henry's condition was attributed by the Pope's physician to Clementina's dietary habits. In her unhappiness she had become ardent in her religious devotions and had embarked on a dangerous regimen of fasting, which had reduced her birdlike frame to little more than skin and bone. Henry did survive and lived to be an octogenarian, but his mother became a highly strung neurotic and resisted all James's entreaties for her to cease fasting.

Eight months after Henry's birth a scandal erupted in the Palazzo Muti. Clementina accused James of having a love affair with Marjorie Hay. The charge, for which there is no foundation on record, arose from several changes in the household that James wanted to make. One of them was to dismiss the nurse, Mrs. Sheldon, who had always sided with Clementina in her vendetta against Marjorie Hay. In James's view Mrs. Sheldon had led his wife astray by making insinuations against Marjorie Hay. At the same time he announced that Charles would receive Protestant as well as Catholic instruction to better prepare him for his life ahead as the King of England, and he appointed James Murray governor to the Prince to see that his wish was carried out. The Catholic Sir Thomas Sheridan was named subgovernor; both were now responsible for educating the boy. Furthermore, Murray was given the title Lord Dunbar, while the Hays were created Lord and Lady Inverness. Thus in one fell swoop James not only eliminated the only friend Clementina had in the palace but also elevated those she considered her enemies. What hurt the Queen most of all, however, was that James was going to make a heretic out of her son.

It was a very low point for Clementina; she could explain her husband's total disregard for her feelings in no other way than that he must be in love with Marjorie Hay. She became uncontrollably hysterical and did what she had often threatened to do: with Mrs. Sheldon in tow, she packed her belongings, left her children behind, and sought sanctuary in the Convent of Santa Cecilia on the nearby via Vittoria. Lady Winifred Nithsdale was immediately appointed to take care of baby Henry's needs (both she and her husband had been pensioners of James ever since their dramatic escape from the Tower of London), while the bewildered five-year-old Charles was put in the care of two aging gentlemen.

All Rome was shocked by the scandal. Within a few weeks news of it had spread throughout Europe. If Clementina had expected public sympathy, she was mistaken. She was heavily censured for abandoning two children, one only eight months old, and for bringing humiliation and embarrassment to her husband. To James's mortification, the spies reported to their governments everything that had transpired in the Stuart household. "Walton" sought out the brother of one of the nuns at Santa Cecilia and learned from him that "the Princess wept freely, and used very exaggerated language." She declared that "her husband wished to bring up her boys as heretics, and rather than permit such an infamy, she would stab them with her own hand. Such speeches, and her declamations against Mr. and Mrs. Hay filled the convent with alarm."

The Pope was sufficiently concerned to send an emissary to question both parties on the issue of Charles's education and James's supposed adultery. Clementina withdrew the latter accusation, but the Pope (now Benedict XIII, who was not especially friendly toward James) temporarily suspended the papal pension and threatened to send the children to Spain for their upbringing if James persisted in his plan to give Charles Protestant instruction. The King was thus forced to give assurances that his son would be educated in true Catholic fashion, and he agreed that a priest would be assigned to the task. However, he was adamant in his refusal to dismiss Lord and Lady Inverness, and so Clementina stayed away from the Muti for almost two years, telling everyone that she feared she would be poisoned if she returned.

Undoubtedly, the children were taken to see Clementina from time to time, although visits are not recorded. It is known by reference that she wrote occasional letters to Charles, but these have not survived. The effect of all this upon "the wee Prince" can only be surmised. He was old enough to have witnessed many quarrels, and like many children of parents who separate, perhaps he felt in some measure responsible. His father feverishly wrote to adherents all over Europe explaining his side of the story in an attempt to stem criticism, and there is evidence that he explained

the circumstances to Charles in terms less than flattering to
Clementina. Many years later, when the Prince was a young man
and his father was constantly advising him to beware of women
because they were foolish and untrustworthy, James used Clementina as an example. As a result, Charles was never comfortable
with the opposite sex; he regarded women as inferior and, like his
father and brother, never sustained a lasting loving relationship.

Sixteen months after Clementina's abrupt departure from the
Palazzo Muti, Lord and Lady Inverness once more begged leave to
quit Rome to make their home in Avignon. Since Lord Inverness
was in poor health, reluctantly James gave his consent. There is
evidence that he wanted to leave Rome himself so that he would be
free to bring up his sons like "proper English gentlemen" without
interference from the Pope, but there was always the problem of
finding a country that would accept him. Many rulers were now
allied with George I's policies in Europe; it was politically expedient for them to ignore the plight of James Stuart. What he desired
most of all was to be welcomed back into the bosom of France,
England's traditional enemy, and to induce Louis XV to support a
restoration. France's treaty promise to England to keep James
beyond the Alps had been signed by Regent Orléans, not by Louis
XV. But Orléans was now dead, and in James's view France was not
bound to honor the agreement any longer. To this end he wrote
several memoranda to the French Court, appealing to "*mon cher
cousin*," but Louis did not respond.

An opportunity for James to test the waters came when he
learned that George I had died in June 1727 and had been succeeded by his son with no public protest whatsoever. England now
was being firmly guided by oligarchic Whigs under the supremely
powerful Robert Walpole, and if there was any opposition to that,
it was from the rival Tory party. Wishful thinking often led James to
confuse Toryism with Jacobitism, and this was one of those
occasions. Recklessly, he decided to leave Italy secretly, and
traveled first to his old protector, the Duke of Lorraine. But James's
presence there was an acute embarrassment to his surprised host,
who was powerless to assist in any way. From there James went to
Avignon, where he stayed with Lord and Lady Inverness and met
with the Duke of Ormonde and other exiled Jacobites. But the life
and soul had gone out of the party. They were few in number,
aging, and impoverished.

The French were furious that he had dared to enter the

country without permission, placing them in jeopardy of war with England. Orders were sent to the commandants of French ports on the Mediterranean to refuse entry to James's family if they tried to enter. The French ambassador in Rome made a strong protest to the Pope, who recalled James immediately. He returned to Rome in January 1728, having expended five months on a journey of utter futility. All he had accomplished was to earn the displeasure of France, and the weary Pope was beginning to rue the day Rome had decided to shelter the Stuarts. In addition, foreign spies increased their vigilance over James's movements so that life became more restricted than ever.

James found that Clementina had left the convent while he was away, but she had taken a villa in Bologna rather than return to the Palazzo Muti. She had also sent for the children; James had to go to Bologna if he wanted his family back. This was a ploy on Clementina's part to make James come to her, for she knew that someday they would all have to return to Rome. In Bologna the couple talked out their differences but agreed to nothing more than not to disagree. The objects of Clementina's complaints had been removed, and therefore, James reasoned, there was no basis for further quarrels. He wrote to Lord Inverness that he had settled matters with Clementina "by giving her and taking to myself an entire liberty. She leads a most retired, melancholy life, and though I have encouraged her to alter it, I dont believe she will, but that's her own business and I shall not constrain her."

The family returned to Rome two months later. James wrote that Clementina was locked up in her room and saw only the maids. ". . . she eats meat this Lent, but fasts to that degree that I believe no married woman that pretends to have children ever did; I am very little with her. I let her do what she will . . ." She was a changed and very subdued Clementina, now twenty-eight years old. All the arguments of old had had only one real basis: that she wanted James's love but he had none to give her, nor to any other woman for that matter. She finally accepted this as her lot in life and plunged further into fanatical absorption with religion.

There had been so much upset and drama in the Stuart household that the Princes were almost lost from view until Charles was eight and Henry four. They were pretty children; the eldest was now well on his way to full physical health, with "arms like a porter," as Dunbar said. He showed promise of being tall, with fair skin inclined to freckle, reddish-blond hair, the generous curving mouth of the Bourbons, and large eyes variously described as hazel, topaz, or brown in color. Henry, on the other hand, was small and ill formed, with the olive skin, black hair, and black eyes of his paternal grandmother; his most conspicuous facial characteristic was a long chin. He was by far the better scholar and quickly surpassed his brother in penmanship and spelling; he had the advantage over Charles in receiving uninterrupted schooling from Jesuit priests.

Henry was known as the Duke of York, the traditional appellation given to second sons of English royalty. He seemed to be the more popular of the two. He talked incessantly and had a way of captivating with clever chatter, while Charles was withdrawn and preferred to spend his leisure hours in the courtyard solemnly shooting birds from the rooftop with a crossbow. He was an expert shot by the age of six, according to the Duke of Liria, who visited Rome at that time, and he could split a rolling ball with an arrow shaft ten times in succession. His interests were physical, while Henry was definitely cerebral in his pursuits. The young Duke of York was no paragon of shining intelligence, but he loved to read and study, which pleased his father greatly.

It was obvious to Charles that James loved Henry better; even in middle age the memory hurt so much that he confessed it to Pope Benedict XIV (1740–58). It was unfair that he had suffered through his parents' and his own torment virtually unaided and that Henry had come along in a time of relative peace. In the peaceful period James also had more hours to spare for his children; he temporarily suspended "affairs of state" after the abortive mission to Lorraine and Avignon. James saw Henry apply himself to study in a way that his elder son never did and this created a deep bond between them that unfortunately excluded Charles.

There were so many wounds for a little prince of eight to overcome, yet Charles could still find it in himself to enjoy certain aspects of life. Love of music and dancing were the only things he had in common with his brother, but only he loved to dress richly, and all his life he spent vast sums of money on clothing. He was not a fop, nor was he effeminate, but he could never resist laces, brightly colored velvets, intricately embroidered brocades, jewels, periwigs, and fine leather boots. He also loved to have his portrait painted by Pompeo Batoni, and he often gave oval-shaped enameled miniatures to adherents; in many of them the clothing he wore reflected a deep fascination with his Scottish ancestry. Again, only he felt this: James desired to be English, Henry was content to be Italian, but Charles wanted to be a Scotsman. In the Highlands of Scotland tartan jackets were never trimmed with ermine tails and gold braid, but Charles did this, and the effect stunned Roman society. He topped off his outfits with a blue bonnet, on which he sported the Jacobite cockade in the form of a white rose, white silk ribbon, or white feather. He was different; he was being noticed, and he loved the attention. He was truly a bonnie prince to behold.

The priest who was "put about" Charles to ensure that he would be a good Catholic was a man by the name of Father Vinceguerra. Very little is known about him except that he was relatively young, very athletic, and humane. There is no evidence that he tried to drill religious dogma into Charles's head; it was already rather too late for that. What he did do was take the untutored boy, assess his attributes and family situation, and give him the best training possible to prepare him for future life. It appeared to the pragmatic Pope Benedict XIII that the chances of Charles becoming King of England someday were very slim— although James was not ready to concede that point—and that it would be best for all if the Prince were trained as an army officer. As it was, the subsidy paid the Stuarts was a drain on the Vatican treasury, and unknown to James, Benedict XIII was not prepared to continue payments or grant royal prerogatives to Stuart successors ad infinitum. It transpired that both James and Charles outlived Benedict XIII, but at this point they had to dance to his tune.

Father Vinceguerra's task was to harden and strengthen the Prince's body to withstand rigor. The two would disappear for days on end into the countryside of Albano wearing rough clothes, sleeping on the ground in all weather, and shooting their own food. They took nothing with them except knives, guns, bows and arrows, a blanket each, and perhaps flasks of water and brandy. Vinceguerra taught Charles how to draw game, skin or defeather it, make a fire, and cook what had been caught.

The terrain selected was the roughest imaginable, and in a short time Charles was scaling heights barefoot like a mountain goat, wading through swollen rivers, hacking his way through thickets, and jumping from boulder to boulder. He was frequently waist high in mud and learned to be tolerant of insects and all climates. He became muscular, and everyone commented on his splendid physique, which, coupled with his taller than average height, drew even more admiration when he washed off the dirt and dressed in velvets and brocades. Years later, when Charles was in Scotland and in desperate straits, followers constantly expressed amazement at his ability to weather any rough passage that came along.

The sibling rivalry never abated. Charles used his physical superiority to hit back at Henry, once calling him a *cacciatore pane bianco*, literally "a white-bread" or "lily-livered hunter." The aggression was all on Charles's side. Henry did his best to make his brother love him, but it was not to be. It has been supposed that the brothers loved each other dearly because of the many affectionate letters written by Henry to Charles, but there are no such letters from Charles to Henry; the affection was one-sided. Charles could not and never did forgive Henry for the fact that their father loved him better. It made matters worse that James tried to force him to be more considerate toward his younger brother.

With a renewed sense of pride after Vinceguerra's training, Charles became pompous and overbearing. The Earl Marischal, who visited Rome when the Prince was thirteen, found that he had "quite got out of the hands of his governors," an unfortunate assessment, for Charles was to meet Marischal again and need his help. Nobody crossed Marischal, a great and respected Scottish patriot who eventually became an adviser to Frederick the Great. He never liked the Prince, and lack of support from him later on thwarted many of Charles's dreams. The Prince had become impossible and unpleasant, arrogant and vindictive, reserving the bright side of his nature only for those who flattered him.

In the summer of 1734, when Charles was approaching his fourteenth birthday, the Duke of Liria wrote to say that he would be coming to Italy to fight in the Spanish service at Gaeta. Spain was attempting to regain by force the Italian principalities she had lost by the terms of the Treaty of Utrecht. Liria's view was that the action would not be dangerous, and he suggested that this would be a good opportunity for the Prince to experience a military campaign. James agreed, provided that Sheridan and Dunbar went along as tutors, for he was now more than exasperated with his son's atrocious efforts at letter writing.

The prospect of Gaeta, an uninspiring landscape on the southwest coast of Italy between Rome and Naples, was not relished by Dunbar or Sheridan, but they had no choice in the matter. French and Spanish officers were curious to meet the son of the King of England in Rome, and Liria was proud to show him off. However, to the despair of Sheridan and Dunbar, Liria also encouraged the boy to drink and carouse nightly with the officers, and Charles, who liked the taste of alcohol, was only too eager to prove he was a man. Thus began a lifelong love affair with the bottle, which contributed greatly to his eventual destruction.

There was little Sheridan or Dunbar could do but send a courier to James telling him what was happening. Back came a letter to Charles from his enraged father instructing him to cease "wine and play" immediately and to spend his time practicing writing. The courier from Gaeta to Rome had brought a token two lines in a slovenly hand from the Prince to his father reading, "My Lord Dunbar has excused me for not having write to you hitherto. I have been very good and umbly ask your blessing." Icily, James ordered Charles to copy letters several times over until they were correct and added, "I am sensible these ommissions proceed from your too natural aversion to all application & that if you do not get the better of yourself & endeavour to cultivate the Talents which Providence has given you, you will soon lose that good character which your present behaviour is beginning to gain you." A clash was brewing between father and son; Charles wanted to be a man, and James was treating him like a child.

When the party returned from Gaeta in September 1734, they met up with James and Henry at the Albano estate. Clementina remained in Rome, too sick to travel. The Prince had many stories to tell and brought back two horses that had been presented to him by Spanish officers. He had had a wonderful time with Liria, who may have used his young cousin to enhance his own image by introducing him as the future King of England. James was sick at heart that Charles had used the experience simply to strut and drink himself senseless at every opportunity. His ego was even more inflated now by the attention showered upon him, and he had learned nothing whatsoever about military strategy. It is a testament to his arrogance that ten years later, the next time Charles was near the scene of a battle, he presumed to instruct the great French Marshal Maurice de Saxe on how to conduct a naval assault!

In January 1735, two weeks after Charles's fourteenth birthday, his mother died at the Palazzo Muti. Clementina was only thirty-four years old, and the Pope's physician, signing the death certificate, named the cause as "scorbutic disease." Clementina had died of scurvy. Although normally associated with mariners subsisting for long periods of time on sea biscuit for rations, scurvy was also prevalent on land in a milder form and affected everyone to some degree. There was as yet no method of preserving leafy vegetables and fruits when out of season, nor was there any knowledge in the eighteenth century that these foods would ward off scurvy. Thus winters brought complaints of arthritis, rheumatism, gout, gum problems, and a whole host of other symptoms of the natural progression of scurvy on land. In the spring months, unless there was a famine, many of these symptoms diminished.

About twenty years after Clementina's death, the Scottish physician Dr. James Lind found the cause of and cure for scurvy after long years of observation and study all over the globe. In his famous *Treatise on Scurvy* published in 1753, Dr. Lind wrote a passage that explained why Clementina became scorbutic:

> I have always observed men of the rigorous orders in the Church of Rome greatly scorbutic. They are remarkable for rotten gums, (part of which is commonly eat away), want of teeth, and a most offensive breath.

Clementina had not been able to walk for some time before her death because connective tissue between each of the bones was affected by repeated fastings. Her teeth dropped out after several weeks of bleeding gums, and black ulcerous sores erupted all over her body, which, near death, exuded a rotting odor impossible to withstand. When she died, the Court was thrown into distracted mourning, according to letters from James and Edgar, and the Princes were ill with weeping and want of sleep as they prayed for her in the last hours.

The funeral was held in the Church of the Santi Apostoli a few yards away from the Muti; her heart rests in an urn in a niche along the aisle of the church. The body was embalmed and buried at Santi Apostoli, but ten years later it was removed for reburial at St. Peter's, where a marble monument and mosaic portrait of the Queen can be seen today.

It was a tragic end to a tragic and wasted life. Clementina had literally destroyed herself out of unhappiness that she had not been able to win her husband's love; she took no pleasure in her children to fill the void in her heart. Unreasoning willfulness, short-sighted obstinacy, and self-centeredness under the guise of piety had brought about her destruction and made an indelible mark on every member of the Muti household. Unfortunately both Princes inherited much of their mother's stubbornness.

James was not entirely blameless as a husband. He was dictatorial; his favorite cry was "I *will* be master of my own house." He was unrelenting and unfeeling toward the girl he had married fifteen years before. As with his children, he gave nothing of himself that would nurture emotional growth, but it had never been a marriage made in heaven. The Queen left some of her jewels to both Princes and favored Henry by assigning to him her *rentes* from Paris, but there were no special tokens of her affection for Charles, giving rise to conjecture that she may have gone to her grave believing he was a heretic. James was omitted from a share in her fortune, for Clementina did what she had often threatened to do and left the bulk of it to the Catholic Church. Some treasures can still be seen in the Sobieski Room at the Vatican. In the end, she had the last word.

Chapter 3

The Twilight of Princes

For the next few years a large question mark hovered over Prince Charles's future. He was filled with adolescent uncertainty about his role in life. He spent his days in idleness and frustrated boredom and was deeply distressed by his mother's death but kept his feelings hidden from everyone.

His family life was not very different from that of many unhappy princes reared in courts across Europe. Like James, their fathers had married a bloodline for pedigree, not for love; this system wrought devastating unhappiness on offspring taught to disregard their biological mother once she had performed her "duty."

Few royal fathers could spare time for the patient nurturing their children needed. Because they were Princes of the blood, the children were expected to be naturally endowed with all the qualities of the anointed that would bring them to adulthood sound in mind and body. Therefore, the only real guidance Charles and Henry experienced came from their separate tutors, confessors, and gentlemen-in-waiting. When they were away at Albano during the summer, they would receive affectionate letters from James addressed to "my dearest Carluccio" or "my dearest Hary" (as he spelled it), "tenderly embracing you from a father that loves you better than himself." But these phrases never varied and were repeated so often that they sounded mechanical. James expected "dutifull submission" from his children. In later years Pope Benedict XIV observed that he considered the Princes ungrateful if they did not show extraordinary affection toward him. On the other hand, when they made an effort to please, James

instantly became suspicious that they were concealing something. The Court at Rome was definitely not a happy place for two
growing boys; they were victimized, albeit unintentionally, by the
circumstances burdening their father.

James's two most overriding concerns were the lack of money
and the lack of a future for the family, particularly for the Prince of
Wales. The Spanish pension had not been paid in years, and
France's payments, which had always been random at best, trick-
led to a halt during the peace that all Europe was enjoying. James
was still receiving the *rentes* on the Hôtel de Ville accruing from
his family's investment, but the French government paid its pension only as long as James and the Jacobites were potentially useful
as a diversion in the event of war with England. But fifty years had
passed since James II's dethronement, and almost two decades
since the last Jacobite rebellion. It appeared in this time of peace
that James had outlived his usefulness as a diversion to either
France or Spain. The bleak financial picture caused the exile to
rely upon the friendly offices of a brother and sister, Claudine and
Pierre Guérin de Tencin.

The Tencins were citizens of France whom James had met in
Paris before he was banished. Pierre was then an abbé; he came to
Rome in 1721 as an aide to the French ambassador. His appointment had been arranged by Claudine, a clever courtesan who
shared her favors with the Regent Orléans, the Duc de Richelieu,
and the writer Fontenelle (by whom she mothered the famous
mathematician and philosopher Jean d'Alembert); several chron-
iclers of the time claimed she also shared an incestuous relationship with her brother. Abbé Tencin actually left France to avoid
the aftermath of an unsavory trial. He had been accused and found
guilty of using Church funds for his own purposes. But he was
welcome at the Vatican because he was a Jesuit and supported the
Pope's desire to win back his fading authority over the French
Church.

Despite instructions from the French government to their
diplomats in Rome that they avoid the Stuarts, Abbé Tencin paid
assiduous court to "*le Roi d'Angleterre*" because, as a monarch
recognized by the Supreme Pontiff, James had the right to vote in
important ecclesiastic appointments. Tencin eventually became
one of the few people outside the immediate Court circle whom
James considered a friend. When Tencin learned about James's
pension problem, he asked his sister to use her influence at

Versailles. She was able to get the pension reinstated and found a way to have the money paid into a Paris bank. Then Abbé Tencin remitted full value from his funds in Rome, thus saving approximately three-fifths of the value formerly lost by exchange difficulties between the two countries. James was suitably grateful, and by the end of 1723 Tencin reported to Claudine that he was confident of the royal vote in his ambitions. His ultimate aim was to become a cardinal, but first he became the Bishop of Embrun. He returned to France in 1724 and enjoyed considerable wealth from an enormous diocese that stretched as far as Lyon; James remained impoverished.

In 1729, the Tencins came to James's aid once again, this time with their own personal funds. When Regent Orléans died in 1726, Louis XV appointed his former tutor, Cardinal Fleury, to govern the country as Premier. Fleury disliked James Stuart intensely, and once more the pension failed to appear. Tencin arranged to send 100,000 livres to Rome through James's Paris agent, Daniel O'Brien. Somehow the transaction became public knowledge; Tencin's enemies circulated a story that he was bribing the exiled King for a nomination to the Cardinalate. The gossip also damaged James. There were those who doubted he would compromise his honor by accepting a bribe, but the charge surfaced again in 1737, two years after Clementina's death.

In that year Prince James Sobieski died, leaving a moiety of the Polish Crown Jewels, titles to land in Poland and Lithuania, and 400,000 florins to his Stuart grandsons. However, Clementina's two sisters and a nephew living in France (the Duchesses of Bouillon and Montbazon, and the Prince of Turenne) brought a lawsuit against their cousins, claiming that the 400,000 florins should be brought into "hotchpot" and divided equally among all Sobieski heirs. The funds were immediately frozen, and James —and later his sons—struggled with "ye lawsuite" for more than twenty years. The Stuarts were so poor that Charles and Henry were forced to sell their inherited land to their Polish cousin, Prince Radziwill, to meet expenses. At this time Claudine de Tencin offered James 30,000 Roman écus (approximately 90,000 livres) to be applied to any purpose he desired. When the next vacancy in the Cardinalate arose in 1739, Pierre Guérin de Tencin emerged as the successful nominee amid further charges of bribery and collusion between him and James Stuart.

As for Prince Charles, James had no idea what his future

would entail after he received from the Court of Spain a blunt refusal to consider a marriage between Charles and the Infanta. The Prince was sent on a tour of Italian states in his seventeenth year, accompanied by a small entourage and Lord Dunbar as the main "gentleman about him," but Charles had by then become rebellious and difficult to manage. "I cannot but tell Your Majesty," wrote Dunbar to James, "that he gives us rather more unease when he travels. But this is only a trouble to his own people, and particularly me who go in the chair with him." It was apparent from Dunbar's letter that Charles had been truculent for some time; undoubtedly the death of his mother, the sparse attention from his father, and not knowing what the future held for him contributed greatly to what plagued the Prince.

The Italian tour was a shock for Charles. Only the Court of Venice would receive him with royal honors and address him as "Your Royal Highness." At other ducal palaces he was received as "the Duke of Albany" (a title his Scottish ancestors had adopted in the fourteenth century), with no other special marks of respect or homage. The British government considered the Prince's reception in Venice an affront to George II and dismissed the Venetian ambassador in London as a warning to others that recognition of Stuart pretensions would not be tolerated.

George II was hardly quaking in his boots because the man he had supplanted was living in Rome and had sired two sons. He had the full backing of Parliament, which acted as the political sovereign, providing central authority, direction, and unity. Britain's acquisition of first a Dutch and then a German ruler brought her allies on the Continent; the nation had prospered and grown explosively in the half-century since she had rid herself of an absolutist monarch. Her navy had cut competitive swaths into French and Spanish trade in North America and the Caribbean, and although Brittania was still a few years away from the rulership of the waves that brought her a vast empire, it was already clear that she would outstrip her rivals.

Voltaire had recently published his *Letters Concerning the English Nation*, in which he praised London as a center of industry, commerce, and scientific discoveries. He was an early thinker of the Enlightenment period but had great trouble publishing many of his writings in his native France, particularly when he praised the free British press and its parliamentary system of government. King Louis XV was an absolutist, supported by a tightly knit aristocracy unwilling to give up an ounce of privilege. It was during his corrupt and ineffective reign that the seeds of the French Revolution began to germinate.

With the exception of Britain, the Continent was struggling through the transition from the absolute monarchical form of government to a more democratic form of government. Those who stood to lose by the change, which they perceived was being brought by heretical Protestant elements, fought every inch of the way. This change took more than a hundred years to come fully into being. It had begun with the dethroning of James II in 1688 and ended with the decapitation of Louis XVI in 1793. The royal Stuarts—James, Charles, and Henry—were thus exactly in the middle of this confusing era, known as the Twilight of Princes. They had to play out their roles for many agonizing years before darkness finally fell.

News coming to Rome from the outside world via the Holland and Swiss gazettes was now augmented by the English magazine *Champions* and by *The London Evening Post*. They brought reports of grumbling in London about taxation and the national debt; these reports were fancifully interpreted by Sir Thomas Sheridan for his pupil to mean that Britons were groaning under the yoke of Hanoverian oppression and were crying out for a return of the Stuarts. Nothing could have been further from the truth, but Sheridan convinced Charles it was so.

The Prince never read anything for himself; he spoke a curious jumble of English, French, and Italian without being able to distinguish one language from another. Although Sir Thomas was fluent in all three tongues, he was not a hard taskmaster. James appointed Francis Strickland, an English Catholic from Lancashire, as another gentleman about the Prince in the hope he would improve his son's Italian-accented English. He also appointed companions such as Henry Goring, son of an old-time Jacobite, and Michael Sheridan, reputed to be the nephew of Sir Thomas. However, these men represented little more to Charles than additional people to manipulate.

Sir Thomas was now past the age of sixty. He had unfortunately trained Charles the same way that James had been trained. As the son of James II's firstborn, Helene, Sheridan may have gone a little overboard in his teachings. The Prince was, by the Grace of God, the anointed son of a king whose mission it was to deliver his subjects from oppression; it was God's will that one day Charles would come into his own and rule his kingdoms. Lord Dunbar became deeply concerned that the Prince's indoctrination was leading to dangerously high expectations that could not be fulfilled. James was also concerned, for in his heart of hearts he now knew that there was but little possibility of a restoration.

To reverse Charles's expectations was not an easy matter, however. He was now almost twenty years old; he loved being called "Your Royal Highness" and clung tenaciously to his dreams. For James to take his son aside and lay out the bald facts would be to abandon the faith in the divine destiny of the anointed. Furthermore, to inform Charles fully would negate James's own posturing as a king—posturing that he dearly loved and would give up only with his life. "There is no help for it," as James often said when events went beyond his control. So life went on as usual, but he felt a measure of guilt that the glorious future he had painted for Charles probably would not materialize. He was also extremely concerned about the young man's laziness, describing him as "backward" and "wonderfully thoughtless for one of his age," spending far too much time on "little childish amusements." Constant criticism like this did nothing for Charles's sense of worth, and he became noted for his glassy-eyed stare and his reluctance to communicate socially.

He was also a spendthrift and a dandy, selling a few of the smaller Sobieski jewels to satisfy his appetite for rich apparel. The remaining gems were constantly in the Luoghi di Monti, Italy's equivalent of a pawn shop, but he redeemed them frequently to wear on special occasions and returned them when he needed money. From a renowned English tailor living in Rome's Piazza di Spagna whose talents were greatly sought after, Charles bought waistcoats in crimson, purple, blue, and yellow satin to wear over white silk ruffle-fronted shirts trimmed with lace. He also commissioned velvet breeches in black, burgundy, and royal blue fastened just above the knee to show off handsome calves clad in white silk hose. His shoes, with silver and diamond buckles, were crafted by the finest Italian cobblers; his favorite jacket was of coral-colored velvet, lavishly embroidered with silver thread and lined with silver tissue.

On grand occasions Charles wore the blue sash of the Order of the Garter, pinned by the Cross of Saint Andrew set in a dazzling sunburst of diamonds. The reddish-blond royal ringlets had long since been shorn, after a visiting Irish officer had inadvertently glimpsed the Prince with a headful of curl papers. Charles was so afraid of being thought effeminate that Lord Dunbar had to write the officer and beg him not to relate to anyone what he had seen. Now Charles sported a collection of manly periwigs; the long, full wigs favored by his father had gone out of fashion.

Fashion was all anyone talked about who had been to Paris. Charles yearned to travel abroad like other young men of his age. Confined to Rome and its environs because of his father's identity, he grew to loathe the Papal City, and he escaped to hunt in the countryside at least a half-dozen times every year. Only at carnival time, when Charles and Henry were asked to lead off the dancing at the traditional balls preceding Lent, did he enjoy the city. During the festivities, Rome was filled to capacity with foreign visitors who came to hear the music and watch the famous horserace from the Piazza del Popolo down the entire length of the Corso to the Palazzo Venezia. Young aristocrats competed for rich prizes such as a silver chalice or a valuable work of art.

The race was preceded by a parade of Italy's weathiest noble families. They came in glittering coaches drawn by magnificent horses and flanked by grooms and footmen richly liveried in the colors of the household to which they belonged. It was the Roman Mardi Gras; citizens and countryfolk promenaded down the Corso dressed in their finest to see and be seen, or they hung out of windows of rooms rented for the day, tossing candied sweets to the throng below. Charles loved the carnival atmosphere, complete with operas and comedies in the evening, but he rarely accompanied his father in public anymore because James still insisted on conducting himself like a king. No one could approach or speak with him unless an elaborate formal introduction had been previously arranged, which had the effect of making most people avoid him. The King had wisely decided against formal protocol for his sons, although each was still addressed as "Your Royal Highness" and known by his title of Prince of Wales and the Duke of York.

Many Europeans who came to Rome at carnival time were bright, well-educated young men who, like the Stuart Princes, frequently congregated for evenings at the Villa Borghese. The youthful foreigners could converse fluently in at least two languages on subjects such as politics, the Enlightenment authors, metaphysics, science, and the arts. They had seen the greatest cities and knew the latest news, but Charles, who had no knowledge of these things, found himself hopelessly out of his depth. He would disguise the fact by retreating alone into the garden to shoot at birds, a habit he had not outgrown, while Henry remained with the company chatting amiably in broken English.

One of these visitors was David Lord Elcho, son of the Scottish 5th Earl of Wemyss. He came to winter in Rome in 1739 and stayed for the following Spring Carnival. He was seven months younger than Charles and shorter in stature, as he discovered when James gleefully placed them back to back to show off the Prince's exceptional height of five feet ten inches. Although the Wemyss family was traditionally Presbyterian and supported the Protestant succession, Lord Elcho's grandfather had been deprived of the post of Grand Admiral of Scotland by George I. Thus excluded from Hanoverian favor, he and Elcho's father tended to be sympathetic to James, as many displaced Scottish families were.

When James heard Elcho was in Rome, he sent for the young man to introduce him to Charles, and thus began a stormy association that lasted many years. Elcho accused the Prince in later times of conduct ranging from fraud to brutality, but at this period he knew nothing at all about him because "Prince Edward never talked much to those who came to pay him court."* Elcho recorded Charles's curious penchant for killing blackbirds and thrushes in the gardens of the Villa Borghese, and also that he had taken up golf, a game imported from Scotland.

Lord Elcho accompanied the Prince to a *chasse* held at the Duke of Gaetani's estate in Cisterna. In his yet unpublished *Journal*, written in French, the young Scot gave us a glimpse of the wealth of wild game available in Italy and of the vastness of the estates commanded by privileged families. Coaches took hunting parties from an estate's main château deep into the woods for the first day's activity, snipe shooting. Peasants swarmed the area beating down undergrowth, while others busied themselves pitching large tents for the noontime meal. By the end of the day, after more than two hundred fifty long-billed snipe had been bagged, the hunters returned to the château for an evening concert and a magnificent supper. The next day everyone rode to another part of the estate, where deer and wild boar roamed freely; they returned

Many referred to the Prince by his second name of Edward to avoid confusion with several royal scions named Charles.

at dusk with twenty-five carcasses. On the third day the *caccia-tores* went to a private lake, where an enormous wooden pavilion had been built with a large dining room in the center surrounded by several bedrooms. Each hunter had his own separate rowboat; by day's end they had slaughtered no fewer than six hundred wild ducks.

James had prayed for war in Europe so that he could thrust himself to the forefront once more. He got his wish toward the end of 1739, when the War of Jenkins' Ear broke out between England and Spain over trading rights in Central America. A year later, in December 1740, a distinctly separate European war was started by a fledgling king, twenty-eight-year-old Frederick II of Prussia (later known as "the Great"). He had succeeded his late father the previous May. In October the Habsburg Holy Roman Emperor Charles VI (who had caused Clementina's arrest at Innsbruck two decades before) also died, leaving a female heir, twenty-two-year-old Maria Theresa. Because she was a woman, Maria Theresa could not assume the title of Holy Roman Emperor. It was hoped that her husband, Francis of Lorraine, would succeed. However, her father had had the foresight to secure an agreement of ruling groups in Habsburg territories and in every major European state that his daughter would inherit his scattered dominions after his death. This agreement was called the Pragmatic Sanction, and it was also ratified by King George II. Habsburg territories included mineral-rich Silesia in Poland, Austria, Bohemia, Moravia, Hungary, the former Spanish Netherlands (present-day Belgium), and Milan, Parma, and Piacenza in northern Italy.

One European ruler who did not ratify the Pragmatic Sanction was Charles Albert of Bavaria, who desired the Imperial title of Holy Roman Emperor for himself. Charles Albert was a Stuart and a Bourbon, the son of the Duc d'Orléans and Henrietta, daughter of Charles I of England. France decided to back Charles Albert, thus withdrawing from support of the Pragmatic Sanction. Upon learning this, Frederick of Prussia decided that if treaties were to be broken, he would march his crack toops into Silesia and take it for himself. Thus began a conflagration that eventually engulfed all Europe, the War of the Austrian Succession.

When it began, Maria Theresa was pregnant. She had been Archduchess of Austria and Queen of Hungary for only two months. She had had no time to organize a cohesive army, nor to consolidate administration in her far-flung empire, which was made up of subjects speaking at least eight different languages and countless dialects. It was a diabolically cunning move for Frederick to steal Silesia; he had cannily predicted the aftermath accurately. Charles Albert of Bavaria, now free to press his claims to the Imperial title, believed he should also be King of Bohemia. Augustus of Saxony was bent on taking Moravia, and Philip V wanted to retrieve Milan, Parma, and the Kingdom of the Two Sicilies, which had been lost to the Habsburgs in the Treaty of Utrecht.

By supporting Albert of Bavaria, France hoped to acquire the Austrian Netherlands and German territory in the bargain, while Britain financially subsidized Maria Theresa and moved troops into Flanders to reinforce the Dutch. Britain also subsidized the King of Sardinia, in the hope that he would help defend Maria Theresa's Italian territory against the Spanish and strengthened her Mediterranean fleet, operating from bases in Gibraltar and Minorca. Whatever else was going on in Europe, the Lords of the Admiralty kept their focus on the ultimate goal, to cripple the French and Spanish navies and create a clearer gateway for Britain into the New World.

The European situation rekindled hope in James that something could be done for his cause. He found himself at meetings with three men who also saw the conflict as a means to achieve their ends. They were Cardinal Tencin; Cardinal Aquaviva, the Spanish ambassador to the Vatican; and newly elected Pope Benedict XIV. These three had been friends for many years and shared a desire to bring France and Spain under papal control and create a solid Catholic bloc capable of dominating the New World. But the kings of France and Spain (Philip the uncle and Louis the nephew) had been at odds for many years; some way had to be found to unify them, or the New World would never be Catholic.

It was some time before the four men could agree on a course of action that would satisfy all their aims. An early meeting generated a memorandum from James listing the advantages to both France and Spain of acting together to restore him as King of Great Britain. Once on the throne, James promised to declare the Treaty of Utrecht illegal because he, the legitimate King of Great Britain, had not signed it. By this measure the Austrian Netherlands and the Italian possessions would be returned to Spain; and he would agree not to assist the Dutch if France chose to take Holland. Furthermore he would recall the Royal Navy from the

New World "because Great Britain is sufficient unto herself"! There were other desperate schemes, such as a promise to renounce in favor of Charles once he was restored and a marriage between Charles and Princess Henrietta of France.

It was Cardinal Tencin who fed some of these schemes into James's head. But the wily old exile knew exactly what he was doing, and he was on his guard for false promises. James never admitted to either Louis or Philip that he knew his restoration as King of Great Britain would never take place by popular demand. He did not have to admit it; they already knew that the only way James Stuart could become King was to restore him by force, and then to continue to drain their resources to keep him on the throne by force. Why would they want to do that, particularly when Spain already had her hands full with the war against England, and when France was uncommitted, on the sidelines? The French were likely to stay out of the fray as long as Fleury was Premier, because the ninety-year-old Cardinal's policy had long been pacific and was not likely to change. "As long as Cardinal Fleury governs," wrote James to Marischal, "I own I shall expect nothing from France except there be a war with England."

Yet James still kept up the pretense that he enjoyed massive support in both England and Scotland. For one thing, it was widely rumored that Tencin was a strong candidate to replace Fleury when the old man died, and James hoped that the Cardinal could hold sway over Louis XV, who was reported to be lethargic and uninterested when it came to affairs of state. But James was also wise enough to count on nothing. From his own experience he knew that Tencin was a self-interested man, regardless of the promises he made to do his utmost to restore James. James had to ask himself several hard questions: What if Tencin did not become Premier? If he did, why would he want to restore James Stuart to the British throne? What would be the advantage to him and to France? Would Louis XV approve of the proposal?

James had never met the French King. He knew much about his character from agents and spies, but Louis was still largely an unknown quantity. The fact that he had never once written a word to James, either by his own hand or that of a secretary (nor had Philip of Spain), lay uneasily upon James's thoughts. If the French helped to restore him, what other concessions would he have to make apart from recalling English merchant vessels from overseas trade and restoring the territories to France and Spain lost by the

Treaty of Utrecht? Would he have to cede territories—Ireland, perhaps, or Scotland, or maybe even England? It was said that the old Sun King had withdrawn support from James's father because he had refused to cede Ireland to the French. In fact, among the last instructions James II had left for his son was a warning never to divide the kingdoms of Britain, or France would swallow them whole.

It was clear to James that France and Spain did not have his interests at heart. Their negligence in paying pensions over the previous twenty years and the refusal of either King to give a daughter in marriage to Charles demonstrated that. There was a reason why Philip and Louis kept James impoverished and power-less. At some point this may have been explained to Prince Charles, but we cannot be sure.

In the Twilight of Princes, Louis and Philip felt as yet un-threatened by the changes in the wind. But they did feel threat-ened by hereditary superiority. Philip, James, and Louis all descended from Henry IV of France in the Bourbon line; James was the great-grandson of Henry IV, Philip was a great-great-grandson, and Louis a great-great-great-grandson. James Stuart was the most senior Bourbon of them all. How much the birth sequence colored relations among the three Kings is difficult to assess since it was never openly discussed among them, but the evidence suggests that it was in the interests of the other two to keep James Stuart in exile. Helping James regain his British kingdoms was never part of any plan formed by Philip and Louis. As the French King asked in 1744, "If the people of England really want James Stuart to be their King, why should he need my help?" It was an excellent question.

James knew and understood all these things only too well. Among the three Kings he was by far the most astute, even if he was the least in terms of power. At the outbreak of war in 1739 and 1740, James realized that if he and his Jacobites were given any consideration at all, it would be for the purpose of creating turmoil in Britain. James did not know what the policies of Louis and Philip might be in the conduct of the war, but he was more than willing to lend himself to any diversionary ploy they could conceive—with certain reservations. He would extract the utmost for his family from the situation. He was guided by the fact that there was absolutely no future for his eldest son in Italy. James had come to the conclusion that the only avenue open to Charles was as a military officer in the service of either France or Spain. But those countries had shown reluctance to cooperate in the matter. If he allowed himself to be used to create a diversion in Britain without appearing to his "subjects" to be a willing dupe, then perhaps the Kings of France and Spain would give his son a place in the world in return.

James's strategy meant that he had to deceive his followers. Here our history radically departs from histories that claim that James was the innocent dupe of France and Spain in what followed. For the next four years James counted on the loyalty of the Scottish Jacobites to strengthen his hand at the bargaining table. He wrote letters to adherents saying his hopes were high that France would soon act to restore him, although he had no foundation for any such hopes. His intention was to rekindle interest in the Jacobite cause among his far-flung followers so that they would be ready when he needed them. There is no evidence that Charles was aware of the extent of his father's mendacity at this time, mendacity that was to change form as the various Continental conflicts unfolded. For the moment, the Prince was to do merely as he was told.

To put his plan into motion, James had to do something about the waning fires of Jacobitism in Scotland. Many of the chieftains of the traditionally loyal clans were scattered throughout the Continent and were impoverished since their attainders in 1715 and 1719. They had long since lost touch with their homeland, and hundreds of their clansmen had found employment in the British army and navy. Thousands more had emigrated to the New World to escape poverty. In Scotland the largest clan, Clan Campbell, policed the Highlands for the Hanoverian government, and northern clans such as the MacKenzies, MacLeods, and Mackays and many MacDonalds had washed their hands of James Stuart after he abandoned them in 1716. As if that were not bad enough, it was well known that Scots could be called en masse to the banner on the word of one man alone, and that was Lord Marischal, who was living in exile at Boulogne sur Mer. He was a true Scottish patriot and was widely respected for his sagacity. If for one moment he suspected that the French were supporting a rebellion in his homeland for their own purposes, he would put a stop to it merely by spreading the word. Marischal was so influential that every important Scot looked to him for leadership.

Although it hurt his pride, James was mindful of Marischal's power and sensibilities. So he never consulted the Earl at any time about the tack he would take. He wrote to Marischal and to the Duke of Ormonde in Avignon on a monthly basis (both received royal pensions), but he gave them little information except family news. Neither man would have condoned his negotiations with Spain, because they were convinced that the Spaniards had used the Jacobites for their own purposes in 1719.

James had learned through Cardinal Aquaviva that Spain was willing to finance a Jacobite rebellion for her own ends, but only if Louis also supported the scheme. James suggested that a suitable reward for allowing this to happen would be for Charles to become Governor of Navarre, which stretched from the Bay of Biscay in the southwest corner of France into Spain's northern border, then extended eastward to the Mediterranean. But the demand was too grandiose and met with no response from Madrid. James was forced to revise his demands downward; he suggested that Prince Charles join the army of Don Philippe, one of the King of Spain's sons. Again there was no response.

Pope Benedict XIV, a kindly man, was squarely behind James's demands. He was deeply distressed at the treatment the exile had received over the years from his fellow kings and cousins. When no word came from Madrid regarding Charles's future, the Pope levied an additional 6,000 écus a year from Spanish bishoprics, abbeys, and sinecures, to be paid to the Stuarts for life. This effectively doubled the papal allotment granted twenty years before, but the increase did not cover the interim inflation of prices. Benedict further decreed that the income from the Bishopric of Malaga was to go to the Stuarts after the death of the current recipient, Cardinal Alberoni. Now fallen from power and living in Italy, Alberoni had been Spain's chief minister at the time of the abortive 1719 Spanish-Jacobite effort. It was as if Benedict were forcing Spain to repay what he believed she owed to the Stuarts.

To be of use to the Catholic powers, James had to organize his scattered adherents from his base in Rome. Problematically, he knew Marischal would not cooperate. In March 1740, a thoroughly scurrilous Scotsman by the name of William MacGregor (or Drummond) of Balhaldies arrived in Rome. "Balhaldy," as everyone called him, was the forty-two-year-old son of Alexander MacGregor of Balhaldies, chieftain of the clan; he made his living by flitting back and forth between Britain and Paris to spy on the

English for the French Court. He presented the outward appearance of a gentleman, but he was detested by honest men such as the perspicacious Marischal. Balhaldy was a carefree bachelor who spent his ill-gotten gains in the bawdy houses of London and Paris. He "was master of enough bad French," said his enemy John Murray of Broughton, "to procure himself a whore and a dinner." Nevertheless, he kept his own counsel and was sufficiently skilled at lying and cheating his way through life that many were taken in. But not James, who knew him of old.

Balhaldy said he represented a quartet of Central Highland chiefs calling themselves the Association of Highland Gentlemen. They claimed to be eager to assist the King's cause. In the event of a rebellion three of the chieftains wanted to be named Lords Lieutenants, which would give them authority and power over more than sixty major clans throughout Scotland. Naturally, none of the other clan chieftains was to know. One of the chiefs was Simon Fraser, Lord Lovat, a notoriously evil man who had gone over to the government side during "the Fifteen" to save himself from attainder and forfeiture of estates. He wanted to be named Lord Lieutenant over all the clans and territories north of the River Spey. The second chief was the impoverished Sir James Campbell of Auchinbreck, chieftain of a cadet branch of the mighty Campbells; his naming as Lord Lieutenant over Argyllshire was thought necessary to woo other clan members from the progovernment Duke of Argyll. Campbell of Auchinbreck was so poor that he was on the point of emigrating to the West Indies, along with other members of his clan, but Balhaldy said that if James paid Campbell a pension of 300 pounds sterling a year, he could be persuaded to stay at home. The third chief was Donald Cameron of Lochiel, known as "Young Lochiel" or "the Gentle Lochiel." His father had come out in "the Fifteen" and had suffered attainder afterward. The father, "Old Lochiel," had been forced to live in France in poverty, reviled by Paris society because he had no title, as were many Scotsmen. Old Lochiel wanted to be elevated to the Peerage, and Young Lochiel wished to be made Lord Lieutenant over the Western Highlands, including the Inner and Outer Hebrides.

James brought up the subject of Marischal in his talks with Balhaldy because it was very unlikely that the Earl would agree to what was being planned, and most Scots would expect him to be named Commander in Chief. Balhaldy suggested the mild-mannered Duke of Perth for the position, with Lovat and Campbell of Auchinbreck acting as lieutenant generals as well as Lords Lieutenants. He stated, "It is further thought necessary that Lord Mareshal have no extraordinary powers by which he may have influence to form and model mens minds, so as to cary what he certainly thinks right . . . least thereby a door be opened to faction and dispute which is not so easily shut again."

Lords Lieutenants had the power to call men together to form fighting companies. They were also authorized to issue commissions to officers so that they could raise their own companies. Fighting would most certainly break out if James gave Lovat, Campbell of Auchinbreck, and Lochiel absolute authority over fiercely proud clans such as the MacDonalds (the second largest clan in Scotland), the MacLeods, the Macleans, the MacKenzies, the MacNeils, the MacPhersons, the Ogilvies, the Chisholms, the Sinclairs, the Grants, the Gordons, the Stewarts of Appin and Ardshiel, and the Murrays—just to name a few. But a civil war in Scotland could be most advantageous for France, and James realized that Balhaldy was not serving the Association of Highland Gentlemen as much as he was catering to his French paymasters. James refused to sign patents naming the Lords Lieutenants until France gave "some assurance of her good dispositions towards me." Indeed, he refused to put his signature to anything until the King of France brought him and his family out of Italy. Since this was the last thing Louis wanted to do and James knew it, from 1740 onward he plotted to force the French King's hand.

Simply stated, James's strategy was to tell his people that the King of France was going to restore him, and he would arrive in person to lead the expedition. With Balhaldy's help, he had to create a semblance of Jacobite unity so that Louis would be tempted to try to use them for his own ends. Then James hoped he and his family would be invited to France, where Louis would be honor bound to treat them well. Balhaldy left Rome with a signed order creating his father, Alexander MacGregor, a knight and baronet, with the title to devolve upon Balhaldy after his death. He was also authorized by James to borrow money for Campbell "from any of our faithful subject [sic] it can be safely got from, and to give our obligation for it in our name to be paid at our Restoration with interest."

Naturally, Balhaldy was not going to advance the money himself. When he arrived in Scotland he turned the task over to the unsuspecting John Murray of Broughton, who, in his eagerness to ingratiate himself with Rome, had assumed the duties of secretary for the Association. Murray was gullible enough to sincerely believe he was engaged in the King's work, and so he advanced the money to Campbell of Auchinbreck himself. Balhaldy also brought James's instructions to the chieftains with "vassals" who were leaving Scotland in droves for the New World "to hinder and divert all by safe means the pernicious humour of transporting themselves to our plantations in America or elsewhere, this being mean and ignoble in them not to learn by our example to suffer in so good a cause."

At a meeting in Edinburgh called by Balhaldy, the group was assured that a rebellion was in the making with positive commitments of assistance from foreign powers. Balhaldy said that arms and ammunition had already been purchased and that money would be available for raising men and victualing. He led them to believe a restoration on James's behalf was "an assured thing" and that it was planned for the autumn of 1741 or the spring of 1742. The Scotsman knew this was a gross deceit, but he had no qualms about lying to his countrymen.

Telling the others that he was to do the King's work at the Court of France, Balhaldy left Scotland; he would not return for two years. He sent occasional messages back to John Murray of Broughton saying that all was in readiness for an uprising and that he would receive word soon. Further carrying out James's orders, Balhaldy met with the handful of English Jacobites in London— Lord Barrymore, Sir John Hynd Cotton, Sir William Watkins Wynn, and a few others. None of them was foolish enough to believe that a restoration of James was possible, but nevertheless Balhaldy returned to the French Court with glowing accounts that "three fourths of the landed gentry" in England were zealous for the Stuart cause. He was asked to provide the Englishmen's signatures, which, of course, none of them would commit to paper; he complained plaintively to James, "If this continues to be their direction, I doe not see a possibility of Your Majestys deceiving that court." Although James suspected that there was little chance of fooling the French, Balhaldy's journeys back and forth across the Channel were useful for stirring up gossip among the Paris Jacobites about the impending arrival of their own King to lead an invasion. The gossip was also useful to the French because it reached the ears of English spies. It was said that George II was concerned enough to stay in England when he heard there was a plot to restore James Stuart. Since France's main interest in the Continental war was in acquiring Holland and more German lands, they were quite happy for George to stay in London so that he would not lead his Hanoverian soldiers to join up with Maria Theresa's Austro-Hungarians.

Matters were moving very slowly because the aging Fleury steadfastly refused to commit his nation to war, even though several French politicians urged him to do so. The old man was tired and failing rapidly. Anticipating his death, Cardinal Tencin returned to Paris in the summer of 1742 after renewing his promise to James that if he became Premier he would do everything in his power to help his family.

In that same year a violent quarrel erupted between Charles and Henry that James later said "was the foundation, and I may say the key, of all that has followed." Most details of the quarrel were contained within the walls of the Palazzo Muti, but it would appear that Henry had become a religious fanatic, keeping company only with Jesuit priests. Based on observations of the Duke of York by others later on, it would also appear that he was homosexual. Although homosexuality was prevalent in Italy and on the Continent, it was anathema to Charles, and he was embarrassed that people sniggered behind his brother's back when he turned the genuflection into a flamboyant display. We know more about Henry's attitude and mannerisms from observers who criticized him in 1745, when he was in France.

Charles still labored under the delusion that one day he would be King of England. Henry's excessive piety troubled him as well as the discovery that James was encouraging him toward a career as an ecclesiastic in the Catholic Church. From Lord Dunbar and Strickland, the Prince came to know that prejudice against his family's religion had been the major obstacle to a Stuart restoration; he could not understand why Henry was being allowed to continue in this way. It would appear that James was preparing a future for Henry in the event that the family never reached France, but Charles had no inkling of his father's concerns at that time. Without consulting James, the Prince took it upon himself to speak to Henry about his excessive devotion to religion and about the harm it would bring to the cause. When that had no effect, Charles prevailed upon Strickland to help; he also asked Lord Dunbar to draw up a detailed description of Henry's activities to present to James.

When news of the dispute between his sons reached the

King's ears, he was grieved beyond measure, for he had always blithely assumed that total harmony existed between them. The nature of the quarrel hit at his very heart and soul, because he too had become very pious in his later years. He did not speak with either Henry or Charles at this time, but he questioned members of the household, including John Constable (Henry's governor), Mr. Dicconson (a tutor), and Henry's confessors, Fathers Ildefonso and Ramilles, as to who was to blame for fostering trouble between the two Princes. Dunbar's report was highly critical of Henry. It detailed that he rose at daybreak and attended Mass sometimes four times in a day, then returned to his apartments, where he spent several hours praying so loudly that he could be heard from outside the door of his suite. He ate sparsely and pored over theology books well into the night so that dark circles appeared beneath his eyes. Dunbar was convinced that Henry's regimen was "ruinous to his health" and that if he persisted, "he would arrive at the age of twenty-two without having cultivated his understanding or acquired a reasonable degree of such knowledge as is the chief duty of his station at present both towards God and man."

It was years before James came to terms with the enmity between "my children." However, he had been so involved with plots and intrigues that he had failed to see the trouble brewing. True to his penchant for blaming others when the household was upset, he later accused Strickland of "putting wrongfull notions into ye Prince's head," and for a while he was even displeased with Dunbar. But eventually he laid the blame for the quarrel upon Prince Charles.

James realized that his sons would have to be separated as soon as possible. His anxiety to see the Prince placed in a gainful occupation in France increased. The King worried that Charles drank too much wine and that he could not afford his own expensive tastes. He wrote to Tencin that the Court of France would have to support the Prince because he simply could not, for Charles had a habit of running up charges without his father's knowledge or permission. Year-end accounts for 1743 showed that the King spent 3,825 livres on himself, Henry spent 8,143 livres, but Charles spent 31,198 livres.

At last, in February 1743, word was sent that Cardinal Fleury had died at the end of the previous month. James waited eagerly for the naming of Tencin as Premier of France, but instead Louis XV surprised everyone by declaring he would appoint no Premier. He intended to take over the reins of government himself.

Chapter 4

Charles Goes to Paris

Vain, vacuous, selfish, handsome, lazy, profligate, and easily bored—all these adjectives describe Louis XV, the weakest monarch France had suffered in a long time. In his thirty-three years of life, Louis had always been ruled, first by Orléans and then by Fleury; but now he was delighted to be master of his own fortune at last. He played with government like a child with a new toy. Although he had inherited a Council of five men, one of whom was Cardinal Tencin, the King preferred to discuss affairs of state with his mistress, Madame de Châteauroux, and rarely uttered a word at Council meetings. He was secretive and impenetrable and was famous for his ability to carry dissimulation to great lengths. Unknown to his own ministers, he corresponded with secret agents abroad and opened private letters to members of his Court. No one could predict what his next mood or decision would be.

He was married to the long-suffering Maria Leczinska of Poland (a kinswoman of Clementina Sobieska). By her he had fathered ten children, seven of whom survived. But she had become drab and embittered by the parade of women Louis had cast his eye upon. The King often indulged in long evening suppers, drinking champagne and playing backgammon until five or six in the morning. Then he amused himself by strolling across the rooftops of the Palace of Versailles, talking to ladies down chimneys before going to bed. He slept during the day, rose at five o'clock in the evening, and held court or conducted business at night.

Claudine de Tencin, probably informed by her brother, told the Duc de Richelieu, "The Council is really laughable. Scarcely anything is said which concerns the State. Those who wish to occupy themselves seriously with such affairs are obliged to give up any such desire owing to the lack of interest which the King seems to take in them and the silence he keeps." Cardinal Tencin had been appointed to the Council as minister without portfolio in August of the previous year, but the French government itself was in chaos. Four men were mainly responsible for the conduct of government, but each ran his own department while jealously guarding his responsibilities from the others. The only efficient one among them was Philibert Orry, the Controller General. The others were the Marquis d'Argenson, the Secretary of State for War; M. Maurepas, now in his early thirties, who had held state office since the age of twelve, the Minister of the Marine; and the weakest of them all, the diminutive, stammering M. Amelot, Secretary of State for Foreign Affairs. He was so inefficient and muddle-headed that rumors circulated that he would soon fall from power.

Argenson and Maurepas used Amelot to handle matters with which they would rather not be involved. They also set him up as a scapegoat when things went wrong. For a while, however, they allied themselves with the timorous Secretary of State for Foreign Affairs in order to prevent Tencin from gaining a foothold in the government. They objected to him for being a Jesuit and pro-Pope, for his past misuse of funds, and for the methods he had employed to acquire his Cardinal's hat. They were also aware that Tencin and James had often been closeted in meetings with the Pope, although they had not been successful in discovering the substance of those meetings. Because Cardinal Aquaviva of Spain was also involved in the gatherings in Rome, they suspected they had something to do with the Pope's plan to marshal the might of France and Spain under his mantle. Everyone, it seemed, had a scheme for universal domination.

The French ministers were afraid that Cardinal Tencin would gain the King's ear and persuade him to embark on a rash project backed by the Pope involving James Stuart. Tencin had already suggested as much at a Council meeting. Some saw possibilities for creating and supporting a Jacobite rebellion in Britain, and the suggestion was not rejected out of hand; but nobody wanted the Stuarts on French soil. Seeing how detested the name of James Stuart was in the French Court, Tencin withdrew from too active a hand in Council affairs and waited to see if the passage of time and the progress of the European war would bring a more favorable occasion to present a plan to Louis.

The task of communicating the Council's position to James's Paris agents was assigned to Amelot. Tencin gladly handed over correspondence from Rome, saying that he wished to devote himself only to his flock at Lyon—an announcement that was greeted with general skepticism. But he kept one document back. It had been sent to him by James in February 1743 and contained a "secret" that Tencin divulged only to Louis. Plenty of references to this "February packet" can be found in subsequent letters from Rome, but not a trace of the packet's contents remains in James's files or in French archives.

We can only make an educated guess as to what the secret was, based on later events and on comments in subsequent letters. Most certainly it involved James's renunciation of his claims, bringing the family out of Italy, and a future for Charles. We may automatically assume that renunciation would mean renunciation of his claim to the throne of Great Britain in favor of Charles. But this would not make sense in 1743. In the first place, neither France nor Spain recognized James; only the Pope did, so there would be no value in renouncing. Also, what was he renouncing but a throne that he could not hope to gain without military assistance from the Catholic powers? As for renouncing in favor of Charles, it is plain that he had nothing to renounce under his present circumstances. However, if we consider the pecking order of the Bourbon line, and that James was the most senior with a lusty young son capable of siring children, James may have believed that Louis would be attracted to the idea of giving one of his daughters in marriage to Charles. In that event, the "renunciation" so often referred to in heavily coded private correspondence of this period, would have been of the Stuarts' claim to be masters of France. For instance, James had several times claimed his full title to be "James VIII of Scotland, the II of Ireland and England, *and* King of France." His father before him had also claimed France among his domains because the Scottish Royal House of Stuart, by virtue of centuries of intermarriage with French royalty, was closer in line to the Crown of France than was any Frenchman.

It was the rights and title of James's senior proximity to King Henry IV of France that he had to renounce to Louis and Philip of Spain. Henry IV had once been King of Navarre, and then became King of France in 1589. James had humbled himself by asking for a mere Governorship of Navarre for Charles, but Louis and Philip would settle for nothing less than a full renunciation of his Bourbon claims *before*, and if, anything would be done for

Charles. This James steadfastly refused to do because the Kings of France and Spain would make no promises about the Prince's future. The situation between the three Bourbon cousins reached a stalemate because both Louis and Philip had sons of their own for whom they had great plans, and neither could see any possible advantage to marrying even their younger daughters to Prince Charles Edward Stuart.

The pot may have been sweetened in James's February packet by suggestions that he would do his utmost to whip up the unsuspecting Jacobites so that they could be used by France. James's underhanded part in this scheme is probably what Amelot was not to know. But there was an even larger secret that James and his family kept to themselves: this was that the papacy (friendly as the present incumbent was) could no longer afford to recognize the Stuarts because the lack of diplomatic relations with Britain and with the powers friendly to her was economically disastrous for Rome.

If James and Charles understood at this time that the latter would not gain royal recognition in the future—and much of what followed indicates that they did—it would explain why James insisted upon being brought out of Italy. Obviously, it had to be a closely kept secret, one that must never be allowed to reach the ears of the King of France. For if that happened, James would have nothing to bargain with, and his only remaining value to the French would be his power to command the Jacobites. However, James had many enemies among the foreign Cardinals at Rome, including the French ambassador who replaced Tencin. Again, judging from what followed, it would appear that Louis did discover the Stuarts' tenuous position in Rome. But James, unaware of that, continued desperately to try to gain recognition for Charles, which had to be accomplished before he died.

The February packet and later dispatches contained James's suggestions for organizing a rebellion. He was to issue declarations and addresses to the Scottish and English nation, to the Lord Mayor and Aldermen of the City of London, and to the universities of Oxford and Cambridge. Concurrently, he would release patents for Lords Lieutenants and commissions for officers, and he would name Commanders in Chief for both England and Scotland. These actions would have the double effect of keeping George II and his soldiers at home while convincing the Jacobites that the rebellion was truly for the purpose of a restoration. James repeated his request that in return for these actions the Stuarts be brought to France and both sons given places of honor. When he perceived that the Court of France was not willing to entertain the notion of a marriage between Charles and one of the French princesses, James again suggested the Governorship of Navarre for Charles or, alternatively, a commission in either the French or the Spanish army.

Because Cardinal Tencin was deliberately keeping out of Stuart affairs for the moment, it was several months before James could get the French ministers' reactions to his proposals. He knew, however, that they were initially lukewarm. When English soldiers were moved into Flanders in the spring of 1743, James hoped this would make the French take a closer look at his plan. In the meantime, Tencin reported that one of France's objections to the scheme was general disbelief that James commanded an adequate number of Jacobites to be of use. James relied on his agents, Daniel O'Brien, Balhaldy, and Lord Francis Sempill, to convince the Court that he did.

James's most trusted and valued representative in Paris was Daniel O'Brien, who flawlessly reported happenings at Versailles for 10,000 livres a year. The King also needed the services of dishonest men: Balhaldy, to journey back and forth across the Channel, and Sempill, as an additional stationary agent in Paris. Sempill had eased himself into quasi-favor with James several years before, when he had assumed management of the dwindling "English correspondence" from London that had all but come to a halt. However, because Sempill was largely dependent on the 4,000 livres a year from James and had an ailing mother to support, he never admitted to anyone how small in number and how ineffective the "English correspondents" were. It would appear that Sempill had a contact in the War Office in London who occasionally fed him intelligence useful to France. Sempill earned a small pension from the French Court for passing the information along. He was so afraid of losing his usefulness either to James or to the French that he constantly exaggerated the strength of Jacobite support in England. James was fully aware of Sempill's exaggerations, but his skill in making them was precisely what James needed at Versailles. For the previous three years Sempill had been working hand in glove with Balhaldy at James's behest.

James relied heavily upon Colonel Daniel O'Brien for the "true lights" on any given situation. He was the son of an Irish

Jacobite who had followed James II into exile and then had taken roots in Spain, where Daniel had spent his childhood and many adult years. He had been an officer in the service of both France and Spain. To see what Amelot was doing and to keep an eye on Sempill and Balhaldy, it was necessary for him to brave the halls of Versailles from time to time. O'Brien disliked the journey because he was disdained at Court, and it was said Louis XV was prejudiced against him. This may have been because of his connection to James or because he was a commoner with no title (James later created O'Brien Lord Lismore in 1746), or there could have been a more personal reason. It was well known that the sixty-year-old O'Brien was being openly and frequently cuckolded by his wife Elizabeth,* who was twenty-eight years her husband's junior. Some said she had been a conquest of Louis; her name was also linked with the Duc de Richelieu. She eventually left O'Brien to live with the Archbishop of Cambrai, an illegitimate son of Regent Orléans whose mistress she had been for some years.

It is small wonder that O'Brien absorbed himself in the voluminous reports to Rome, which often took up more than sixty handwritten pages a week. That his letters and private life have hitherto been ignored is largely due to the wrongful assumption that Balhaldy and Sempill were James's trusted agents, instead of merely being used by him. Another impediment to the identification of O'Brien (whose mother tongue was Spanish) as keeper of the King's secrets has been that he always wrote heavily coded letters in a difficult-to-read hand in atrocious eighteenth-century French. Moreover, he used cant terms in a cipher shared only by himself and Rome. It has always been easier to peruse Balhaldy's and Sempill's letters, which were written in English, and to assume these men had the King's ear. But it is among the letters of Daniel O'Brien that the real story unfolds.

O'Brien's reports to James from Versailles were not encouraging because, although Amelot agreed that a Jacobite rebellion would be useful to France at some stage, it was perfectly obvious that neither he, nor Louis, nor any of the other ministers had any intention of bringing James and his family to France. Amelot

---

*Elsewhere her name is given as Margaret Josepha, but her contemporaries called her Elizabeth. The O'Briens had a son in 1736 known as Viscount Tallow; he later succeeded to the Lismore title and to great riches. Since O'Brien was not a wealthy man, Tallow may actually have been the natural son of the Archbishop of Cambrai.

would not say so outright but fobbed off O'Brien with wait-and-see tactics while he plotted ways to take advantage of the unrest that he knew Balhaldy was fomenting in Scotland and England.

Amelot had met John Murray of Broughton in March 1743, when the Scotsman came to Paris from Edinburgh to check on what Balhaldy had been doing in the three years since he had said a rebellion was definitely in the making. Murray and the others (who no longer called themselves the Association of Highland Gentlemen) were told that Fleury had been the impediment. Since the Premier had recently died, Murray sought an update of the situation. Balhaldy introduced young Murray to Sempill, who also assured him that France was intent on restoring James Stuart. Balhaldy and Sempill instructed Murray to tell Amelot that Scotland was ready to rise.

Murray was obviously putty in the hands of the two agents, for although years later he wrote in his *Memorials* that he had doubted Amelot's sincerity at that gathering in March, he neglected to add that he wrote to James claiming to be completely satisfied with the meeting. Balhaldy also persuaded Murray to complain to James about Marischal's presence at Boulogne sur Mer. Everyone knew he was the most logical Commander in Chief for Scotland, but as yet James had made no mention in letters to Marischal of any plans for a restoration, and the Earl injected doubt into many people's minds by saying so. Balhaldy wanted Marischal gone from Boulogne. His hope was that James would order him to Avignon out of harm's way, but the King could do nothing about the situation without bringing suspicion upon himself. The "tracasseries" among his people were only just beginning.

Amelot was beginning to wonder if the fragmented Jacobites could ever be useful when Daniel O'Brien came to see him late one evening at the end of May, accompanied by an imposing gentleman who had just made a secret dash across the English Channel at great personal risk. The man was the Earl of Wemyss, Lord Elcho's father. His twenty-four-hour visit to Paris from his home in the north of England is believed to have been made at James's instigation. He told Amelot that he was willing to raise the nobility from the areas of York, Durham, and Lancaster, provided the French assisted with arms, money, and men.

The reason for this secret meeting in Paris may have been that James wanted to convey the impression that Jacobite supporters also existed in the middle regions of the British Isles, and coming so soon after Murray's visit, he hoped the Earl of Wemyss could convince Amelot that the Stuarts still commanded enough respect in their homeland that France could not wash their hands of them easily. Why the Earl of Wemyss undertook this mission for James is hard to fathom. He certainly had no intenton of raising men; nor did he wish to see civil strife in the land. Nevertheless, his appearance at Versailles made a great impression upon Amelot.

As the French government muddled along without direction, Louis's mistress, Madame de Châteauroux, a twenty-seven-year-old courtesan, was using her wiles on the King to divert his ever-wandering attention and to sate his extreme vanity. Châteauroux was the only person who shared Louis's innermost thoughts and schemes. Their grandiose plots coupled with his meddling in military affairs would ruin the nation.

Louis resurrected the House of Bourbon's old ambition of universal monarchy, a special passion of the old Sun King, whereby France would dominate Europe and then the New World. The King's first step was to secretly ally with his uncle, Philip of Spain, by proposing a marriage between the Dauphin and the Infanta (the one Charles had once hoped to wed). Louis then planned to march on the southern Netherlands to drive a wedge between George II and his Hanoverians; this would prevent them from coming to the assistance of Maria Theresa. Her defeat would mean victory for the Spaniards in Italy. Louis hoped to take Hanover, Holland, and the southern Netherlands from her for himself. With these prizes in hand, the French King anticipated being able to wrest considerable concessions from England during the inevitable peace negotiations.

At the end of May Tencin at last gained a meeting with Louis. He learned that none of the schemes for universal monarchy in the House of Bourbon included restoring the cast-off James Stuart. Louis was determined to carry on the policy of Fleury and Orléans of keeping James as far away from his Jacobite "subjects" as possible, including the soldiers, mostly Irish, in the French and Spanish service. Cardinal Tencin brought up the matter of a future for Charles. He relayed the news to Rome that Louis first wanted James to renounce all his royal claims and titles.

Everything was now "*sur le tapis*," as James said. Matters were "on the carpet" and out in the open. It was only too clear that the French King wished to rid himself of the Stuart nuisance. This was reminiscent of what had happened between James II and Louis XIV. Gossip at that time had had it that the Sun King and Orléans had somehow connived to bring about the fall of the Stuarts to provide a spare throne for Orléans and his descendants. Times were different now. Louis XIV was intelligent, and James II was not. Half a century later, the intelligence was reversed; the titular James III could outthink both Bourbon kings put together. Although he was not coming from a position of power, he was not ready to give up. He realized that Cardinal Tencin had to be a servant of his own government now, and James responded to the request that he renounce all his claims and titles (and Louis was probably more concerned about Bourbon-line supremacy than anything else) by saying that he would consider it only after Charles had been adequately provided for. Matters reached this impasse in the middle of June 1743.

On June 19, George II surprised everybody by arriving in Flanders and personally leading the English and Hanoverian troops to join up with Maria Theresa's Austrians. En route, the Pragmatic Army, as it was called, was marching toward supply stores at Hanau when he walked into a trap; the French army under Marshal Noailles staged a surprise attack at Dettingen, on the banks of the Main River. George moved part of his force into the southern end of Dettingen, while twenty-four thousand Frenchmen lay concealed in the northern end. The remainder of Noailles's men were hidden by bluffs and riverbanks along the southern and western boundaries, ready to obliterate the Pragmatic Army between two fires once they had all marched into Dettingen. However, youthful impetuosity caused the Duke of Gramont, who was in command of the French troops in the northern part of the village, to show his hand far too soon. He commenced the attack after only a small body of George's soldiers had entered Dettingen. In order to engage the enemy, Gramont was forced to move farther into the village than had been originally planned, and Noailles (Gramont's uncle) had to cease his battery for fear of killing his own men. George II quickly recovered from the surprise and charged the French. He sent them scattering in retreat across the Main, where hundreds were drowned or trampled to death by their own cavalry. Although the Battle of Dettingen can hardly be called a military victory, it was regarded as such by many Englishmen. Handel composed a special piece of music in honor of it. Although George II wore Hanoverian uniform and was present at Dettingen in his capacity as Elector of Hanover, British history marks this battle as the last time an English king personally led his soldiers to victory.

In the streets of London, news of the Battle of Dettingen inflamed the age-old English hatred of the French. But angry voices were also critical of George, who was blamed for bringing England to the brink of an expensive war merely to benefit Hanover. So no war was declared against France in retaliation for Dettingen. Louis took advantage of the situation to pursue his goal of universal monarchy.

Neither Hanover nor the Netherlands had been taken, and Maria Theresa's Austrians were firmly entrenched along the Rhine. Louis decided that an alliance with Frederick the Great would be of great advantage, and in the middle of August he took the extraordinary step of sending no less a personage than Voltaire to Berlin to plumb the depths of the Prussian King's mind. This plan was conceived by Madame de Châteauroux, who knew—it was no secret—that the middle-aged philosopher and the young warrior King had shared an intimate relationship for the past seven years. Letters between them had been intercepted in which they addressed each other as "lover" and "mistress." After two months Louis received Frederick's curt refusal to ally with France. The Prussian king was content to let the European powers dissipate their energies fighting among themselves while he built his country into a major European power.

In the meantime, Louis had sent an equerry named James Butler to join Balhaldy in England. Butler's cover for the journey was that he was going to buy English horses for the French army, but he deliberately let slip a story to the Jacobites in Paris that he was going to London to finalize a restoration of James Stuart. Undoubtedly, this was for the benefit of the growing number of Jacobites being influenced by Marischal. They were saying that they would not participate in a Scottish rebellion unless the French proved to them it was genuine and that a simultaneous descent on England was planned.

Butler's real mission had nothing to do with preparing the way for a Stuart restoration. It was to bring back a current account of ships in English ports and troops in garrisons. The French were particularly interested in trying to capture Tilbury Fort at the mouth of the Thames and the Essex port of Maldon. These were vital British supply links with Holland, which had recently allied with England.

While Voltaire and Butler were away on their separate missions, Louis intercepted letters from Admiral Matthews, who commanded the English fleet in the Mediterranean. Matthews begged the admiralty for relief because his ships were in great need of repair and his men were dropping like flies from scurvy. Conditions were so bad that no English ships had sailed from Gibraltar and Minorca since the end of July. The French took advantage of this absence to send a fleet to rendezvous with Spanish ships at the port of Toulon. From there the Franco-Spanish forces planned to march to Turin and join with Charles Emmanuel of Sardinia, who they supposed was an ally, and then to drive Maria Theresa's Hungarian soldiers out of northern Italy and the Rhine.

By the middle of October, when Butler, Balhaldy, and Voltaire returned to Paris, however, the English had already made their move. In early September, seemingly out of nowhere, Admiral Matthews had swooped down on Toulon and bottled up the French and Spanish ships in a blockade that was to last for six months. At the same time the King of Sardinia, who had been dallying with France and Spain while accepting subsidies from England, decided to form an alliance with George and Maria Theresa. Crippled by the loss of ships and unable to attack Maria Theresa from the south, the French were forced to take a new look at the Jacobite scarecrow.

Louis began to correspond with Philip. The appearance of an attack on Britain would be extremely useful to both France and Spain at this time, and he hoped to assemble ships at Dunkirk to be ready in January. The date was moved back to February and then March, partly because of bad weather but mostly because the best ships were bottled up at Toulon. As early as September, Sempill had written James asking him to send the wording for the declarations and manifestos to be printed, but the King had refused to do so. Although he had long since ceased to talk of returning to France himself, he still hoped for an invitation for Charles, and he decided to hold on to the declarations until he had received satisfaction on that matter. He notified Sempill of his decision and added the ominous warning: "I should be sorry any private ones were actually sent out at this time."

According to Balhaldy's yet unpublished version of what happened at Versailles when he returned from England, Balhaldy asked Amelot for permission to journey to Rome and to return to Paris with the declarations and Prince Charles. Amelot told him to travel to Rome via Switzerland and trace a safe route through the Alps that he could use to quietly return with the Prince and reenter France at Belfort on the Swiss border so that no one would know of their arrival. In a subsequent meeting Amelot changed his mind about Balhaldy returning with the Prince. The Scotsman was told that if Charles wanted to travel to France via Belfort under his own steam, he could leave Rome on January 12, 1744, "after the expedition set out." Balhaldy then asked for a letter from Louis to James explaining why Louis had delayed sending for the Prince. Not until November 23 did Balhaldy get his answer. It was that Louis had declined to write because he feared the letter might be intercepted while Balhaldy was in transit to Rome. The Scotsman then asked how he was supposed to persuade James to allow his son to leave Rome with no official invitation. He was told that Louis would write "as soon as the expedition took place"! (The "expedition" was no more than an assembly of ships at Calais and Dunkirk in the first week of January. It was contrived to persuade the British that an invasion was planned so that Admiral Matthews would abandon the blockade of Toulon. The ruse did not work.) These were the salient points contained in Balhaldy's acount, which was committed to writing under duress from James. It was to form the slim foundation for James's future claims that "the King of France has called for my son."

Balhaldy's account does not jibe with letters written by Louis to Philip dated December 6 and 10, 1743, a few days after Balhaldy set out for Rome. In those letters and in the subsequent replies from Madrid, Louis and Philip referred to George II as "His Britannic Majesty" and to James as "the Chevalier de Saint George," leaving little doubt as to which person they believed was entitled to occupy the throne. According to the French King, Balhaldy's mission was to bring back the declarations only, for the Jacobites did not expect either James or Charles to be in France, because "surrounded by spies as he is, his departure from Rome cannot be kept a secret."

In the last days of November Balhaldy set out for Rome by way of the Swiss and Italian Alps with another Scotsman, Duncan Buchanan, as his traveling companion. Buchanan was clerk to Aeneas MacDonald, the Scottish banker in Paris, but he was looking for other employment because MacDonald's bank was failing. For three weeks on the journey they suffered incredible hardships, making their way through snowbound passes. They encountered Maria Theresa's soldiers in encampments along the route, but at last they arrived in Rome on December 17, 1743.

When James learned that they had come only for the declarations and not for the Prince, he was beside himself with anger and railed furiously at Balhaldy. The two men could not have arrived at a worse time, for James had been sick with "a defluxion on my gumms" and sores on his feet, symptoms of a nutritional deficiency disease that struck most Europeans in the winter. Lord Dunbar was suffering from what was known as gout, and arthritis crippled his hands so that he had not been able to write letters in months. Dicconson, Henry's tutor, had died in October, and Lord Nithsdale had taken to his sickbed and died the following February. Charles and Henry were still at daggers drawn and kept as far away from each other as possible, and all Italy, from Reggio di Calabria to the Gulf of Genoa, was under quarantine due to a north-bound Sicilian plague that had claimed hundreds of lives each week since spring.

When James simmered down, he made Balhaldy write several memoranda* relating in full the details of his meetings at the French Court: what exactly was said and who had said it. The slippery-tongued Scotsman was cornered, for he knew that whatever he wrote would be used against him if he dared to lie. The King also told Balhaldy to draw up a complete itinerary of the towns he had passed through on his way to Italy, the miles between each, and the details of Austro-Hungarian encampments he had encountered on the way. At heart he disbelieved Balhaldy's story that Charles was to set out on January 12, and suspected the Scotsman was lying to cover his failure to secure an official invitation. But James acted as if he were going to send Charles through Switzerland to Belfort. He caught the loquacious Scotsman neatly by asking about quarantine procedures. Although there were none for travelers into Italy, the requirement of a stay of five to eight days was mandatory for those leaving Italy; and this had been in force for months. But when questioned, Balhaldy did not know these regulations, which told James that part of the Scotsman's mission had not been to clear the way for the Prince's departure.

On December 23, James signed the commissions for the Lords Lieutenants of Scotland and commissions naming Lord Marischal

---

All unpublished, these were discovered by the author in the Stuart Papers, unsigned and filed out of date order. This explains why they have been overlooked heretofore.

Commander in Chief of Scottish forces and the Duke of Ormonde Commander in Chief of English forces. There were also declarations and manifestos addressed to the Church of England, the universities of Oxford and Cambridge, and the Lord Mayor and Aldermen of the City of London. James kept copies of these documents in his files; they were later found by historians and published as if they had actually been printed and issued at the time. They were sent to Paris with Balhaldy in a sealed package to be delivered to the King of France (which it is known he did receive), but some of the documents were neither printed nor distributed, and Marischal and Ormonde did not receive their commissions until very late in the proceedings.

James also wrote a personal letter to Louis:

Rome, December 23, 1743

My Brother and Cousin:

Mr. MacGregor arrived here last Tuesday and communicated to me the resolutions and intentions of Your Majesty as he was charged to do, the account of which has penetrated me with such strong sentiments of attachment towards Your Majesty that words will not suffice to make the extent known. I candidly avow to Your Majesty that my first impulse was to defer the departure of my son until I could receive more precise orders and instructions from you, but upon reflection of the probity of Mr. MacGregor and the eminent virtues of Your Majesty, I believe that I might on this occasion bypass the usual rules without risking your disapprobation of anything that might befall your court, so that finally I have determined not to constrain the ardor and vivacity of my son to go where his duty, his honor, and Your Majesty call him . . . He will leave, therefore, in conformity with what Mr. MacGregor related, about the 12th of the coming month . . .

The only authority James had for his action was the passage in the memorandum he made Balhaldy write, even though the Scotsman later qualified the statement by saying that Louis had thought better of the plan and would send for Charles after an expedition had set out.

In his letter to the King of France, James was careful not to mention by which route Charles would enter France, but he led Balhaldy to believe it would be through Belfort. On December 24 he sent the Scotsman back to Paris. Duncan Buchanan was to remain behind in Rome and accompany the Prince on his journey later. Balhaldy was to take the short route to Paris via Genoa and Antibes. From there he was to go through Avignon, then north-ward to Paris via Lyon. He was to be accompanied every step of the way by Bandini, the Pope's postmaster, who was to take charge of all documents, including orders that Balhaldy was to open at various stages of the journey. The Scotsman was humiliated by the procedure, which also included daily reporting back through Bandini by way of the Pedone, the highly efficient papal commu-nications link between Rome and Avignon, but the message was clear. James did not trust him, and Balhaldy knew he had better carry out his instructions to the letter because his future knight-hood hung in the balance.

Bandini and Balhaldy reached Siena on Christmas Day, and the Scotsman's usual braggadocio failed him when he was forced to admit that he had been wrong about quarantine regulations. With that knowledge, he said, "my heart sunk into my heels." He had encountered the most difficulty at Massa, where quarantine was usually rigidly enforced before anyone could enter the state of Genoa. The postmaster at Massa remembered his coming through a week before with his friend "Mr. Graeme." (Balhaldy and Buchanan had traveled incognito as Messrs. Malloch and Graeme.) Balhaldy bribed the postmaster with five chequins to give him billets of health as if he had been at Massa for some days; he said that Mr. Graeme would soon be passing through with another gentleman and that "it would favor me much if he pro-cured their billets of health as he done us." Balhaldy also learned that "the name and badge of Courier is necessary to open all gates and barriers in the way to Massa which they doe to no other."

From Genoa they went overland to Cannes but were stopped and questioned by both the town's commandant and the governor of the province. This delayed them considerably, so that they did not reach Antibes until December 30, six days after they had left Rome. On the way Balhaldy picked up the information that it was not possible to enter any French port along the stretch of the coast where the Ligurian Sea meets the Mediterranean without under-going quarantine. The two men reached Paris on or about January 6; en route Balhaldy opened orders from James to make himself scarce in England as soon as he had delivered the package to the Court of France. There was reference to a letter James received from Balhaldy dated at Paris on January 10, 1744. Unfortunately, this was either lost or destroyed, for no trace of it can be found.

James deliberately changed his mind about the departure date, moving it up three days to January 9. He wrote to Lord Sempill to explain that he intended to organize a hunting party to provide Charles cover for his escape from Rome. How much the Prince knew about the background of his journey is uncertain. He was fully aware, however, that there was no authentic invitation and that he was to arrive in France *publicly* in an attempt to shame Louis into treating him honorably. Disguises, a boat, passports, and other documents were required to put the plan in motion. James secured the cooperation of the Pope, Cardinal Aquaviva, and Jean-Louis de Tencin, the Cardinal's nephew, who was the ambassador from Malta to Rome. The "Bailli de Tencin" (he had the rank of Bailly in the Order of the Knights of Malta) believed James when he said the Court of France had called for his son, as did the others, and he probably believed this had come about as a result of his uncle's work. But there is no evidence that Cardinal Tencin knew anything at all about this stage of the proceedings.

Through Bandini's reports, James learned that there were encampments of both Spanish and Austro-Hungarian soldiers between Rome and Genoa and that passports would be necessary to get Charles through that stretch of country. Cardinal Aquaviva was only too happy to comply with safe-conducts through the Spanish camp, but getting documents from Maria Theresa's Hungarian ambassador was another matter entirely. Bailli de Tencin went to the ambassador, Monsieur de Thun, and said he wanted passports for his friend the "Marquis Spinelli" (Charles) and an accompanying Neapolitan officer. (When Thun later found out Bailli de Tencin had lied, life in Rome was made so uncomfortable that he escaped to Paris for a while.) It had already been decided that accompanying the Prince, in addition to Duncan Buchanan traveling as "Mr. Graeme," would be François Vivier (the "Neapolitan officer"), a Frenchman who had been a groom at the Palazzo Muti for some years, and Monsieur Godinet, Bailli de Tencin's steward.

On January 4, five days before the plan went into execution, Buchanan and Godinet left Rome by coach. They intended to go ahead to Massa, to make arrangements with the postmaster to get through quarantine, and then to wait for Charles and Vivier to arrive. However, a short distance outside Rome, Buchanan and Godinet learned that nowhere in Italy could fresh horses be obtained for carriage-borne traffic. Only "post" horses were available for those riding horseback. This meant that they had to return the carriage to the Muti and start out again the next day astride horses. This early hitch was actually rather fortunate because a heavy snow fell on the day Charles and Vivier left Rome, and if they had had to rely upon a coach, they would never have passed through the mountains.

Privy to the plan were Sir Thomas Sheridan, John Stafford (a gentleman-in-waiting), James Edgar, Lord Dunbar, Strickland, Father Vinceguerra, John Townley (who had replaced the late Mr. Dicconson), and the Duke of Gaetani, from whose estate the hoax was to take place. Only the Duke of York was unaware that anything was happening. Why he was kept ignorant is unclear, except that Henry was given to walking around dressed entirely in black "like a Monseigneur" and praying loudly. He was also highly excitable, and perhaps it was feared that he would give everything away. However, the most likely reasons for Henry's being kept in the dark were that he simply would not have approved, since he wanted to stay in Italy and devote himself to the Church, and that information leaking from the Muti was suspected to come from Henry's household.

Security was indeed a problem. On January 7, Sir Horace Mann, the British resident envoy to the Grand Duke of Tuscany in Florence, wrote one of his frequent reports to the Duke of Newcastle, England's secretary of state. Mann now had complete charge of all espionage agents throughout Italy, including Walton in Rome; he had been keeping a close eye on the Stuarts for the past few years, ever since Walton reported as early as 1739 that James was brewing restoration plots. For the previous two months Walton had found it difficult to extract secrets from the Muti, owing to the death of his inside informant in October. Since Mr. Dicconson, of Henry's household, was the only person to have died in October, one can assume that he had been the inside informant all along. Mann began his January 7 report to London with news about the Spanish and Austrian encampments, then he went on:

> . . . other letters mention the great motion that has been observed in the Pretender's house, and that it is generally believed they tend to the Eldest son's departure from Rome, to which the Pretender himself seems averse till he sees on what foundation. My utmost attention is employed to be informed of every thing that relates to that family, and I hope I shall not fail of having the earliest notices of any thing that should happen.

On the morning of January 9, 1744, well before dawn, spies watching the Muti saw nothing unusual about the assembling of coaches, horses, grooms, and retainers there. It had been given out that the Prince of Wales and the Duke of York were to engage in the *chasse* at the Duke of Gaetani's estate in Cisterna; indeed, it had been their habit to do this, always leaving at dawn, at least six times a year for several years. The brothers usually traveled in separate coaches, since Henry liked to stop at every shrine to pray, and this time was no exception.

Leaving Henry's party hitching horses to coaches at the Muti, Charles and his retinue drove south through the city past the Colosseum to the Porta S. Giovanni, leading to the Via Appia. A key had been left for them the night before so they could unlock the gate, but once outside the city walls, Charles stopped the carriage and was heard to argue with Sheridan about wanting to continue the journey on horseback. Vivier and John Stafford were already waiting with three saddle horses, and although Sheridan appeared to remonstrate with Charles, sometimes in English and sometimes in Italian, the Prince insisted on riding horseback to Cisterna by way of Albano, and he told Sheridan not to tell his father or brother. For the benefit of watching spies, Sheridan continued to protest, saying that the Prince would catch cold and the journey would be dangerous on the bad winter roads, but Charles prevailed and rode off with Vivier and Stafford, calling out that he would reach Cisterna long before Sheridan.

The gatekeepers and other witnesses to the scene gave little thought to this exchange because the Prince's headstrong obstinacy was well known. Their attention was further diverted when Sir Thomas fell into a ditch, on purpose, so that no one would see which direction the men took. At a safe distance from Rome, Charles took off his wig and put on a courier's uniform with a large cap covering his eyes, while Vivier donned the uniform of a Neapolitan officer. They gave their cast-off clothes to Stafford, who was to hide at Albano. Later that evening the gentleman-in-waiting sent a message to Henry at Cisterna saying that Charles had fallen off his horse but was not seriously hurt. Stafford asked Henry to send two shirts to Albano for the Prince because they meant to stay there for a couple of days, and he begged him not to mention anything of the accident to the King in case he should be concerned.

In the meantime, Charles and Vivier rode northward on the road to Cardinal Aquaviva's house at Caprarola, some thirty miles away. The snow that had been falling since the previous night still persisted. For eleven and a half hours they plowed through massive drifts. At Caprarola, Aquaviva gave the two men fresh post horses and passports, and Charles was given the badge of a Spanish courier from Cività Castellana to speed his way through quarantine stations. It was now seven o'clock on the evening of the ninth, but Charles and Vivier pressed onward through the night, suffering dreadful hardships while crossing over snow-clad Mount Radicofani. The courier badge and passports enabled them to acquire fresh horses at each crossroads. They must have been taken for men engaged on a mission of desperate import connected with the war.

They continued traveling night and day without sleep; they finally reached Massa at four o'clock on the afternoon of the eleventh. There they met Buchanan and Godinet, who had bribed the postmaster for quarantine clearances for four men. Since the snow had put their arrival at Massa a day behind schedule, the party of four left the same evening, after the Prince and Vivier had snatched a few hours of much-needed sleep. Their destination was Genoa, where Cardinal Aquaviva had arranged for a Catalonian *felucca,* the swiftest craft on the Mediterranean, to await their arrival of January 12 in a quiet corner of the harbor. It was not until the following evening that the Prince and his party arrived at Genoa. They immediately set sail (Charles had now assumed the identity of the Marquis Spinelli) and made for Savona, hugging the coast tightly to avoid detection by any English warships that might be patrolling the waters. The light craft put in to port in the early-morning hours of January 14.

The Prince and his companions were forced to stay at Savona for six days before they could continue onward to their ultimate destination, Antibes. That there would be a delay of some days was part of James's schedule. In his planning he had estimated an arrival date at Antibes of January 20, allowing for time to satisfy the quarantine requirements, which Balhaldy had earlier warned were strictly enforced at ports of entry. The receiving port for France was Monaco, farther on down the coast from Savona, but the winter storm had brought fierce squalls, high seas, freezing rain, and icy waters, so that it was impossible to put out to sea. Still-existing logs of British ships in the area supporting the Toulon blockade record dangerous weather conditions from January 14 to 20, and even they dared not brave the open sea.

The Prince must have spent an agonizing six days at Savona

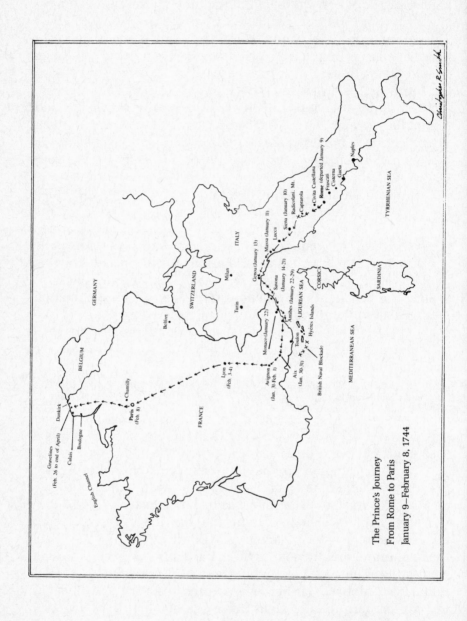

The Prince's Journey
From Rome to Paris
January 9–February 8, 1744

wondering whether his departure from Rome had yet become public knowledge. His great fears were that the foreign ministers had already been informed by their spies and that a message might already have been sent by Sir Horace Mann to Admiral Matthews. But incredible luck was with them. Not until January 18 did the foreign ministers first begin to suspect anything unusual about the Prince's absence, which meant that, including the day of the ninth, Charles had a ten-day headstart. James had once estimated that no more than three days could pass without the Prince's absence from Rome being detected, so this was remarkable. The success was entirely due to all those who had gone to the *chasse* at Cisterna.

The hunting party decided to move the venue from Cisterna to Fogliano, where they were told they were to meet Charles on Monday, January 13. It was then that Henry first learned, from a letter sent by his father, where Charles had really gone. He took a couple of days to respond to James's letter but appeared to take the news surprisingly well. He even entered into the spirit of the plot by sending wild geese, pheasant, and ducks to friends in Rome, as if they were gifts from Charles. The problem with the charade was that the Duke of Gaetani's wife, who was about to give birth to a child in Rome, kept urging her husband to return home. She could not understand why he stayed away hunting so long at such a time. It may have been the length of the hunt that eventually caused suspicion in the Papal City.

On January 18, James was openly questioned about his son's disappearance. He knew perfectly well how the Prince and his party were faring because a Pedone post rider had relayed their progress from every stop on the way. James admitted that Charles had gone to France and that his reason for doing so was to accompany the King of France on a military campaign. Although Louis had given no such promise, the least James hoped for was that his son would be allowed to accompany the French King to Flanders.

In Florence, Sir Horace Mann, who had promised his government the earliest notice of anything that happened, had been utterly hoodwinked, and his understanding of what had actually transpired was imperfect. Not knowing that there were four men, he circulated a description of only two, the Prince and Godinet. He mistakenly said the Prince's eyes were blue when they were a brownish color, but otherwise he described Charles accurately—

tall, long-faced, fair-skinned, with a large mouth, curving lips, and
large expressionless eyes. Sir Horace described Godinet as being
around forty years of age, with brown hair and a round face. The
earliest Admiral Matthews could have received this description of
the two men was about the time the party of four was making ready
to set sail from Savona.

On midnight of January 21 the *felucca* slipped out of Savona
without lights and eased into the harbor of Monaco. There they
waited out the daylight hours until dusk, then made sail for
Antibes, arriving at seven-fifteen that evening. From the quayside
a letter was sent to the port's commandant, Villeneuve, asking if he
had received orders from the Court of France to allow them entry,
but there was no such document. James had not expected there to
be. He wrote a letter dated January 2 to Sempill asking him to relay
to Amelot that Charles would leave three days earlier, on the ninth
rather than the twelfth. In that letter James said he had changed his
mind about Belfort and was sending his son through Antibes,
where his estimated date of arrival would be January 20. James also
said he expected that orders from the Court of France giving
permission for his son to enter the country would be waiting at
Antibes. James did not really expect any such orders to be there; he
simply did not want to be accused by France later on of not
informing them of the time and place of his son's entry into
France.

On January 21, when Sempill received James's January 2 letter,
he was thunderstruck. This was the first he had heard of the
Prince's coming to France; Balhaldy, supposedly now in England,
was not available for questioning. Sempill went immediately to
see Amelot, who furiously denied ever saying the Prince could
come to France and told Sempill to write James and tell him so.
Sempill did, but it was already too late. Amelot's great mistake,
and the most likely reason for his eventual dismissal from office,
was that he was so querulous and confused that he did nothing to
stop the Prince's entry. It would have taken four days for such an
order to reach Antibes from Paris, but none arrived.

At Antibes, Commandant Villeneuve did not know the identity of the men who had arrived in the Catalonian *felucca* while he
was at supper—he only knew that they had not fulfilled the
quarantine requirements at Monaco. He sent a note to the *felucca*'s
master, ordering him to sail to Monaco to obtain the necessary
quarantine documents; until he did so, no one aboard the vessel

would be allowed to disembark at Antibes. The next morning (January 23), when the *felucca* still had not left Antibes, Villeneuve went to investigate. He was astounded when a tall, fair-skinned young gentleman introduced himself as the son of the King of England in Rome.

Charles played his part beautifully. It was obvious he was prepared for this dubious reception at Antibes. He announced that he had an urgent packet to be immediately dispatched to the minister of war, the Marquis d'Argenson. It was also to Argenson that Villeneuve sent a letter at two o'clock that afternoon:

. . . The prince is attended by three people; he gave me the packet and requested me to send it with all diligence. He told me that at first his orders were to pass through Switzerland and he actually had a carriage waiting at Belfort, but that plans had changed and he departed suddenly from Rome with an order from Cardinal Aquaviva for a boat to carry him from Genoa to Antibes . . .

When I arrived at the harbor to see who were the passengers in question, a longboat arrived from an English ship anchored at the mouth of the port and asked for refreshments which I gave them. But I suspect the request for provisions was a pretext. The longboat also boarded a fishing boat that left the harbor this morning. The master of the vessel told them that a Catalonian felucca had arrived, and the English informed him of the departure of the Prince from Rome. They are sending cruising ships to stop all feluccas. We have seen no English ships off the coast for ten days, except one yesterday morning and one this morning which is now actually in the harbor.

It is extremely puzzling that this mysterious British ship appeared at all at Antibes—an unfriendly port—when Toulon was being blockaded not far down the coast. Furthermore, not one logbook of the British fleet in the Mediterranean (all of which are still intact) recorded a call at Antibes. The British ships were all lying off the Hyères Islands (where there were ample provisions), opposite the port of Toulon. So where did the mystery ship come from?

One fragmented clue suggests that the Stuarts actually hired the ship and paid the English boatmen to play their part so that Villeneuve would be sufficiently alarmed to let the Prince pass on. The Italian coastline was fairly littered with English deserters who had been press-ganged into service; they faced death from scurvy unless they jumped ship. Finding men to do the task and rigging a vessel with appropriate colors would not have been difficult. The basis of this suggestion is a heavily water-damaged and torn letter dated from Siena the previous December 26, when Balhaldy and Bandini were making their way to Paris from Rome. It was written in a polished hand and signed "J. Stuart." This may have been John Stuart, a strange figure who kept carefully in the background. He stayed devotedly by the Prince's side during his dying days and was said to have accompanied Charles to Scotland, although no record of his participation in that country's rebellion appeared at the time. It would seem that he had been sent by James to accompany Bandini and Balhaldy part of the way through Italy. The portions of his letter that can be read are as follows:

> All I can do is just to acquitt myself . . . that I wou'd write from Sienna. There was too much reason for my Suspicions, tho' they did not tally exactly with the Persons [Balhaldy's?] designs, he had not yett entirely form'd his Scheme, but was thinking that without the Walls of Rome was the most favorable occasion he should meet with. He has two Wretches . . . in the Enterprise . . . Storke & has been Midshipman on board Adm. Matthews & the others name I dont yett know. I shall quitt him either here or att Florence & on my ' arrival shal give you more particulars.

Stuart then signed off and added a curious postscript in which three or four words are missing at a time:

> 'tis with the utmost difficulty I shal be able to . . . & if you had not exactly . . . perhaps finished the . . . I shal keep my word if . . . only say this that he is perhaps the horridest Rascal the Earth ever bore.*

He sent this letter to James Edgar. Sketchy though this piece of evidence may be, it may contain the answer about the ship that called at Antibes to ask questions about Charles. Certainly no English ship was in the harbor on that date or on any day during this entire period. "John Stuart" may or may not have been referring to Balhaldy as the person trying to form a design, but it is clear that somebody not fully trustworthy was planning something with two "wretches" of English seamen, and it had been Stuart's task to report to Rome on the matter.

*Unpublished letter, Stuart Papers, Volume 254, fo. 113.

It is a tribute to the cleverness of James's secret plans and his covering his tracks that it has taken more than 240 years to discover how he actually got Charles into France. But there are one or two mysteries left, and we still have not yet got the Prince to Paris. Along with his and Villeneuve's dispatches to Argenson, Charles wrote another curious letter, which was penned for him by Godinet. The addressee was not identified; although the index to the Stuart Papers says it was sent to Sempill, he did not receive it, and the high-toned form of address and style of writing was not the usual manner employed when writing to "Lord Simple," as Charles came to call him. It could only have been sent to Amelot, who was, according to Balhaldy, the person in the French government who had first mentioned the departure date of January 12 and who knew that Balhaldy and Buchanan had journeyed to Rome as "Messrs. Malloch and Graeme." This particular letter gave notice that "Messrs. Graham and Malloch accompanied by two people" had arrived at Antibes, which has made historians believe that Balhaldy was at Antibes with the Prince. But he was not at Antibes; he was reportedly in England, or perhaps he had been ordered to Belfort.

Another point about this letter is that since Charles had already declared his true identity, why was it necessary to use code names? The document may have been written in an attempt to implicate Amelot by using Jacobite code names, so that when the inevitable questions arose later, Charles could say the French government had known all along that he was coming. Louis XV did eventually order a search through Amelot's files a few months later, and the discovery of this letter, with Jacobite code names, may have been part of the justification for the man's dismissal.

The alarmed Villeneuve never doubted the authenticity of the "English ship." He became fearful for the safety of the son of the King of England. He hid the *felucca* in a corner of the harbor with everyone still on board, then notified the governor of the province, the Marquis de Mirepoix. This was exactly according to plan. The Marquis was an old friend of James's, and his brother, the Bishop de Mirepoix, owed his position to James's ecclesiastical voting power. There is little doubt that Mirepoix was part of James's plot. He told Villenneuve to grant permission for the *felucca* to stay at Antibes for eight days. If by that time no word had been heard from Paris, the Prince and his party should be considered to have satisfied the quarantine and allowed to enter France. Eight days were leniently counted from the time the felucca had been at Monaco, and on January 29, Charles wrote to Rome that they had all been released into the custody of "M"—Mirepoix. When later questioned by a letter from Amelot, Villeneuve naturally referred the matter to his governor; Mirepoix's response to questioning was that he had not received orders to stop the Prince.

From Antibes the party rode on horseback to Aix. They arrived there late at night on January 30, after having great difficulty finding decent horses at each of the sixteen post stops along the way. They decided to buy a coach and set out for the Papal City of Avignon on the morning of the thirty-first. At Avignon they did not see the Duke of Ormonde or even make any contact with him, as would have been expected if Charles had believed that an invasion of England on his family's behalf was the reason for his journey. Nor was Ormonde delivered his commission as Commander in Chief of the English forces at this time. These omissions proved to be major flaws in James's plan, and they aroused great suspicion among the Jacobites later on. The party was housed by Lady Inverness (her husband, John Hay, had passed away in 1740) and by the vice-legate of Avignon, Nicholas Lercari, who also acted as the Stuarts' legal counsel. The report to Rome from Avignon was that Charles and party had eaten heartily and slept soundly.

The next stop was Lyon, where they arrived on the afternoon of February 3. They left at dawn the next morning for the last leg to Paris. By now the older men, Buchanan and Godinet, were exhausted and "quite rendu," as Charles declared, adding that if they had had to go any farther, he would have had to tie them to the coach with his luggage! Finally, on the evening of February 8,* Charles and his bedraggled entourage quietly arrived in the French capital, to face a very unsure welcome the next day.

*This is the first time February 8 has been given as the date of the Prince's arrival in Paris, and also the first time how he accomplished the entry into France and who accompanied him have been fully explained. All other accounts not only state that Charles was invited by Louis XV but that he arrived on February 10. This was the date Charles wrote to his father saying he had reached Paris "on Saturday," which was February 8, 1744.

Chapter 5

The Expectant Heir

Charles wrote to his father: "I have met with all that could be expected of the King of France, who expresses great tenderness, and will be careful of all my concerns." This was not, however, the real picture. Louis was away at his residence in Marly when the Prince arrived, and he absolutely refused to receive him or to take responsibility for his presence in Paris. Charles's early letters were worded very carefully because it was common knowledge that mail leaving the city by "the ordinary" post was opened and read before it was sent on its way. Louis had bribed the postmaster general to bring his dispatches of special importance, which they perused together every Sunday afternoon.

Charles always sounded overly optimistic in letters to his father, and even after a safe cipher system had been arranged between them, he tried to hide several of the drawbacks of his life in Paris. He had not gone through all this danger and physical hardship just to return again, and he was unwilling to be recalled to Rome "with ye melancholy prospect of spending my life there." He intended to stay away forever. Even though James had another twenty-two years of life ahead, father and son never saw each other again.

The Prince had at last broken free from family bonds; he was a "master of his own fortune," with a life of his own to lead and mistakes of his own to make. Having come this far, he did not doubt that his derring-do would impress the French King (Frederick the Great was impressed when he heard about it), and his expectations were very high that Louis would treat him respectfully. But the French King had been upstaged; he was acutely embarrassed and angered beyond measure.

Andrew Thompson, the British ambassador in Paris, protested Charles's presence in France as a violation of the Treaty of Utrecht, but the French explained his arrival as the act of a rash young man who had made the journey without consulting anyone. Philip of Spain was also mystified; he had been notified by Aquaviva about his unwitting part in getting Charles out of Italy in the belief that the King of France had called for him. This was not the plan Louis had outlined to Philip; therefore the French ambassador in Madrid, Vaureal, was instructed to find out what he could from Amelot.

Replying on February 27, Amelot said that the Chevalier de St.-George had taken an "imprudent step" in sending his son to France after being told to wait for news of an expedition before doing so. "I do not yet understand for what reason he changed this plan," said Amelot. "If he had sent him through Switzerland there would have been little inconvenience because he could have been hidden. But that was not possible at Antibes where he was obliged to make himself known because the commandant had no forewarning." Louis also wrote to Philip asking permission for Charles to join Don Philippe's army because he could not now send Charles back to Rome without bringing shame and dishonor upon himself. But Spain wanted nothing to do with the embarrassing situation.

Within a week of Charles's arrival, Lord Marischal and Lord Elcho arrived from Boulogne and found the Prince sipping tea at Sempill's house on the rue Estrapade. Charles appeared to be nervous. He gave Marischal James's commission as Commander in Chief of Scotland and said that Louis had invited him to be on hand for an invasion attempt in his father's name and that ten thousand men were presently assembling at Dunkirk under the command of the Comte Maurice de Saxe. Charles appeared to really believe that an invasion on his family's behalf was going to take place, for he told Marischal and Elcho to report to him at Dunkirk at the end of February.

Lord Marischal was perplexed, for there had been no prior discussion by letter with James about a restoration attempt; his experience in the uprisings of 1715 and 1719 had rightly led him to believe that when France and Spain involved themselves with the Stuarts, it was only for their own ends. Marischal knew that James was well aware of this, for both he and Ormonde had often discussed the matter with him. He could not understand, therefore, why the King appeared to be willing to play into France's hands again. Nor could he see how James could expect him, as Commander in Chief of Scottish forces, to call out the clans for a project he and the chieftains knew nothing about.

Meanwhile, the aging and infirm Duke of Ormonde hurried from Avignon to meet with Marischal in Paris. We do not know if his journey came as the result of a request from his old friend or because he had just received by messenger his commission as Commander in Chief of English Jacobite forces. All we know is that Ormonde briefly talked with Marischal and Sempill and did not see the Prince before he returned to Avignon. As Marischal bluntly stated in a letter to James some months later, "As to the Duke of Ormonde, it is very plain he was not only excluded from the secret but was to be from any share in the execution. The time he was advertised shows this. . . . Either the Lord Sempill must have abused your majestys name to have him excluded or the Court of France must have had such designs as they knew the Duke of Ormonde would not be assisting to." Marischal was unaware that James's main concern was not for a restoration but that France give royal recognition to his sons and their descendants. The Earl also did not know that the Vatican could no longer afford to extend royal prerogatives to the Stuarts.

Marischal decided to clear up several questions by paying a visit to Versailles, but first he borrowed money to have a suit of clothes made, for his garments were threadbare and shabby. Because both Marischal and Ormonde had suffered confiscation of estates by the British government in retaliation for their adherence to the Stuarts, James paid each of them a small monthly pension. This income was supplemented by whatever their families in Scotland and England could afford to send. In Marischal's case, there was certainly not enough money to spare for the silks and velvets sported by the fashionable gentlemen of Paris, where "clothes make the man" was an unavoidable aspect of social intercourse.

Still believing that James counted on France to restore him as King of Great Britain, Marischal presented himself in his new clothes to Amelot at Versailles to find out exactly what lay behind French schemes. He was annoyed to find that Sempill had represented the military affairs of Scotland in a very unrealistic fashion. Sempill had asked Amelot for money to outfit and arm twelve thousand clansmen, whereas Marischal knew nothing could succeed without at least twenty thousand, and even these would not suffice unless an equal number of Englishmen were prepared to join under a trusted leader such as the Duke of Ormonde. Part of the reason for the Duke's quick return to Avignon was that he knew that not even a tenth of that number of Jacobites existed in England. When Marischal met with Amelot and told him that money would be needed for twenty thousand Scots, the minister insinuated that he was inflating the numbers to pocket the money for himself. Insulted and outraged, Marischal checked further and learned that no plans for a rising in Scotland were being made at all; only a strike on England was being talked of. Given the minuscule support in that country for the Jacobite cause, Marischal realized immediately that the French aim in the so-called restoration was nothing more than to divert George II from sending troops to Europe. It was a scheme to which he would not lend himself, nor would he encourage any of his countrymen to participate.

Charles left Paris on February 26 with Balhaldy and Lord Caryll, Sempill's brother-in-law, but he was sequestered at Gravelines, twelve miles from Dunkirk. Balhaldy journeyed back and forth from Gravelines with messages, but when Marischal insisted on speaking with Charles, he was told the Prince had taken a necessary "incognito," that his abode was secret, and that he could see no one.

Approximately ninety-five hundred men were brought to Dunkirk—mostly Swiss, Corsican, and Monegasque mercenaries, with a few French regiments such as Languedoc, Bauffremont, Eu, and Royal-la-Marine. But there was no appearance of the famous regiment raised by the Prince's uncle, Marshal Berwick, the illegitimate son of James II and Arabella Churchill and half-brother of James. The greatest number of officers were from Monaco; the rank and file consisted of grumbling, exhausted, ill-equipped men. Balhaldy had brought Lord Barrymore's son to Dunkirk and paraded him among the officers and soldiers, so that many of them believed he was the Prince. They had no way of knowing what Charles looked like, and nothing was done to dispel the general belief that Master Barrymore was Prince Charles. Marischal was curious about this, and about the fact that he never saw the Prince with Saxe. He was also highly concerned that preparations at Dunkirk and Calais were inadequate for an invasion of England, let alone an expedition to Scotland. The French "fleet" (the cream of the crop was still trapped at Toulon) was a very sorry assemblage of unarmed privateers in need of repair. Added to them were small fishing vessels requisitioned from their normal routine of catching mackerel.

Because Marischal was prevented from seeing the Prince (not that the Prince showed any willingness to receive him), he warned Charles by sending several letters to Gravelines. One advised him to "guard against being made a tool of France to hurt your natural subjects and that such snares will be laid for you I can make no doubt." But the Prince saw things differently. He told Marischal that he would "doe nothing that is rash or foolish so far as I can judge," but in the same breath he vowed to go to England, even without any troops, "to relieve His Majesty's subjects or perish with them . . . I am determined to be with them at whatever rate it is and live or die with them." This was the same headstrong impetuosity the Earl had observed in the boy several years before; such empty, valorous boasting irritated the older man, then and now.

Other letters from Charles at Gravelines were filled with similar foolishness. He flattered himself that enough charisma was embodied in his person that all Britain would fall at his feet. He was so confident of this that he told Marischal that he was sending Buchanan to make contact with the English Jacobites. They would then send a small boat across to France for the Prince, who was filled with heroic visions of fighting to the death, even if nobody stood with him. Summoning great patience (audible sighs can often be detected in his letters), Marischal responded:

> Besides the concern I have for your person, and doe not take it amiss that I tell you with my ordinary plainnesse that I have more for it since reading your letter, that to go single unless you are invited by concert of the principal people both for credit and good sense, would be forever the destruction of the cause, and fix perhaps forever the family of Hanover in Brittain.

What was occurring at Dunkirk was, in the words of Jon Manchip White, Maurice de Saxe's biographer:

> nothing more than military vaudeville, which also happened to chime in very well with Maurice's general strategy: a concentration of troops at Dunkirk need only thrust north-east along the Flanders coastline to drive a wedge between Great Britain and her allies. Ten thousand men would never serve for a full-scale invasion of the

British Isles: but they could very easily constitute the spearhead of a larger striking force. Furthermore, their mere presence at Dunkirk procured a useful advantage for the French, in that they frightened the British into withdrawing a substantial number of their regiments from the Continent in order to swell the garrison at home.

The Dunkirk military operation had only two objectives: to force George to withdraw troops from Flanders, and to break the Toulon blockade. The Brest fleet had been cruising the English Channel since the end of January under the command of Admiral Rocquefeuil. After Charles's arrival in France, Rocquefeuil was sent orders by Argenson and Maurepas that he was engaged upon a mission to restore James Stuart as King of Great Britain. He and the Commanders at Calais and Dunkirk (Bart and Barrailh) were contemptuous of the imbecilic orders, which were written with no knowledge of their situation and treated the naval commanders as if they were fools.

Admiral Rocquefeuil, for instance, was ordered to engage the English Home Fleet under Admiral Norris, then to sail to Brest to accompany the Dunkirk transports across the Channel to the mouth of the Thames. They were to look for a white flare from two English ships, whose captains, according to the information Balhaldy had given the French, were willing to join the French fleet. The French naval commanders were aware that the instructions were impossible to carry out both because Norris's fleet was superior and because the southern English ports were protected by offshore islands and shifting sands whose secrets only the local pilots knew. They also understood the English very well, including their prejudice against Catholics and James Stuart. As for looking for a white flare, Rocquefeuil threw up his hands in horror. On these March-tossed, fog-shrouded seas, he could barely see from one end of his main deck to the other, let alone see some far-off white flare. There is no evidence that he carried out any order from Versailles relative to any attempt to restore James Stuart, or that he believed this was his real mission.

A desperate problem afflicting all European seafarers during this famine period was scurvy. Seven hundred of Bart's men were sick at Calais, as he himself told Marischal, and Rocquefeuil's matelots were in a worse condition. His fleet of about twenty ships was being decimated in Channel squalls brought by the spring equinox; he was forced to return ship after ship to Brest for repairs.

He pleaded with Versailles to recall him "before all His Majesty's ships are lost." Finally, one terrible night he lost eleven vessels, some with all hands on board; by the time the Brest fleet limped home to port, Rocquefeuil had also died at sea—of "apoplexy."

The same storm wrecked the transports at anchor in Calais and Dunkirk. Although the English had been sighting and making reports on French ships for some time, they gave no serious consideration to intercepted messages about an invasion to restore James Stuart until Charles arrived in Paris. Admiral Matthews then deployed some of his ships from the Mediterranean to guard the home coast; this allowed the French and Spanish to break through the Toulon blockade in a battle as bloody as any in European naval history. News of this French victory reached Paris at the time when it was discovered that George had recalled six thousand men from Flanders. This was what Maurice de Saxe had been waiting for. He instantly abandoned Dunkirk for the Flanders front without notifying Charles that he was departing for good. In fact, the two had never met face to face.

Saxe left some soldiers at Dunkirk, as if his mission had not been abandoned, in order to persuade the watching English that an invasion was intended to go forward. But Saxe also falsely led Charles to believe there would be a further attempt on England as soon as the Brest fleet recovered from its losses. He suffered no pangs of remorse for the deception. For one thing, he had put up with insufferably haughty letters from the Prince at Gravelines that contained advice with no more foundation than arrogance. Charles pretended to be an expert on the relative strength of the French and English fleets (which he knew nothing at all about) and complained to the forty-seven-year-old Saxe that Admiral Norris had been "sillily" allowed to slip through their fingers. The Comte de Saxe, who had once enjoyed a love affair with Charles's aunt, the Duchesse de Bouillon, was not sorry to leave Dunkirk without meeting the Prince. For his part in the operation, Saxe was promoted to Marshal of France on March 26, and a few days later Louis XV declared war on England and Austria.

It was Marischal who broke the news to Charles that Saxe had gone. "It is several days since I judged what would happen," he wrote, adding that he was "afraid that those who give your Royal Highness assurances of the French King's being not determined to give up the expedition until it is fully executed speak on very ill grounds." As usual, Marischal was right. He had a talent for seeing things as they really were, which was why most people respected him. But Charles was agonizingly slow in realizing that he had been literally abandoned at Gravelines. He clung to the belief that his stay "at the seaside" was for an assault on Britain; he was encouraged in this by Sempill and Balhaldy. Marischal eventually lost patience with the Prince's refusal to see or talk with him. The Prince was being influenced by Balhaldy, who naturally wanted to keep Marischal out of the way; and the Earl had precious little time for a man who could not think for himself.

Saxe left Dunkirk around March 16. By the end of April, Charles found himself still waiting at Gravelines, cut off from all company and forbidden to be seen in public. He was confused, forlorn, lonely, and perhaps a little frightened. He asked James to send Sir Thomas Sheridan to him as soon as possible, and he also wanted the painter Pompeo Batoni to send a miniature of the family, including his mother and brother (the "Quin and the Duk"). Because Louis was in residence at Versailles and wished to give no appearance of condoning the Prince's presence in his country, Charles was not allowed to return to Paris.

When mail had not arrived from Rome after a couple of weeks, Charles complained that he was "in anciety because their is too posts due." He was "in the dark" as to his present situation and had no "sifer" by which to send coded letters. He was prevented from seeing anybody, as he told James, "which obliges mee to read more than ever" and was "affred of growing too fat which will appear very surprising to you."

At the end of April, after two months at Gravelines, Charles went to Chantilly to stay briefly with his upright and stuffy cousin the Bishop of Soissons, a son of Marshal Berwick. Finally, on May 11, the Prince was allowed to return to Paris, but he found that King Louis had departed for Flanders without him. A letter from James dated May 22 said: ". . . and now I hear the King of France is actually arrived in Flanders and nothing of your going to the campagne, and I always understood you were to make it there." James also urged Lord Sempill to press for permission for Charles to go to Flanders. When Lord Marischal learned of this, he wondered how the Prince could possibly reconcile joining the French army to fight against the very people he had recently sworn to die among. The Earl was so wearied by his suspicions of Charles, James, Sempill, Balhaldy, and the Court of France that he took to his sickbed at Boulogne.

Amelot had disappeared from office by the time Charles returned to Paris. There was no official explanation why. Amelot had approved a payment of 3,000 livres and 1,500 louis d'or to the Prince when he first arrived—that may have been his fatal error. But there was no more money forthcoming now that the minister was gone. Charles had already spent what he had been given, plus a further 10,000 livres James had placed on deposit with his Paris bankers, the uncle-and-nephew team of John and George Waters, usually referred to as Old Waters and Young Waters. Most of this had gone toward splendidly outfitting himself in anticipation of accompanying Louis to Flanders, "for an officer when he goes to a campaigne must be at a great expense as to horse forniture, and other things that can't be avoided." So read Charles's explanation to his father.

Although James pleaded with him to manage his money carefully, Charles began to look for a house of his own and hired two valets. Buchanan was still with him, and he sent to Avignon for George Kelly, a retainer of the Duke of Ormonde, to act as his secretary. George Kelly has been described as a nonjuring parson and may have been an Anglican, as most of the people around Ormonde were, but James did not approve of Charles's choice, fearing Kelly would relate private matters back to the Duke. The King had earlier asked Sir John Graeme,* also from Avignon, who had acted briefly as James's secretary of state in 1727, to report to the Prince. Although Sir John stayed in the Paris vicinity for five months, Charles refused even to see him, and his choice of Kelly prevailed.

A struggle of ferocious proportions was occurring between James and Charles, even at a long distance. The one wanted freedom; the other wanted control. James had sent Sir Thomas Sheridan and John Stafford off to Paris at the end of April, but they were delayed at Genoa because of the Anglo-Spanish war and did not reach Paris until June 2. From his initial letters back to Rome, it is clear Sheridan had been asked to report on the Prince's conduct; later Michel Vezzozi, valet to the late Lord Nithsdale, was sent to do the same. Both spied upon Charles for James, at least for a while.

Of great concern to the King was his son's fondness for

---

* Because of Buchanan's use of the code name "Graeme," confusion has resulted, and it has always been reported that Sir John accompanied the Prince out of Italy. This was not so.

alcohol. When Charles was at Gravelines, James had written: "I suppose you will not always be locked up but whether in publick or in private, for God's sake, dear Child, be on your guard as to wine and play. . . . I hope you will never give me ye heartbreak to ever hear you fail in them." This letter was prompted by reports to Rome from Godinet (Bailli de Tencin's gentleman), from Lady Inverness at Avignon, and possibly from François Vivier and Buchanan, that Charles's penchant for liquor had been very much in evidence throughout his journey from Rome. Furthermore—and this explains the Prince's reckless declarations to Marischal that he would go to England alone if necessary—he had taken a firm notion to settle for nothing less than the crown of three kingdoms. Charles talked as if he, and not James, were going to be King. He began to distance himself from his father's and brother's Romanism by criticizing the Church and the Pope. These matters had been the subject of an "indifferent speech" Charles made when passing through Avignon, prompting James to warn his son to resist being swayed by "fashionable and popular" notions of religion.

In Rome, James called a meeting with Strickland and Dunbar to find out how they had tutored the Prince to effect this surprising development. Specific details of what was discussed at the gathering are unknown; but James immediately dismissed Strickland, banishing him from Italy and warning him never to go near the Prince again. Lord Dunbar also fell out of the King's favor, although he stayed on at the Muti for a few more years before he retired to Avignon to live with his sister.

Henry also was questioned by his father about the quarrel he had had with Charles three years before. Once outside Italy, Charles had apparently told several people about the argument and had discussed Henry's Jesuit training in unflattering terms, catering to the popular Jacobite view (which prevailed among Catholics as well) that the Duke of York should not have been educated by Jesuits. James was surprised to discover that Charles had tackled Henry directly on the subject of religion "and other delicate matters." He reminded Charles that "you are not his father." It seems obvious from the King's appalling ignorance of his sons' development that neither prince had had the benefit of paternal guidance as they were growing up. Blaming Strickland for everything, James began to fret that the schism between his sons would split the family forever.

James also felt uneasy that Charles was forming ideas of his own about his mission and purpose in France. He knew there was no guarantee that successive Popes would continue to recognize the Royal House of Stuart, so it had been his fond hope that Louis would honor Charles as a prince of the blood and make a soldier out of him, after which he would send Henry to France and perhaps follow himself. But if Charles were determined to settle for nothing less than restoration of his family to the kingdoms of Great Britain—a dream James had long ago given up—this would upset much careful planning on the King's part.

Until his family's future could be settled, James was intent on remaining in good standing with Pope Benedict XIV. It is doubtful that Charles had been taken fully into his father's confidence or that he thoroughly understood the delicate position of the entire family. The Prince's indiscreet utterances en route to Paris, fueled by his favorite brandywine, had also reached the ears of the Pope by way of the Pedone communication channel. James feared that his son was burning the papal bridge behind him.

In May the Prince leased a hilltop house with a sweeping view and little garden in what was then considered the countrified air of Montmartre. Sheridan and Stafford found him there when they arrived in Paris in the first week of June, restless and tired of "this lurking," from which he hoped soon to be free. The Prince was going out nightly, but he was forbidden to declare his identity or to appear publicly as a prince. This made the affront hard for Charles to bear. Sir Thomas, now past seventy, was delighted to be reunited with his pupil once more. He discovered he had not only "increased his broth" but appeared to be taller. Charles showed Sir Thomas the secret; he had adopted the Paris fashion of wearing shoes with heels two inches high!

All did not go well between Sheridan and Charles, however. At the beginning of July a distraught Kelly came from Montmartre to see Daniel O'Brien in Paris with the tale that Charles had taken up with the disreputable MacDonnell of Glengarry. Together they went drinking every day in neighboring *ginguettes*—low-class taverns. Young Glengarry, as he was known, was heir to the chieftainship of the clan, but he had no money or morals and was a well-known toper. Kelly told O'Brien that he was afraid Glengarry had won Charles over to his "irreligious" way of thinking and that Glengarry had told the Prince not to trust Cardinal Tencin, Daniel O'Brien, or Sir Thomas Sheridan because they were all papists.

It is not clear what other views Glengarry expressed on religion, but it is known that Kelly upbraided the Scotsman in Charles's presence. It troubled him most that Charles was quarreling with Sheridan and refusing to show him letters or allow him to assist with coding and decoding. Sir Thomas had wanted to pay a visit to Cardinal Tencin at Versailles, but Charles had forbidden him to leave the immediate vicinity of Montmartre. The Prince was acting in accordance with everything Glengarry said and seemed to be completely under his spell.

It seems strange that Charles could be dominated so easily and quickly by someone he barely knew. Clearly he needed to be managed. He was out of control, and not just with his drinking and talking. He was in debt in the amount of 30,000 livres. O'Brien suggested they write to Rome for advice, but Kelly said the matter was far too urgent to wait six weeks for a reply. Something had to be done about the Prince's behavior immediately before news of it reached the King of France.

O'Brien decided upon a course of action that would carefully hide the Prince's "weakness," his "youth and inexperience," and the fact that he was "too simple" for a man like Glengarry. He wrote James that a letter from him might bring his son to his senses, and he counseled Sheridan to stay where he was and assert himself. He did not write to Tencin for fear of precipitating a scandal that might hurt Charles. Newly arrived in Paris, Sheridan had not yet had time to find out what O'Brien knew, which was that although James counted on Tencin to help his family, the Cardinal now had little inclination and no influence at Court to do so. He was, in fact, doing everything possible to disassociate himself from the Stuarts. He had come under uncomfortable scrutiny and suspicion from Louis, who had seized his papers as well as Amelot's to see which of them was responsible for the Prince's public arrival in France.

When, at the end of April, Amelot was gone, everyone assumed he was the guilty party. Actually, he was as innocent as Tencin in the matter. Although the Cardinal stayed on at Court, he was very reluctant to involve himself with Charles for fear of guilt by association. For the same reason he withdrew from Council meetings so that he could not be accused of passing information on to James Stuart. He owed the family no favors and had used James for his own ends; now the Stuarts were becoming an embarrassing liability.

On the morning of Tuesday, July 7, the day before Kelly returned to Montmartre, Sheridan found the Prince tipsy and in rare good humor. He said that of course Sheridan could visit Cardinal Tencin and to bring a compliment in his name. By the afternoon, with Sheridan proposing to leave for Paris that evening, Charles's mood had become brooding and distorted from the liquor he had been drinking all day. He now withdrew his permission and said he would rather Sir Thomas deferred the visit until the weekend.

On Thursday there was a major clash between them when Sheridan threatened to leave the Prince's service for good. Supposedly, Sir Thomas was free to do as he chose because James had paid him only until the end of April. Thereafter, his monthly stipend of 100 livres was to be Charles's responsibility. But the Prince had no money and was living on credit extended to him by Young Waters without his uncle's knowledge. Sheridan's threat to quit the Prince's service proved to be empty, for he was an old man with no prospects of employment in Paris, and he did not want to return to Rome. Although Sheridan had detested life at the Palazzo Muti, James was divesting himself of surplus staff in order to conserve his meager finances, and there was no place for Sir Thomas as long as Charles was gone.

Far from being the evil genius behind the Prince, as has often been asserted, Sir Thomas Sheridan was a victim of circumstances whose only recourse was to come to terms with his master's drunken whims and to represent him as best as possible. In late August 1744, Sheridan traveled to the French army encampment at Metz, to which Louis had transported his court and advisers, including Madame de Châteauroux. Part of his mission was to see if Louis would accept Charles into the French army, but the main reason for his journey was that the Bishop of Soissons, acting as almoner for the army, had written to say he had something urgent to impart that could not be entrusted to a letter.

The bishop was the son of Marshal Berwick, whose glorious military career had come to an abrupt end in 1734, when he was killed by a cannonball. In that same year the bishop's brother, the Duke of Liria, had taken Charles to the Siege of Gaeta, perhaps in hope that James could help him. The bishop's older brother, the Duke of FitzJames, commanded the FitzJames Horse regiment in the French army and had inherited the bulk of his father's estates. Soissons was an upright, God-fearing man who was a cousin not only of Charles but of Sheridan as well. He told Sir Thomas that Louis XV was so resentful of how he had been tricked by the Prince's public arrival in France that he was determined to do nothing at all for him.

Soissons had every reason to know the King's mind. On August 7, Louis fell so dangerously ill at Metz that it was feared he would not live. The fever continued for some days, and it was being reported that the King was already dead. Soissons was called to administer the last sacrament, but strict moralist that he was, he refused until Louis sent Madame de Châteauroux away. Apparently, her presence at the front was heavily criticized by officers, who felt she was dictating to the King, and they complained that they had no access to their monarch in matters of importance. At the insistence of the bishop, Louis signed an order vowing that he would never see her again. There was confession and repentance, and who knows how much was said about the Stuarts during the King's feverish delirium, but it was enough that Soissons felt he had to warn Sheridan.

The French population flocked to the churches to pray for Louis, and the Queen and the Dauphin rushed to Metz from Paris. But the King had already begun to recover when they arrived. He was able to return to Paris in the middle of November, but he broke his word about putting Châteauroux away forever. By now he was furious at Soissons's ecclesiastical parade at Metz, and he ordered him to repair to his diocese and remain there. The mistress was reinstated at the end of November but died of a mysterious fever ten days later, on December 8. For fear of reprisals against her coffin, she was buried without ceremony in a quicklime pit in the early hours of the morning. The King's grief for Châteauroux was short-lived. Four months later she was replaced at Court by his most famous mistress of all, Madame de Pompadour.

The affair at Metz did nothing to predispose Louis to the Stuarts; the mention of their very name rankled him, and the Council, including Tencin, was only too aware that Charles had become a liability who could not be sent back to Rome without risking dishonor to the King of France. By refusing to pay him a monthly subsidy, they hoped he would be forced to leave France, or at least retreat to Avignon. Charles wrote a haughty letter "incisting" that either Louis give him a place in the army or else furnish troops to restore his family to the throne of Great Britain. Charles's demands were regarded as irrational in the light of

France's own intelligence reports describing how the English would rather board up their houses and take to arms than suffer the imposition of a Catholic king at the hands of the French. Louis angrily wondered aloud what he was supposed to do for a royal family whose own subjects did not want them. If they had, the Stuarts would have no need of French help.

James was distressed to hear how Charles was being treated. As he wrote to his son on August 7:

> Your going into France without any authentick invitation or call puts the King of France no doubt more at liberty to act as he pleases towards us. This is a misfortune 'tis true, tho you know we could not reasonably act otherwise than we did at the time.

Publicly, however, James continued to insist that the King of France had called for his son and that therefore he should maintain him. Louis denied it and stubbornly refused to give Charles an allowance. The 30,000-livre debt from the summer threatened to double by the time winter set in. James would send no money—even though Charles had asked for his jewels—because that would defeat the purpose of forcing Louis to support the Prince. He hoped public opinion would eventually bend Louis; indeed, many people were questioning why Charles was being kept incognito. They knew nothing about the background, so a certain amount of sympathy was extended toward the Prince. When he could afford to lease the Montmartre property no longer, the Archbishop of Cambrai (Madame O'Brien's lover) lent him his "country hows." Charles wanted to be as close to Paris as possible, but Cardinal Tencin brought news that the Court of France would agree to a monthly allotment of funds only if the Prince removed himself far away from Paris—preferably to Avignon. Defeat stared Charles in the face, for there was nothing beyond Avignon but Rome.

Sir Thomas had already told James by letter what he believed was the only value of the Prince to France for which he might obtain permanent subsistence and perhaps royal recognition. That was that Charles could land in Scotland and create a rebellion in the summer of 1745. Sheridan had been to the army front again and had discovered that summer was the time when the French were most likely to plan a major attack on the Pragmatic Army, now led by Charles's cousin, the Duke of Cumberland, son of George II.

James was against a campaign in Scotland alone, but Sheridan was six weeks away from advice and was told to make his own determination on how best to proceed. James did not know that Sheridan and the Prince had already made up their minds to go to Scotland, even if the French sent no troops with them. They planned to start a rebellion and were sure Louis would support it militarily and financially once it was underway. There were indications that Spain was also interested in supporting a Scottish diversion. At no time did Charles and Sheridan consider the consequences to the Scots if plans failed. The fate of Scotland was considered less important than gratifying the expectations of the royal heir.

Sheridan was now determined to get Charles's affairs with the Court of France out of the clutches of Sempill and Balhaldy, who were either unaware of the French King's true feelings or—worse still—misrepresenting them. It was essential to get rid of Balhaldy first. Too many Scots now mistrusted him, and the Prince needed to establish a direct link with the northern Jacobites. Charles and Sheridan had heard from Balhaldy that John Murray of Broughton, secretary to the former Association of Highland Gentlemen, was coming to France from Edinburgh, and a secret meeting was arranged at stables near the Tuilleries. Murray met first with Sheridan and Kelly; then on September 20 the prince joined them, but Balhaldy was excluded from these and all other meetings thenceforward.

John Murray of Broughton has often been blamed for misleading Charles about the strength of Jacobite support in Scotland, but nothing could be further from the truth. Murray was merely a sycophantic dupe, gullible to a fault, who was used by Charles and Sheridan. Sir Thomas now followed his master's drunken dictates, for his survival gave him little other choice. He wrote down this resolve during the September 20 meeting with Murray, Kelly, and Charles:

> To be particularly inform'd what measures may be taken to secure Scotland supposing even that no party cou'd be for ye present form'd in England we being resolved to be master of one of our Kingdoms at any rate.

It was utterly ridiculous to suppose Scotland could be "secured" as a Stuart kingdom unless the English cooperated. Even James knew this was impossible; but Sheridan seemed strangely out of touch with reality. Another note in Murray's hand written at the same meeting read:

> The Princes resolution of going to Scotland Without Forces to be keept private from the King, Lord Marshall and the Court of France but att the same time to acquaint those in Scotland who may be trusted.

Charles also wrote a letter to the former members of the Association of Highland Gentlemen to say he would soon appear at the head of "the King's faithfull subjects in order to bring about his restoration which has been too long and too earnestly wished for by them." Another address was sent to the MacLeod and Mac-Donald chieftains of the Inner and Outer Isles, asking what they would undertake "for the service of their king and the good of their country," supposing he found money to pay for the broadswords he understood would be needed by the Highlanders. He also requested that they state the number of French forces necessary for a landing in Scotland and asked what proof they wanted of support from English Jacobites. However, there is no evidence that these chieftains gave Charles any encouragement; nor does a copy of their response exist, although they claimed they told Charles not to come.

Other instructions Murray carried back to Scotland were to caution Elcho and his brother-in-law, James Steuart of Goodtrees, not to tell Marischal anything of the plan. But Marischal had removed himself from Boulogne to stay with Ormonde at Avignon for a while. He could not speak as freely as he would have liked because he suspected that Charles had cooperated with the French scheme at Dunkirk. He hoped that his absence from the coast would discourage others from being used in further French designs, and his stand at Avignon was heeded by many as a warning not to get involved.

Murray of Broughton was asked to raise money in Scotland, and Lord Traquair was to see if he could make contact with Jacobites in London. But he refused to be a part of any plan unless Lord Marischal sanctioned it. The Duke of Perth was asked to find a ship to get the eighteen hundred broadswords Charles was arranging to have manufactured in Holland, but the vessel foundered at a home port, and a letter was sent from Scotland saying it would be some time before another could be found. Before too long it was apparent that those in Scotland were getting cold feet. Murray and others now urged Charles to consult with Lord Marischal before going any further. But Marischal was the last person from whom the headstrong Prince would seek advice because he knew that the earl, with all good reason and sense, would advise him against doing what he had already made up his mind to do. Eventually, Murray of Broughton sent a message saying that perhaps this was not the time for His Royal Highness to come to Scotland.

But Charles had long given up relying solely on Murray and the Scots in Edinburgh. Other interesting events had transpired to bolster his and Sheridan's hopes. In December 1744, a petition was presented to the Prince by Sir Hector Maclean, the perennially absent chieftain of the clan, whose territories spanned the small western islands of Eigg, Muck, Coll, and Tiree. Maclean had been attainted and lived in Paris, as did the joint presenter of the petition, John Roy Stuart, a long-time adherent to the Jacobite cause. If one single document solidified Charles's and Sheridan's resolve to go to Scotland, this was probably it.

> The humble representation and petition of Sir Hector Macleane and John Roy Stuart to His Royal Highness the Prince in their own name and by the desire of the following Chiftains of Clans; the number of whose men as each proposes to bring to the field is here specified, viz:

Sir Hector Macleane	800
Macleod	800
Sir Alexander MacDonald	800
The Family of Clanranald	800
Glengarry	500
Keppoch (MacDonald of)	300
Stuart of Appin	500
John Roy Stuart	300
	4,800

> Which with officers makes upp a
>   brigade of above . . .   5,000

That nobody but Maclean and Stuart had signed this document did not matter to Charles. What was important was that these men had pledged themselves to him, and that the names of MacLeod, MacDonald of Clanranald, and Sir Alexander MacDonald of Sleat were on the list. Between them and Maclean he counted on support from the entire western region of Scotland not covered by chieftains of the former Association. The Prince was so confident of a massive following that he borrowed 120,000 livres from Young Waters, again without Old Waters knowing about it. By that time, Charles already owed 60,000 livres to the latter, part of which he had used to pay off some of his accumulated debts. He intended to use the new loan to pay for broadswords and other weapons, as well as to acquire a ship to transport him to Scotland. It was left to James later on to pay off the entire debt of 180,000 livres.

"As long as there is life there is hops ses the proverb," Charles wrote in the winter of 1744. He was trying to mediate a violent argument that had broken out between Sir Hector Maclean and Lord John Drummond, the Duke of Perth's half-uncle. Drummond had received a colonel's commission from James the year before to raise the Royal Scots regiment in French service. Louis XV had honored that commission and had provided money for outfitting the regiment, which was the signal for many Scots to scrabble for commissions. However, many of them, Maclean included, did so only with a view to obtaining money from the French for their own use. Their claim to be able to command vast numbers of Highlanders to follow them was far from true. When Lord John Drummond heard that Maclean, with Charles's approbation, intended to apply to James for a lieutenant colonel's commission in the Royal Scots, he raised objections, saying that Maclean had no military experience whatsoever. He also claimed that Maclean had been away from Scotland for so long that most of his clansmen had forsaken their homeland for Canada and America and that those remaining were dominated by the pro-Hanoverian Campbell Duke of Argyll. Many Macleans had intermarried with Campbells, so Lord John doubted that Sir Hector could rally more than a few score men to his name.

As it happened, James did not grant the commission to Sir Hector. He told Charles not to do or say anything that would offend Lord John, but Charles had already taken Maclean's part in the dispute, which almost ended in a duel. He felt that Drummond "would rather sacrifice me and my affairs than fail in any private views" and that he was liable to have his "throte cut." But the Prince knew nothing about the interclan rivalries in Scotland, and since Drummond had been part of the Association, his opposition may have been responsible for the lackluster correspondence from Edinburgh.

However, at the end of 1744 Charles was looking in yet another direction for support. At his father's suggestion, he had written to Lord Tyrconnel, who had commanded the Irish for James II at the Battle of the Boyne, and to Lord Clare, commander of an Irish regiment for the King of France. Tyrconnel was now employed by Frederick the Great as an adviser on French affairs, and Clare was actively serving Louis. Although they could be of no practical help, they did introduce Charles to a group of Franco-Irish ship-owners who had become immensely wealthy through the repugnant but lucrative trade of transporting slaves to the colonies. Among them were Antoine Walsh, whose father had built and captained the ship that had brought James II from Ireland after the Boyne; Daniel Hegarty (or d'Heguerty), one of the founders of a Masonic order dedicated to a Stuart restoration; and Walter Rutledge, a banker and shipbuilder operating out of Dunkirk. These men were delighted to be of service to the Prince, who was trying to find a ship after being disappointed by the Duke of Perth's efforts. Walsh pledged the use of his frigate *Du Teillay*, which was lying at Nantes, and Walter Rutledge offered the *Elizabeth*, an English ship he had acquired after the bloody battle at Toulon Harbor, although she was lying at Brest waiting for repairs and would not be ready until the summer of 1745. The Prince still had not yet taken delivery of the broadswords from Holland, so there was little to do but wait.

News from Rome was not very cheerful. James had been seriously depressed and melancholy following a "defluxion" on his gums that had spread to his face, but he was taking care of Charles's dog, Stellina, "who was put to bed some months ago of one puppy, which I keep, tho it be very ugly." A few months later: "Poor Stellina is dead in parto and left four puppies behind her." James also suffered from bleeding feet, so his doctor would not allow him to attend a service commemorating the tenth anniversary of Clementina's death when her remains were moved from Santi Apostoli to the higher church of St. Peter's. Henry continued to write flowery letters of affection on a regular basis at James's behest, doing his best to please his father, who kept urging the brothers to love one another. Charles barely bothered to acknowledge receipt of Henry's letters unless it was in a postscript to Edgar or James. The Prince did send some sheet music to Edgar for the Duke, saying it was a rarity because "all the musick in Paris is not worth a straw." And Henry reported that life in Rome was very boring ("for realy wee are agrowing as dull as cat's") and that soirees were lifeless because "what with the fewness of the ladys and what with the want of my dear brother the country dances went very ill."

To his credit, Henry, who was aware of what Charles had been saying about him, made every effort to be genial. But the Prince was preoccupied, and his brother's letters were meaningless to him. He did write warmly to James Edgar, who seemed to be the only person in Rome capable of writing positive letters. On January 16, 1745, two weeks after his twenty-fourth birthday, Charles notified Edgar that he was going to leave Paris.

> I am going in to or three days to my country howse when I will be at full liberty to have the spleen. It is now to months I have not handeled a gun becose of the bad weather and cold for which I would be called *cacciatore di pan bianco* by the Duke iff he new it; in revenge for my calling him so formerly. As soon as I am arrived at Vizjames I intend to begin again to shute but not when it rens. You see by this that according as one advanses in years one gets reason. Adieu. Charles P.

The "country howse" was put at the Prince's disposal by Anne, Duchess of Berwick, the marshal's widow and mother of Liria, Soissons, and the Duke of FitzJames. Their father had left the brothers adjoining estates near Soissons, between Senlis and Chantilly, about seven hours' coach ride (or fourteen leagues) northeast of Paris on the road to Calais. FitzJames was away in Flanders, and his main residence was at Lille, so Charles had the use of his country home, which was also called FitzJames, just for himself and his entourage. Withdrawing to this estate saved him from having to retire to Avignon, although it was Sheridan's opinion that Avignon was where Cardinal Tencin really wanted them. Tencin was able to procure a payment of 5,000 livres per month for the Prince, which was only half the amount required to maintain the household. Tencin was also able to pry loose a lump sum of 30,000 livres to satisfy some debts, provided Charles maintained his incognito and lived in a private manner.

Despite his agreement to stay away from Paris, Charles spent the latter part of February and most of March 1745 in that city, thoroughly enjoying himself and ignoring his promise to keep incognito. He seemed to be flaunting Louis's authority and doing as he pleased; he made contact with his mother's relatives, the Duke de Bouillon, the Prince de Turenne, and the Montbazons. He had supper with them on January 10 before he left Paris and afterward accompanied them to an opera and masked ball. The entire city was ablaze with weeks of celebrations in honor of the wedding between the Dauphin and the Spanish Infanta. In the middle of February he was smuggled into a grand *bal masque* at Versailles by the King's equerry, Butler (the same man who had gone to England eighteen months before to meet up with Balhaldy), where Charles saw Louis and all his family. He fancied Louis had arranged it, although there was no exchange between them; but that hardly seems likely. The King was furious when he heard that the Prince had been present at several balls where people had guessed his identity.

One of the reasons Sheridan and Charles spent so much time in Paris was that the concierge at FitzJames was trying to profit by overcharging them for game animals on the estate, fish from the river, chickens, and firewood from the forest. When Charles accepted the invitation of a neighbor to hunt at his estate, the concierge hid all the saddles and bridles so that he was unable to go. Sheridan felt the man's insolence was due to his master; they did not seem to get along with the Duke of FitzJames as well as they did with Clementina's relatives. Five thousand livres a month was not enough to meet the salaries of retainers and servants (James had to make up arrears later on), much less pay for food or entertain guests. In Paris they stayed either at the Hôtel Dauphin or at the Hôtel de Bretagne, both on the rue Croix des Petits Champs. Debts were beginning to mount up again, and it was common knowledge among Paris tradespeople that Charles had not only left the house at Montmartre owing rent but had also sold some of his landlord's furniture to pay his debts. The hoteliers insisted upon some surety that their accounts would be paid, and O'Brien was called upon to stand as guarantor.

The household was now made up of Charles, Sheridan, Kelly, Stafford, Michel Vezzozi, who had arrived the previous November, three servants named Ferbos, Florio, and Tournier, Duncan Buchanan (Vivier seems to have disappeared from the scene), and John William O'Sullivan, an Irish Jacobite who had sought out the

Prince in January 1745. Charles remembered O'Sullivan's visiting Rome some years before. He was a fat, well-fed man who had once been tutor to children of French Marshal Mallebois; he had seen military action once when his master took him along as aide-de-camp on a campaign to Corsica. The Prince put him to work at FitzJames managing household accounts and dealing with the troublesome concierge.

O'Sullivan was easy-going and his heart was in the right place, but he was not qualified to be named, in his own words, "Adjutant-General, Inspector, and all sorts of other things besides" for the Jacobite army Charles was to form in Scotland the following August. His dubious "military experience," and that of an old Irish toper named Sir John MacDonald, who had been a captain of carabiniers in a Franco-Spanish regiment, was the total military expertise upon which Charles could rely while planning his voyage to Scotland. Other hangers-on were Aeneas Mac-Donald, the failed banker who had once employed Buchanan, and Sir Hector Maclean. The one thing they all had in common was that they were subservient and unemployed and seemed to be mesmerized by the hot-headed Prince.

Despite their former resolve to keep matters secret from the Court of France, desperation for money led Sir Thomas to meet with the Marquis d'Argenson and propose that Charles go to Scotland alone. The minister's view was that as long as they were foolish enough to make the attempt, he was not going to stop them. He made noises about the possibility of being able to spare a regiment or two, but he would part with no funds because the French were preparing for their summer campaign against the Pragmatic Army. Cardinal Tencin went on record as saying he also approved of the idea, and Maurepas, the minister of marine, issued passes for the ships Walsh and Rutledge had acquired. James was furious when he heard Tencin was actually encouraging Charles to go to Scotland alone; when he found out about the purchase of broadswords, he called that a waste, but he trusted that Sir Thomas Sheridan knew what he was doing.

One can imagine the French ministers smirking under their powdered perukes at the idiocy of this young Prince. Of course, they wanted Charles to leave for Scotland with his two ships, and they suspected he was desperate enough to finance the enterprise himself if necessary. Marshal Saxe left Paris for Flanders in March to give battle to the Duke of Cumberland heading the Pragmatic

Army; writing years later, Argenson said he wished the Prince had sailed at that time. Although France defeated Cumberland at the Battle of Fontenoy on May 11, the victory might have cost fewer lives if Cumberland had also had his cousin's voyage to Scotland to contend with. As it was, the war dragged on for another three years. Now Prince Campo Florido, the Spanish ambassador in Paris, began to take an interest in what Charles was planning.

Chapter 6

The Road to the Isles

It became imperative for Charles and Sheridan to leave for Scotland as soon as possible after the Battle of Fontenoy. It was feared that a peace would be negotiated that would stipulate banishment of the Prince from France. At the end of May, Charles and Sheridan disappeared from FitzJames, saying they were accepting an invitation from the Duc de Bouillon to hunt on his estate at Navarre in the southwestern region of the country. At the same time, instructions were given to O'Sullivan, Sir John MacDonald, Aeneas MacDonald, Buchanan, and others to report to Nantes on June 11 and address themselves to Antoine Walsh, from whom they were to receive instructions. In Sir John MacDonald's case, Walsh directed him to an inn beyond the bridges of the Loire River flowing through Nantes, and since he was known to many of the Irish merchants established in the city, he was told to keep well out of sight until he was contacted again. The men all stayed at different places under assumed names and were instructed to avoid any recognition of the others if they should happen to encounter them in public places.

In the meantime, from Bouillon's residence at the Château de Navarre, Sheridan, Kelly, and Charles wrote letters to various people asking for help. Although these were dated June 8–11, none was delivered until the end of July, after the Prince had gone and had safely arrived in Scotland. This was because there was great reason to fear that his ship would be captured or forced to turn back by the English fleet off the west coast of Britain. Stafford, Rutledge, and Pierre Gallet, a servant of Aeneas MacDonald, were to wait at Nantes for news of the Prince's landing in Scotland; then

111

they were to deliver letters to Paris, Avignon, Rome, and Madrid. Stafford was assigned to take letters to Spain for Sir Charles Wogan, now following in Don Quixote's steps as Governor of La Mancha, and for Sir Thomas Geraldine, another Irish Jacobite living in Madrid. Both were instructed to ask the King and Queen of Spain for money, arms, "and at least Irish Officers if troops could not be spared." Wogan did not receive his letter, dated June 8, until July 26. Letters written from Navarre were also sent to O'Brien, the Marquis d'Argenson, Louis, and James and to Marischal and Ormonde, asking them to use their influence to gain "succours" from the Court of France.

During the last week of June, Walsh's small frigate *Du Teillay*, mounting eighteen to twenty guns, lay in wait at the port of St. Nazaire, a few miles from Nantes, and Walter Rutledge was at Brest making ready the sixty-eight-gun *Elizabeth*. The latter was to carry ten cases containing eighteen broadswords each and other weapons that Charles had purchased with the 180,000 livres he had borrowed from Young Waters. According to a list he furnished Edgar, these included 1,500 "Fusis" (*fusees*), a good quantity of powder, twenty small field pieces, "two of which a mule may carry," balls, flints, "durks, Brandy & etc." His personal cassette amounted to almost 4,000 louis d'or coins.

Despite his father's warnings that Strickland should be avoided at all costs, the Prince sent a message to Avignon, where Strickland had gone, to ask him to join the party at Navarre. Michael Sheridan, Sir Thomas's nephew, was also part of the group, and Sir Hector Maclean was sent ahead to Edinburgh to organize matters there. Unknown to anyone at the time, two of the chieftains to whom Charles had written the previous September—Norman MacLeod of MacLeod and Sir Alexander MacDonald of Sleat on the Isle of Skye—had been to see Duncan Forbes, Lord President of the Court of Sessions of Scotland, and had told him everything they knew. When Sir Hector made an appearance in Edinburgh, he was immediately arrested and held for questioning. MacLeod and MacDonald were not necessarily responsible, for news of Charles's plans could have leaked from many quarters.

The most likely source was MacDonald of Glengarry, who had introduced the Prince to Paris's *ginguettes*; he was identified by historian Andrew Lang as the infamous "Pickle the Spy." For several years Glengarry had remained on the fringe of Jacobite affairs and had pretended to help the Prince, but all the while he was sending bulletins to the English government under the code name Pickle.* Murray of Broughton had been unwittingly using the services of Glengarry to carry messages back and forth between Edinburgh and Paris. In fact, Glengarry had arrived in Paris on June 24, bringing Murray's letter that told the Prince not to come to Scotland, but he found that Charles had already left the Paris vicinity. It is known that the Prince did receive this letter before leaving France, but he simply ignored it and pressed ahead.

O'Sullivan's written account of the adventure related that Charles, Sheridan, and Kelly were the only persons who commanded the secret of the expedition to Scotland until everyone was assembled at Nantes. O'Sullivan must have had some idea of what was afoot since he was involved in arranging for the broadswords to be transported and loaded onto the *Elizabeth* at Brest; he was also responsible for acquiring several cases of pistols, an armored breastplate, a bed, and a "set of Pleat" for the Prince, who wished to please the Scots by wearing the kilt. Not until June 25 did Charles arrive at Nantes to meet with the group known in Jacobite folklore as the "Seven Men of Moidart," but at least fourteen or fifteen conspirators congregated in the city on the Loire.

The men Charles had known from Rome—Sheridan, Michael Sheridan, Strickland, and Vezzozi—were there. Also present were Kelly, O'Sullivan, Sir John MacDonald, Buchanan, and Aeneas MacDonald, who was the brother of Donald MacDonald of Kinlochmoidart. It was hoped that Aeneas, through his brother, would be able to influence others of his clan who hesitated to join because of the anticipated hostility (already a reality) of Mac-Donald of Sleat. A tenth member was Antoine Walsh; and one of Lochiel's men, Donald Cameron, was also on hand to pilot the ships through the treacherous waters to safe harbor at their intended destination in the Hebrides Islands. A young priest of about Charles's age, the Abbé Butler, had somehow attached himself to the party. He had been in Rome a few months after Charles left, and James had given him letters of introduction to the Archbishop of Cambrai. Butler may have met the Prince when he was borrowing Cambrai's country house. He was selected to carry back messages from Scotland to Paris and Rome as soon as the

*No one ever suspected Glengarry during his lifetime. It was a century after his death that Lang unmasked him as Pickle the Spy.

party reached its destination. This accounts for a dozen people. Since John Stuart (who is thought to have given the report from Siena about negotiations with English seamen) had a talent for remaining as inconspicuous as possible, it is not certain he was at Nantes, yet the chances are he sailed with the rest of them because later reports maintained he was with the Prince in Scotland. John Townley, who had replaced the late Mr. Dicconson, was also on board. James had dismissed him as well as Strickland because he could no longer afford to maintain a large household.

The fifteenth member, then, was the only man of meritorious blue blood Charles could offer to the Scots in Scotland as a leader in the wake of Lord Marischal's withdrawal. The Jacobites in Paris, who were influenced by Marischal, refused to have anything to do with Charles. This was clear evidence to the Prince that the Scots would follow only one of their own, and his pride was immeasurably wounded, affecting his later conduct. However, he found living in Paris the toothless, gout-ridden, fifty-five-year-old William Murray, the 2nd Duke of Atholl, who had been attainted in 1715. William's younger pro-Hanoverian brother, James, was now enjoying the title of the Duke of Atholl and the estates surrounding Blair Castle in Perthsire. William, therefore, was referred to by the Scots as "the Jacobite Duke of Atholl," but in France he was known as "the Marquis of Tullibardine." Charles persuaded Tullibardine, who seemed older than his years and was aging quickly, to accompany him to Scotland. As an inducement, the Prince promised to pay the wages of Tullibardine's Paris housekeeper while he was away. It has often been wondered why Tullibardine made the decision to go to Scotland, but the reason could have been that he wanted to see his native land once more before he died. He had little more than a year to live. No Scotsman ever returned home looking and acting more like a French popinjay than Tullibardine, from his velvet-ribboned wig to the diamond-studded buckles on his high-heeled shoes. He was so arthritic that he could barely walk; he was usually carried in a sedan chair with a lace-trimmed handerchief dangling from his pale, soft-tipped fingers.

These were the men Charles brought to Scotland from France. They were, according to the Chevalier de Johnstone, who joined the Jacobite army in Edinburgh as an aide-de-camp, "very bad counsellors, and altogether ignorant of the nature and resources of the country, and the character of the Highlanders . . . one of the greatest oversights in the Prince's whole conduct was his coming over without an officer of distinction."

When Walter Rutledge brought the *Elizabeth* from Brest to join up with the *Du Teillay*, he was asked to deliver a letter to Louis from Charles. Written in French, with Sheridan's help (the Prince never mastered the writing of important letters and documents without assistance), it read:

> After having tried in vain all methods of reaching Your Majesty in the hope of obtaining from your generosity the help necessary to enable me to play a role worthy of my birth, I have resolved to make myself known by my actions and to undertake alone a project to which even a small amount of help would guarantee success. I am bold enough to flatter myself that Your Majesty will not deny it me. I would never have come to France if the expedition planned more than a year ago had not made me aware of Your Majesty's good intentions towards me and I hope that the unforeseen accidents which rendered that expedition impracticable for the time being have not changed anything. May I not flatter myself at the same time that the Signal Victory which Your Majesty has just won over his enemies and mine (for they are the same) will have brought about some change in the situation and that I can reap some advantage from this new blaze of Glory that surrounds you. I beg Your Majesty most urgently to consider that in upholding the justice of my rights he will be putting himself in a position to achieve a solid and durable Peace, the sole object of the War in which he is now engaged.

By July 12 the *Du Teillay* with everyone on board had sailed the short distance from St. Nazaire to Belle-Île,* where they anchored to ride out contrary winds and wait for the *Elizabeth*, which eventually joined them later that day. Except for the coast-skimming hops of the *felucca* from Genoa to Antibes, Charles had never been on an ocean voyage before. He was a very poor sailor and fell victim to seasickness almost immediately, but as he wrote to Edgar on July 12, "I finde the more I strugle against it the better." He was heartened by the sight of sixty volunteers on board the *Elizabeth* "which tho few will make a show, they having a pretty uniform." Their leader was a Captain d'O (or Eu—an unusual but not uncommon name in France) who had been listed in Marshal

---

Originally known as Belle Isle—beautiful island.

Saxe's complement of troops at Dunkirk more than a year before as an ensign standing by in case of need. He was a mercenary; his brother was also aboard the *Elizabeth* as a lieutenant.

Charles sent his last letter to James from Belle-Île with a nine-page effort he had written at Navarre. The sixty volunteers were mentioned, but inexplicably the Prince said an additional seven hundred men were on board the *Elizabeth*. This simply was not true. He was mindful that his enterprise might be judged as downright folly by the courts of Europe, and perhaps he lied in an attempt to assure his father that he was not being rash. Whatever the reason, the men he met at Nantes and Captain d'O's volunteers aboard the *Elizabeth* (which never did reach Scotland) were all he had.

His long and rambling letter of explanation to James was obviously constructed with Sheridan's assistance, for the spelling was reasonably accurate. The Prince said he had discovered that France's first attempt was not genuine and that the Scots were aware of this. He claimed the Scots "wou'd rise of themselves in spite of all I cou'd say or do to prevent it," but this also was untrue. He spoke of the "scandalos usage" he had received at the hands of France, which was why he was stealing off without informing Louis beforehand. He told his father he was doing all this "without even letting you suspect there was any such thing a Brewing" because he was afraid James would have "absolutely forbid my proceedings, thinking that to acquire Glory I was Capable of doing a desperat action . . . Let what will happen, the stroke is struck and I have taken a firm resolution to Conquer or to Dye and Stand my Ground as long as I should have a Man remaining with me. . . . It is most certain the Generality of People will judge of this enterprise by the success, which if favorable, I will get more honour than I deserve. If otherwise, all the Blame will be put on the F.C. [French Court] for having pushed a Young Prince to shew his Mettle, and rather dye than live in a state unbecoming himself. . . . I wou'd perish as Curtius did to save my Country & make it happy; it being an indispensable duty on me as far as lyes in my Power. Your Majesty may now see my reason for pressing so much to pawn my jewels which I shou'd be glad to have done immediately, for I never intend to come back, and Money next to Troops will be of the greatest help to me."

On July 5 Old Style—the British dating system that we shall use from now on—the two ships set sail from Belle-Île for Scotland. Michael Sheridan appears to have been the only member of the original group aboard the *Elizabeth*, while the Prince and the others were aboard the *Du Teillay*. Sailing without lights except for a small illumination for the compass, they saw nothing for several days but small merchant vessels, which avoided them. Then a squadron of eight English ships suddenly appeared off the coast of Ireland. Walsh decided to change course, hoping that nightfall would give them cover, but at the break of day it was discovered that two ships still remained with them. One sailed off, presumably to notify the rest of the squadron, but the other, a sixty-four-gun man o' war named the *Lion*, stayed to give battle to the intruders.

Captain d'O was very young and inexperienced. He came aboard the *Du Teillay* for advice, and it was decided that the *Elizabeth* would engage the English ship and cover the Prince's vessel because she had more men and guns aboard. That she also carried the heavy load of weapons and artillery Charles had purchased severely restricted her maneuverability.

She engaged the *Lion* for four and a half hours. Captain d'O, his brother, and several of the crew were killed, and Michael Sheridan was among the wounded. The English captain was also killed, and when night fell the *Lion* disappeared. The *Elizabeth* was in no fit condition to do anything but return to Brest. Charles had ordered Walsh to go to the *Elizabeth*'s aid during the battle, but Walsh knew that one twenty-four-pound ball would sink his small ship, and he refused to obey. The story may be apocryphal, but it is said he locked the zealous Prince in his cabin and crowded all sail until the *Du Teillay* reached the island of Barra—MacNeil territory—at the southern tip of the Outer Hebrides.

Aeneas MacDonald's sister was married to MacNeil of Barra, so he and Kelly set off in a small boat for the island. But they found that MacNeil was away from home. While those aboard ship were waiting, a man o' war appeared and tried to come close all that day (July 21) and the next, but the winds blew so strongly that she was kept out at sea. Duncan Cameron, the pilot, then set out in a longboat to find another pilot more familiar with the local area, and eventually the *Du Teillay* was guided to the tiny island of Eriskay, which gives its name to the hauntingly beautiful song "Eriskay Love Lilt."

On July 23, on this small patch of sea-swept land that lies between Barra and the island of South Uist, the Prince first set foot on Scottish soil. He was wearing not a kilt but the robes of an abbé, the disguise he was wearing when he left France. Local tradition has it that seeds of a pink convolvulus, not indigenous to the Hebrides, had attached themselves to his clothing while he was waiting in France; they are said to have dropped and rooted in the spot where Charles landed, still known in the Gaelic language as *Cladach a' Phrionnsa*—"the Prince's Shore." The flower still flourishes on Eriskay.

The weather that greeted *Tearlach* Mac Sheumais* ("Charles son of James") was typically Hebridean. The rain, lashed cruelly by gale-force winds, could have swept a man off his feet. Lead-colored clouds hung low and rolled so swiftly that they almost seemed part of the stark, granite-strewn landscape, which was devoid of trees. In the summer months the Gulf Stream often brings warm winds and clear skies to brighten silver sands and encourage golden marsh-marigolds, purple Jacob's Ladder, daisies, buttercups, clover, and the pink-tufted thrift flower, which grows by the edge of the sands. But the skies were angry when Bonnie Prince Charlie arrived.

The driving rain forced him to seek shelter in a crude hut. It was made of granite boulders, cunningly selected so that no cement was needed to keep out the elements. The roof was sod, battened down with rope and weighted with more stones. A small opening in the roof allowed some of the aromatic, teal-blue smoke from a peat fire to escape, but most of it remained to blacken the walls and challenge the eyes and lungs. Under this small roof a family usually sheltered its livelihood—chickens, black cattle, and sheep—with little separation between living quarters. It was a typical dwelling of the lower orders of clan members who lived as vassals of their feudal lord, the chieftain.

In return for a small patch of land called a tack or croft upon which to live, these melodic-voiced Gaelic speakers historically had pledged to leave hearth and home whenever their chieftain called them into battle. Although those days were mostly over by 1745, a Highlander was the fiercest adversary anyone could have the misfortune to come up against in war. The Highlanders' fame as fighting men was known all over Europe; and strong-limbed,

---

*Pronounced "tcharlach," with a very soft ch ending, from whence comes the diminutive Charlie.

Gaelic-speaking men formed shock-troop regiments in every major army on the Continent.

In the tiny, smoke-filled "black house" of tacksman Angus MacDonald (for they were now in MacDonald country) Charles spent his first night in Scotland. His host had no idea who the Prince was, but he went to the trouble of catching flounder that he smoked over the bare peat fire for supper. As clouds of blue haze billowed into the tiny room, Charles kept going to the door for fresh air. "What a plague is the matter with that fellow," asked Angus testily in Gaelic, "that he can neither sit nor stand still, and neither keep within nor without doors?" This was Aeneas Mac-Donald's version of the story, and it amused everybody so much, it was repeated far and wide. Some said the Prince's fidgeting exasperated Angus so much that with characteristic Highland bluntness he said he hoped the devil would take the man.

The *Du Teillay*, anchored off Eriskay, had hoped to put in at the island of South Uist, barely two miles to the north, the home of Clanranald's brother, Alexander MacDonald of Boisdale. Some stoic messenger braved the stormy night and brought Boisdale to see Charles and company the following morning. Boisdale wasted no time informing them that MacDonald of Sleat and MacLeod had alerted him and others of the possibility Charles might make an appearance, but that if he came without troops, nobody intended to join him and he might just as well return to France.

"Every body was strock as with a thunder boult, as you may believe," wrote O'Sullivan in his account, "to hear yt sentence & those dispossitions in the Contry, especially from MccCloud, who was one of those yt said he'd be one of the first yt wou'd joyn the Prince in case even he came alone." There is no evidence, save Hector Maclean's list naming MacLeod, Sleat, and Clanranald, that any such promise had been made; yet the Prince spread the word that it was so.

Most of the group was for returning to France at that point, but there was no changing Charles's mind once it was made up: He was going to stay. Thus on the evening of Thursday, July 25, under cover of night, the *Du Teillay* slipped away from Eriskay to avoid the large man o' war that was still visible in the Sound of Barra and made for the mainland. She threaded her way across the Sea of the Hebrides through the islands of Skye, Eigg, Muck, and Rhum until she reached the sea-Loch of nan Uamh between Arisaig and

Moidart. This was the home of Kinlochmoidart, Aeneas Mac-
Donald's brother. Aeneas took a boat to fetch his brother back to
see the Prince. He returned with Kinlochmoidart, another brother,
and Clanranald's son, Young Clanranald, who happened to be
visiting.

It was now Friday, July 26. The log of the *Du Teillay* chronicles this as the day "Conversations began." Charles suggested to
Young Clanranald that he should raise his men to join the cause,
which alarmed him greatly because he could not go against the
wishes of his father. He and the Prince were closeted together for
an afternoon. Kinlochmoidart, the first man to declare for Charles,
helped sway Clanranald against his better judgment. He stipulated, however, that his commitment was good only for six months
if other chiefs did not join. Donald of Kinlochmoidart was captured four months later, when he vainly attempted to contact Sir
Alexander MacDonald of Sleat and MacLeod on the Prince's
behalf. He was hanged at Carlisle in October 1746.

They did not appear to have any sense of the seriousness of
what they were all getting into. The gaunt rocks of Loch nan Uamh
sheltered the anchored *Du Teillay* as curious MacDonalds came to
see the Prince. A large tent had been erected on the frigate's deck;
there visitors were cheerfully welcomed by Tullibardine, who had
known many of them since "the Fifteen." A great variety of wines
and spirits was set out under an awning; perhaps this explains the
ease with which certain promises were made. One account,
thought to have been written by the Gaelic poet Alexander Mac-
Donald (the widespread duplication of names led to people being
known by the region where they lived or the work they performed), tells of a visit to the *Du Teillay*. The writer had not
expected to see His Royal Highness, who was meeting privately
with Clanranald.

> After being 3 hours with the P., Clanronald returned to us, and in
> about half ane hour after there entered the tent a tall youth of a most
> agreeable aspect in a plain black coat with a plain shirt not very
> clean and a cambrick stock fixed with a plain silver buckle . . . a
> plain hatt with a canvas string haveing one end fixed to one of his
> coat buttons; he had black stockins and brass buckles in his shoes;
> at his first appearance I found my heart swell to my very throat. . . .
>   I at this time taking him to be only a passenger or some clergy-
> man, presumed to speak to him with too much familiarity, yet still
> retained some suspicion he might be one of more note than he was

said to be. He asked me if I was not cold in that habit [the writer was wearing a kilt]. I answered I was so habituated to it that I should rather be so if I was to change my dress for any other. . . . Severall such questions he put to me; then rising quickly from his seat he calls for a dram. . . . Having taken a glass of wine in his hand, he drank to us all round, and soon after left us.

Kinlochmoidart was sent to Edinburgh with letters to Murray of Broughton, the Duke of Perth, and Lochiel, notifying them of the Prince's arrival. He was also given some louis d'or to exchange for guineas because the Scots would not accept foreign coins as payment for food. Clanranald killed a stag and some kids, which he brought to the ship; then he went off to the Isle of Skye to see what he could do to persuade MacLeod and MacDonald of Sleat to change their minds. Their answer was still the same: Go back to France.

Those on board ship were surprised that although they stayed at anchor in Loch nan Uamh for several days, the government garrison at Fort William was not notified. They were being introduced to traditional Highland hospitality—and indeed the Prince owed his life to that code later on—whereby a guest in that territory could never be betrayed. Hospitality was often the only thing a Highlander had to give; the unwritten rules were—and still are—very carefully cherished. It was even suggested to Charles that he go to Skye and be a "guest" of MacLeod and MacDonald of Sleat, which would effectively prevent them from cooperating with the government by being forced to honor the code. But Charles failed to heed the advice, and besides, his business was now chiefly to take place on the mainland.

Young Clanranald left to recruit for Charle's army. He appointed MacDonald of Glenaladale as his second in command to work with O'Sullivan, who was cutting his teeth as quartermaster-general for an army as yet unformed. This was a far cry from O'Sullivan's arguing with the concierge at FitzJames over the price of fish from the river. Together he and Glenaladale organized unloading twelve out of twenty field pieces that were luckily stored aboard the *Du Teillay*. The eighteen cases of broadswords and other weapons had returned to Brest in the *Elizabeth*'s hold. The Prince's intention was to send the *Du Teillay* away so that there would be no more talk of his returning to France.

The first response from Murray of Broughton in Edinburgh

was an attempt to dissuade Charles from staying; Lochiel sent his brother, Dr. Archibald Cameron, with the same advice. But Cameron found Charles to be powerfully persuasive, using arguments that his honor, conscience, and self-interest demanded that he should do his utmost to establish the King upon the throne for the good of his own country. As for Murray of Broughton, Sheridan wrote to him that it was on the strength of his promises that the Prince had come in the first place, and that it would be laid at his door if he did not keep his word.

Why did so many clan leaders give their word and pledge their men to "Tearlach" at this time? The answer is mostly moral blackmail combined with the effects of liquor on empty bellies. During sessions of potent imbibing, the men signed a "deed of association," promising to be faithful to the Prince and call out their vassals. If any tried to back out when he sobered up, the tactic was to royally reproach him in front of others and trap him by calling his honor and word into question. Many a man caught in this fashion then grudgingly went off to raise troops from among impoverished tacksmen, often using force and threats to make them follow. Some vassals were whipped, and others had their cows butchered one by one until they promised to "come out," bringing whatever weapons they had. Often these were nothing more than rusty broadsword relics of former days—scythes, peat cutters, hoes, and other farm implements.

Angus MacDonald of Scotus and Alexander MacDonald of Keppoch had now joined. Each chieftain was given fifty or a hundred guineas, depending on the number of men he could pledge. There were promises of titles and preferment to be bestowed upon those early joiners, and at all times Charles gave positive assurances of French help—help that he had no assurance would come. In his own mind he had no doubt he would succeed in creating an action that would shame Louis into sending reinforcements. Only his personal feelings of right, destiny, and the duty others owed to him prevailed. Sense and responsibility were completely absent.

Charles made his headquarters in a farmhouse at Borrodale, near the head of Loch nan Uamh, to which hundreds were drawn by the most powerful persuader of all—food. The nucleus of the Jacobite army was not composed of loyal followers of the House of Stuart. It was composed of men whose families had been on the edge of starvation for more than a year because of failed crops due to the harsh Scottish winters of 1743 and 1744. For six months before the Prince's arrival, not a scrap of oatmeal was to be found in the upper Highlands, and there was no money to purchase meal from the nearby garrison at Fort William. The shortage was so severe that many people had developed "the itch," a rash on the arms and legs brought on by malnourishment, perennially afflicting those in this part of the country.*

Before he left Scottish waters, Antoine Walsh captured two sloops carrying sacks of barley and oatmeal and promised to release the captains only on condition they sold their cargo to the men assembled at Moidart and Arisaig. "It was a Vast succor in that jouncture," wrote O'Sullivan, "for the poor people had not a Scrap of meal for above six months before. The prince bought the meal & got it distributed proportionably to the numbre yt was in each familly; people came from all parts to get their proportion. Before this succor, the prince nor those of his suite had no other bred, but what he got out of Forte William, where he sent from time to time to by some sacs of meal, & the Garrison was not the wisser for it."

At a council of war it was agreed that the royal standard should be raised on August 19 at Glenfinnan, where all the chieftains and their men were to gather for a reading of the Royal Proclamation. Murray of Broughton had now joined the Prince and was created secretary, adopting an officious manner that eventually offended everybody. On August 18, the Prince and his party left Borrodale and moved inland along the peaceful shores of Loch Shiel. On the way they met up with Old Gordon of Glenbucket, a veteran of "the Fifteen," who had recently captured Captain Swettenham, an English army engineer on his way to strengthen the fortifications at Fort William. The Prince granted Swettenham's release upon his promise he would not take up arms against him for a year and a day, and the captain was as good as his word; he later went to London and gave glowing reports of Jacobite strength.

News was already spreading that Bonnie Prince Charlie had arrived in Scotland, but Lord President Forbes in Edinburgh was having little success in raising troops to oppose the rebels. He was hampered by the lack of ready money for their subsistence, a lack

---

*"The itch," which was actually scurvy on land, was being studied in Edinburgh at that very moment by Dr. James Lind, who found a cure eight years after "the Forty-five."

of weapons, and a rumor circulating that those who joined King George's army would be bound for the rest of their lives in that service. For want of food, thousands of able-bodied men had left Scotland in the spring to join the Dutch service (Charles had sent word to Holland to recall them), and those remaining uncommitted refused to take up arms for King George if their relations sported the white cockade of the Stuarts in their bonnets.

Today a simple stone monument to Bonnie Prince Charlie rises above the serene beauty of the loch shore at Glenfinnan, where the ragged band of Highlanders waited two hours for the arrival of Lochiel and MacDonald of Keppoch's men, who had promised to appear. It was an anxious wait, but finally the skirl of the bagpipes pierced the air as seven hundred Camerons and three hundred MacDonalds of Keppoch came over the mountaintop and threaded their way down a zig-zag path toward the cheering men in the glen below. When order was restored, the Marquis of Tullibardine read the Royal Proclamation in English, stating that King James VIII of Scotland and III of England and Ireland was asserting his just rights to claim the throne of three kingdoms. Casks of brandy were unstoppered as men whooped and tossed their bonnets into the air, drinking the Gaelic toast *slainte an Righ*—"the King's health." With that exception, precious few had understood a word of Tullibardine's ceremony.

For two days the Jacobites waited at Glenfinnan for Young Clanranald, who had not yet rounded up all the men he had promised to bring. O'Sullivan set about trying to form companies of fifty men, each with a captain, lieutenant, and four sergeants. He found this a difficult task because the Highlanders insisted on remaining with their "tribes" and would not mix or separate. They also insisted on double officers (two captains, two lieutenants, and so on), regardless of their strength. Since one chief might have sixty men and another only twenty, the system caused untold confusion later on.

MacDonald of Keppoch's men had already engaged in one action by ambushing two companies of soldiers on their way to Fort William. As the government troops passed over Spean Bridge, Keppoch's piper set up an eerie drone. Then the barefooted MacDonalds ran from their hiding place with incredible speed, brandishing the terrible broadsword and screaming at a pitch to match the *pibroch*, the music of the bagpipe. The government troops "were struck with such an accountable panick as with one consent to run of without so much as taking time to observe the number or quality of their enemy," wrote Murray of Broughton. A dozen MacDonalds, including the piper, had struck terror into the breasts of fifty men who, after being chased for six miles, surrendered when Keppoch himself caught their captain and threatened to cut him to pieces unless the rest laid down their arms. Four or five government soldiers were killed and a dozen or so were wounded, but the MacDonalds escaped without a scratch and brought their captives to Glenfinnan. The prisoners were given an option to join the Jacobites, but they refused. Even so, Charles insisted on humane treatment, finding them a roof to sleep under at night while his Highlanders cheerfully slept outdoors. Eventually they were released on condition they agreed to serve Charles whenever he called, but none ever kept his word.

From Glenfinnan, the Jacobites moved westward toward Fort William, along the shores of Loch Eil, to the house of another of Lochiel's brothers, John Cameron of Fassifern. Loyal to the government, he had taken himself off to Fort William to avoid being implicated in the cause his two brothers espoused, but his wife remained and gave the Prince a clean bed for the night. Here Charles "made as good chear as he cou'd anywhere, & God knows he wanted it . . . for he himself eat but very little bread for a long time before, & alwaise marched afoot at the head of the men as he continued almost all the time he was in Scotland." However, he drank from morning till night and eventually became very ill for two or three days.

On August 26, the Jacobites reached the home of Young Glengarry's father at Lochgarry Castle after making a detour over treacherous mountain passes to avoid the guns at Fort William. There were not enough horses to transport the baggage and field artillery, and it was discovered that O'Sullivan had made the gross mistake of burying as much equipment as possible at the western end of Loch Eil. This included the twelve small cannon, powder, ball, "picaxes, Shouvels, hatcheds & ca., yt we cou'd not get the men to carry; the garrisson of Forte William was informed of it, wch is within six or seven miles, & took it all," confessed O'Sullivan.

It was a worried Sheridan who told Sir John MacDonald "in confidence" what O'Sullivan had done. Sheridan was also being cast aside. This did not worry the old man as much as did Charles's drinking and his propensity for giving too much credence to a man of O'Sullivan's limited talents and experience. The Prince, who hated to be contradicted and expected obedience, found the ultimate fool and toady in John William O'Sullivan. The association would be the ruin of them all.

Young Glengarry was at Lochgarry Castle, having recently returned from his futile mission in France to stop the Prince. He reported that Lieutenant-General Sir John Cope, Commander in Chief of Forces in North Britain (Scotland), had assembled 3,800 men to repel any advance by the rebels at the mountain pass of Corrieyairack. Cope's forces were to march from Fort Augustus near Corrieyairack, the middle of three forts stretching from west to east across Scotland. (Fort William was the western garrison, and Fort George overlooked the Moray Firth on the eastern coast.) Largely because of the Jacobite rebellion of 1715, the British government had built these three garrisons along the foot of the mountains to check the wild Highland inhabitants beyond, who were often forced by hunger to raid the Lowlanders for food and cattle.

A council of war was called at Lochgarry Castle, to which neither O'Sullivan, Sir John MacDonald, nor Francis Strickland was invited. The Prince heard complaints from the Scots about his "foreign" advisers, who knew nothing about the country, and the mountain men outlined a plan whereby General Cope could be defeated at Corrieyairack. Young Clanranald joined them about this time (Charles had not waited beyond two days for him at Glenfinnan), and two hundred Stuarts of Appin, led by Stuart of Ardshiel, also made an appearance, while Young Glengarry was given two or three days to raise more men.

Altogether, the Jacobite army was augmented by the addition of six hundred men at Lochgarry, but because everyone who wrote an account was most secretive about numbers, it is not possible to give the exact strength of Jacobite forces, particularly since some men had already left and gone home and others were leaving daily. However, the best estimate is that the Jacobites at this time numbered only approximately 1,200 men. Nevertheless, everyone was in high spirits; casks of French brandy were not buried at Loch Eil. Murray of Broughton was put to work composing a proclamation countering an August 4 announcement in *The London Gazette* that a reward of 30,000 pounds would be given to anyone who captured the Young Pretender. There is a story that Charles suggested a retaliatory reward of 30 pounds for the capture of King

George. It is a tribute to Highland hospitality that the reward was never collected, even though the Prince later found himself among clans who vehemently opposed him.

Charles did not have his day at Corrieyairack. But General Cope's men were untrained, and many had never seen service. The government soldiers would have to approach the pass from the south by a series of steeply ascending zig-zag paths; a mere handful of Jacobites coming from the north could easily hold Corrieyairack. And Cope had also been plagued by daily desertions as his men passed through hostile Atholl country, where the local people made their passage as difficult as they could. Food was hidden, and Cope was given wrong directions on his way to the mountains, and although the Duke of Atholl (Tullibardine's brother) was a staunch supporter of George II, his people were not of the same mind. General Cope rightly judged it suicidal to tackle the Jacobites at Corrieyairack. He decided to retreat to Inverness, leaving a clear road open for the Jacobites to push southward toward their goal of entering the capital city, Edinburgh.

From his home at the foot of the Monadhliath Mountains near Corrieyairack, Cluny (Ewan) MacPherson, chieftain of Clan Chattan ("the Cat"), played a double game. He sent messages to Cope with intelligence of the Jacobites' movements, yet at the same time he was flirting with the idea of bringing his three hundred Mac-Phersons to join the rebels. Before he could make up his mind, a party of Highlanders came in the night, kidnapped the MacPherson chieftain, and brought him before the Prince. No doubt bottles were unstopped and toasts toasted, and by the end of the evening Cluny MacPherson had been persuaded. Never was an army put together in such piecemeal fashion, its principal officers having floated into duty on a sea of brandywine.

The fleet-footed Highlanders came over Corrieyairack "like lightning" and went to Garvamore, where it was supposed Cope was encamped, but they learned that he had taken his army to barracks at Ruthven on his way to Inverness. The Highlanders were for pursuing Cope eastward to Inverness, hoping to find very fine plunder there, but they were bitterly disappointed to learn that Charles planned to march southward along the River Garry toward Blair Atholl, where he hoped to recruit more men.

It was August 29 and a very hot day, the first fair weather Charles had seen in the five and a half weeks he had been in the country. In late August and September, Scotland bursts into its most colorful bloom. The mountains are covered with pink-purple heather; deep purple thistles grow by the roadside, along with blue cornflowers, the shy yellow lady's slipper, and the prickly gorsebush, whose yellow flowers are as sunny as shining egg yolks. As Charles contemplated his southward march, out on the moors sphagnum mosses in orange and many shades of green were thrusting out tiny, star-shaped white flowers, and a variety of fluted-edged lichens spread over granite rocks.

It was a day for washing. The Highlandmen had brought their women and families along with them. On this day the women washed clothes in the River Garry, thrashing the homespun garments upon rocks to beat them clean. There were "boys of 8 and old grey-beards of 80," according to a witness who saw the extraordinary army pass by. Many a Highland babe was born by the roadside.

Apparently to appease the Highlanders, a time-wasting attack was made on the Ruthven barracks. It was carried out by O'Sullivan, against his better judgment, and included MacDonald of Lochgarry (a cousin of Young Glengarry), Old Gordon of Glenbucket, and Lochiel's brother, Dr. Archibald Cameron.* Only sixteen government soldiers and one sergeant remained at the Ruthven barracks, while O'Sullivan had sixty men. Yet so inept was he that two of his men were killed and three were wounded as they set alight a barrel filled with combustible material to flush the enemy out. The Highlanders were repulsed and forced to rejoin the main body of the army without having captured the arms and meal they expected to find. The attack on the Ruthven barracks was a disappointing blunder, and O'Sullivan was "very sorry to have attempted it."

Meanwhile, the Jacobite army pressed on to Blair Castle, Tullibardine's ancestral home. The old man was greeted joyously by Athollmen who had not seen him in thirty years and who crowded around to press kisses on his hands. To many he was the real Duke of Atholl; perhaps they expected better things from him

*Cameron has the dubious distinction of being the last man known to have been executed for his participation in the Jacobite rebellion of 1745. His death by hanging came eight years later in 1753, when he was sent to Scotland on a mission for Charles, but he was betrayed by Young Glengarry and members of his own clan, who by that time wished no more of the turmoil wreaked upon them by "this Prince with a Polish mother and an Italian grandmother."

than from the government-supporting brother who had taken his title. Like Cameron of Fassifern, the incumbent Duke of Atholl had fled Blair Castle for fear of being tainted with the Jacobite brush. Tullibardine, however, was of no use to the Athollmen or the Prince, beyond displaying French fashions on his bent-over frame and reading proclamations whenever the occasion demanded.

The day after Charles's arrival at Blair Atholl on September 2, a review of troops revealed that many Highlanders had deserted. Their chieftains were sent to look for them. They caught up with several parties who explained that they were disgruntled because Charles had not pursued Cope and given him battle. They were brought back, but it was obvious that the men were thirsting for an action that would reap them some spoils of war, while the leaders were trying to delay such an action as long as possible. They feared the Highlanders would return to their homes as soon as they secured some booty.

On September 3, Charles left Blair Atholl on his way to meet up with James Drummond, the Duke of Perth (a Jacobite title not recognized by the government). He sent Lochiel and a body of men ahead to secure the city where James was to be proclaimed King and Charles his Regent. On September 4, the Prince stopped at Nairne House, between Dunkeld and Perth, to dine with Lord Nairne, a cousin of Atholl and Tullibardine; then he continued toward Perth. He was resplendent in the "set of pleat" trimmed with lace and gold braid as he rode through the city on a borrowed horse, but there were no wild cheers of acclamation, for the citizens in general were "not well dispos'd."

The Prince stayed in Perth for a week to try to raise money and more men. He had come with but one guinea in his pocket, all that remained of the 40,000 louis d'or. The Perth Magistrates appeared to be too stunned to do anything but acquiesce to Jacobite demands, and public cess and excise funds amounting to 500 pounds were seized. Murray of Broughton was sent off to Dundee to see what could be collected there, while Charles borrowed from many of the gentlemen visiting him, and "in seven or eight days there was a raisonable somme gethered up." The loans, he said, were to be repaid with interest as soon as his father was in full possession of his three kingdoms.

The Duke of Perth himself provided 200 or 300 pounds. He was thirty-four years old, an affable man who had spent the first twenty years of his life being educated at the Scots College in Paris.

He suffered from a lung ailment that may well have been tuber-
culosis,* and he died the following year as he was escaping to
France. The Chevalier de Johnstone described Perth as "brave even
to intrepidity, a perfectly upright man, endowed with a great deal
of sweetness of character, was of a feeble genius, and intermeddled
with nothing." He had no military experience to speak of and
never pretended to have any; yet Charles created Perth the most
senior lieutenant-general of the Jacobite army. He was one of two.

The other lieutenant-general was of a vastly different character and later became Charles's nemesis. He was fifty-one-year-old
Lord George Murray, younger brother of the Duke of Atholl and of
the kerchief-carrying Tullibardine. This was the third time Lord
George had taken up arms on behalf of King James. He had been
involved in "the Fifteen" and in the Spanish-Jacobite attempt of
1719; most of his life had been spent living down previous
transgressions after being pardoned by the government. He was
the fifth son of wealthy parents, an unenviable lot in life for an
aggressively ambitious man, and he viewed the rebellion of 1745
as his last chance. Little is known about Lord George's practical
military experience except for the Chevalier de Johnstone's statement that he "had a natural genius for war, which, cultivated by
the study of the military art, had truly rendered him one of the
greatest generals in Europe." This was undoubtedly an exaggera-
tion, for Lord George Murray did not possess the quality of an Earl
Marischal, but he was certainly far superior to the Duke of Perth.
Maxwell of Kirkconnell said that although Perth was "much
beloved and esteemed," if the Highlanders could pick their choice
of a general, "Lord George would have carried it by vast odds
against the Duke of Perth." Lord George was, Johnstone admitted,
"fierce, haughty, blunt and proud" and "desired always to dictate
everything by himself, and knowing none his equal, he did not
wish to receive his advice." From the outset he had annoyed many
by firmly and self-importantly assuming leadership of the Jacobite
army.

Lord George Murray entered the Prince's service under a
cloud of suspicion. A MacDonald woman who had lived in the
neighborhood for a long time reported to Sir John MacDonald that
Lord George intended to raise the men of Atholl, then take them

---

*Contemporaries said that Perth's ailment was due to his chest having been crushed by a
barrel when he was a boy.*

over to the government side. This was, at least, what Sir John, who was jealous of Lord George's strength and competence, told the Prince. The substance of the story made no sense to anyone who knew Lord George, particularly the fighting men and Scottish chieftains, but the people who came over from France were fond of keeping the rumor alive.

The army was joined by men such as Lord Ogilvy, Oliphant of Gask, Robert Mercer of Aldie, and Maxwell of Kirkconnell. Their amazement at the poor quality of men chosen by Charles to launch the daring enterprise could not be hidden. O'Sullivan "committed blunders on every occasion of moment"; Sir John MacDonald was frequently intoxicated; Aeneas MacDonald was maligned and disliked by even his own clansmen; Sir Thomas Sheridan was a bigoted Catholic with archaic ideas; Strickland was sickly and dropsical; the decrepit Tullibardine (left behind at Blair Atholl to recruit) was fawned over by a retinue of flighty Frenchmen; Hay of Restalrig, an incompentent man recruited by Murray of Broughton to purchase the army's food, fell short of his duties so that the Jacobites often went hungry; and the offensively self-assertive Murray of Broughton bustled about looking down his nose at anyone from north of Perth.

It was said that Secretary Murray of Broughton prevented chieftains from seeing the Prince, but Charles had his own way of creating divisiveness. He had no liking for the proud Lord George because he was competent and he naturally commanded authority. These were qualities the Prince wished he had and tried to feign, but in the skirmishes that followed it was to Lord George, not to the Prince, that all turned for leadership. This was not the way Charles had imagined himself in his dreams, and from the beginning he set up a childish and destructive competition against the only person in the Jacobite army who knew what he was doing.* Rarely did the Prince consult with men who knew the people and the territory, and in the seniority dispute between Lord George Murray and the Duke of Perth—an issue of more concern to the fighting men than to the principals—Charles hit upon the idiotic solution of giving them alternate command of left and right

---

*One anonymous, tongue-in-cheek observer wrote: "Had Prince Charles slept during the whole of the expedition and allowed Lord George to act for him, according to his own judgment, there is every reason for supposing that he would have found the crown of Great Britain on his head when he awoke."

wings and command of forces on alternate days. It was a wonder that men of sense remained committed for very long, but it was usually not until they had publicly declared for the cause that inherent evils were discovered. By then it was too late to withdraw.

At Perth, Lord George made the decision that unless he wrested control from the sycophants who surrounded the Prince, the Jacobites would have little hope of success. He was galled, for instance, that Sir Thomas Sheridan would dare to instruct him on how to treat his countrymen. The Lord Provost of Perth had been imprisoned on Charles's orders for nonpayment of exacted taxes. "We must show these kind of people our power," intoned Sir Thomas, "or they will spit upon us." With much difficulty Lord George was able to obtain the Lord Provost's release, but more and more of the Scots were coming to resent these strangers accompanying the Prince who had risked neither men, money, titles, nor property. Yet it was their words and counsel that carried most weight with Charles.

At Inverness, Lieutenant General Sir John Cope had persuaded only one clan, the Munros, to join him. All told, the English commander now had approximately two thousand men because of sickness and desertions; but he was daily expecting to be reinforced by six thousand soldiers, to be pulled from Dutch service and shipped across the North Sea to Scotland. When he heard the Jacobites had marched south, Cope notified eighty-five-year-old General Guest, in command of Edinburgh Castle, to hold the city until he could transport his men southward by ship to meet up with the reinforcements from Holland. This information was relayed to the Jacobites by their spies in Cope's camp, and they resolved to march to Edinburgh as quickly as possible to capture the city before Cope could get there.

Leaving Perth on September 11, the Jacobite army passed through Dunblane and then Stirling. As O'Sullivan described the march, they passed "in sight & even within Cannon Shot of the Castle of Sterling, in very good order. Collors flying, pipes playing & makeing the best appearance he cou'd with his little Army. The Castle fired several Cannon Shots at him as he past, & tho' the bals came very near, & even one or two past over their heads, not one man stured out of his rank, but answer'd by several Howsa's."

Beyond Stirling was the historic site of Bannockburn, where the worthy King Robert the Bruce had defeated England's Edward II in 1314. Beyond that was Falkirk and Linlithgow, where the rebels hoped to surprise a regiment of government dragoons led by the hapless Colonel James Gardiner. Gardiner and Colonel Hamilton, commander of a second dragoon regiment, were the only forces standing between the approaching Jacobites and Edinburgh. Their physical condition was appalling, for the lack of food that afflicted the Highlands was even more severe in Scotland's more densely populated middle and lower regions. As Murray of Broughton had told Charles in March of that year (it was one of his reasons why an expedition to Scotland should not have been attempted in 1745), a plague had hit the black cattle, and many had to be destroyed. The men's legs and thighs were covered by purplish-black bruises and were so swollen that they could not get their boots on. Their gums bled; many had already lost teeth; and an extreme lethargy and melancholia overtook them so that they cared not whether they lived or died. Their horses had wanted forage for many a day and were in no fit condition to carry riders on their backs. The dragoons made no pretense at a defense of Edinburgh but took off over Colt Bridge, three miles west of the city, and made for the open countryside as soon as they saw the first rebels approaching. The incident became celebrated in Jacobite annals as the Canter of Coltbrig.

From his camp two miles away, Charles sent the following summons to the Lord Provost, Archibald Stewart, and the Magistrates of the City of Edinburgh on September 16:

Being now in a condition to make our way into this capital of his Majesty's ancient kingdom of Scotland, we hereby summon you to receive us, as you are in duty bound to do. And in order to it we hereby require you upon receipt of this to summon the Town Council and take proper measure in it for securing the peace and quiet of the city, which we are very desirous to protect. But if you suffer any of the Usurper's troops to enter the town, or any of the cannon, arms or ammunition now in it, whether belonging to the publick or to private persons, to be carried off, we shall take it as a breach of your duty and a heinous offence against the king and us, and shall resent it accordingly. We promise to preserve all the rights and liberties of the city, and the particular property of every one of his Majesty's subjects. But if any opposition be made to us we cannot answer for the consequences, being firmly resolved at any rate to enter the city, and in that case, if any of the inhabitants are found in arms against us, they must not expect to be treated as prisoners of war.

A deputation of the magistrates came out to treat and talk of conditions, but Charles would hear of none except that the city be delivered over to him unconditionally. They returned beyond the walls and said they would come back in two hours to give the Prince a final answer. As the deputation was coming out from Edinburgh by a wicket gate for the second time to treat once more with the Prince, the guard was rushed and disarmed by Highlanders. Bonnie Prince Charlie was now master of Scotland's capital.

Chapter 7

The Battle of Prestonpans

Just before noon on September 17, 1745, all was in readiness for Charles to march triumphantly into Edinburgh. The only hitch of any consequence was that General Guest and King George's troops were still in possession of the castle and its guns. So the Jacobite force had to make a wide circuit and enter the city from the south, where the men were protected by the heights of Arthur's Seat and Salisbury Crags. The Duke of Perth rode to Charles's right and the newly joined Lord Elcho to his left, "and all the hillskippers in rank and file." The procession made its way to the park fronting the Palace of Holyrood, where the Prince dismounted from the bay gelding that had been presented to him by the Duke of Perth. He displayed himself to the throngs of people who crowded around to press kisses on his hand. "One would have thought the whole inhabitants of Edinburgh were assembled there," wrote Maxwell of Kirkconnell, "and all seemed to join in the loudest acclamations . . . The joy seemed universal. God Save the King echoed back from all quarters of the town. The ladies particularly distinguished themselves on this occasion."

The Prince was certainly an impressive sight. He wore a light-colored peruke topped with a blue velvet bonnet that was ringed with gold lace; a tartan short coat; and a waistcoat and breeches of red velvet. On his breast the Order of St. Andrew was pinned to a blue sash wrought with gold. Completing the outfit were military riding boots and a sword with a silver hilt. Charles stayed on foot for some minutes, acknowledging the people; then, so that more could get a view of him, he remounted his horse and moved slowly through the cheering throng toward the Palace of Holyrood, the

135

ancient seat of the Stuart kings. A gentleman stepped forward, unsheathed his sword, and holding it aloft in the air, led the Prince to the entrance of the palace. In this dramatic way James Hepburn of Keith chose to declare his support for the Stuart cause. Charles reached the suite of apartments that had been made ready for him, stepped out onto the balcony, and graciously acknowledged the cheers of the citizens below. It must truly have seemed to many that, in the words of an old Jacobite song, at last "the King had come into his own again."

There are two Holyroods; the Abbey, long since a ruin, and the Palace, begun in 1501 by James IV of Scotland in preparation for his marriage to Margaret Tudor, sister of Henry VIII. Today Holyrood Palace is usually associated with Mary Queen of Scots (the Prince's great-great-great-grandmother), Lord Darnley, Bothwell, and the brutal murder of Rizzio. But Charles Edward Stuart may have reflected that only sixty-five years before, his grandfather had exercised at Holyrood the prerogatives of royalty as a representative of his brother, Charles II. His great-grandfather, Charles I, had been christened at Holyrood and had spent his childhood years there. It was at Holyrood that his great-great-grandfather, James VI of Scotland, was brought news that his cousin Queen Elizabeth I was dead and that he was now King of England. Since that event in 1603, the career of the Stuarts had certainly been turbulent; now the last of their line had come to reclaim the family fortunes in the name of his father.

In the few short weeks since the raising of the standard at Glenfinnan, Charles had accomplished a great deal, swiftly and unopposed. It is small wonder that, as he stood on the balcony of Holyrood Palace, he was the darling of the crowd and the idol of the women. Even the Whigs among them had to admit that he was impressive. "The figure and presence of Charles Stuart were not ill-suited to his lofty pretensions. He was in the prime of youth, tall and handsome," said one observer. Other grudgingly conceded that although he looked like "a gentleman of fashion," in their estimation the enterprise he had undertaken was "above the pitch of his mind, and his heart was not great enough for the sphere in which he moved." The Reverend Alexander Carlyle, a young man of twenty-three at the time, wrote: "The commons in general, as well as two thirds of the gentry at that period, had no aversion to the family of Stuart; and could their religion have been secured, would have been very glad to see them on the throne again."

For the most part Charles was warmly welcomed in Edinburgh. The afternoon was reserved for the formal proclaiming of his father as King James VIII of Scotland at the Market Cross. Those who could find no room to stand in the streets hung out the windows of the city's tall houses; gaily colored handkerchiefs fluttered from every building.

Making his way to the city to witness the events of the day was the author of *The Woodhouselee Manuscripts* (believed to be Patrick Crichton of Woodhouselee), whose colorful narrative ridiculed the Jacobite attempt at pomp and ceremony on this occasion. Written in broad Lothian Scots, the manuscript is a rollicking, scathing diatribe on the Highland "rowges" and "scurlewheelers." He described the Highlanders the day before their entry into Edinburgh; "and on they came with there bagpipes and plaids, rusty rapiers, matchlocks, fyerlocks, and tag rag and bob taile was there." He was in a very angry mood, for he believed the Lord Provost of Edinburgh, Archibald Stewart, had cooperated with the "enemie," who were "invited to come in at discretion." However, curiosity drove him to the city, which he entered "by the Bristol Port which I saw to my indignation in the keeping of these caterpillars. A boy stood with a rusty drawen sword and two fellows with things licke guns of the 16 centurie sat on each side the entry to the poors howse, and these were catching the vermin from ther lurking places abowt ther plaids and throwing them away."

Undaunted, he went on until he reached the head of the stairs that led to Parliament Close, where he "cowld scarce pass for throng." Here he came across a minister of his acquaintance and inquired of him, "ar these the scownderalls have surprised Edinburgh by treachery?" To which the minister replied, "I had reither seen it in the hands of Frenchmen, but the divell and the deep sea are both bad." On he went through the crowds looking for a vantage point. "I saw from a window near the Cross, north syde of the High Streeat, this commick fars or tragic commody. All these mountan officers with there troups in rank and fyle marched from the Parliament Closs down to surrownd the Cross, and with there bagpipes and loosie crew they maid a large circle from the end of the Luickenboths to half way below the Cross."

The Market Cross was draped with a Persian carpet and five heralds richly dressed in formal costume stood in attendance. Although the Jacobite accounts speak of a fanfare from the heralds, the author of *Woodhouselee* tells us, "they came attended but with one trumpet." As the Highlanders were forming, he had an opportunity to examine their poor weapons. "I observed there armes, they were guns of diferent syses, and some of innormowows lengh, some with butts tured up like a heren, some tyed with puck threed to the stock, some withowt locks and some matchlocks, some had swords over ther showlder instead of guns, one or two had pitchforks and some bits of sythes upon poles with a cleek, some old Lochaber axes. The pipes plaid pibrowghs when they were making ther circle thus they stood rownd 5 or six men deep." Inside the circle were the officers, "speciall favowrites," and Mrs. Murray of Broughton, resplendent in a magnificent white dress. To lend a semblance of pageantry to the occasion she was mounted on a white horse and held an unsheathed sword throughout the ceremony. "All the streat and the windows and forstairs were crowded and sylence being made the manefesto was read in the name of James 8 of Scotland England France and Ireland King. . . . Chalmers the herald pronunced all this manefesto and declaration with ane awdable strong voice. I cowld hear at my distance distinctly, and many much further. . . ."

After James's declaration came the reading of Charles's commission as Prince Regent, then his manifesto, which began:

> By virtue and authority of the above commission of regency granted unto us by the king, our royal father, we are now come to execute his majesty's will and pleasure, by setting up his royal standard, and asserting his undoubted right to the throne of his ancestors.
>
> We do, therefore, in his majesty's name, and pursuant to the tenor of his several declarations, hereby grant a free, full, and general pardon for all treasons, rebellions and offences whatsoever, committed at any time before the publication hereof against our royal grandfather, his present majesty, and ourselves. To the benefit of this pardon we shall deem justly entitled all such of his majesty's subjects as shall testify their willingness to accept of it, either by joining our forces with all convenient diligence; by setting up his royal standard in other places; by repairing for our service to any place where it shall be so set up, or at least by openly renouncing all pretended allegiance to the usurper, and all obedience to his orders, or to those of any person or persons commissioned, or employed by him, or acting avowedly for him.

The manifesto continued on at some length, promising higher commissions and a whole year's pay to all officers in the army or

navy in the service of the "foreign usurper" if they would immediately take arms for their "natural sovereign." These monies were
to be paid "as soon as our kingdoms shall be in a state of
tranquility." Assurances were given that the Church of England
would be maintained as established by law, as well as the Protestant Churches of Scotland and Ireland. Charles stated his aversion
to religious persecution and declared that churches, universities,
and his father's subjects would retain full enjoyment of all their
rights. The Prince commanded all revenue and customs officials
to deliver the collected public money to him immediately, and he
called for every male between the ages of sixteen and sixty to
repair forthwith to King James's standard to assist him in the
recovery of his just rights.

An ominous note crept into the last paragraph of Charles's
manifesto.

> Lastly, we do hereby require all mayors, sheriffs, and other magis-
> trates of what denomination soever, their respective deputies, and
> all others to whom it may belong, to publish this our declaration at
> the market crosses of their respective cities, towns, and boroughs,
> and there to proclaim his majesty, under the penalty of being
> proceeded against according to law, for the neglect of so necessary
> and important a duty; for as we have hereby graciously and sin-
> cerely offered a free and general pardon for all that is past, so we, at
> the same time, seriously warn all his majesty's subjects, that we
> shall leave to the rigour of the law all those who shall from
> henceforth oppose us, or wilfully and deliberately do, or concur in
> any act or acts, civil or military, to the hurt or detriment of us, our
> cause or title, or to the destruction, prejudice, or annoyance of those
> who shall, according to their duty and our intentions, thus publicly
> signified, declare and act for us.

The document obviously did not take into consideration the fact
that by far the majority of its readers had been born after James II
vacated the throne in 1688. George II was the fourth monarch since
then to interrupt the Stuart succession, and by 1745 he had been
on the throne for eighteen years. Many must have been perplexed
by talk of "full and general pardons" and threats of dissenters
being proceeded against according to the "rigour of the law."

After listening to James's declaration, dated from Rome, and
Charles's, dated from Paris, the *Woodhouselee* author sneered
caustically, "Thus the winds [that] blew from Rome and Paris were

to work our thraldome." Copies of the documents were liberally distributed to the assembled citizens at the close of the ceremony. The Highlanders were then dismissed "with bagpipes playing and a fashion of streamers over their showlders and the chime of bells from the High Church steaple gave musicall tunes all the whill."

On the evening of the seventeenth a ball was held at Holyrood House. The next day there was much work to be done. Bread had to be baked for the Highlanders; quarters and arms had to be found. Charles was very careful about billeting the men he needed within the city walls so as not to inconvenience private citizens. "The Burgesses and people of fashion were not harrassed with common fellows for their guests," said Murray of Broughton, whose disdain for the Highland men with whom he allied himself is frequently evident in his *Memorials.* "Only publick houses and people of low rank was burthened with them."

The "common fellows" required inside the city as guards were under strict orders not to touch a drop of alcohol. They were given straw beds to lie upon in Parliament Close and the Tron Church. The main body was encamped at Duddingston, just outside Edinburgh, well away from the castle guns. On September 18, an order went out for a thousand tents, each for six men, six thousand pans "for readying their victwals," and shoes and stockings for six thousand men. Although the Prince had barely half this number, the strategy was to inflate orders for provisions in order to hide their weakness. For the same reason, Highlanders at Duddingston were drilled and redrilled to confound anyone who tried to count them.

The antiquated guns and other weapons had to be replaced, for "not above one-half of the Highlanders was completely armed," said Maxwell of Kirkconnell, a major in Lord Elcho's company. A stand of arms was found in the city, but half of them were "good for little." So an order went out to the citizens of Edinburgh and the surrounding countryside to turn in all the weapons they had in their possession. All the supplies and provisions were to be paid for. Charles was adamant on that point, and the writings of the period, both Jacobite and Whig, make it clear that the Highlanders always paid a fair price for what they needed.

Some of the accounts by James Gib, the Prince's Master of Household for a brief period, are printed in *Lyon in Mourning.* From them we learn that in 1745 beef was two and a half pence per pound, chickens were six pence each, and ducks cost eight pence. Butter could be obtained for four pence a pound, and ale was one shilling and four pence a gallon. A thousand oysters for the army cost only four shillings, while eggs were two pence a dozen and milk was two pence a pint. For those who would further compare 1745 prices with those of today, random extracts from Gib's account are of interest:

	£.	s.	d.
to a goun and peticoat to the citchen girle		13	5
to 5 yard lining for shirts and making		6	4
to 22 sheep	5	1	0
to a colored pigge		3	0
to 6 dozen oranges		18	0
to ½ dozen Lisbone wine		10	0
for 3 sheeps heads singing [singeing]			1½

To Charles both the invaded and the invaders were his father's subjects; he did everything possible to make things run smoothly. Money was scarce because all specie had been locked up in the castle, which had not been captured by the Jacobites. The funds received at Perth had run out, so on the morning when he entered Edinburgh, Charles borrowed 1,500 guineas from Lord Elcho. We hear a great deal about this loan for years afterward. Other funds were to come from the cess and excise accumulated in each town, while each day brought hope that the long-awaited gold from France that Charles spoke of would arrive.

Meanwhile, General Cope had shipped government troops from Aberdeen to Dunbar, where he hoped to find that the Dutch reinforcements had landed to assist him. The disembarkation at Dunbar took place on September 17 and 18. There Cope heard the news of Edinburgh's capitulation and learned to his dismay that the Dutch had not yet arrived. He held a council of war, and although it was the opinion of Colonel Gardiner and some other officers that the Royal Army should await the Dutch, Cope judged it best to march on Edinburgh without further delay.

Already he had been the victim of the ministry's procrastination and disorganization. He feared that to wait much longer would allow aid for the Jacobites to arrive from France. He was also afraid that the northern clans who had not yet committed themselves would march to join Charles once the news of his success at Edinburgh reached them. Cope had good intelligence from John Home, the historian, as well as from others who had seen the Highlanders in Edinburgh. Home had counted the men at Duddingston as they sat down to an evening meal and estimated that they were two thousand strong, roughly equal to the number of Cope's forces. Taking into consideration the decrepit state of the Highlanders' weapons, their lack of artillery, and the fact that the castle was holding out against them, Cope made his decision to march. On September 18, he wrote to Tweeddale, Secretary of State for Scotland, "I march tomorrow morning, and will do the best I can for his Majesty's service."

Late on the afternoon of Thursday, September 19, the news was brought to Charles that Cope had left Dunbar that morning and had reached Haddington, seventeen miles from Edinburgh, where he intended to camp for the night. Charles was delighted that at last his Highlanders were to be given a crack at King George's troops, which they had been long awaiting, and he was probably further elated that the general was making his move without waiting for the Dutch. He left at once for Duddingston with his officers and called a council of war, where it was decided to march and meet Cope in battle well away from Edinburgh.

After John Home's tally of two thousand, the Jacobite ranks swelled by the addition of another five hundred clansmen from the MacLauchlans, from the Grants of Glenmoriston, and from the men of Atholl. Glenmoriston's men reached the camp on the morning of September 20, having made an all-night march. Dirty, tired, and bewhiskered, the chieftain hurried to present himself to the Prince. But he was rewarded by a sarcastic comment from Charles on his ill-kempt appearance. Rightfully indignant, Glenmoriston riposted, "Sir, it is not beardless boys who are to do your business."

Another tactless action attributed to the Prince that day was that he called the chiefs together to ask how they expected their men to behave in battle. This annoyed many who were experienced fighters and leaders; they never thought they would be called upon to answer for their clansmen. MacDonald of Keppoch replied for all, assuring Charles that the gentlemen of the clans would lead the attack with one accord, and that since the clansmen loved the cause as well as their chieftains, they would certainly share the danger with their leaders. On hearing this,

Charles resolved to lead the attack himself. However, he was dissuaded from this course when it was pointed out that even if his army were victorious, all would be lost if he were killed.

On the morning of September 20, Charles presented his sword at the head of his army and cried, "Gentlemen, I have flung away the Scabbard. With God's assistance I don't doubt of making you a free and happy people. Mr. Cope shall not escape us as he did in the highlands." There were very few Gaelic-speakers who understood what was being said, but a cheer went up, and the sky was filled with flying blue bonnets. They began the march with high hopes of a solid victory. They progressed toward Musselburgh and from there along the post road toward Pinkie. At the south side of Pinkie Gardens, Lord George Murray, who was leading the vanguard, received word from a scout that Cope had left Haddington and was at or near Preston. The two armies were about three miles apart. Lord George's immediate reaction was to strike out across fields without waiting for the Prince's command in order to reach the ground of Falside Hill before Cope did. "In less than half an hour, by marching quick, I got to the eminence. I went very slow; after I had got possession of the ground, I intended waiting till the rear was fully joined. We then marched in order, advancing towards Tranent, and all the way in sight of the enemy."

Although Lord George had the high ground, he was king of a castle that Cope had already rejected. The village of Tranent lay atop a long, broad ridge that sloped down to a plain approximately 150 feet below. Assembled on the lower terrain, drawn up in battle order, were Cope's 567 dragoons, 1,624 footsoldiers, six 1½-pounder galloper guns, and six small mortars. Only half a mile now divided the opposing sides, who, to the delight of the country people assembled to watch, began to hoot, jeer, and yell defiance at one another. It took considerable effort to restrain the Highlanders from rushing pell mell down the slope and falling upon their adversaries then and there. However, close examination of the ground revealed that it was a treacherous boggy morass broken up by hedges, ditches, and willow trees. Here and there were plots of land surrounded by stone walls and trenches; a broad water-filled ditch ran along the entire base of the hillside. No force could hope to charge the plain below and maintain impetus and military formation. Colonel Ker of Graden was sent to reconnoiter, mounted on a little white pony. Amid fire from Cope's men, Ker coolly surveyed the area and confirmed the suspicion that in charging the "uncouth piece of ground," the flower of their force would be subjected to merciless fire.

Cope had previously rejected the plateau now held by the Jacobites because it was unsuitable for his cavalry; the ridge was so broad that he ran the danger of being outflanked. The lower ground of flat reclaimed marshland between the villages of Preston and Seaton was ideal for his purposes. It extended about a mile and a quarter east to west, and a mile from north to south. The northern boundary was formed by the seashore and the coastal villages of Port Seaton, Cockenzie, and Prestonpans. To the west was the ten-foot-high wall of Preston House,* which ran almost the length of the field from north to south. Anticipating Charles's approach through Preston to the west, Cope ordered breaches to be made in this wall; just enough masonry was torn away that his artillery could be effective. To the east was the village of Seaton, and running along the southern extremity of the battlefield was the road leading to Edinburgh, little more than a narrow cart track. On the south side of this track, or "defile" as it was termed, was a water-filled ditch that was six feet across and as deep as it was broad. Beyond that was the marshy incline stretching toward Tranent.

When the Jacobites appeared at Tranent, Cope wheeled his troops around from their position facing Preston to form a diagonal line across the plain facing southwest. His right flank stretched toward the sea; his left reached the ditch at the bottom of the slope; in front were the partially breached walls of Preston House, and his rear offered clear ground to Seaton in case of retreat. The government army appeared impregnable to the Jacobites. "The more we examined it, the more we were convinced of the impossibility of attacking it, and we were all thrown into consternation, and quite at a loss what course to take," wrote the Chevalier de Johnstone, who was aide-de-camp to both Charles and Lord George Murray. In the face of this predicament, the strong personalities at variance among the Jacobites took action independently of one another, with inevitably clashing consequences.

The chain of events began when Lord George rushed to take

Sometimes known as Grange House, this belonged to the eccentric George Erskine of Grange, brother of the Earl of Mar, who had commanded the Jacobite Rebellion of 1715. Cursed with an insane wife, Lord Grange had connived at her abduction to a remote area in the Hebrides.

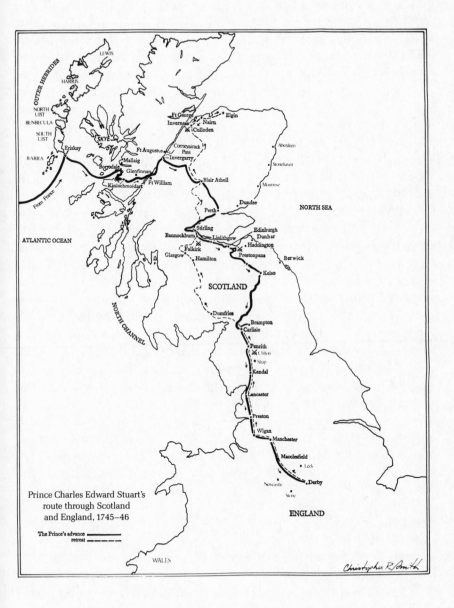

Prince Charles Edward Stuart's
route through Scotland
and England, 1745–46

The Prince's advance ▬▬▬▬
retreat ▬ ▬ ▬ ▬

Christopher R/Smith

the high ground without waiting for orders. At the time that had probably seemed the best course to follow, but Lord George did not know the country as well as he had claimed. We do not know what Charles's verbal reaction to the situation was, but it would have been in keeping with his character—and his dislike and distrust of Lord George—to rebuke him publicly. The Prince did take half the army and march westward to determine the possibilities of attacking through Preston. He took the Duke of Perth with him while the remainder of the army stayed at Tranent under Lord George. Perth was little better than a submissively acquiescent attendant to the Prince; it had never ceased to rankle Lord George that his commission of general was dated later than Perth's, thus making the latter the senior of the two.

While Charles marched westward and Lord George conferred with village people who knew the area, O'Sullivan either took it upon himself or was ordered by the Prince to post a contingent of Lochiel's Camerons in the Tranent churchyard at the village's northwestern extremity. Almost immediately they were discovered by Cope's men, who brought up two galloper guns and proceeded to bombard them, wounding some. Lochiel was incensed that his men had been so needlessly exposed, and he begged Lord George to authorize their withdrawal, which he did. Soon afterward, O'Sullivan came upon Lord George and asked him why he had removed the Camerons. Their presence in the churchyard was vital, he said, if the attack was to be made from the west, where Charles had taken his party. Lord George stated in no uncertain terms that he had decided that the attack would take place from the east; that he would accept the responsibility of persuading the Prince of the practicability of his plan; and that the Camerons were withdrawn because they served no purpose where O'Sullivan had placed them. The exchange was quite heated, for Lord George, who was never one to mask his feelings, had long considered the Irishman weak, sycophantic, inadequate, and a nuisance. It did not help that O'Sullivan was an obvious favorite with Charles.

Lord George's decision to move eastward from Tranent along the ridge in the direction of Seaton was based on information from Robert Anderson of Whitburgh, the Younger. As a boy he had often gone snipe-shooting in the area, and he knew of a hidden path at the east end of the ridge leading through the bog to the plain below. Lord George ordered an immediate reconnaissance of the ground to see if it would be feasible to mobilize an army by that route. Finding Anderson's story accurate, he hurriedly sent a message to Charles to join him and then marched out of Tranent. For him, time was of the essence. He still hoped for action that day, but darkness was due to fall in another couple of hours.

As if the division between the officers were not enough, the clansmen were squabbling among themselves as well. The most unhappy were the MacDonalds, who had the largest representation, under the combined families of Clanranald, Keppoch, Glengarry, and Glencoe. Traditionally the MacDonalds had the right hand in battle, a right bestowed upon Angus MacDonald, Lord of the Isles, by King Robert the Bruce as an honor in gratitude for having been hidden by MacDonald for nine months after the Battle of Bannockburn. The right could be yielded to another clan only by the MacDonalds themselves, as it was in the Battle of Harlaw, when they gave the honor to the Macleans.

Earlier, when Charles's army had assembled at Perth, this ancient right was challenged by the other clans. So to keep the peace a system of drawing lots was devised and agreed upon among the chiefs. The men knew nothing about it until they were told that Lochiel and his Camerons had drawn the lot that would give them the right-hand position in the battle with Cope. The MacDonalds were furious; they felt that if Old Clanranald, their chieftain, had been leading his men instead of Young Clanranald, this system would not have been imposed on them. The same was true of Keppoch and Glengarry's men; they too were led by younger sons. The grumbles and complaints grew throughout the day, threatening to erupt into mutiny. At length the Gentle Lochiel, as he was known, appeased the men by promising that if there were no action with Cope on the twentieth, which seemed likely with the approaching dusk, he would concede the right hand in battle to the MacDonalds the following day.

Meanwhile, back on the plain, the movements of the Jacobites during the afternoon had so amazed Cope and his officers that before night they shifted position no less than four times, to be ready for the attack. The first position, as we have seen, was facing Preston. Then, when the Jacobites appeared at Tranent, they moved again. They shifted once more when Charles took his party to the west, and again when he returned to join Lord George Murray to the east. By this time it was twilight; Cope's perplexed army was stretched along the foot of the morass facing it, so that when darkness fell the two armies were opposite each other with a few hundred yards of impossible bog between them.

When Charles joined up with Lord George, the schism between them widened further. The general was still anxious to make the attack, even in the failing light; but Charles, who knew nothing about the other's plans because he had not been informed of them, had left a brigade of five hundred Atholl men posted in the village of Tranent. Realizing that twenty percent of the army was missing—and they were his own men—Lord George exploded. He threw his gun onto the ground and swore he would never again draw a sword for the cause if the brigade were not brought back. The officers were horrified by this outburst, which O'Sullivan called an "extreme mark of disrespect to the Prince," and it was unfortunate that Lord George allowed his volatile temper to get the better of him. All day long, the two fiercely independent men had been playing childish games—making moves without informing one another, countermanding each other's orders. Perhaps Charles believed that Lord George intended to betray him, but the Prince was totally inexperienced in military matters, although he would not admit it, and Lord George held more sway with the chieftains and their clansmen than did Charles. Their argument was resolved by calling a council of war and putting the issue to a vote. Lord George was outnumbered; by far the majority decided to postpone action until the following day.

Charles settled down for the night with his plaid wrapped closely around him. Taking a sheaf of pease for a pillow, he lay on the bare, stubble-covered field surrounded by his Irishmen. Lord George bedded down some distance away. Although the night was cold, the order went out that no fires were to be lit, and strict silence was enforced upon the men as they lay in close order of battle. Cope's men were barely four hundred yards away, and the Jacobites could see the lighted fires all along his front line. Old Captain MacDonald of the French carabiniers wrote later that he could scarcely believe the seeming disregard of the Highlanders, who slept soundly that night. He stayed awake, unnerved by the sound of the voices of the men they were to fight the next day.

The hour chosen to mobilize the men was three A.M. on September 21. They were to march along the ridge in the direction of Seaton, toward the hidden path known by Anderson of Whitburgh, which led down to the plain a mile before Seaton. All had to be accomplished in total silence, which must have been extremely difficult, for the first maneuver was to keep Lochiel's promise and move the MacDonalds to the head of the column to give them the right hand in battle when they formed on the plain. While this maneuver was going on, Charles learned that during the night Lord George had sent a message to his Atholl Brigade ordering them to join the main body of the army. Charles was furious because he had posted the men at Tranent to keep watch on the road to Edinburgh and to prevent Cope from slipping off under cover of darkness to retake the city. "He at first seemed resolved to make them return, but when he reflected that their march, if discovered by the enemy, might induce them to believe it was the whole army and occasion them to alter their dispositon or occasion any confusion or distrust among his own people, he judged it safer and better to put up with the disappointment, tho' he could not help complaining that his orders had been neglected on so material a point."

In spite of the Jacobites' attempts to maintain complete silence, even to the point of leaving their small troop of horses behind, their movements were heard by Cope, who immediately alerted his army. It was assumed that the Jacobites were going to Seaton to pick up the road that would lead them to the east side of the lower plateau. This erroneous assumption led Cope to underestimate, almost by an hour, how long it would be before both armies came face to face.

In an almost leisurely manner, King George's men repositioned themselves to face east with the artillery to their right, and officers were sent to recall the outlying parties of guards. One officer rode off through the morning mist and half-darkness toward a group of what he thought were his own men, but he found himself entangled with a party of Highlanders. They had made their almost-soundless descent long before they were expected. The officer raced back and gave the alarm, immediately pointing the Highlanders out to the artillery guard; the outlying parties hurrying back to the field could not find their regiments. The dark shapes of the Highlanders forming before them were thought by some to be bushes. An English officer later wrote, "It was so dark that I could not distinguish one of the pickets, who was marching within twenty-five paces, who they were." The Royal Army was aghast at the premature appearance of the Jacobites, but none knew of the existence of the path that Anderson of Whitburgh had found in his youth.

The Jacobites had problems forming up in the darkness. The

Duke of Perth, who had command of the right, led the MacDonalds forward; but being unable to see the enemy's position, or incapable of judging in the dark how much room he would have to leave for Lord George to form the left flank, he marched too far toward the sea. When daylight began to creep through, a gap was visible in the line. The first rays of sunlight played on the metal trappings of the Royal Army. Several of the Jacobites later said that at their first sight of the Redcoats, of the superior number of their horse and artillery, they expected to be swept off the field.

The Highlanders began a slow march toward the enemy in complete silence. The aim was to get close enough to fall upon them in the manner they were best suited for—hand-to-hand combat.

The left flank, commanded by Lord George with the Camerons, Stewarts of Appin, the Atholl Brigade, and MacGregors, advanced obliquely toward Cope's cannon in an effort to close the gap in their ranks. Since they were in the direct line of artillery fire, they concentrated on shooting at the ordnance guard as they advanced. As this was happening, an old untrained cannoneer fled from his post, taking his powder flask with him. Every other gunner and the ordnance soldiers, following his example, took to their horses, leaving Colonel Whitefoord completely unaided to discharge the cannon. Somehow, single-handedly he managed to fire off five of the guns at the approaching Highlanders. Some fell, including Major James MacGregor, son of the famous Rob Roy MacGregor. At that the enraged clansmen broke into a run "with incredible impetuosity." The attack was on with a vengeance.

As bagpipes began their eerie drone, the Highlanders ran toward the enemy, screaming at a pitch to match the *pibroch* and flinging away their hampering plaids, which exposed their nakedness underneath. Those who had no taste for muskets threw them away and brandished axes, scythes, and the terrible broadsword. Cope's front line panicked in the face of this onslaught and fired a straggling irregular volley too soon. This "infamous puff puff and no platoon" had little or no effect on the ferocious horde of bare-limbed men thundering down upon them "with a swiftness not to be conceived." The footsoldiers turned and fled, some without having fired a shot, all with clean bayonets. But the Highlanders were too fleet-footed for them "& the broadswords played their part, for with one stroke, armes & legs were cout off, & heads split to the Shoulders, never such wounds were seen."

The dragoons' horses reared and plunged a terrified path away from the carnage, unrestrained by their riders, who were "ducking their heads at every pop" while trampling their own men in their flight. Those with scythes did terrible work to the beasts before the battle was over. Long believing that horses were used in battle to bite and tear them asunder, the Highlanders used their scythes to hack at their legs and rip open their bellies until they fell, bringing their riders down with them. Witnessing the massacre on the front lines, the rear ranks of Cope's army began to give way "and the rest followed in tens and twenties."

There was only one direction in which they could flee: toward the wall of Preston House, in the desperate hope that they could clamber through the breaches or escape via the cart track below Colonel Gardiner's house. "They were on the plain like a flock of sheep which after having run away, gathers together and begins to run again when seized by a fresh fear." Both avenues of flight were death-traps, where "the Highlanders made a terrible slaughter of the enemy." The walls of Preston House, torn down the day before for their defense, now became a prison. Very few managed to get through the breaches because they were too high, and most were hacked to pieces as they fought to scrabble their way to the other side. Soon bodies lay in heaps along the base of the wall; the narrow track between the houses was stopped up with the mutilated bodies of horses and men. The battlefield was literally soaked with blood and littered with dismembered arms, legs, hands, and heads.

All attempts by Cope and his officers to rally the men failed utterly. At one point the Earl of Home managed to get 450 men together to make a stand, including dragoons, but on the order to attack they "could not be brought to move one foot." Some officers behaved shamefully by running away, but many stood their ground. Colonel Gardiner was one; he had long been in poor health and was in no condition to be on the battleground at all. On perceiving the cowardly behavior of his regiment, Gardiner, who "seemed determined not to survive the odium," stood fast and was cut down, mortally wounded.

Charles, who had taken no part in the action, was appalled by the bloodshed. Mounting his horse, he galloped all over the field, pleading with the Highlanders to stop the killing, crying that Cope's men were also his father's subjects and that he did not wish for their deaths. But in less than fifteen minutes the rout was total.

Even then Charles and his officers had difficulty restraining the exuberant clansmen. Once in full tilt of battle there seemed to be no stopping them. Some of the enemy were chased for more than a mile before their pursuers were called off. Fifteen minutes after the battle was over, Murray of Broughton noticed that the pile of bodies by the wall of Preston House had diminished somewhat; "nine of ten found their feet, for to evite [evade] death numbers threw themselves on the ground, the great part not so much as wounded." They probably hoped to make their escape through the swarms of country people who were picking their way through dead bodies and divesting them of clothes, weapons, and anything else of value.

It would be far from true to say that none of the Highlanders gave quarter. The Camerons took many prisoners; so did Lord George Murray. He came across a group of Cope's men who were trapped at the foot of the morass preparing to defend themselves, even though they were hopelessly outnumbered. He ordered the Highlanders to put up their arms and give the enemy a chance to surrender as prisoners. ". . . nothing gave me so much pleasure that day than having it so immediately in my power to save those men, as well as several others."

The battle had been so fierce and bloody that the prisoners were "doubtful whether they were to be treated as prisoners or rebels." They were made to turn their coats inside out to denote their status, but Alexander Carlyle, who took no part in the action and whose sympathies were with the government, wrote that he saw many with turned coats trying to escape even after they had been given quarter. "The Highlanders, when they could not over-take them, fired at them, and I saw two fall in the glebe." Carlyle walked around the field to observe the aftermath and was able to assure frightened prisoners that the wounded were being treated well. He further ventured that he had seen nothing that would lead him to believe the prisoners would be treated badly. Indeed, the Prince's first concern was with the great number of the enemy's wounded. ". . . the Chevalier gave orders to have the wounded dressed and carriages provided to take them of [sic] the field, which was executed by his Surgeons wt all the care and expedi-tion imaginable, to the great loss of the wounded of his own army, who from being neglected till most of the troops were taken care of, their wounds festered, being all gun Shott and mostly in the legs and thighs." Every house in the area was filled to capacity with the wounded. Even Colonel Gardiner could not be granted the right to die in his own house because there was no room. A friend found his badly hacked body sometime after the battle. He had been stripped almost naked by the pilfering country people, but he was still alive. He was carried to the Manse at Tranent, where he died later that day without uttering a word.

The account of dead, wounded, and prisoners issued by the government army headquarters listed five hundred killed and fourteen hundred taken prisoner, nine hundred of whom were wounded. Probably many of the prisoners were merely camp followers. Murray of Broughton's figures differed from Cope's; he stated that eight Redcoat officers and three hundred private men were killed, four to five hundred wounded, and "almost all" were taken prisoner. The latter is true, but the disparity between the numbers of dead and wounded would depend on whether the count was only of those killed on the battlefield or included soldiers who later died of their wounds. Also, Cope's tally could have been inflated to gain sympathy or to shock the ministry into action, while Murray of Broughton's could have been minimized in the face of later charges against the Highlanders of barbarism at the Battle of Prestonpans.*

Very few of the Redcoats escaped. We know that 175 certainly did, but the number is unlikely to have been more than 200. Most took the road south by Lauder and Coldstream, following orders to repair to headquarters at Berwick to join up with the Dutch. At a village near Coldstream the refugees halted for the night at a place where Sir John Clerk of Penicuik was also lodging on his way into temporary exile until the tumult ended. He overheard a violent argument among the escaped officers. "We thought hell had broken louse, for I never heard such oaths and imprecations, branding each other with cowardice and neglect of duty."

The Jacobite losses were minimal, but again an exact count is impossible to ascertain. The official report stated that four officers and thirty men were killed, and seventy or eighty were wounded. Maxwell of Kirkconnell came near to agreeing with this. He said forty men were killed, which included three or four officers, and about sixty or seventy were wounded. On the other hand, when Charles wrote to Tullibardine, who was still recruiting in the

---

*In Jacobite correspondence this battle is frequently referred to as the Battle of Gladsmuir, to satisfy an ancient prophecy stating that "in Gladesmoor shall the battle be."

north, he mentioned losing only twelve soldiers. Such a low figure was probably given to impress the uncommitted clans with the impact of their undeniably total and complete victory. Whichever way the figures are compared, a conservative estimate is that for every Jacobite killed at Prestonpans, Cope lost at least ten men.

Many stories of individual cowardice and valor surround the Battle of Prestonpans: the officer who snatched up a white cockade and escaped disguised as a Jacobite; the Highlander who stayed with a man he had mortally wounded to comfort him until he expired. But accusations against Cope and his officers of shameful cowardice and negligence pervaded all. The general was lampooned in song and verse, some of his officers even turned against him. Cope even demanded a public inquiry to clear himself of blame for the humiliating defeat.

An official inquiry was held after a few months; the lengthy testimony of Cope, his officers, and several witnesses was later published anonymously. Every aspect of the battle and of the events leading up to it was examined to piece together what had happened. Emphasis was placed on the cowardice of the dragoons, who were Irish with no particular feelings of loyalty toward King George. The poor health of their commander was a demoralizing factor; Colonel Gardiner had been so weak on the way to the battle site that he could not summon the strength to mount his horse. Instead, he was brought from Haddington by coach. His presence could hardly have been inspiring to his dragoons, who had not yet lived down their flight from the Highlanders at the Canter of Coltbrig. Gardiner had no faith in his men, either, for he told Alexander Carlyle before the battle that he felt they would not stand by him in action.

The inquiry lasted five days. More than forty witnesses were examined as the presiding officers strove to make sense out of the shameful defeat at the hands of men thought of as a ragged, uncivilized, and poorly armed rabble. Strategists and logistics experts have since pointed out what Cope should and should not have done, but the exercise is useless. Many reasoned that tactical errors *had* to have been responsible for the defeat. But precious few of these experts ever faced this fierce fighting body or witnessed the bizarre specter of strong, shaggy-haired, bare-limbed men attacking with lightning speed, the sun glinting on their murderous weapons and bloodcurdling battle cries and the high scream of bagpipes above it all. No commander could have overcome the tide of sheer terror that swept the field and rapidly infected each and every soldier. The board of inquiry heard considerable evidence that Cope and some of his officers had been relentless in their efforts to rally the men. Perhaps Cope himself came closest to summing up the defeat when he said, "The manner in which the enemy came on, which was quicker than can be described . . . possibly was the cause of our men taking a most destructive panic."

At the close of the hearing the general was given an honorable acquittal. He was later posted to a high command in Ireland and died in 1760. No monument marks his burial place at the Church of St. James's, Westminster; songs that mock his name still survive even today. Robert Burns (not born until fourteen years later) penned the most famous of them all. Based on the story that Lord Mark Kerr had greeted Cope on his return to Berwick after the battle by sardonically congratulating him on being the first general to bring news of his own defeat, Burns composed the following verses, to be sung to the tune of the lively old Scottish song "Will Ye Go to the Coals in the Morning":

> *Sir John Cope trod the north right far,*
> *Yet ne'er a rebel he came naur*
> *Until he landed at Dunbar*
> *Right early in the morning*
>
> *(chorus:)*
> *Hey Johnnie Cope are you wauking yet,*
> *Or are ye sleeping I would wit;*
> *O haste ye get up for the drums do beat,*
> *O fye Cope rise in the morning. . . .*
>
> *It was upon an afternoon,*
> *Sir Johnnie marched to Preston town;*
> *He says, my lads come lean you down,*
> *And we'll fight the boys in the morning.*
>
> *(chorus) Hey Johnnie Cope, etc.*
>
> *But when he saw the Highland lads*
> *Wi' tartan trews and white cockauds,*
> *Wi' swords and guns and rungs and gauds [cudgels and*
> *   iron bars]*
> *O Johnnie he took wing in the morning. . . .*

Sir Johnnie into Berwick rade,
Just as the devil had been his guide;
Gi'en him the warld he would na stay'd
To foughten the boys in the morning. . . .

Says Lord Mark Car, ye ar no blate [not backward]
To bring us the news o' your ain defeat;
I think you deserve the back o' the gate,
Get out o' my sight this morning.

(chorus)

Chapter 8

To England and Back Again

After the Battle of Prestonpans, Charles made the mistake of believing that he and his Highlanders were invincible, that his victory had been God's will, and that fortune would continue to smile on him. When news circulated that the Jacobites had not only defeated Cope but captured all his baggage and equipment as well, many Edinburgh citizens were delighted, particularly the ladies, who "became passionately fond of the young Adventurer and used all their arts and industry for him in the most intemperate manner," according to Duncan Forbes. Borderline Jacobites became fervent enthusiasts overnight "and talked of nothing but hereditary rights and victories." The joy was no more than a temporary madness, however; it simmered down when it was discovered that many of the Highlanders had gone home with the loot they stripped from the dead bodies.

It was suggested that Charles pursue Cope to Berwick, whither he had fled to await the landing of Dutch reinforcements. But only fifteen hundred Highlanders remained, and of these many disappeared when they were ordered to bury the men they had killed. Charles was getting used to the singular temperament of these mountain men of war. They prided themselves on being fierce fighters and thus would not allow themselves to be used as pack animals to transport equipment (this was one reason why O'Sullivan earlier had to bury weapons at Loch Eil); nor would they pick up a spade to dig trenches or graves. They refused pointblank to comply with the Prince's orders because such toil was far beneath their dignity. "Those who should bury the dead are run away, as if it was no business of theirs," complained Charles in a

157

letter to his father. "However, I am determined to try if I can get people for money to undertake it, for I cannot bear the thought of suffering Englishmen to rot above the ground." The Prince sent out orders that he expected no public celebrations to mark his victory because "he was far from rejoicing att the death of any of his father's subjects' even when they had appeared in action against him."

His pressing need was to find more recruits and men like Lord Lovat, who had promised to join but had still not come out. Word of the victory was sent northward in the futile hope that it would sway MacLeod and MacDonald of Sleat; Lord George sent several letters to Tullibardine urging him to hurry in the raising of approximately a thousand still-uncommitted men of Atholl. During almost six weeks at Edinburgh, Jacobite ranks were swelled by the addition of Lords Pitsligo, Balmerino, Ogilvy, Nairne, Lord Louis Gordon, and Lord Nithsdale (son of the man who had died in Rome seven months before); the Earl of Kilmarnock; and eventually Lovat sent his eldest son to lead out the Frasers. But the Prince was never master of more than forty-five hundred men and even that for only a brief period of time.

The patents signed by James at the end of 1743 creating three Lords Lieutenants were presumably still in Balhaldy's hands, but the Prince seemed to be unaware of their existence. That was just as well because of the three intended recipients—Lovat, Lochiel, and Campbell of Auchinbreck—only Lochiel had joined Charles; the others had little faith in the enterprise. Even Lochiel had argued hotly against becoming involved when he discovered that the Prince had come without French assistance, but it is said that he was shamed into action when Charles flung at him: "Very well, stay at home and read in your newspaper of your Prince's fortunes."

In London the news of Cope's defeat was greeted with disbelief that such "raw ragmuffins" could triumph over the government forces. The pulpits rang with sermons denouncing the Popish Prince, and Henry Fielding, the author of *Tom Jones*, began to publish a newspaper called *The True Patriot*, which was dedicated to ridiculing the Highlanders and to assassinating the Prince's character. He published a song set to the tune of "Lillibullero" that was "proper to be sung at all merry meetings":

> *Brother Sawney hear you the news*
> *Twang 'em, we'll bang 'em and hang 'em up all*

An army's just coming without any shoes
Twang 'em, we'll bang 'em and hang 'em up all

(chorus)
To Arms, to Arms Brave Boys, to Arms
A true English cause for your courage doth call
Court, country and City
Against a banditti
Twang 'em, we'll bang 'em and hang 'em up all

The Pope sends us over a Bonnie Brisk Lad
Twang 'em, etc.
To court English Favor he wears a Scotch Plaid
Twang 'em, etc.

(chorus)

Four more verses, each to be followed by the rousing chorus, ran as follows:

A Protestant Church from Rome doth Advance
And what is more rare he brings Freedom from France

If this should surprize there is News stranger yet
He brings Highland Money to pay England's Debt

You must take it in Coin which the Country affords
Instead of broad pieces he pays with broad swords

And sure this is paying you in the best Ore
For who thus is once paid will never want more

In the next few issues of his weekly newspaper, Fielding kept his readers inflamed against the "savage inhabitants of wilds and mountains," but he cautioned that they should not be confused with the majority of Lowland Scots who were loyal to the Crown. Indeed, the Scottish worm was beginning to turn, for the majority of Lowlanders had no desire to be associated with the "barbarians" dressed in smelly rags and now covered by sores from "the itch."

The initial enthusiasm in Edinburgh died down as numerous manifestos and declarations were issued by the Prince. One dated October 9 "Given at our Palace of Holyrood House" warned and commanded "all His Majesty's Liege Subjects, whether Peers or Commoners," to pay no obedience to King George's summons for a meeting of Parliament to be held at Westminster on October 17. The only authority for any such gathering, it went on, could come only from "the King our Royal Father," and if any subjects from his ancient Kingdom of Scotland should act contrary to his express commands, "the Transgressors shall be proceeded against as Traitors and Rebels to their King and Country, and their Estates shall be confiscated for his Majesty's Use, according to the Laws of the Land; the pretended Union of these Kingdoms being now at an End."

Observers were not sure Charles had reason to suppose he was master of the kingdom. Although Mackinnon of Mackinnon came through from the Isle of Skye with 120 men, word was received from MacLeod and Sleat that they were solidly behind the government. Neither Edinburgh Castle nor Stirling Castle had been taken by the rebels, and Forts William, Augustus, and George were still in government hands. The Duke of Argyll had now recruited opposition to the Jacobites from the MacKays and Sutherlands as well as the Munros, and the six thousand Dutch reinforcements had at last arrived from Flanders. In addition, a further three battalions of the guards, eighteen line regiments, nine squadrons of cavalry, and four artillery companies from the Continent were also on their way to Scotland to join the regular troops already there by the latter part of October. Three groups were formed: Field Marshal Wade was in command of a contingent marching to Newcastle; the second group was en route to Lancashire under Major General James Oglethorpe; and a third force remained in the south of England to guard the coast in case of a French landing.

The French had already made a landing of sorts. In September and October two ships bringing cannon and ammunition put in at Montrose and Stonehaven. One of them, the *Esperance*, carried the lately recovered Michael Sheridan and a Monsieur du Boyer, the Marquis d'Eguilles; the latter was sent over by Louis XV to find out exactly what was happening and how long he could count on the Scottish sideshow to continue. At this time the French were working on secret plans to capture Brussels, and far from being shamed into supporting Bonnie Prince Charlie as the Prince had expected, Louis planned to use the foolish enterprise for his own ends.

The appearance of the Marquis d'Eguilles, who was being

introduced by Charles as the French "Ambassador" to his "Court" at Holyrood, fed hopes among the Jacobites that French troops would set sail with the first fair wind. This led many of them to support a decision that Charles had already made—to march into England. But others were not willing to take this enormous step until French reinforcements arrived; the Jacobites hung on at Edinburgh for six weeks, often quarreling among themselves.

In the meantime, Irish merchant Antoine Walsh returned to France and reported that the Prince had assembled five thousand men. Charles actually had only a tenth of that number then, when Walsh left Scotland, but perhaps Walsh was following orders to misrepresent Jacobite strength. Other reports received in Rome (which may have come from Charles himself) said he had ten thousand soldiers, and various Paris sources claimed that the Jacobites numbered twenty-five to thirty thousand. It is said that Charles rewarded Walsh by creating him an earl of Ireland, but this the Prince had no power to do. He did recommend it to his father and suggested that Walsh apply to Rome for the warrant, but Walsh made the mistake of trying to bribe James Edgar for the honor.

Abbé Butler carried various dispatches to Rome, including Walsh's request and letters from Charles to his father written upon his arrival in the Outer Isles. Butler found the Court in residence at Albano, and at Walsh's behest he offered Edgar money. "I own to you I was not a little surpized when Abbé Butler offered me money in your name," wrote the affronted secretary to Walsh on October 20. "In the situation I am in it is what I have never taken from anybody and if I ever had nothing could engage me to accept of it from one who had done such essential service to the prince and the good cause." This was intended merely to soften the blow of how empty the honor really was. It could not be ratified until the Great Seal of Ireland had been stamped on it "after the restoration of the Royal Family." As it was, Walsh could "on this side of the sea take upon you the title of an Earl, but His Majesty does not think it proper that you should at present assume that title and when he gives you leave to do it he must require that you should give over all manner of trade and commerce because it would be a dishonour on such an high rank and dignity." So much for a Stuart earldom!

James was at Albano alone when Butler arrived with the dispatches from Scotland. He had sent Henry off to Paris by way of Avignon, accompanied by John Constable, on August 29 (New

Style, or August 18 Old Style; it was the day Charles left Borrodale for Glenfinnan). It had always been James's intention that the Duke of York follow his brother into France and that Louis should provide for them both. But in view of the way Charles had been treated, it is surprising that Henry was allowed to leave Italy. The French, however, encouraged Henry's arrival because his presence would make it appear to the British government that Louis intended to support the Scottish rebellion; this would force George to keep his troops at home. It was given out in Paris that the Duke of York was to head an expedition for England, a plan that James did not believe would materialize. But the exile was still cooperating with French plans in the hope that Louis might be grateful to his family in the future.

Henry was in no fit condition to travel and was gravely ill when he reached the home of Lady Inverness at Avignon, having suffered "four severe fittes of an ague" at Orgon shortly before. Flood conditions kept Henry at Lady Inverness's town house, to which the Duke of Ormonde sent his physician to care for the ailing Prince. It was a gallant gesture; Ormonde himself was exceedingly ill and died a few weeks later. Lady Inverness found Henry "eaten up with buges," which she attributed to poor lodgings on his journey. After a stay of three weeks, he still had not regained full health. Nevertheless, Henry and Constable pressed onward in a coach acquired by Lady Inverness. Although the Duke of York suffered another fit on the way, they eventually reached Paris in the last week of October.

The sickness afflicting Henry was the same as that afflicting most of Europe. The Continent and England had been cursed by atrocious weather conditions in 1743, 1744, and 1745, and everyone—from the Highlanders to Marshal Saxe, Lord Dunbar, James, and Henry—was afflicted. To what degree each was afflicted varied according to the treatment they received or what food was available. Marshal Saxe, for instance, manifested an unmistakable progression of symptoms of nutritional deficiency; Dunbar experienced what Dr. James Lind called "flying rheumatic pains"; and James's gum and face defluxion gave way to deep melancholia. He wailed in a letter to Henry that "All places are melancholly to me when I have not my Bairns about me, for tho I thought I loved them a great dale yet I did not think it was so much as I now feel it." He wrote this about five months before Charles himself became sick.

James did not seem surprised that Charles had gone to Scotland, although he told Lord Sempell that he was afraid the enterprise would not succeed without France's participation. He pawned Charles's jewels, and a large sum of money was also provided by the Pope; but the King urged O'Brien to keep these funds secret for fear the French would provide nothing if they knew how much was at the family's disposal. James claimed in a letter to Charles that Henry had also pawned his jewels to help the cause, but this was not true. James was still pathetically trying to endear the brothers to one another, but secretly he wrote Henry: "I would not make haste to wear them or produce them for it is no secret that we have pawned jewels for a considerable value and you know what I writ to the Prince about yours, so that on many accounts, which you will easily comprehend I should think it would be more prudent not to produce these till it may please God that our affairs take a good turn." Although James had often pled poverty, records made by Waters at this time show the banker had received from Rome a total of 595,930 livres to be disbursed by O'Brien's authority. Some of it was to be used for Henry's expenses when he arrived in Paris, but O'Brien told James that in view of Charles's known extravagance he judged it best to send him only 1,000 louis d'or at a time before the rest disappeared for the subsistence of impoverished clans. This 1,000 guineas he sent with Michael Sheridan on board the *Esperance*.

At the end of October, Charles sent Kelly from Edinburgh in the company of one James Carnegie with letters and dispatches for the Court of France. They sailed from Montrose, taking the Holland route, but were arrested on arrival and were forced to burn all the papers they had brought with them. One of the documents contained an urgent request from Charles that the French provide an experienced commanding general. The fact that he had not brought such a one with him was severely hampering his recruitment efforts and was making nonsense out of his incessant claims that Louis XV was solidly behind him. Although Lord Marischal would have been the most popular choice for lieutenant general in Scotland, many a Jacobite was deeply grateful that Lord George Murray was on the scene to represent their interests. It is possible that officers suspected Charles was looking overseas for a foreign commanding general, and they rallied all the more around Lord George.

When Kelly and Carnegie were released from Holland, they went on to Paris and reported that Charles had twelve thousand men. After being questioned thoroughly by Lord Marischal, however, they revised this downward to eight or nine thousand men. They were not the best emissaries to appear before the French government, according to Henry, "and so committed some blunders which they might have avoided had they been well guided." Kelly and Carnegie's artifice may not have been polished enough for the wily members of the French Ministry, for there was a feeling among the latter that they were still not hearing the truth when the figures were revised downwards. They were justified in their suspicions. Kelly and Carnegie's revised figures represented twice as many troops as Charles actually had. As for Charles's request for a commanding general, Lord Marischal again refused the dubious honor, as did Lord Clare (now known as the Marquis of Thomond). Henry was desperately trying to find a willing general "whether it be a Ming's subject* or a foreigner."

At the beginning of November, Sir William Gordon of Park, son of Viscount Kenmure (who had been executed for his part in "the Fifteen") also left Scotland for Paris in company with Alexander Gordon, a Jesuit priest who possibly was Sir William's brother. They, too, claimed that Charles had twelve thousand men, but lies were now flying both ways. The French said the Duc de Richelieu was preparing to head an expedition into England; the Marquis d'Argenson signed an agreement with O'Brien to provide the Irish regiments that were in French service; but there were continual delays. At first the excuse was that the ships were in poor repair; then it was contrary weather; and finally it was that no French ships could get through because the British were guarding every port. Only Lord John Drummond, commanding the Royal Scots in French service, was able to get off aboard the frigate *France* with his regiment and a few Irish volunteers paid by O'Brien—approximately a thousand men—but poor weather prevented them from sailing until November 29 (N.S.).

Also at the end of November, Walter Rutledge managed to get his ship *Le Neptune* to Stonehaven, on the east coast of Scotland, carrying unspecified stores of arms, ammunition, and money. They were paid for out of funds James had sent from Rome. Waters's accounts show that 24,151 livres were expended to reimburse Rutledge in the amount of 1,000 guineas; the remainder was to be made payable to Sir Thomas Sheridan. Apparently James

*A man from China.

agreed with O'Brien that Charles should not be entrusted with the management of any more than 1,000 guineas at a time.

Unlike Dunkirk in 1744, which had been widely suspected as a feint to mask action on the Flanders front, not a soul knew that the French planned to take Brussels or that Saxe was preparing to begin as early as January 1746. The timing was unusual. Armies traditionally retired in winter to quarters to make ready for action in the spring, but as long as Charles Edward Stuart held out, Saxe intended to take advantage of the situation. By September Philip of Spain and Louis XV agreed to give Charles 100,000 crowns each and to provide equal quantities of arms and ammunition, but their plan was to delay sending any help as long as possible and to send only a little at a time. By this tactic they hoped to spin out the Scottish affair through the spring and summer of 1746 to prevent the English and Dutch from returning to Flanders.

The Jacobite army left Edinburgh on November 3 and crossed the River Esk into England on the eighth. They avoided Wade's army at Newcastle, estimated at eleven thousand strong. On the way the Prince lost at least a thousand Highlanders due to desertions. Not only were the mountain men far from home, reluctant to penetrate any farther into foreign territory; there was also a lack of confidence in the leadership. The chieftains and their men could plainly see that Prince Charles and Lord George Murray did not like one another. The Jacobite general's annoying habit of being persistently right was seen by the Prince as an affront to his Divine Wisdom. Charles wanted deference, not advice. Unused to having his word questioned, especially in the peremptory, brusque manner that was Lord George's style, Charles took to conferring more with Murray of Broughton, Hay of Restalrig, Sir Thomas Sheridan, the Duke of Perth, and the Irishmen he had brought with him. This meant that Lord George and the Scottish chieftains were usually excluded from decision making. But the decisions affected them more than anyone else. If things went wrong, it was they who would face the tortures of fire and gibbet, while the Irishmen could secure their parole by claiming French nationality.

Lord George Murray found it impossible to stand quietly by and allow this inexperienced, arrogant youth to dictate measures with no more foundation than divine right. "Lord George did not altogether neglect making his court," wrote Maxwell of Kirkconnell; "upon occasions he was very obsequious and respectful, but he had not the temper to go through with it. He now and then

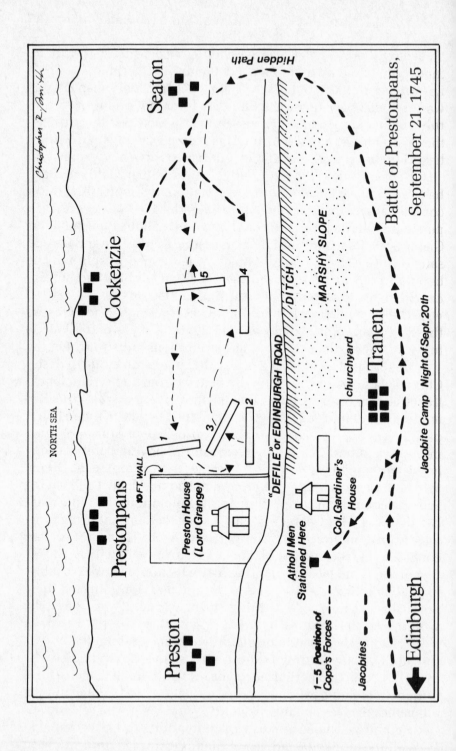

Christopher R. Smith

NORTH SEA

Preston

Prestonpans

Cockenzie

Seaton

Hidden Path

10 FT. WALL

Preston House
(Lord Grange)

1

3   2

5

4

Atholl Men
Stationed Here

Col. Gardiner's
House

"DEFILE" or EDINBURGH ROAD

DITCH

churchyard

MARSHY SLOPE

Tranent

Edinburgh

Jacobite Camp   Night of Sept. 20th

Battle of Prestonpans,
September 21, 1745

1—5 Position of
Cope's Forces - - -

Jacobites ▬ ▬ ▬

broke into such violent sallies as the Prince could not digest, though the situation of his affairs forced him to bear with them." Lord Elcho appended his view of Lord George, which was that he was "a man of spirit, very brave, and one that would not himself be ruled by anybody—and with good reason. As head of the Scots, the prince and the Irish did not like him. The Scots on the other hand liked him much and had great confidence in his capacity."

It irked Charles the most that Lord George Murray and not he had the confidence of the entire fighting body of men. The latter's common sense placed a frustrating brake on the Prince's impetuosity. Charles kept unsavory gossip circulating about Lord George's loyalty. Lord Elcho claimed that one of the Irishmen had said he had orders to assassinate Lord George if he made a move to betray the Prince. But interestingly enough, Charles could not conduct a smear campaign among the Scots because the calumny was rejected by them. He had set up a clique that excluded most of the Scottish nobility—the men who had actually provided money for the campaign.

Lord Elcho, one of the few Scots looked upon with favor by Charles, was also one of his most vehement critics. He pointed out that men of noble birth who had risked their all were never invited to dine at the Prince's table, and if the Prince should happen to pass by them, they were given disdainful looks, as if they were no more than "common dragoons." Elcho had raised a handsome body of horse guards, and he was a member of the Prince's council; this afforded him ample opportunity to form an opinion of the Prince he had known in Paris in 1744 and at Cisterna five years before. He was appalled at Charles's abysmal ignorance of the history, geography, constitution, and laws of the nation he had come to conquer. Elcho felt Charles was strongly influenced by Sheridan, "a zealous Irish Catholic very attached to religion and his country." According to Elcho, the Prince's head was filled with notions of absolutism. To him the word *subject* was synonymous with *slave*.

The rot in morale had already set in by the time the army reached Carlisle, the gateway to England. Perhaps drawing upon his brief experience when fourteen years old at the Siege of Gaeta, Charles decided that to take Carlisle, trenches should be dug around the Castle. This strategy was strongly opposed by Lord George and by the Highlanders. It was completely unnecessary and difficult to perform in the ice-bound November ground. But

His Royal Highness had given an order, and it was to be obeyed without question. At this point, approximately ten percent of the Highland force simply gathered their families and belongings together and struck out for home.

The decrepit castle, manned by ancient militia volunteers, easily fell to the Jacobites. A deputation was sent to negotiate the terms of surrender. When Lord George attempted to discuss the city's capitulation with Charles, Charles curtly informed him that it was a civil matter and "no General officer had any concern about it." When Lord George later learned that the Duke of Perth and Murray of Broughton had been sent to treat with Carlisle's dignitaries, he was insulted.

It alarmed the other Jacobites because Perth was a Roman Catholic. Laws preventing Catholics from holding public office were still in force in England; and charges of popery and arbitrary power had beset Charles ever since his arrival. To have sent the Duke of Perth to negotiate capitulation of the first English city to fall into Jacobite hands constituted a blunder of enormous proportions.

The only avenue left to Lord George was to resign his commission, which he did on November 14, but he offered to continue serving in the ranks as a volunteer. His letter began: "I cannot but observe how little my advice as a General officer has any weight with your Royal Highness . . ." He went on to reaffirm his attachment to the Royal Family, "in particular to the King, my master." Charles smarted at this singling out of James as worthy of Lord George's attachment; he accepted the resignation the same day, saying he was "extremely surprized you shou'd throw up yr commission for a reason which I beleeve was never heard of before. I am glad of yr particular attachment to the King, but I am very sure he will never take anything as proof of it by yr deference to me. I accept of yr demission as Lieutenant General, and yr future services as Volunteer."

Having the Duke of Perth in sole command under the Prince was wholly unacceptable to the Jacobites. Perth was well liked, but his religion was fuel for Jacobite detractors, and the fact that he was self-admittedly inexperienced in military matters fostered loud protests from the chieftains. They demanded that Lord George be reinstated. Now it was Perth's turn to resign, having "nothing at heart but the Chevalier's interest." Charles was forced to ask Lord George to resume his commission. He did, but the relationship between the lieutenant general and the Prince, which had been tenuous from the beginning, worsened as time went on.

It was now the end of November, and the weather was bitterly cold, with snow on the ground. The Jacobites had avoided Field Marshal Wade at Newcastle by taking the Carlisle route, which had not been anticipated by the government army. An attempt was made to relieve Carlisle, but after two days of struggling through deep snow, Wade was forced to return to Newcastle. As many as a thousand of his men were sick and exhausted from an arduous and unsuccessful campaign in Flanders.

The English people grew angry that Charles Stuart had brought his cause to afflict them when their defenses were low. "In what light can you imagine you must appear to us in such an undertaking?" demanded Henry Fielding in an open letter to Charles, published in his third issue of *The True Patriot*. He railed vigorously on the content of the proclamations Charles had issued in Edinburgh, particularly at one in which he disclaimed any pretensions toward absolute power. "Those who know any thing of your father and of your own behaviour in Scotland, will, I am afraid, give little credit to this declaration," said Fielding, and he went on to ridicule the Prince's claim that his cause was the same as that of the people of England. Fielding wrote that Charles would not have "one vote in a thousand" if the issue were placed before the electorate.

Fielding reserved his most heated rhetoric for the Highland "banditti," the Catholic Church, and for the fact that Charles was under the protection of the very country with which England was engaged in a war. He tried to be fair to Catholics in London who were in no way supportive of the Stuarts, reporting that many had sold their homes and possessions to seek anonymity in the country.

But he was merciless when it came to Highlanders. Fielding described them as "sons of rapine," although rape was unheard of among their ranks. Fielding and others painted such a lurid picture of Highland Scots that it would be more than a century before the damage was undone.

Partly to demonstrate to the Prince that he was not a traitor, and partly because Charles claimed to be in touch with numbers of powerful English Jacobites, Lord George acquiesced to penetrating farther into England. News arrived that Lord John Drummond had landed in Scotland; this was seen by many as the beginning of massive French support. Thus, leaving a hundred men behind to hold the garrison at Carlisle, the Highland army separated into two divisions and left the city on November 20 and 21.

Although the rebels could not have been much more than three thousand strong due to desertions and sickness, the split divisions hid their true numbers. At each town they demanded shelter for six to eight thousand men. George II's son, the Duke of Cumberland, returned from Flanders to command the government troops that guarded England's south coast. Lord Elcho and approximately fifty red-and-blue-uniformed horse guards, the most presentable soldiers at Charles's disposal, always headed the first division, commanded by Lord George. The Prince himself led the second division, made up of the rest of the horse (the equine strength of the Jacobite force was estimated by spies to be no more than a hundred animals) and of the clans not in Lord George's division. Charles "never dinn'd nor threw of his clothes at night, eat much at Supper, used to throw himself upon a bed at eleven o'clock, & was up by four in the morning. As he had a prodigious strong constitution, he bore fatigue most surprisingly well." This was the report of the adoring sycophant O'Sullivan, but according to Lord Elcho, Charles was rarely sober.

At each town, public money was collected on pain of military execution, and James's proclamation was read. But the Jacobites were invariably greeted by sullen faces or by hoots and jeers from the brave. James Gilchrist, the Postmaster of Dumfries, had joined the rebels to spy upon them for the government. He sent his intelligence to Viscount Irwin in London. "Now that we have seen this army," wrote Gilchrist in November, "it gives us no small concern to think that a whole kingdom should have been so shamefully intimidated with such a pack of tatterdemalions, for two thirds of them are no better and great numbers of them marching without breeches, stockings or shoes."

Soldiers were given two shillings a day, but officers paid for food out of their own pockets and would take no money from the Prince as long as they had funds of their own. Sometimes they offered country people more than was necessary, which gave offense on a number of occasions. Tom Richardson, Postmaster at Penrith, observed the Highlanders and sent the following report to Viscount Irwin:

> They march with droves of black cattle and sheep, three wagons of
> biscuit and cheese which they sit down at noon to eat, at night and

An Incident in the Rebellion of 1745
by P. D. Morier

Flora MacDonald
by Allan Ramsay
(Scottish National Portrait Gallery, Edinburgh)

Prince Charles Edward Stuart in his early thirties
by Jean-Louis Tocqué
(In the collection of the Duke of Atholl at Blair Castle, Perthshire.
Reproduced by permission of Mr. W. Drummond-Moray)

Clementina Walkinshaw
*(Reproduced by permission of the
Duke of Atholl)*

Louise de Stolberg
*(Reproduced by permission of The
Rector and Trustees of Stonyhurst
College, Lancashire, England)*

Prince Charles Edward Stuart c. 1785
by Hugh Douglas Hamilton
(National Portrait Gallery, London)

Charlotte, Duchess of Albany
attributed to Hugh Douglas
Hamilton
(Scottish National Portrait Galle
Edinburgh)

Henry Stuart, Cardinal York
after Pompeo Batoni
(National Portrait Gallery, London)

morning get a little oatmeal, which they buy up at their own price or take away wherever they can get it, and constantly carry it in a leathern bag for their subsistence; every one has a sword, a target, a gun and a dirk. The rear always push forward the front, and they march in a very great hurry. They wish much to be in Lancashire and Wales, and offer ten guineas to any volunteer that will go to the Chevalier.

An anonymous letter to Irwin described the Jacobites' arrival at Kendal. The bellman had been instructed to go around the town telling everyone that private as well as public houses must supply bread and ale for the oncoming army. Butchers and bakers were to work double time, and food was to be brought in from the surrounding countryside for which a modest price would be paid. The writer observed the Highlanders and verified former reports that they ranged in age from eight to eighty and were laden down with muskets, broadswords, targets, and pistols. Undoubtedly some of the weapons had been taken from dead soldiers at the Battle of Prestonpans, but it was too much equipment for most to carry comfortably. He counted no more than a thousand men in Lord George's division. It was, he said,

a sight worthy of ridicule to every observer and matter of joy to all lovers of their country that no better than such trumpery are come to invade us. Such a number of Scotch black cattle I never saw except the droves that go into the South for Slaughter, and I doubt not so are these. I should be ashamed to be their Colonel. How they get any listed for so low a post as captains I wonder. Then came their horses that looked as if their masters had made bedding of what they poor beasts should eat. I am sure the greatest part could not be exchanged with us for mules. I saw some of poor Johnny Cope's horse, who have great reason to curse their new king, for whatever they may get by him they have lost a deal, a deal of flesh and many a good meal. You will excuse my being merry; my spirits were quite raised at such a comic scene as this procession from first to last. I assure you it gave me great joy to see such sorry fools as they are. Had King George been with me today he would have been very merry.

A similar tone pervaded reports from Lancaster and Preston as the Jacobites headed south for Manchester. Charles was dejected that the recruits he imagined would flock to his banner did not materialize. To stir up enthusiasm for his cause, as he rode into Manchester there were bonfires, bell-ringing from church steeples, and a cheering throng to escort the Prince to his lodgings; but it was all arranged by advance men. Charles's conversation that night at table was, "in what manner he should enter London, on horseback or a foot, and in what dress." But although he had counted on at least fifteen hundred men to join him at Manchester, he had to be content with approximately two hundred unemployed people; they had intended to offer their services to whichever army first reached the city. In command of this dubious rabble, dubbed the Manchester Regiment, he placed Francis Townley, who may have been the brother or other relative of John Townley, who had replaced Mr. Dicconson in Rome at the end of 1743.*

At Manchester, Lord George Murray and several Highland officers seriously began to consider a retreat. From a captured government spy they learned that Cumberland's army numbered 2,200 horse and 8,250 foot. Perhaps believing reports that the Jacobites were going to Wales, they were encamped at Stone, less than fifty miles to the south. Field Marshal Wade, his strength now reduced to ten thousand men, rapidly proceeded toward Manchester via forced marches. The Jacobites left the city and were at Leek on December 3. Somehow Charles had been able to persuade Lord George and the chieftains to go farther into England. Their progress was actively hindered by countryfolk, who disassembled bridges over swollen fords and streams along an easterly route to Derby, about 120 miles from London as the crow flies.

O'Sullivan picks up the story of the march to Derby on the night of December 4:

> We had a fine moon-light night, & we had need of it, for we marched by by-roads, & if it was not for the hard froste, we cou'd never get our Artillery out of them. From hence we arrived the next day at Darby, where his Royal Highnesse was parfectly well recd. Bon-fires on the roads, the Belles ringing; we arrived a little leat, it was really a fine sight to see the Illuminations of the Town. The Princes raison for stricking to the left towards Darby was, yt he expected by yt to gain two days march on Cumberland, & of consequence to arrive at

---

*A year later, Francis Townley was one of the captives of "the Forty-five" who were rounded up and publicly disemboweled in London. These prisoners were among the last to suffer that barbaric practice. It was ultimately abolished in England as a form of public punishment.

London before him, yt was alwaise the Princes design, since Comberland avoided to come into an action.

Sir John MacDonald of the carabiniers was more than deluded in his account of the same proceedings:

> All we knew of the enemy was very vague, being only founded on reports or on their own published reports in the papers. We only knew that these were in three corps of unknown strength two of which we had left behind us, Wade's at Newcastle, Oglethorpe's at Yorkshire. The third commanded by Prince William [Cumberland], the strength of which was not known to us, was on our route to London. It was therefore impossible to judge of the possibility of our advance. I have heard since that it was not superior in numbers to us. We had, I think, a little over 5,000 men who would certainly have defeated 15 thousand English. It is true that in retreating before us to the neighbourhood of London they could have reinforced themselves from the army guarding London, but it is probable that when we approached that great city many people would also have joined us; I heard there were 30 thousand ready to do so. We were also told that the City of London in council had decided to send a deputation to meet H.R.H. on his arrival, that the Duke of Hanover had given orders to have everything ready for the departure of his family, but that he had replied to those who wished him to go also, that he intended to remain and die King of England.

The thirty thousand assembling in London were by no means Stuart partisans but were men from the towns and countries bordering London who were incensed by the gall of "barbarous North Britons" in general and the Popish Prince in particular. Henry Fielding's colorful rhetoric had whipped up passions to such a degree that the Jacobites would have been massacred had they come closer. Fielding correctly assessed from reports filtering in from the north that Charles commanded only 2,300 foot, but he vastly overestimated the number of horses at 450. The Prince was opposed by at least forty thousand combined militia and government troops at various locations. Penetration as far as Derby had been a great mistake. They arrived in that city, according to Henry Fielding, "after one of the longest Marches which hath perhaps been heard of. —Many of them dropped down as soon as they came into their Quarters, and most of their Legs were swelled with their Fatigue. Add to this, that a Distemper at present rages among them, which as it must retard their March, by weakening them, will cause them to leave so strong a Scent, that their Pursuers will be infallibly sure of hunting them down."

At Derby, Lord George, the chieftains, and their men had had their fill of the Prince's impossible dreams, futile hopes, and empty promises. Despite the overwhelming odds—to which he seemed to be blind—the Prince blithely planned to march onward to London in the hope that large numbers of the government army would defect to his cause. But the Jacobite general refused to be responsible for what must amount to total annihilation. The rash young man had been indulged long enough—too long, in fact—and Lord George Murray had to bring him down to earth once and for all.

The Prince was lodged at Exeter House, on Derby's Full Street. In the surrounding neighborhood the Gaelic-speaking clansmen, who had no idea of the awesome numbers opposing them, quarreled among themselves, vying for the services of cutlers to sharpen their dirks and broadswords for the battle they had been promised. The Prince emerged from his quarters on the morning of December 5 and found his general waiting to accost him. With steel in his eye and voice, Lord George stated in a manner brooking no argument that in his opinion and everyone else's the time had come to retreat to Scotland, join the forces that Lord John Drummond had brought from France, and regroup to determine future strategy.

Perhaps noboby but James had ever addressed Charles in that manner before. The Prince was astonished both by Lord George's implacably firm attitude and by the nature of the proposition. He expostulated that it had always been agreed the army would march on and that the clans had "assured me they were all resolved to pierce or to dye." But Lord George reminded him that the advance had always been subject to review. He insisted upon a council meeting, few of which had been held since the army entered England, so that Charles could hear for himself what the leaders of the clans had to say on the matter. Hastily rounding up everyone he could, Lord George met with the Prince and his entourage in the handsome oak-paneled drawing room of Exeter House later that morning. As the reasons were set out for not going forward, Charles glowered; his displeasure was expressed with very bad grace. Lord Elcho reported: "The Prince heard all these arguments with the greatest impatience, fell into a passion and gave most of the Gentlemen that had Spoke very Abusive Language, and said they had a mind to betray him."

Of those assembled at the meeting, which included all the chieftains, only two people favored going forward. The Marquis of Tullibardine, Lord George's brother, was one who sided with Charles, and Young Clanranald may have been the other. The rest, including Sheridan, O'Sullivan, and Murray of Broughton, were all for turning back. "I never saw any body so concerned as he was for this disapointmt," wrote O'Sullivan, "nor never saw him take any thing after so much to heart as he did it." This was putting it mildly. Charles was shattered. For the first time in his life the wisdom and leadership qualities that he had assumed were part and parcel of his birthright had been put to a vote, and the verdict was a resounding one of no confidence.

Preparations for the retreat began immediately. All the way back to Scotland Charles childishly sniped at Lord George and contradicted him at every turn. Even before the border was reached, many gentlemen realized that the cause was lost and made for the coast to find a ship to take them to France. Several were apprehended and later executed. Highlanders pressed northward, eager to get home, but the countryfolk who had earlier allowed themselves to be intimidated now gave full vent to their anger when they realized the rebels were in retreat. Not a few mountain men disappeared from the straggling ranks and turned up in an unknown English ditch with their throats cut.

Yet many townspeople took pity on them; in one case they buried at public expense the stillborn child of a MacPherson woman who had followed her man. The civil-war-in-the-making, which did not end until April 1746, brought out both the worst and the best in people on both sides. None of them fully comprehended what had caused it all. Certainly one contributing factor to its prolongation was an ingrained concept of respect for royalty on the part of many. O'Sullivan, for instance, frequently concerned himself only with the feelings of the Prince and was far too charitable in his judgments. "I cant imagine how he resisted," wrote O'Sullivan of the Prince, "in those great marches we made"—as if others much older and sick in body had not also traversed the same ground. But men such as Lord George, Elcho, and the chieftains were not willing to deify Charles in the same manner. In Scotland he often had to account for his actions to men who deferred to him no longer.

Some of the incidents during the Jacobites' expedition into England would have been comical had the surrounding circumstances not been so tragic. Many had to do with the attitude of the people of the Lowlands toward the wild mountain men. O'Sullivan tells the story of a Quaker woman near Carlisle in whose house Charles lodged for the night. By this time stories had been spread that Highlanders raped, pillaged, burned, and destroyed everything in their path and that they lived upon human flesh. When Sir Thomas Sheridan and Lochiel were meeting with Charles in his room, they heard a groaning noise coming from under the bed and found a frightened little boy trying to hide. They sent for the woman of the house. "The poor woman began to cry & beged the Prince to spare yt child, yt it was the only one she had of seven; the child was drawn from under the bed. Yu never saw a woman in yt condition; she thought the child wou'd be set upon the Spit as there was not much to eat in the house . . ." When Sir Thomas calmed the woman down, she related all the frightening stories being circulated about the nature of Highlanders.

It was two days before the government troops learned of the retreat from Derby. By then, December 8, the Jacobites had reached Manchester, where they heard that General James Edward Oglethorpe was expected daily. The Oglethorpes had once been Jacobites (hence the general's first given names) and had gone into exile with James II. Oglethorpe's two sisters still lived in Paris and were constantly meddling in Jacobite intrigues, much to King James's annoyance and to the embarrassment of their brother. General Oglethrope had never quite won the confidence of King George, although in 1736 he founded the State of Georgia, naming it for the King. In 1745, he was still trying to prove his loyalty to the crown. The Jacobites took the road back to Manchester, then to Wigan, Preston, and Lancaster with Oglethorpe chasing them all the way. His mounted advance guard coolly observed the ragged retreat from every hilltop.

Uppermost in Charles's mind was how to salvage his wounded pride, how to show he was still in command and that he knew what he was doing. He also tried to convey to the Marquis d'Eguilles that he had leadership qualities because he still hoped for a French or Spanish command if all failed in Scotland. Charles began to sneeringly refer to the retreat as a headlong flight from the enemy, and he made it perfectly plain that it had not been his decision but Lord George's. When Oglethorpe was only a day's march from Lancaster, Charles affected bravado by insisting on staying the night. It was only with difficulty that he was persuaded to move on. He also refused to call council meetings, and delays were seriously jeopardizing the safety of the main army, especially those bringing up the rear.

In his book *Marches of the Highland Army*, Lord George Murray wrote that on their way to Derby Charles was always the first up in the morning and had the men in motion before the break of day. He usually marched alongside them on foot, wearing a philibeg and sporting a blue bonnet atop his peruke while he delivered phrases of Gaelic that he had learned. He fancied the Highlanders thought him a fine fellow then. However, as the army retreated, Charles had neither time nor concern for the Highlanders, particularly those bringing up the rear. He rose late in the morning, after the vanguard had commenced its march, and held up the rearguard, which could not leave until His Highness was ready. Then he rode straight on, having the advantage of a mount. The danger of attack from the enemy to the rearguard was so acute that they became unwilling to await His Royal Highness's pleasure. "And now few there were who would go on foot if they could ride; and mighty taking, stealing and pressing of horses there was amongst us. . . ."

The Jacobites avoided action for as long as possible, but so did the government army, whose attitude at this point seems to have been that from Scotland the rebellion had sprung and in Scotland it would be finally crushed. Onward the rebels moved, through Kendal and Shap on the road to Penrith. Beyond Penrith lay Carlisle and the border. The Duke of Perth, now acting only as a volunteer, asked leave to return home to raise some men. He took only thirty or forty escorts with him, and they met with such animosity from the townspeople at Kendal and again at Penrith that he was forced to fall back to the Kendal area and await the main Jacobite army.

It was December 16, four days away from Charles's twenty-fifth birthday, according to the British calendar. In ten days the Prince had gone from believing that masses of English would flock to his cause to knowing from the Duke of Perth, who had lost a servant to the mob's fury at Kendal, that the entire country was up in arms against him. There was even a rumor that Charles had taken all the money he could lay hands on and tried to escape. The rumor was unfounded, but many were beginning to question Charles's constant talk about giving fight to the enemy.

Now the shoe was on Lord George's foot; he began to goad the Prince. "As your Royal Highness is always for battles be the circumstances what they may," he said caustically, "I now offer you one three hours from this time with the army of Wade which is only about three miles behind us." Lord George took smug satisfaction in reporting to the Prince that he had paid some men sixpence a head to carry cannon balls northward because O'Sullivan had fallen down in his duty as quartermaster and failed to arrange transportation. The general knew exactly when to approach the Prince to emerge personally triumphant—in the evening, when the brains of Charles and his cohorts were addled by drink. In many respects self-righteousness was the only weapon Lord George had left, although he had the support of bitter chieftains, whose men were diseased and dying or lying at night in the rainsoaked mud because no one would give them shelter.

Lord George was joined at Shap by John Roy Stuart "and his regiment," which, since nobody ventured numbers, must have fallen disappointingly short of the hundred that had been promised and was probably nearer to thirty or forty men. He had come over from France with Lord John Drummond but had detached himself from the Royal Scots in French service to meet the retreating Jacobites. Charles, no longer anxious to loiter in the rear, was at Penrith pushing toward Carlisle, but his standing orders not to abandon ammunition kept the baggage train constantly behind, uncomfortably aware of the enemy's presence on hilltops around them. The government troops now appeared two by two with "a prodigious number of trumpets and kettle-drums." Glengarry and Cluny MacPherson's men charged up a slope and were able to disperse them. Whether the government soldiers were obeying orders not to attack or whether they were genuinely driven off is not known. Lord George sent an urgent message to Charles asking for reinforcements before the rearguard was cut to pieces. The reply was that none could be spared and that all haste should be made by the baggage train to join the van at Carlisle.

At the village of Clifton, Lord George was joined by the Duke of Perth, who had returned from Charles's camp to offer his help. The hatchet was wisely buried between them in a situation they recognized was none of their own making. In the skirmish of Clifton Moor, which took place on the night of December 18 under a moon often obscured by scudding clouds, the Stewarts of Appin and the Stewarts of Ardshiel came together with the Murrays of Atholl, the MacPhersons, and the MacDonalds of Glengarry to form a fighting force of a thousand men commanded by Lord

George. They were outnumbered four to one, but this was no deterrent to them; they planned to strike at night in guerrilla fashion. They had already worked out an escape route, and all was to be accomplished with lightning speed. Lord George was extremely bitter that Charles's delaying tactics had placed him in this dangerous position, but he was also going to take this opportunity to demonstrate to the Prince and his Irish "experts" just how Highlanders should be used in battle.

Hedges, stone dykes, and narrow roadways flanked the government encampment at Clifton. Knowing how inferior the Jacobite numbers were and believing they were taking cover behind hedges and stone walls, government troops settled down for an exchange at daybreak. But the kilted Highlanders cut their way through prickly hawthorne "being very uneasy to our loos'd tail'd lads" and fell upon their adversaries pell-mell. Government issue of metal skullcaps broke many rusty Highland weapons that night, but fifty swords were taken from the slain dragoons. Forty were killed or wounded before the Jacobites fled down lanes too narrow for cavalry to follow. They had left thirteen of their dead behind.

Charles, it was reported by Lord George, "seemed very well pleased" with what was called "The Skirmish of Clifton Moor," but his coldness continued, and if Lord George was trying to impress this Prince, it was wasted time and effort. Charles would not rest until he had established himself as the supreme authority in military matters. This burning desire cost the lives of many more men before he was finished.

Chapter 9

Master of His Own House

The Prince spent his twenty-fifth birthday fording the swollen River Esk at Longtown. Congratulations were reserved until Charles reached the other side so that it could be said he was both in England and in Scotland on his birthday. Charles was no swimmer, and the locals warned that the Esk was not fordable after the torrential rains. The first to be sent across were the "highest horses" with mounted guides to see if the current could be negotiated. Only after struggling against the powerful waters did they reach the opposite bank.

The Highlanders looked upon the crossing as a sporting challenge and a test of their own mettle. They marched into the water six abreast, each holding on to another's collar. "I was astonished to see how the Highlanders crossed this river, which I could scarcely cross on horseback," said Sir John MacDonald. When it came to be the Prince's turn he went in with all the horse at the army's disposal to break the flow of current so that he would not be swept away. There was a certain amount of gallantry to this maneuver, for he judged that a solid mass of equine flesh would divert the torrent and make things easier for the men coming behind. Little by little the army crossed over to Scotland; the only losses were two female camp followers who were drowned. But the artillery and a great deal of baggage had to be abandoned.

There was no hearty celebration on the other side, however, either for the Prince's birthday or for the army's return to Scotland. An unmistakable wave of resentment and suspicion toward Charles permeated the ranks of the chiefs, who saw scaffolds and entrail-burning fires staring them in the face unless limits were placed on their young leader. It angered them that just before the Esk crossing, approximately four hundred men had been ordered to stay behind at Carlisle to hold the garrison captured on the southward march. This was suicidal madness in view of Cumberland and Wade's proximity to the Jacobites; few expected ever to see the men again. Those left behind were the Manchester regiment, commanded by the hapless Francis Townley, whose capture came at Carlisle; Old Glenbucket's regiment, whose dropsical leader mercifully died before he was brought to trial; Francis Strickland, who also succumbed to dropsy in prison three days after he was taken; and men from Perth's, Ogilvy's, and John Roy Stuart's regiments.

The decision to leave the men at Carlisle was made solely by the Prince, who refused to change his mind, despite the fact that not one person agreed with him. The only reason for it that anyone could fathom was that his pride would not allow him to leave England without claiming to be master of at least one city. That situation lasted only ten days.

The garrison at Carlisle surrendered to the Duke of Cumberland on December 30. The double-chinned, rotund son of George II, whose cruelty later earned him the name Butcher Cumberland, said he trusted the rebels would have "no sort of claim to the King's mercy, and I sincerely hope will meet with none." They did not. Nine (including Francis Townley) were hanged, drawn, and quartered, while those who survived imprisonment were transported to the American plantations to serve as slaves.

By January 6, 1746, the army had retraced its steps as far as the Stirling area, having passed through the openly hostile city of Glasgow and losing at least five hundred deserters on the way. Lord George Murray's letter to the Prince of that date expressed not just his own feelings but those of the chiefs as well:

It is proposed that His Royal Highness shou'd from time to time call a Council of War to consist of all those who command Battalions or Squadrons; but as severals of those may be on partys, and often absent, a Committee should be chosen by those Commanders, to consist of five or seven, and that all Operations for the carrying on the War shou'd be agreed upon, by the Majority of those in His Royal Highness presence, and once that a Measure is taken, it is not to be changed except by the advice of those, or most of them, who were present when it was agreed on.

That upon any sudden Emergency such as in a Battle, Skirmish, or in a Siege, a Discretionary power must be allowed to those who command. This is the Method of all Armys, and where so many Gentlemen of Fortune, not only venture their own and their Familys All, But if any Misfortune happen are sure of ending their lives on a Scaffold the most Dismal Consequence cannot but ensue.

Had not a Council determined the Retreat from Derby, what a Catastrophy must have followed in two or three Days! Had a Council of War been held the Army came to Lancaster, a Day (which at that time was so precious) had not been lost. Had a Council of War been consulted as to leaving a Garrison at Carlisle it would never have been agreed to, the place not being tenable, and so many brave men wou'd not have been sacrifized, besides the reputation of His Royal Highness Arms.

It is to be considered that this Army is an Army of Volunteers, and not Mercenarys, many of them being resolved not to continue in the Army, were affairs once settled.

On the same day that he received Lord George's letter, Charles, assisted by Sheridan, made a lengthy reply. The letter reveals that the Prince had apparently assumed the role of senior general, formerly held by the Duke of Perth.

When I came into Scotland I knew well enough what I was to expect from my Ennemies, but I little foresaw what I meet with from my Friends. I came vested with all the Authority the King cou'd give me, one chief part of which is the Command of his Armies, and now I am required to give this up to fifteen or sixteen Persons, who may afterwards depute five or seven of their own number to exercise it, for fear if they were six or eight that I might myself pretend to ye casting vote. By the majority of these all things are to be determined, and nothing left to me but the honour of being present at their debates. This I am told is the method of all Armies and this I flatly deny, nor do I believe it to be the Method of any one Army in the World.

I am often hit in the teeth that this is an Army of Volunteers, and consequently very different from one composed of Mercenarys. What one wou'd naturally expect from an Army whose chief Officers consist of Gentlemen of rank and fortune, and who came into it meerly upon Motives of Duty and Honour, is more zeal, more resolution and more good manners that in those that fight meerly for pay: but it can be no Army at all where there is no General, or which is the same thing no Obedience or deference paid to him. Every one knew before he engaged in the cause, what he was to expect in case it miscarried, and should have staid at home if he could not face Death in any shape: but can I myself hope for better usage? at least I am the only Person upon whose head a Price has already been set, and therefore I cannot indeed threaten at every other Word to throw down my Arms and make my Peace with the Government.

I think I shew every day that I do not pretend to act without taking advice, and yours oftener than any body's else, which I shall still continue to do, and you know that upon more occasions than one, I have given up my own opinion to that of others. I staid indeed a day at Lancaster without calling a Council, yet yourself proposed to stay another but I wonder much to see myself reproached with the loss of Carlile. Was there a possibility of carrying off the Cannon and baggage, or was there time to destroy them? and wou'd not the doing it have been a greater dishonour to our Arms? After all did not you yourself instead of proposing to abandon it, offer to stay with the Athol Brigade to defend it?*

I have insensibly made this answer much longer than I intended, and might yet add much more, but I choose to cut it short, and shall only tell you that my Authority may be taken from me by violence, but I shall never resign it like an Idiot.

Although Charles spoke of obedience and deference and claimed he would never resign his authority, more and more people, Catholics as well as Protestants, were deciding that they would not forfeit their lives and fortunes to uphold the Prince's blatant assertion of absolute, arbitrary power. Some opted for laying down their arms and making peace with the government as a way out, but that decision brought imprisonment. The remainder were trapped with no recourse but to make the best fight of it they could. Some were for retreating beyond the mountains; others wanted to make for the coast. But Charles continued to talk of victory and believed himself to be a conqueror. "I cant see nothing but ruin and destruction to us all in case we should think of a retreat," he wrote. "Wherever we go the Ennemy will follow, and if we now appear afraid of them their spirits will rise and those of our men sink very low." He was playing for time. That the Spaniards had already sent money and that Lord John Drummond had brought some small pieces of field artillery from France, the Prince looked upon as positive signs of more help to come, but he was living in a fool's paradise.

*Charles had rejected this offer.

The day after their reentry into Scotland, Sir Thomas Sheridan wrote a letter from Dumfries to Daniel O'Brien. He sent it via a Colonel Brown, an aide-de-camp to Charles, who acted as a shipboard messenger between France and Scotland. As O'Brien's response shows, Sheridan actually wrote him three letters from Dumfries, but only the letter to be shown to the Court of France still exists. In it Sheridan gave a glowing account of their exploits into England and back, depicting the Jacobites as a force from which the superior English army had run. They would soon make themselves masters of Stirling Castle and all the forts to the north, he wrote, after which they intended to march on England once more. He acknowledged the small assistance of money and arms from Spain and was pleased that Louis had given Lord John Drummond's regiment permission to come to Scotland, which he regarded as a sign of His Most Christian Majesty's "continuing friendship upon which we base our principal hopes." It was an "ostensible letter," meant to be shown to the Marquis d'Argenson for whatever it might produce. Sheridan's two missing letters to O'Brien may have contained the truth of their situation, which had to be hidden from the Court of France. Sir Thomas and Charles were naive enough to believe the facts would not be known in France.

Sir James Steuart of Goodtrees, Lord Elcho's brother-in-law, had left for France from Edinburgh before the Jacobite army marched into England. He was fully aware of the woefully inadequate number of men Charles commanded at that time; it had fallen to approximately fifteen hundred by the end of January 1746. Not only was Steuart forthright with the French, he also wrote to Rome and gave James accurate accounts, astonishing the King with reports of the small numbers. It was not the situation that his son had represented to him.

Steuart, like Lord Elcho and their mutual friend Marischal, was a plain-spoken man who had nothing to gain by relating anything but the truth. His accounts could also be verified by several of the men brought over by Lord John Drummond, who, when they realized the army in Scotland was not twenty-five thousand men as they had been led to believe in Paris, promptly returned to the Continent. O'Brien realized that his energies would be better spent finding ships to rescue the Prince than persuading the French to pour money into the Jacobite cause. He began this work at the end of February, but he was constantly thwarted in his efforts, and almost three months passed before he was able to get any ships to the Western Isles.

Henry and a few French and Spanish officers appeared at Boulogne as if a massive invasion were in the making; this was a show on the part of France. News was also leaked that various French regiments were bound for Scotland, including FitzJames's, Berwick's, Clare's, and Lally's, and the Duc de Richelieu was rumored to be making a descent on Wales. But only 120 FitzJames men came through; the rest were never intended to. This French ruse was successful; the result was that Cumberland deployed part of the Royal Army to guard the south coast. As O'Brien warned Sheridan, all Louis was interested in was keeping English troops occupied on the home front while France successfully conquered Brussels. In Paris everyone was talking about the "total defection" of the Prince's army, and O'Brien warned Sheridan never to believe any of France's promises "because they always make a show."

Louis XV treated Henry exactly the same way he had treated Charles at Gravelines. The Duke of York did not receive a penny for his subsistence in four months, although he was eventually granted a monthly income of 4,000 livres in March. He was confined to close quarters at Boulogne under the pretext of an impending invasion. Just as Charles had done, Henry solicited leave to join the French army in Flanders and was refused. After a short while at Boulogne, which he considered a "vile hole," he requested permission to live in Paris, but that was also denied. Boulogne's taverns were now filled with men lately returned from Scotland who could not understand why Henry was applying for service in Flanders when he should have been more concerned about his brother. A growing number no longer wished to be called Jacobites. There was an increasing, uneasy sense that the Stuarts were up to something with the French Court that they did not fully understand.

Henry spent a very uncomfortable twenty-first birthday at Boulogne on March 6. He could not afford to buy a coach to take the air, and he hated to walk the streets on foot like a commoner, particularly because the hostility of the Boulogne community was directed at him. They criticized the severity of his long black monseigneur's coat, which was tightly buttoned from foot to neck, his black stockings, his black shoes, and his flat black hat with a small crown and wide brim. They made fun of him as he walked to church with his hands clasped tightly together, his fingertips touching his lips.

There was no humility about his pious air; although his dress was simple, his approach and elaborate manner of genuflecting were intended to draw attention toward himself. From Avignon, Paris, and Boulogne came an avalanche of criticism about Henry's conduct and manner. It was too Romish, too pompous, too effeminate, they said. When O'Brien related all this to James, he swept it aside with a simple explanation: "I am used to hearing such things."

Outside Italy, respect for the Stuarts was at a nadir. "There is no help for it," James said when he heard about the further tracasseries in the Jacobite camp. All he had left to hope for was that Louis would allow his sons to live permanently somewhere in France. As for himself, he said he preferred the Italian climate; but he hoped that the King of France would permit him to visit his sons from time to time.

But in Scotland Charles was not willing to give up so easily. In January the Prince stayed at the house of Sir Hugh Paterson at Bannockburn, near Stirling. Here he met Clementina Walkinshaw, who later became his mistress and the mother of the only child he ever had. We know very little about Clementina Walkinshaw except that she was about the same age as Charles and was named after his mother. Surviving portraits show that her looks were decidedly plain. She was the daughter of John Walkinshaw of Barrowfield, who had served James at Avignon a quarter of a century before. Barrowfield had done his utmost to find a European court that would accept James prior to his banishment to Rome; he was also involved in the search for a bride that led to Clementina Sobieska. However, neither he nor his wife (Sir Hugh Paterson's sister) was now living, and Clementina's marriage prospects seem to have been bleak.

There is no evidence of any sexual union between Charles and Clementina at this time; indeed, that would hardly be likely while she was in her uncle's care. She was lonely and overlooked; and although the Prince always received much attention, at heart he was also lonely, and they may have talked together. Charles was always extremely shy and awkward in female company. Yet he treated women like subservient creatures, after the pattern of his father. Whether the Prince was still virginal at the age of twenty-five is difficult to say, but there had been a hint of sexual adventure when he cavorted with Young Glengarry in the Paris *ginguettes*. Not until he returned to France did Charles show a deeper interest in the opposite sex, but Clementina Walkinshaw, who eventually followed him there, was the least of his considerations.

The Jacobites avoided going through Edinburgh during their retreat. The city was now occupied by Lieutenant General Henry Hawley, who had been appointed to replace the aging Guest. His first order had been to erect gallows in anticipation of the soon-expected exchange with the rebels. By mid-January, Charles's forces were bolstered by reinforcements—Lord Strathallan from Perth; some Farquarsons, Frasers, MacKenzies, MacLeods led by Lord Cromarty; and even four hundred men raised by Lady Mackintosh, whose husband was aligned with the government. At this point Charles reached his peak of five thousand men—seven thousand if O'Sullivan is believed. Other reports by the Chevalier de Johnstone and the government placed the number at eight thousand men, counting Lord John Drummond's French troops; but even if there were eight thousand, the number dwindled drastically after yet another of the Prince's ill-conceived sieges.

The attempt by Charles to capture Stirling Castle was a further waste of time. As usual, others were set up to take the blame if the siege should fail. Charles placed the Duke of Perth in command of the men, and a supposed French engineering expert who had come over with Lord John Drummond was put in charge of the physical execution of battering the Castle into submission. He was of the Gordon family but had resided so long in France that his airs, lace-trimmed clothing, and mannerisms were wholly Gallic and in comic contrast to the scratching, matted-hair Highlanders. He called himself the Marquis de Mirabelle; the Highlanders laughingly called him Monsieur Admirable. Even O'Sullivan had to agree that he was a "headstrong ignorant fellow yt wou'd go his own way & follow no mans advise." The Chevalier de Johnstone recounted that the Highlanders discovered Mirabelle "was totally devoid of judgment, discernment, or common sense; his figure being as ridiculous as his mind."

The siege was a dismal failure. Mirabelle tried to reduce the formidable Stirling fortress with a lightweight battery, which he positioned so that the gunners were in mortal danger from the shells hurtling from the castle. He ordered the Highlanders to fetch sandbags from distances far away; they stood with arms folded, refusing to do the work, which they considered beneath their dignity and a waste of precious time. In the end some of the French regulars brought by Lord John Drummond were the ones to fetch and carry.

The bewigged and perfumed Monsieur Admirable directed yet another display of the abysmal military judgment of Bonnie Prince Charlie. Hawley's English numbered eight thousand, although twenty percent of them were unfit to march. His ten regiments were augmented by the Black Watch Regiment, by Sir Robert Munro and his clan, and by the Argyll Militia. With the Jacobites in retreat, Hawley believed that he had ample time to prepare to meet the rebels, and in an almost leisurely manner he marched his troops from Edinburgh toward Stirling. He halted at Falkirk, nine miles east of the Prince's quarters at Bannockburn House. He believed that the Jacobite army would take a defensive position at Bannockburn.

Hawley made his quarters at Callendar House, the home of Lord Kilmarnock, who had come out for the Prince. He availed himself of Lady Kilmarnock's unwilling hospitality, partaking liberally of wines and spirits throughout his stay. When Hawley received a report that the Jacobites were marching on Falkirk, he dismissed it, feeling quite sure that the Prince was in no position to take the offensive.

Meanwhile, after he was brought news of Hawley's march, Charles adopted the air of a commanding general. For two consecutive days (January 15 and 16) he drew up his army in battle order on Plean Muir, south of Bannockburn. According to O'Sullivan, the reason for this was so that "every one may know their Ground." Lord George felt that to wait for the superior force would be fatal and that the only wise course would be to launch a surprise attack. This was, after all, the way Highlanders were used to fighting, and eager for a skirmish, many had become impatient with the Prince's trying out of textbook battle formations.

After two fruitless days Charles grudgingly agreed to Lord George's proposal to march on Falkirk. Even so, when the army came to the flooded River Carron, which lay between them and Falkirk, Charles sent O'Sullivan from the rear with a message ordering Lord George to wait until morning. Exercising the "discretionary power . . . to those who command" that he had outlined in his letter, Lord George persisted in the march, having found the Carron fordable at Dunipace Steps. By midnight of the sixteenth the Jacobites had taken possession of Falkirk Muir, a hundred-foot-high plateau not far from Callendar House, where Hawley's sensibilities were becoming more addled by the hour. Throughout the evening he had received messages that the Jacobites were in motion on the Hill of Falkirk. He had paid little heed to them, but a final urgent message sent him scattering to his horse, his head uncovered, looking like a man "who has abruptly left an hospital table."

It was January 17, and the wind was blowing fiercely on Falkirk Hill. The rain drove hard into the Highlanders' backs, but Hawley's men faced the full brunt of the tempestuous weather. Having heard stories—certainly once true—of the Highlanders' dread of horses, Hawley ordered his cavalry forward in the late afternoon as darkness was beginning to fall. They went "at a grand trot piercing into their ranks, driving all before them and trampling the Highlanders under their horses feet," wrote the Chevalier de Johnstone. But then, as at Prestonpans, the trampled men reached up and stuck bayonets and broadswords into the horses' underbellies. They pulled the riders down and slew them with pistols because the battle was so thick that there was no room to swing the broadswords. ". . . the resistance of the Highlanders was so incredibly obstinate," wrote Johnstone, "that the English cavalry . . . were in the end repulsed and forced to retreat."

The Highlanders pursued with dirks and swords. They ran as fast as the enemy's horses, dragging several men to their deaths in full view of Hawley's ranks. Those of the government cavalry who could escape plunged a terrified path back through the ranks. As Hawley was later forced to report of his own men to Cumberland, "suche scandalous Cowardice I never saw before. The whole second line of Foot ran away without firing a Shot." The scaffolds that Hawley had earlier erected in Edinburgh to choke the life out of the Jacobites were now used to punish his own men. Thirty-one of Hamilton's dragoons were hanged for desertion, and thirty-two of the footsoldiers were shot for cowardice. Other officers were dishonorably discharged following a humiliating public ceremony. In the case of one Captain Cunningham, "his sword [was] broken over his head, his sash cut in pieces and thrown in his face, and lastly the provost-martial's servant giving him a kick on the posteriors, turned him out of the line."

All accounts say that there was a great slaughter by the Jacobites at the Battle of Falkirk and incredible disorder in the Royal Army. The MacDonalds under Young Clanranald were the least restrained in plundering and killing that day. The battle, in which Charles took no part, lasted no more than twenty minutes and netted the Jacobites a useful haul of tents and mortars, seven pieces of cannon, powder, a few hundred muskets, "and a great many hampers of good wines, & liquors & other provisions were found in the Town," related the well-satisfied O'Sullivan. On the Jacobite side, approximately fifty were killed and sixty to eighty were wounded. The government's loss is reputed to have been four hundred slain men, many of them officers, including Sir Robert Munro, chieftain of the clan. His death was deeply regretted by the Jacobites, even though the Clan Munro had taken the government side.

Something that occurred the next day was taken by the superstitious Highlanders to be a very bad omen and sent them home in great numbers. Young Glengarry's brother Aeneas (or Angus) was accidentally shot by another MacDonald, of Keppoch's clan, as the man was cleaning his firing piece. Although the dying Glengarry forgave the other with his last breath, dejection and desertion were rife.

Other Jacobites, however, were for pursuing the government army to Edinburgh to consolidate the victory. Charles rejected the idea. His mind was set on returning to Stirling, where he had left the Duke of Perth in command of a thousand men, to make another attempt to take the Castle. With the Duke of Cumberland returning from the southern coast to reinforce Hawley, Charles's insistence upon spending more time at Stirling was scarcely creditable. How many men left his army for good at this point is difficult to assess, but two thousand is a reasonable estimate.

Charles went back to Sir Hugh Paterson's house to be nursed by Clementina Walkinshaw for an ailment described to everyone as "a cold." He was falling victim, slowly but surely, to a debilitating series of maladies associated with malnutrition. Scotland's food stores could not support all the military activity it had recently seen, and many men were on the edge of starvation.

Why did Charles persist in the impossible siege of Stirling Castle? If it were merely to compete with Lord George Murray, as several suspected, he could have certainly chosen a vehicle that had more promise of success. The answer lies in an aspect of politics of which only Charles and Sheridan were fully aware at the time—the old fear, long harbored by James, that France intended to divide Britain and keep her weak so that later on the Bourbons could conquer the nation.

Daniel O'Brien confirmed in his dispatches to Sheridan that Louis XV had been conferring with the King of Sardinia, who was now dissatisfied with the terms of his alliance with George II and Maria Theresa. Louis was already planning what he would extract from George under the terms of a future peace settlement, but he would need the cooperation of the King of Sardinia as well as that of Philip V to strengthen his position at the bargaining table. One of the early propositions was that George II would remain King of England, but Scotland was to be given over to the Stuarts.

Charles and Sheridan vainly attempted to capture Stirling and the forts to the north, after which they planned to march back into England. As for the matter of the three crowns, it was to be all three or none for Charles. That he expected to capture the Scottish forts and then England with only the small forces at his disposal testifies to his stubborn willfulness and to his belief in miracles; or perhaps he had simply lost touch with reality.

Bad news filtered through to Scotland about the state of affairs on the other side of the Channel. The real state of affairs was not at all what Charles had been representing to the chiefs. From Boulogne, Sir James Steuart sent urgent word to his wife, Elcho's sister, to leave Scotland and make her way to Holland. And he was not the only man arranging for his family's escape to the Continent. These departures were motivated by the news that there were no French troops waiting for embarkment at Boulogne and that France was providing no money.

All the histories say the rebellion was financed by France; and some louis d'or, known as the Treasure of Loch Arkaig, did eventually find their way to Scotland. But the coins had been converted in Paris from Spanish pistoles. Only Spain and the Pope provided money. Spain's subsidy was a monthly allotment equal to 400,000 French livres, to be used for the payment of two thousand men supplied by France. The Spaniards also gave leave to twenty-five or thirty Irish officers (including Sir Charles Wogan) to meet up at Boulogne with those two thousand troops. But after waiting several weeks with no appearance of any men, most of the Irish went back to Madrid and sent warning letters to James. A few hung on idly at the coast, collecting 200 livres a month from the Spanish subsidy. Among these was Colonel Felix O'Neill, who would be invaluable to Prince Charles in the months ahead.

In the meantime, Henry had placed the disposition of the Spanish pension in Sir James Steuart's hands. By March the latter had arranged for the first month's subsidy of 400,000 livres to be transported to Scotland via a captured English vessel, the swift-sailing sloop *Hazard*, renamed *The Prince Charles*. When the money landed on the western coast of Scotland, a party of Highlanders tried to transport it inland to the Jacobite encampment. But they were attacked by the progovernment Mackays, led by Lord Reay, and all the gold was taken.

Back in France, aspersions were being cast on the honesty of the men involved in transporting the money, including Colonel Brown. As one of the Prince's aides-de-camp and messenger between France and Scotland, Brown had taken delivery of the funds in Paris for shipment to Scotland. Even Sir James Steuart came under suspicion. Henry went so far as to haughtily demand personal assurances from him that Charles would receive further shipments of money. Cardinal Tencin had apparently warned Henry that if the funds were being managed by Steuart, they were "in a very bad Channel." Affronted, Sir James and Colonel Brown refused to have anything more to do with transporting gold to Scotland.

The other side of that story is that James did not want the Spanish and papal subsidies to be sent to Scotland. He wrote Henry that he should never have allowed Sir James Steuart to manage the money and that all such matters should be handed over to Daniel O'Brien. There was no reason to question the honesty of Sir James or Colonel Brown. The incident only increased the mounting hostility toward the Stuarts, particularly from Lord Marischal and his party. James was afraid that if the money were controlled by Scots, it would be used to finance the escape of hundreds of Highland refugees, who would then apply to him for subsistence. He was also concerned that Charles not waste the money by purchasing further arms from Holland, which he was known to be trying to do. Therefore, on James's orders, future Spanish and papal subsidies were held back in Paris by O'Brien until the final hour, when it became known that all had failed in Scotland. It was then used to finance the Prince's rescue. Not all this was known to the Jacobites at Boulogne, but enough disturbing facts were brought to Scotland's shores and relayed inland to the chieftains by clan runners.

Tempers were fraying in the Jacobite camp due to a scarcity of food and deep anxiety about what the Prince's next arbitrary decision would be. On January 29, Lord George Murray delivered to Charles's quarters at Bannockburn an address signed by the chieftains. They had solemnly declared "in the presence of God" that Charles should retreat into the Highlands north of the Forth River. This reasonable demand couched in the form of a request was softened by the rider that they were "firmly resolved to stand by him and the Glorious Cause we have espoused to the utmost hazard of our lives and Fortunes"—but only if the Prince retreated north of the Forth.

The Declaration of the Chiefs was given to Hay of Restalrig, but Hay decided not to awaken the Prince that night. As Lord George had stated in his cover letter, "We are sensible that it will be very unpleasant, but in the Name of God what can we do?" The next morning, January 30, Charles was presented with the declaration. He struck his head against the wall with a blow that sent him staggering and "exclaimed most violently against Lord George." "Good God!" he shouted. "Have I lived to see this?"

Sheridan was summoned to draft a reply; two of them were penned that day. A meeting was held in the evening, with Cluny MacPherson and MacDonald of Keppoch representing the chiefs' interests, but they were treated to the Prince's "Despotick temper," to which Charles himself later confessed. Neither Keppoch nor Cluny was budged by the royal rages, and Charles was forced to agree to a further retreat. He sent a memorial to the chiefs that he trusted would be shown "to no mortal," concluding that "After all this I know I have an Army yt I cannot command any further than the chief Officers please, and therefore if you are all resolved upon it I must yield; but I take God to witness that it is with the greatest reluctance, and that I wash my hands of the fatal consequences which I foresee but cannot help."

Throughout snow-filled February and most of March, the army moved in small groups toward Inverness. That city lies at the easterly end of the great Glen Mor, which separates the Highlands from the Lowlands by Loch Ness, Loch Oich, Loch Lochy, and Loch Linnhe. Some of the leaders dreaded moving into this territory because they would be bringing most of the soldiers close to home. The chiefs harbored no illusions about the fact that many of the men were still there only because it was the only way they could get food and clothing. But even with both commodities very hard to come by, it was expected that once many of the Highlanders came in sight of their homes and hearths, they would leave forever.

Lord George was the only person keeping the Highlanders

together, but he did so no longer out of conviction for the cause. He felt a keen sense of responsibility toward the men of Atholl whom he had led into the fray. But with each passing day he found it harder to disguise the rancor he felt toward the Prince. He painfully drove home advantages at every given opportunity. He had left his children and a wife he dearly loved to do "my duty to King & Country." One evening he composed a letter to his family to try to explain decisions he had made that would cause them distress. The letter shows that he was prepared to die in battle. Yet as fond as the Prince was of high talk about honor, duty, and fighting or perishing, no one had yet seen him take a personal risk, and too many already knew from the Boulogne grapevine that O'Brien was sending rescue ships for Charles.

At council meetings, now held more frequently as a result of the Declaration of the Chiefs, Lord George took complete charge. He asked for opinions about future strategy, and if Charles tried to interrupt any man's reply, Lord George would threaten to leave the meeting. To avoid senseless arguing, he set up a rule that when he directed a question to someone, no other could speak until the answer had been given. Only after all opinions had been expressed could the Prince speak.

Lord George in effect took control away from Charles. "Are you mad?" asked Lord Louis Gordon; others were also aghast at his daring. But too few stood up to Charles. Lord George wanted to put a stop to the Prince's habit of privately meeting with individuals to persuade them to his way of thinking after a resolution had already been decided by the majority. Lord George intended that having each man express his opinion in council meetings in front of the others would leave no room for anyone to change his mind. But he only succeeded in making Charles more determined than ever to be lord of all. Here again, James set the pattern: one can almost hear his voice ringing out in the frosty braes as it had once done at the Palazzo Muti: "I *will* be master of my own house."

The army spent most of March at Elgin, near Inverness, where Charles's "cold" turned into a "spotted favor." He had once said that all he needed to be a complete Highlander was "the itch," and now he joined the ranks of those driven to distraction by scratching, pus-filled hair follicles on the chest, arms, and thighs. Sometimes there were tingling inflammations of the back as well, like shingles. People could tell where the Jacobite army had been by the scratching posts set up along the road. Since the common though completely unfounded notion was that only those of low birth could be afflicted by "the itch," the Prince's illness was kept a secret. It is likely that his condition was helped by his diet, for although he disdained vegetables, cabbages, onions, and potatoes were probably about all there was to eat, and these vegetables contain ascorbic acid, necessary to cure the ailment. Charles soon made a temporary recovery.

By April the Prince had audaciously commandeered Culloden House, home of Lord President Duncan Forbes. It lay near the River Nairn, six miles south of Inverness. Charles took advantage of the early spring season to hunt, shoot, and fish, but the activity was now not so much a sport as a means of obtaining food. He had recently been crushed by ill tidings, that the gold sent from France had been taken by Lord Reay and the Mackays and that the Duke of Cumberland, in command of all operations in Scotland, had crossed the River Spey with an army of eighteen thousand men. On April 14 they were encamped at Nairn, eight miles from the Jacobite army at Culloden.

William Augustus, Duke of Cumberland, was feeling very pleased with himself on the eve of his twenty-fifth birthday. (He was four months younger than his cousin Charles.) His leadership abilities greatly inspired confidence in his men, who had affectionately called him Billy when they fought under his command at Flanders. He was not a naturally affable man; he was a strict disciplinarian and something of a bully. But he ran an efficient army and took good care of his men. Cumberland was ice cool in the heat of battle and had taken great pains to study the art of warfare during his long months of campaigning in Flanders. He had also examined the testimonies of several officers whose men had run away at Prestonpans, Clifton, and Falkirk. He sought to determine exactly what caused such unaccountable panic when the Highlanders appeared. The Duke of Cumberland did not think upon the matter merely as a military strategist; he was also personally involved. It was his father's throne that Prince Charles was trying to take.

The metal skullcaps he had issued his men had not lessened their dread of broadswords brought down with two-handed force; they could lop off an arm or a leg or sever a man's head from his body with one swift stroke. The caps were not effective. Battlefields were littered with the dead bodies of men who had worn them. They could not withstand a mighty blow of steel and could also be easily tipped off by the point of a sword. The distribution of this useless piece of armor had only lowered morale. A surefire offensive tactic against the Highland method of warfare was needed. At last the Duke believed he had found that tactic.

Cumberland drilled and redrilled his soldiers in hand-to-hand combat techniques, one in particular. When a Highlander raised both arms to strike his enemy with a broadsword, the Redcoat to the immediate right of the man who was about to be struck was to plunge a bayonet under the Highlander's left armpit, straight into the heart. Each Redcoat would be protected by the man to his right, on down the line. Cumberland hoped that the bayonet attack would take the Highlanders by complete surprise because it would come from the least expected direction. It remained to be seen whether the Redcoats executed the new strategy perfectly.

On April 15, the troops were happily celebrating the Duke of Cumberland's birthday with meat from the cattle herds they had driven from the south.* They also ate cheese, bread, and grain-rich ale, while the officers were plentifully supplied with brandy. Eight miles away at Culloden House a dinner of roasted lamb was prepared for Prince Charles and his favorites; they had robbed the Lord President's cellar of sixty hogsheads of claret. Charles is alleged to have pushed the food away, saying that he could not eat when he knew his men were starving.

For several days the Jacobites were reduced to rations of one flour-and-water biscuit per day, if that. Lord George accused Hay of Restalrig of neglecting his commissariat duties by failing to bring tumbrel carts of food from Inverness. Hay, who was comfortably quartered at Culloden House, insisted that supplies would come, but nothing arrived. The army simply had no money, and the men had not not been paid in months. Since December many had taken to roaming the countryside in search of food, terrorizing farmers and stealing their livestock. Even if spare food was available, the farmers sold it to the Redcoats because at least they had money to pay for it.

Murray of Broughton succumbed to sickness and went into hiding to avoid arrest. It may be too harsh to say that he deserted,

---

*Much cattle now in Cumberland's charge had been driven south by the Jacobites, but the herd had to be abandond during the retreat from England.

for he had been given permission to withdraw. But he later named names at government inquiries—testimony that brought many to public execution. The only person Charles now looked to for military advice was O'Sullivan, the former tutor of the children of a French marshal.

Charles had decided that the battle against the Duke of Cumberland would be his to command. It was the first and last battle he would ever command. He brooked no interference, and he was determined that Lord George be given no credit for what he was sure would be a glorious victory. He sent O'Sullivan to reconnoiter a suitable battlefield, but the Irishman's choice of Drummossie Moor, beyond a braeside south of Culloden House, could not have been better for the Duke of Cumberland. It was a flat, open piece of ground that afforded the government troops ample room to pelt a merciless fire upon the Highlanders before they could make an attack. "Not one single souldier but would have been against such a ffeeld had their advice been askt," wrote Lord George later on. It was true. When Cumberland came to review Drummossie Moor, he could scarcely believe his luck. The chances were that the Jacobites could be annihilated before any hand-to-hand combat took place.

Lord George Murray, who had not been consulted, realized the danger. Taking Colonel Ker of Graden and some others with him, he frantically reconnoitered a battle site that would give his men a fighting chance. They found a stretch of uneven ground near Dalcross Castle that would afford far better protection from artillery fire than Drummossie Moor, but the Prince refused to deviate from O'Sullivan's choice.

Shortly after dawn on Tuesday, April 15, the Jacobite army awoke in the parks and gardens surrounding the Lord President's magnificent home at Culloden. They marched southward to Drummossie Moor and lined up in battle order facing northeast. Their eyes scanned the heather-covered brae for Cumberland's men, but while the sound of cannon fire had brought them to that spot, it had been in honor of Cumberland's birthday.

With time to review their precarious situation, the chiefs fell to quarreling instead. O'Sullivan claimed that Lord George had insisted upon taking the right hand in battle along with his men of Atholl; it was the position traditionally held by the MacDonalds. Lord George may have been given command of the right because many MacDonalds had deserted, particularly the Glengarry Mac-

Donalds after the accidental death of one of their number at Falkirk. But the MacDonalds protested as loudly as they had at Prestonpans seven months before, and their clan, led by Clanranald, Keppoch, and Lochgarry, leader of the remaining Glengarry men, sought out the Prince. They literally "begged he would give us our former right," confessed Lochgarry, "but he intreated us for his sake we would not dispute it as he had already agreed to give it to Lord George and his Atholl men."

However, there was no battle that day, for the enemy was far too busy celebrating the anniversary of its commander's birth. Charles walked around the field speaking to individual officers, trying to cajole them to agree to an impetuously conceived plan to attack Cumberland's camp at dawn the next day. No doubt he hoped to take the drunken government troops by surprise, but almost without exception everyone believed it a mad scheme. Even his Irish favorites believed it a "desperate attempt."

During the day some more of Keppoch's men came from Lochaber to join the Jacobite camp. Lord Elcho's reconnaissance verified that all was quiet and inactive in the enemy's quarters at Nairn. At a meeting of officers late that afternoon, opinions about the battle plan began to change, particularly Lord George's. Perhaps he decided that making a surprise attack on Cumberland in his own camp would be no more irrational than exposing his men on the open expanse of Drummossie Moor. Moreover, a surprise attack under cover of darkness would confuse the enemy and buy the Jacobites time to consider escape routes; certainly more of them would survive that kind of parry and thrust than would survive an open-field battle in broad daylight. It was agreed, then, to make a surprise attack, but with a reservation: They could not leave Drummossie Moor and take the Royal Army by surprise unless they marched at night. Since Nairn was eight miles away and there was baggage and artillery to transport over rock-strewn and muddy ground, it was unclear if they could make the march by daybreak of April 16. All agreed to try.

The sequence of events as related in various contemporary Jacobite accounts varies from writer to writer. We do not know at precisely what time on April 15 the decision was made to march on Cumberland at Nairn. We do know that around seven o'clock that evening the officers discovered that a third of the army was missing. It is probable that this discovery generated the hastily convened meeting and Lord George's change of heart.

The desertions had undoubtedly taken place after the men viewed the suicidal expanse of Drummossie Moor; some of those who went off foraging for food never returned. None of the ordinary soldiers knew of the intended night march on Nairn, for it was a closely kept secret. Days after, bodies were found twenty miles from the scene. Many had simply dropped dead from starvation. Livid blue-black wounds on their legs and thighs with protruding growths resembling fungus led some to believe the men had been victims of grapeshot wounds suffered in battle, but most of them had deserted the day before the battle.

When night fell, the army assembled in two columns led by Mackintosh guides familiar with the territory. The Prince tried to spur the men on with talk of the reinforcements that would soon join them, but the Highlanders had heard it all before. Many who did not understand his Italianate, broken English that was borne on brandied breath trudged sullenly over the braeside, treating His Royal Highness to sidelong looks and rancid silence. "Had I but a thousand men I would attack," Charles had often repeated that day. The 4,500 figure usually given for his force at this time is outrageously charitable. A more reasonable estimate is that the Prince had but two thousand bone-weary men left for the Battle of Culloden. They were outnumbered approximately nine to one. A massacre was in the making.

In the wee hours of the morning, the march to Nairn was abruptly halted. Men were dropping in their tracks; hunger and exhaustion had overtaken them. Some who still had strength in their legs slunk off through Kilravock Wood in search of food, while others who had not had the courage to desert in the light of day now hill-skipped homeward under cover of night.

Suddenly a gap was discovered in the middle of the line, half a mile long. The surprise attack could not possibly be accomplished successfully with such a gap. Lord George therefore sent a message to the Prince to close the ranks so that every available man in the army could make the attack simultaneously. Regardless of the urgency of this request, Charles interpreted it as an order. Not stopping to think of the safety of his men or of the success of the mission, he sent orders back to Lord George Murray to attack without waiting for the rest of the army to come up.

Lord George and the other officers were astonished and outraged. With dawn not far away, it would have been suicidal to do as Charles asked, and if they waited for the Prince to arrive, daylight would render a surprise attack absolutely impossible. What thoughts raced through the officers' minds can only be guessed. Some believed that Charles intended to cut and run for the coast if the forward troops met with grief. He and his group of Franco-Irish *picquets* and what remained of the FitzJames contingent had commandeered the best of the starving horses.

Lord George made the only decision he could under the circumstances. He ordered what remained of his bitter army back to Culloden. He was solidly backed in his decision by Lochiel, Lord John Drummond, Keppoch, the Duke of Perth, and the rest of the chiefs. John Hay, who had never been more than a fetch-and-carry boy for the Prince, relayed Lord George's decision to retreat to his master.

Charles rode forward in a hot and furious temper to see what was happening. On his way he met the retreating men. "Where the devil are the men a-going?" he screeched. When told that this group had been ordered by the Duke of Perth to return, he raged: "Where is the Duke? Call him here. What need have I to give orders when my orders are disobeyed? I am betrayed!" He rode in circles on his arthritic gelding calling everyone a traitor, but the men had seen his drunken fury more than once too often.

Perth was finally located in the company of Lochiel. "Good God!" Charles exclaimed in the hearing of men he hoped to impress. "What does this mean? We were equal in numbers and could have blown them to the devil." At this point the Gentle Lochiel, as he was known, and the equally calm-natured Perth steered Charles to a private meeting, where he would not embarrass himself further in front of the men. There they told him quietly but firmly that the Jacobite army was returning to Culloden. Charles continued to shout hysterically that nobody could command his army but himself. But he had already lost command.

Chapter 10

Culloden

The Jacobite army returned to Culloden at about six o'clock on the morning of Wednesday, April 16. At Culloden House the principal officers were "sullen and dejected," having gone the entire night without sleep. They threw themselves "on beds, others on tables, Chairs & on the floors, for the fatigue and the hunger had been felt as much amongst the officers as the Soldiers." A major of Ogilvy's first battalion was sent to post guard, but "a violent favor & transports took him" (hallucinations induced by hunger)—an incident that shattered everybody's nerves.

The night's effort also caused O'Sullivan to faint, forcing him to lie down for a while. His narrative, which was written after he escaped to France, was quaintly worded and flowed relatively smoothly until the events leading up to the Battle of Culloden. The memories were so obviously painful and disturbing that the Irishman literally became incoherent at that point. He mixed the sequence of events, contradicted himself, lied some, and also related nuggets of the truth, but above all, deep distress was evident as the words tumbled one over another.

O'Sullivan's narrative was written for James, who commissioned written accounts from several others as well to get to the bottom of why Charles had left France against his wishes and understand what had happened in Scotland. He had received sporadic letters from his son, but they were either glowingly optimistic or far too brief. James recognized that if he were to learn the truth, it would have to come from other sources. Because O'Sullivan was unemployed and was hoping for an army commission or pension when he wrote his account for James, he was very flattering to Charles, glossing over his foul temper and insisting that the Prince never spoke a harsh word to Lord George. But too many other accounts refute him.

O'Sullivan described an incident during the march to Nairn in which the Prince attempted to cajole Lord George, which left the Jacobite general cold:

> When Ld George was in march the Prince joyns him, takes one of his hands, & sets another hand about his neck, holding him thus, tels him, 'Ld George, yu cant imagine, nor I cant expresse to yu how acknowledging I am of all the services you have rendered me, but this will Crown all. You'l restore the King by it, you'l deliver our poor Country from Slevery, you'l have all the honr & glory of it, it is your own work, it is yu imagined it, & be assured, Dr Ld George, that the King nor I will never forget it. I speake to you my Dr Ld George (the Prince sweesing him) from the bottom of my soul, & I am sure it is to yu we'l owe all, so God Blesse yu.' The Prince continued so holding him by the hand & about the body for above a quarter of an hour. Ld George never dained to answer one word. The Prince continued to walk near him after he quited his hand for a long time, at last seeing Ld George did not speak a word, the Prince took leave of him, saying 'well God blesse yu. Il go & see if all follows.' Ld George took of his Bonnet made a stif bow, & the Prince went off, every body yt was presente was surpris'd at that conduct, thought Ld George had lost his senses, or yt the Prince had Ill treated him before; but there was no such thing, the Prince never sd a hard word to him.

This kind of display of intimacy was obviously what Charles used to get what he wanted, and it was probably how he had been able to talk so many chieftains into following him in the first place. But Lord George now stiffened and remained silent in the face of this wheedling, and the Prince was forced to recognize that lavish praise and coaxing no longer had any effect on the Scots—neither the chieftains nor on their men.

Cluny MacPherson had already taken his clan two months before, ostensibly for spring planting, but there is no evidence that the clan planned to return. Although O'Sullivan seemed to be expecting the MacPhersons to rejoin, this may have been wishful thinking on his part. There is room to believe that the MacDonalds would also have left had the army been near their part of the country.

The discovery that Aeneas MacDonald, the banker, was holding money aroused suspicion about the reason for the lack of food. Was Charles conserving money so that he and his Irish followers could escape? Colonel Ker of Graden's account states that the men had not slept for several nights and that the want of food "occasion'd a prodigious murmuring among the private men, many of them exclaiming bitterly ev'n in the Prince's hearing, which affected him very much." That evening the Prince said he had sent a squadron of FitzJames Horse off to Inverness to purchase meal to make biscuit. Then Charles reposed "with great difficulty having got some bread and whiskie."

The long-awaited food had not arrived when, around eleven o'clock on the morning of April 16, the sleeping Jacobites in the fields and parks surrounding Culloden House were aroused by the sound of cannon fire in the distance and by Cumberland's Campbell pipers calling them to battle. Due to extreme fatigue and hunger many of the men slept on as if they were in comas. Colonel Ker said they "never waken'd till they found the enemy cutting their throats." The Royal Army halted to give the Jacobites time to assemble. More than one man afterward wondered why they had not fallen upon the exhausted men then and there. But Cumberland had drilled his soldiers to such a degree that he was not going to cheat them or himself out of a victory in an orderly battle.

O'Sullivan saw the Duke of Cumberland's army stretched out in perfect battle order on the far side of Drummossie Moor, less than a mile south of Culloden House, as he rode to a small hillside near the house with Lord John Drummond, Captain O'Shea of FitzJames Horse, and Lord Balmerino (who would be beheaded for his part in the rebellion). It is estimated that the Royal Army was fourteen thousand strong that day. Cumberland had intelligence of the Jacobites' aborted march of the night before and had struck camp at five o'clock that morning to march on Culloden. He issued his men a breakfast of bread and cheese, washed down with a tot of brandy, then the march to Drummassie Moor was accomplished with laudable efficiency and order. Many of the troops who had been shamed at Prestonpans, Clifton, and Falkirk were more than determined now to put a swift and grim end to the rebellion. They were told that the Highlanders had been ordered to give no quarter—take no prisoners alive—if their attack the night before had succeeded; they were similarly instructed to give no quarter this day.

No order had actually been issued by the Jacobite army to deny quarter. But the plan of the previous evening's aborted attack may have been conveyed to Cumberland by some of the deserting Highlanders. Many of them had sold their targets and weapons to buy food because they had not received pay in weeks. Because many of the Highlanders had been literally pressed into service, they could have easily gone over to the Hanoverian camp with no impunity, particularly as many had relatives on that side. Charles, they felt, was not fighting for Scotland; he was simply trying to feather his nest by assisting France. Cumberland, however, had at least three Scottish regiments who were fighting not necessarily for him but certainly for Scotland. Besides, the Royal Army was well supplied with food from the transport vessels that lay off the coast and from the cattle they had driven north. Thus, that men defected to Cumberland's camp on the night of April 15 must be considered.

These defectors would have told Cumberland that one-half of the Jacobite army was to fall upon tents, sword in hand, and seize the armory, while the other was to attack the horses and either kill them or set them loose. Mounted dragoons were the most the Highlanders had to fear, but without their horses dragoons were useless in combat. Such a plan suggested that the Highlanders would have given no quarter, vastly outnumbered as they were and making a guerrilla attack by night.

Whether Cumberland gleaned these and other details from Jacobite deserters or from his own intelligence sources, his men assembled on Drummossie Moor were so fired up that they could barely wait to deny quarter. When O'Sullivan saw the Duke of Cumberland's army stretched out before him, he rode white-faced back to Culloden House, where he found that "there was no body to give orders, & none given." He stated at one point that Charles told him to take command, and it appears he did so. But when he presumed to give gratuitous advice to Lord George and the general huffily inquired if he was taking command, O'Sullivan backed down. Actually more concerned with retreat than with fighting, O'Sullivan ordered tumbrel carts to be burned on a bridge over the river so that the enemy could not follow, and he put more energy into plotting an escape route in those frantic hours than he ever gave to how the exhausted clansmen were to fight the massive array waiting on Drummossie Moor. To be fair to O'Sullivan, he initially had no idea that the men would be fighting that day. He assumed, as everyone else did, that they would be beating a hasty retreat.

Charles was in a murderous mood, but his fire was more against the Scots who would not do his bidding than against the enemy. He was being thwarted; he was being disobeyed. Events had not come to pass as he had expected, and it was everyone else's fault. Muttering imprecations of "traitor" and "betrayer" under his whisky breath and declaring that the Scottish nation was made up of treacherous people, he insisted on nothing less than fighting that day.

Keppoch and Lochiel begged him to reconsider, and even the French "Ambassador" d'Eguilles pleaded with the Prince. "I threw myself at his feet," the Marquis reported to Louis XV. "In vain I represented to him that he was still without half his army; that the great part of those who had returned no longer had their targets . . . that they were all worn out with fatigue . . . and for two days many had not eaten at all for want of bread. In the end, finding him immovable in the resolve he had taken to fight at any cost . . . I retired in haste to Inverness, there to burn all my papers and there to think over the means of preserving your Majesty that portion of his troops which might survive the action."

Lord George was tight-lipped on the issue of whether to fight, but he spoke up when he learned that he was again to take the right hand in battle. Far from being an honor, the right-wing position would place his men hard upon the stone wall enclosure of Leanach pastures on Drummossie Moor, leaving no room for maneuvering. For before them lay a boggy incline filled with mud, which was increasing rapidly with the falling rain. He begged leave to reconnoiter the ground further, but Charles, who had assumed command of this battle and had appointed O'Sullivan deputy commander, curtly refused to allow him to.

The Royal Army was so sure of victory that day that officers' wives drove in gilt coaches to observe the battle as if it were a picnic. Of the fourteen thousand soldiers Cumberland brought to the field, probably only three thousand were engaged in actual battle; that was all that was considered necessary. About fifteen hundred Jacobites drew up in line to meet them; their forces were supplemented by local blacksmiths, shopkeepers, farmers, boys, and anyone Charles's scouts could press into service.

Cumberland's guns began a far-flighted cannonade. Balls flew over the Highlanders' heads and reached the position Charles had taken in the rear. One ball decapitated his groom, a man named Daw; evidence suggests that the Prince then withdrew, surrounded by FitzJames Horse.

One or two of the accounts written for James state that the Prince rode up and down the ranks spurring his men on, but it must be remembered that these accounts were penned by impoverished men hoping for pensions from the exiled King. There is no evidence whatsoever that Charles witnessed the Battle of Culloden. Not one man of the Royal Army ever saw him that day. Of his own admission O'Sullivan said he told O'Shea: "yu see all is going to pot. Yu can be of no great succour, so before a general deroute wch will soon be, Seize upon the Prince & take him off." Apparently the ball from the initial cannonade that decapitated Daw also struck the Prince's horse in the shoulder so that with "kicks & cappors he's oblidged to change horses." As Charles rode away, Lord Elcho was reported to have called after him that he was "a damned cowardly Italian!" That particular story has never been substantiated, but if the Prince left early, as is likely, it would explain why the front line of the Jacobite army faced the full force of the now-adjusted range of cannon fire without orders to attack. As their comrades' bodies fell in heaps, the men waited with rage and fury on their faces, but no order to attack came from the Prince.

It is assumed that Lord George Murray finally ordered the attack after his men had faced a full twenty minutes of grapeshot and ball that "swept the field as with a hail storm." From the right the Jacobite army was drawn up with Lord George's three regiments of the Atholl Brigade, taking in Robertsons, Menzies, Rattrays, Mercers under Lord Nairne, Stewarts of Appin, Maclarens, Murrays, Camerons under Lochiel, and Lord Lovat's Frasers, led by Inverallochy. In the center were Lady Mackintosh's men under MacGillivray, Macleans of Drimmin, MacLachlans, MacLeods of Raasay, Farquharsons, Chisholms, and John Roy Stuart's regiment. The left wing, commanded by the Duke of Perth, was made up of MacDonalds of Clanranald and MacDonalds (or MacDonells) of Keppoch, Glencoe, and Glengarry, with a few Mackenzies of Seaforth and Grants of Glen Urquhart and Glen Moriston, plus what was left of the Gordons of Glenbucket, MacGregors, and the regiments of Lords Lewis Gordon, Ogilvy, Elcho, Balmerino, Pitsligo, Strathallan, Kilmarnock, Lord John Drummond, and the Irish Picquets under Brigadier Stapleton.

The Duke of Perth ordered the MacDonalds forward on the left wing, but they refused to enter the hail of metal projectiles from Cumberland's cannons. Lord John Drummond came up, but neither could prevail upon the men to move. Some threw themselves onto the ground, while others broke rank and fled. Only the center section charged forward, led by the heroic Colonel MacGillivray of Dunmaglas.

The Highlanders' usual method of fighting was to discharge one shot from their musket, then throw it away and run upon the enemy with sword in hand before the enemy could reload their firelocks. On this day it was thought that the rain would prevent the Royal Army from firing their pieces at all, but they had kept the powder dry under their coat lapels. The Campbells on the government side kept up an exceptionally steady fire; the wind behind their backs blew sulphur and smoke in the Highlanders' direction. Some Highlanders said they could not even see the enemy through the smoke until the legs of the front-line troops appeared before them, closing in for attack. Dunmaglas's charge veered to the right, crowding the Atholl Brigade, which was already hampered by the wall of the Leanach enclosure. So the force bearing down on the Royal Army's left wing was "in a Sort of a mob, without any order or distinction of Corps." The congestion was so great, said Maxwell of Kirkconnell, that the men threw their muskets away— there was no room to discharge them.

On the other side of the Leanach enclosure, Major James Wolfe's royal regiment opened fire on the Jacobites, who had been herded together like cattle. Dunmaglas's standard bearer was shot dead, and Stewart of Killiechassie, under Lord Nairne's command, lost thirty out of thirty-three men in his company. Nairne's brother, Robert Mercer of Aldie, and his young son, a mere child, were killed; their bodies were never found. Still the Highlanders went on. The Camerons and Atholl Brigade charged the Royal Army's Barrel's regiment and the Munros, who had fled at Falkirk. "Like Wildcats their Men came down in Swarms upon our Left Wing," wrote one of Cumberland's soldiers, "and began to cut and Hack in their natural way without ceremony." But Cumberland's men had been ordered to wait until the Highlanders were within thirty yards. They then fired a volley that dropped the Camerons and Murrays in their tracks. The government soldiers engaged in close combat with those left standing, executing their new bayonet drill to perfection.

Barrel's regiment fell back and split in two, allowing the charging Highlanders to mingle with them. Lord Robert Kerr is said to have run the first Cameron Highlander through with his bayonet, but he was instantly cut down by Gillies MacBean of the Mackintosh regiment, "his head being cleft from crown to collarbone." Lieutenant Colonel Robert Rich, commander of Barrel's, lost his left hand at the wrist to a broadsword, and minutes afterward his right arm was severed at the elbow.

Another of Cumberland's soldiers wrote:

> The Highlanders fought like furies and Barrel's behaved like so many heroes. It was dreadful to see the enemies' swords circling in the air as they were raised from the strokes: And no less to see the officers of the army, some cutting with their swords, others pushing with their spontoons, the sergeants running their halberts into the throats of the opponents, the men ramming their fixed bayonets up to the sockets.

As Barrel's regiment formed two parallel flanks, Munro's and Bligh's regiments moved in to surround the Highlanders, forming a square. "No one that attacked us escaped alive," said one Munro officer, "for we gave no quarter nor would accept of any." Another regiment was ordered in by Cumberland. The carnage was now almost total. The Highlanders were mown down without mercy until dead bodies lay in heaps of three and four deep. Those left standing with no weapons "in their fury and despair threw stones for at least a minute or two before the total rout began."

Barely any of the approximately five hundred men who penetrated Cumberland's lines made it out alive. The wounded were dispatched by bayonets as they lay on the ground. When the MacDonalds refused to fight, Keppoch is said to have drawn his sword, crying, "O my God, has it come to this, that the children of my tribe have forsaken me!" He and his brother Donald ran toward the enemy lines. Donald was the first to be shot down. Then Keppoch fell when a ball shattered his arm, and one of Clanranald's men begged the chieftain not to throw his life away. But Keppoch would go on. He was felled a second time, then rose once more to receive a final bullet in the back. An English officer ran Lord Strathallan through with his sword when Strathallan's horse failed under him, and Lord Kilmarnock was about to suffer a similar fate when Lord Ancrum of the opposition recognized him and saved his life. Kilmarnock may rather have died on the battlefield, for he was taken to London with Lord Balmerino and beheaded on Tower Hill on August 18.

Miraculously, Lord George emerged unscathed, as did Lord Nairne and Stuart of Ardshiel. But nineteen officers and fully half of the entire Atholl Brigade lay dead on the field. Lochiel was carried to a hut after both ankles were broken by grapeshot; his brother, Archibald, was also wounded. MacDonald of Scotus, one of the early joiners, and twenty of his men were killed, as were many other MacDonald officers who braved the field when their clansmen refused to.

The men of FitzJames Horse who had not gone off with the Prince stayed to cover the retreat of the army to Inverness. They were commanded by the valiant Brigadier Stapleton, who rescued many of the wounded from being butchered as they tried to crawl away. Even some of the women camp followers were bayoneted as they picked their way through the bodies looking for their husbands or sons. Stapleton was mortally wounded by grapeshot and died a few days later of his injuries.

Elcho and his major, Kirkconnell, took little part in the action. It appears that they were held in reserve to cover the retreat. Some accounts say that Charles witnessed men fleeing and tried to make them return, but others say he was some distance away at the ford of Faillie over the River Nairn, intending to make for Fraser country. Lord Elcho saw him there after the battle "in a deplorable state." Charles asked only about the Irish officers and never about the Scots because he was obsessed by the idea that they would betray him for the 30,000-pound price on his head! Elcho also said the the Prince had set two Irish officers to spy on Lord George to watch for treacherous conduct; but all accounts state that the Jacobite general fought like a hellion along with the rest of his men.

In retreat, some of Cumberland's soldiers let those Jacobites pass who stayed in a body together; but those who returned singly to the battlefield in search of friends and relatives fell victim to government soldiers who had been reserved as backup troops and had not yet tasted blood. Maclean of Drimmin was cut down when he went looking for his sons, as was Gillies MacBean, who had split Lord Kerr's head open with his broadsword. Officers of the Menzies, Fraser, Chisholm, and MacLachlan clans fell, while others who had taken refuge in a barn were burned alive. As one government soldier said, the moor "was covered with blood, and our men, what with killing the enemy, dabbling their feet in the blood, and splashing it about one another, looked like so many butchers." The official government casualties were fifty killed, 259 wounded, and one missing. Not all the Jacobite wounded were killed on the field; many were taken prisoner. Five hundred and fifty-eight French and Scots were rounded up at Inverness; the rest lay dead on Drummossie Moor. It is not known how many escaped, but very few did.

Charles fell back on Sheridan and his Irish officers for advice as to what to do next. There was not one single Scotsman with him. "He was in total prostration, lost to all hope of being able to retrieve his affairs, having his mind completely imbued with the evil counsels of Sherridan and other Irishmen, who governed him at their will, and giving up every design but that of saving himself in France as soon as he possibly could." So wrote the Chevalier de Johnstone, who also claimed that Elcho and Lord George Murray tried to persuade Charles to rally the army "and try once more his fortune." This could hardly have happened; Lord George himself knew all was lost. It is likely that everyone was deeply distressed by the Prince's conduct in view of all his haughty airs and brave speeches about conquering or dying sword in hand. "All the world has regretted that the Prince did not fall as Keppoch fell, leaving an unblemished fame," wrote historian Andrew Lang in 1900, "that he did not ride back, if it were alone . . . and die with glory."

Instead, Charles rode to Gortuleg (now Gorthlick), twenty miles away from Culloden, and met up with Lord Lovat of Fraser for the first time. This meeting may or may not have been prearranged; the Prince was welcome to stay only that one night. Although Lovat had sent some of his Frasers to join Charles's army, he himself had not come out. This later made no impact on the government, however, when they caught up with the wily old chieftain. He was beheaded in London in April of 1747.

Meanwhile, Charles issued a number of confusing instructions from Gortuleg to those who had fought at Culloden. Lord George and the chieftains were told to go to Ruthven in Badenoch (not be be confused with the Ruthven where barracks were attacked the previous year) and await the Prince. That same evening Charles wrote a letter to Cluny MacPherson, who had not appeared at Culloden. Charles called the day's events a mere "ruffle" and told him to hasten with his clan, not to Ruthven but to Fort Augustus—which had been taken earlier by the Jacobites—and to appear there on April 18. Two or three days later, Lord George learned from Cluny the contents of his dispatch from the Prince, and he guessed immediately what was afoot.

In his paranoid belief that he would be betrayed by Scots, Charles had sent conflicting orders to the leaders; he fully expected that they would be leaked to the government. He had no intention of appearing either at Ruthven or at Fort Augustus but had already struck off westward across the mountains on foot with O'Sullivan and a recent Irish arrival, Colonel Felix O'Neill. The Prince was hoping to find French ships waiting for him on the coast or in the Outer Isles. He issued the conflicting orders in a selfish bid to buy time to cover his tracks and make his escape. As Lord George dryly observed, the orders had been sent "to cover H.R.H. from being pursued, which I wish it had taken effect. . . ."

Young Michael Sheridan was sent to the surviving chieftains of Culloden on April 16 to tell them to go to Ruthven. He accompanied them part of the way before leaving on some pretense. He had also brought money for food, but on April 18, upon orders either from Sir Thomas or from the Prince, Young Sheridan went back to Ruthven, retrieved the money, and then rejoined the Prince. There is no evidence whatsoever that Young Sheridan had any choice in this act.

The reason Charles gave for his disappearance was that he believed the Scots would try to collect the reward on his head. Yet in all the months that the reward had been offered, no one had made any attempt to collect it; nor did they in all the dreadful months that followed.

Lord George Murray never saw the Prince again, although he made one last parting shot in a letter he wrote the day after the Battle of Culloden. He wrote it before he realized that he and the others had been used to cover Charles's escape; this accounts for its remarkably restrained tone under the circumstances. Doubts have been raised about whether the Prince actually received the letter because its contents are usually quoted from a copy in the possession of the present Duke of Atholl. But another copy exists in the Stuart Papers* that leaves no room to doubt the Prince

---

* *Stuart Papers at Windsor Castle, Vol. 273, fo. 96.*

received it. He did not, however, reply to Lord George. After all was said and done, he was powerless to make any responsible answer to the charges laid at his door.

May it please your Royal Highness:

As no person in these kingdoms ventured more franckly in the cause than myself and as I had more at stake than almost all the others put together, so to be sure I cannot but be very deeply affected with our late loss and present situation, but I declare that were your R.H. person in safety, the loss of the cause and the misfortunate and unhappy situation of my countrymen is the only thing that grieves me, for I thank God, I have resolution to bear my own and family's ruine without a grudge.

Sr., you will I hope upon this occasion pardon me if I mention a few truths which all the Gentlemen of our army seem convinced of.

It was highly wrong to have set up the royal standard without having positive assurance from his most Christian majesty that he would assist you with all his force, and as your royal family lost the crown of these realms upon the account of France, the world did and had reason to expect that France would seize the first favorable opportunity to restore your August family.

I must also acquaint your R.H. that we were all fully convinced that Mr. O'Sullivan whom your R.H. trusted with the most essential things with regard to your operations was exceedingly unfit for it and committed gross blunders on every occasion of moment: He whose business it was, did not so much as visit the ground where we were to be drawn up in line of battle, and it was a fatal error yesterday to allow the enemy those walls upon their left which made it impossible for us to break them, and they with their front fire and flanking us when we went upon the attack destroyed us without any possibility of our breaking them, and our Atholl men have lost a full half of their officers and men. I wish Mr. O'Sullivan had never got any other charge in the army than the care of the bagage which I have been told he had been brought up to and understood. I never saw him in time of Action neither at Gladsmuir, Falkirk nor in the last, and his orders were vastly confused.*

The want of provisions was another misfortune which had the most fatal consequence. Mr. Hay whom Y.R.H. trusted with the principal direction of ordering provisions of late and without whose orders a boll of meal or farthing of monie was not to be delivered, has served Y.R.H. egregiously ill. When I spoke to him, he told me, the thing is ordered, it will be got etc but he neglected

---

* *Jacobites referred to the Battle of Prestonpans as the Battle of Gladsmuir.*

his duty to such a degree that our ruin might probably been prevented had he done his duty: in short the three last days which were so critical our army was starved. This was the reason our night march was rendered abortive when we possibly might have surprized and defeat the enemy at Nairn, but for want of provisions a third of the army scattered to Inverness and the others who marched had not spirits to make it so quick as was necessary being really faint for want of provisions.

The next day, which was the fatal day, if we had got plenty of provisions, we might have crossed the water of Nairn and drawn up so advantageously that we would have obliged the enemy to come to us, for they were resolved to fight at all hazards, at prodigious disadvantage, and probably we would in that case have done by them as they unhappily have done by us.

In short Mr. O'Sullivan & Mr. Hay had rendered themselves odious to all our army and had disgusted them to such a degree that they had bred a mutiny in all ranks that had not the battle come on they were to have represented their grievance to Y.R.H. for a remedy. For my own part I never had any particular discussion with either of them, but I ever thought them uncapable & unfit to serve in the stations they were placed in.

Y.R.H. knows I always told I had no design to continue in the army: I would of late when I came last from Atholl have resigned my commission, but all my friends told me it might be of prejudice to the cause at such a critical time. I hope your R.H. will now accept of my demission. What commands you have for me in any other situation please honor me with them. I am with great zeal Sr., Your R.H. most dutifull & humble servant

Signed, George Murray

Ruthven 17th April 1746

I have taken the liberty to keep 500 pieces which shant be disposed upon except you give leave.

Lord George's remarks in this letter about Hay and O'Sullivan have often been quoted, but the third paragraph, accusing Charles of wrongfully setting up the standard without assurances from France, has usually been omitted by writers and historians, all of whom believed the Prince had been invited to France and that his Scottish enterprise was backed by that country. Therefore, Lord George's comments on that subject have been ignored or at best regarded as sour grapes on his part.

We now know the well-kept secret of 240 years—that France neither invited Charles nor financed him. The question is: How did Lord George find out? The most logical answer is through Sir James Steuart of Goodtrees in Paris, to whom Marischal must have revealed many of his suspicions. Steuart must have then written warning letters to Elcho and others, who passed the information on to Lord George. James was complaining in Rome that neither Marischal nor Goodtrees was answering his letters at this time. He seemed to be more than a little concerned about what they had discovered—and how they had discovered it.

Charles traveled from Gortuleg along the shores of Loch Ness through Invergarry and reached Borrodale Farm on April 23; it was near Arisaig on the western coast, where he landed nine months before. He left Sir Thomas behind. The old man had been in no condition to make the arduous journey over wild mountainous territory; it had to be accomplished at great speed in order to reach the French ships that O'Brien said would be sent to the coast. In a letter dated April 23 (written for him by Hay of Restalrig), Charles told Sheridan that he was "still of the same opinion we have traitors among us which has made me take my party." He enclosed an address for the chiefs, to be shown them "when you think proper only I think the longer you can defer showing it the better."

In the address to the chiefs, Charles stated grandiosely that when he came to Scotland, his only view had been to do all in his power for their good and safety. "But alas! I see with grief, I can at present do little for you on this side of the water, for the only thing that can now be done is to defend your selves till the French assist you"! He said he was going to France instantly, "however danger-ous it may be," to persuade the French Court either to assist them "effectually and powerfully" or at least to procure them such terms as "you would not obtain otherways." This was sheer nonsense. France had done little if anything and certainly had no power to bargain for the prisoners awaiting execution and depor-tation. The Marquis d'Eguilles had secured a cartel for the Irish and French, but there would be no mercy for the Scots.

However much he tried to deceive himself—and the fatuous phrases used by this untrained youth constantly irritated grown men—Charles was literally running away, and to many of the old-time Jacobites, history seemed to be repeating itself. This was exactly what James had done in 1716. The Prince continued at length in the address trying to explain his departure to the chiefs. They had apparently been talking among themselves and had hit on the truth of the matter. "It is thought to be a Politick," said

Charles, "tho' a false one, of the French court, not to restore our Master, but to keep a continual civil war in this Country, which renders the English government less powerfull and, of consequence, themselves more. This is absolutely destroyed by my leaving this Country, which nothing else but this will persuade them that this Play cannot last."

There seems to be a contradiction here. If the "politick" was false, why did Charles think it necessary to put a stop to the "Play"? And if he recognized that the French were furthering civil war in Britain, why had he lent himself to their schemes? Charles may have been trying to convince the chiefs that he was being noble by leaving, but they were solidly behind Lord George Murray, who was wondering why the Prince had come to Scotland in the first place.

There is no evidence that any of the chiefs received the Prince's address; moreover, it is highly doubtful that Sheridan would have distributed such a conceited and self-contradictory document. The cover letter contained a last sentence written in the Prince's own hand telling Sheridan to "Follow me as soon as you think it Convenient. Adieu. Charles P.R."

Sir Thomas never saw the Prince again. With Hay of Restalrig, Lord Elcho, Lord John Drummond, the Duke of Perth (who died at sea), and some others, Sheridan escaped to France on May 3 aboard the *Mars*, one of two ships sent by the French to Scotland. The heartbroken old man was then summoned to Rome by James, although he was reluctant to return. There he died the following November.

Charles missed the *Mars* and her companion ship, the *Bellona*, when they arrived at Loch nan Uamh on April 30. He was so terrified of betrayal or arrest that he had fled to the island of South Uist with O'Sullivan and Felix O'Neill, hoping to gain protection from the Clanranald MacDonalds. According to a letter written by O'Brien, the *Mars* and the *Bellona* were sent by the French in early April—the first real assistance—not to take men away but to bring money to sustain the rebellion. Between the two ships was a total of 1,200,000 louis d'or; but when the captains heard that all was lost at Culloden, they left only 400,000 louis d'or, the papal money from Spain that had been accumulating in Paris until a safe method could be found for transporting it. The coins were landed in seven caskets. One was stolen by MacDonald of Barrisdale's men, and the remainder were transported inland to Loch Arkaig, where they were delivered to Murray of Broughton, now apparently recovered from his illness.

When Murray was apprehended by the government, the Treasure of Loch Arkaig, as it became known, was transferred to Lochiel and his brother, then to Cluny MacPherson, who had taken refuge in a hidden cave on Ben Alder with some of his clansmen. Only the men who buried it knew precisely where the money was. In the transferral, much of the money disappeared, and Charles later accused Cluny of embezzling it. The Treasure of Loch Arkaig was the source of bitter feuds and quarrels for years to come; some may still lie underground in a forgotten place.*

Just before the Prince had fled to the Outer Hebrides, the government retook Fort Augustus and strengthened Fort William. Lord Loudon, in command of soldiers in Skye, was ordered to proceed to the mainland via Arisaig and Moidart, laying bare the land as he went. Many of the clans were on the verge of turning in their arms. Glengarry's men had already given themselves up at Fort Augustus. The people who assisted the Prince during his flight had been awaiting reprisals from the government ever since Culloden. Those who were suspected merely of tending the wounded or of giving shelter to refugees from the battlefield were shot or had their houses burned and their cattle driven off. As the Redcoats moved in bands through the hills and glens, they pillaged, raped, and systematically destroyed everything in their path. The atrocities were not committed solely by English officers, as has often been reported, however. By far the worst offenders were soldiers under the command of some of the Lowland Scots officers.

The Jacobite prisoners at Inverness were treated like animals. Several were manacled together so tightly that the metal sank deep into their flesh and could not be seen. Doctors and surgeons were forbidden to treat them, and they died of gangrene. Those who still showed signs of life after their bodies were hauled in cartloads from the battlefield were unceremoniously dispatched by a bullet in the head or a blade to the throat. The prisoners were asked to deny their belief in the right of the Stuarts to occupy the throne. Although most of them did, they were still summarily executed.

Those who survived were transported to England aboard

---

* About thirty years ago, gold Spanish coins were found in the hoofs of cattle in the Loch Arkaig area. It is believed that these were part of the hoard landed for the Prince's use.

prison ships. One anonymous survivor said that at least six or seven times a day, bodies were weighted with stones and tossed overboard whether alive or dead. These men may have been granted a favor, because butchery at Kennington Common awaited many. Some with money or influential connections were able to buy pardons, but most could not. Those who were still able-bodied when they reached London were shipped farther south to Tilbury Fort at the mouth of the Thames, there to await transportation to the American colonies.*

The Duke of Cumberland received news that the Belgian cities of Tournai and Hainault, which were of vital importance to the British forward defense system on the Continent, were in danger of falling into French hands. Cursing his cousin Charles for forcing him to withdraw valuable troops from the Continental theater of war, Cumberland immediately made plans to go to Flanders—too late, as it happened, to save Tournai or Hainault. Those cities fell to Marshal Saxe in May and June.

Before he left Scotland, Cumberland placed the search for the Prince in charge of William Keppel, the 2nd Earl of Albemarle, the son of a Dutchman who had served William of Orange. Albemarle was an old, gouty soldier with an acid temperament who had had a command at Cumberland's front line during the Battle of Culloden. Denied service on the Continent, which was where he wished to be, Albemarle came to passionately hate Scotland and the Scots, and he increased the atrocities with renewed vigor. Writing about the prisoners in a letter to the Duke of Newcastle in London, Albemarle stated that he wished from his heart that "His Majesty had ordered the whole to be executed the same day." His mood and the mood of his soldiers was of mounting wrath; it increased with each day the Prince remained at large, for it bespoke of "convincing proof of the disaffection of that great part of the country" in which they intended "to root out if possible even the very name of Jacobitism and Rebellion."

If Charles had waited on the mainland of Scotland for the French ships, it would have prevented much rampage, rape, murdering, and marauding. As it was, his hiding in the outer islands led to even more misery for the Highlanders over the course of the next five months.

* *The Reverend Robert Forbes, Bishop of Ross and Caithness, later collected stories from eyewitnesses and survivors, then assembled them into three volumes for the Scottish History Society called* The Lyon in Mourning.

Chapter 11

Over the Sea to Skye

Donald MacLeod of Gualtergill, in Skye, was as fine an island boatman as anyone could find. For most of his seventy years he had made his living by piloting ships and fishing in the Sea of the Hebrides, which runs into the waters of the Minch, separating the Hebridean Islands from the mainland of Scotland. Skilled seamanship has always been a hallmark of Hebridean mariners, for they daily negotiate one of the most notoriously treacherous bodies of water in the world. Over the centuries the Minch has been a graveyard for countless thousands of ships and boats, sucked to the bottom by whirlpools or blown upon jagged underwater rocks by sudden gale-force winds powerful enough to sweep grazing sheep and cattle off clifftops.

Four days before the *Mars* and *Bellona* arrived, Charles learned that patrols of soldiers were searching for him only a few miles away. Increasingly impatient to escape from the mainland, he sent for Donald MacLeod of Gualtergill. He planned to make his way by sea to Stornoway, the largest port and town in Lewis, the most northerly island of the Outer Hebridean archipelago. At Stornoway, Charles hoped to hire a ship to take him to the Orkney Islands and from there to Norway, Sweden, or Denmark; then he would seek a route to France. Undoubtedly, this was why Michael Sheridan was sent to take back the money left for food for the Jacobite army. The hiring of a ship was going to be an expensive proposition.

The Prince and his party had very little clothing with them, so Charles hastily had a jacket, vest, and breeches cut in the Highland manner from a long riding coat. O'Sullivan similarly converted an old blue coat and assumed the name "Mr. Sinclair." The Prince was to masquerade as O'Sullivan's son, Young Sinclair. Colonel Felix O'Neill donned a kilt and changed his name to MacNeil. They planned to tell strangers that they were merchants who had been shipwrecked on the Isle of Tiree and were looking for a replacement vessel to continue their journey northward to the Orkney Islands. Among the members of the party was a Catholic priest, Father Allan MacDonald, and eight natives of the Outer Islands who were to act as oarsmen. According to Donald MacLeod, who gave his testimony to Bishop Forbes after he was arrested for helping the Prince, Charles was distraught. "You see, Donald, I am in distress," he said. "I therefore throw myself into your bosom, and let you do with me what you like. I hear you are an honest man, and fit to be trusted."

Charles first suggested that MacLeod take letters to Sir Alexander MacDonald of Sleat and to Macleod of MacLeod in the belief that they would help him, but Donald told the Prince this would be foolish. Both men were actively engaged with the government troops in searching for him, and they were only twelve miles away. Donald found a stout eight-oared boat; at dusk on April 26, although ominous storm clouds were gathering, they put to sea from the very spot Charles had first set foot on the mainland.

Not long after they left shore, the storm descended with thunder, lightning, and lashing rain. O'Sullivan tells us that the waves became "mountains." At every moment the boat threatened to overturn, and all hands were busily baling. The Prince was knocked flat by one wave, and O'Neill and O'Sullivan were thrown on top of him by another. As still more waves swamped the boat, they heard a cracking noise and felt sure that all was lost. Charles begged Donald to head for land, but Skye was the closest, and too many warships were riding out the storm in her harbors. Besides, it was safer to stay out at sea than risk being dashed upon the offshore rocks. Luckily the wind was behind them. Donald stoically held on to the rudder while Father MacDonald and the sailors prayed aloud for the preservation of them all.

On the morning of April 27, they were blown toward Rossinish on the desolate island of Benbecula, sandwiched in between the outer islands of North and South Uist. Near the shore they found a small shieling, typical of the temporary shelters for local fishermen and tacksmen tending sheep and cattle dotted all over the islands. Usually little more than four walls of immovable granite boulders, the structures provided a shelter area of about forty square feet. Many had no roof at all unless the shieling was used frequently, as was the one at Rossinish. Even roofless enclosures provided some protection from the wind and rain because it is a rare Hebridean rain that falls straight down; it is borne laterally by the wind with stinging speed straight over the top of roofless enclosures. From Rossinish O'Sullivan watched amazed as he saw a ship with sails furled and masts broken being scudded by the wind and disappearing beyond the horizon inside a quarter of an hour.

The men made a fire with heather to dry out their clothes and cook what food they had been able to carry with them in a chest. They had half a lamb, some meal in a leather bag, a little butter, and cheese. A wooden bowl for making bread and an iron cooking pot were "all the battery of cuisine" that survived the journey, but the pot was discovered to have a hole in the bottom. The Prince watched with amusement as one of the boatmen stopped up the hole with linen rags; the makeshift repair sufficed while they cooked the lamb. There was not enough meat for everybody, and Charles ordered the men to kill a cow near the shieling, promising to leave money for the owner.

The group stayed in Benbecula for two days waiting out the storm, then set off again in the eight-oared boat toward Stornoway. Lewis and Harris combined, known as the Long Island, constitute the largest land mass in the Outer Hebridean archipelago. Although they have two distinct names, they are not separated by water. The tiny islet of Scalpa lies off the east coast of Harris like a dislodged piece of a jigsaw puzzle. There Charles and the others were brought to stay with Donald Campbell, who was known to the boatman Donald MacLeod. They waited at Campbell of Scalpa's house while MacLeod went on to Stornoway to procure a ship.

The caution was necesary. Lewis and Harris were populated by Presbyterians; the southerly isles were Catholic. People coexisted harmoniously despite their religious differences—and still do—but Lord Seaforth's Mackenzies and the MacLeods of Lewis were very hostile toward the Stuarts. The elder Seaforth had fought in the rebellions of 1715 and 1719 and had forfeited his estates after he fled to France. He was eventually pardoned in 1726 and allowed to come home, but he had lost everything and nurtured a deep grudge against the Stuarts, a sentiment shared by many of his people. He died in 1740.

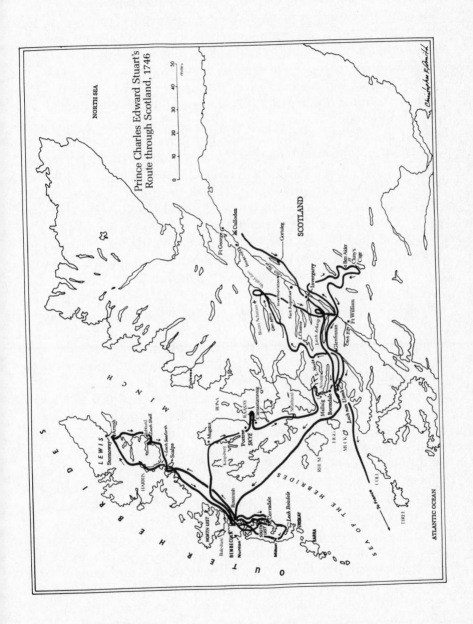

Prince Charles Edward Stuart's
Route through Scotland, 1746

Every Stuart King from Charles I to the exiled James III had made promises to these islanders in exchange for support for the Stuart cause, but the promises had never been kept. The people had also suffered government wrath when Marishchal and his Spaniards landed there in 1719. They had made up their minds that there would be no more.

Donald MacLeod had been to Stornoway many times before to buy meal for the Isle of Skye, so he had no trouble obtaining a ship on the same pretext. He then sent for the Prince, O'Neill, and O'Sullivan. With a guide and one of Clanranald's sons, who had been sent to help when they first landed in Benbecula, they rowed to the top of Loch Seaforth, running deep inland up through Harris. This was far safer than rowing along the Minch's coastline, which was by now crawling with English ships due to the appearance of the *Mars* and *Bellona* a few days before.

From the head of Loch Seaforth the party made its way by foot sixteen miles over peat bogs and rock-strewn terrain to Stornoway. They had hoped to reach the town by midnight on May 4 so that Charles could sneak aboard ship under cover of darkness to avoid being seen by government vessels in the harbor. But they lost their way "in the wildest contry in the universe." Not until daybreak on the fifth, having walked all night in a continual heavy rain, did they find themselves near Arnish, just outside Stornoway. They sent the guide to tell Donald MacLeod of their arrival and waited in the open with no shelter, unable to lift their heads because the rain lashed painfully on their faces. "I declair to you," wrote O'Sullivan, "the Prince was blew wth cold, & so was every body. The Prince was in a terrible condition seting aside cold & hunger without even complaining, he had not a Shoe to his feet, all tore to pieces, they held only with coards . . . his toes were quit stript."

From Stornoway, Donald sent the guide back to Charles with food and brandy and the message that they were to go to the house of Mrs. Mackenzie of Kildun, near Arnish, for safety. A kindly woman, she gave Charles a blanket that he carried for the rest of his travels, some warm milk, eggs, butter, biscuits, and whisky. She also offered the men a clean bed so that they could sleep for a while. They could not possibly stay, however. The whole town of Stornoway was in an uproar because the Hebridean grapevine had brought word that MacLeod was procuring a ship to carry the Prince to France. A hundred and fifty townsmen had armed themselves and were prepared to fight. Rumors grew out of proportion; it was even being said that Charles had come to Lewis with a band of five hundred men to plunder the island. Hostility was so rife that two of MacLeod's original eight boatmen took off, wanting nothing further to do with the Prince.

At this same time, the *Bellona* and the *Mars*, with Sheridan, Michael Sheridan, Hay, Elcho, Lord John Drummond, and the Duke of Perth on board, were engaged in naval combat with H.M.S. *Greyhound* and *Baltimore* at the mouth of Loch nan Uamh. The French ships were able to outgun the smaller English vessels and eventually managed to limp away to France after a furious battle.

From Arnish the party left Lewis in the rowboat, hugging the coast to stay out of sight of warships in the Minch, which Charles mistakenly fancied were French. But the boatmen recognized them as English vessels. In order to avoid capture, they hid on the tiny uninhabited island of Iubhard at the mouth of Loch Shell, which was used by Lewis and Harris fishermen to wind-dry piles of herring, cod, ling, and kelp. Shelter was an unroofed enclosure this time, but between Macleod and Mrs. Mackenzie they had obtained a good store of brandy, tobacco, several pairs of shoes, sugar, and a butchered cow. As they sat drinking brandy by the fireside, Charles struck up boastful talk about marrying the King of France's daughter and constantly drank to her health. Macleod's report to Bishop Forbes said Charles spoke affectionately about Louis and was confident that he would be able to assist him. The Prince would have everybody believe he was friend and confidant of the King of France and that he had actually met him and the Dauphin. It was not the first time he had told such stories.

They stayed in Iubhard until May 10 and then returned to Scalpa. There they found that Campbell had left his house because he was unwilling to harbor the Prince any longer. So they sailed to Benbecula, dodging warships all the way, with not much more for sustenance than meal and salt water. Charles had tried his hand at making oatmeal cakes with the brains of Mrs. Mackenzie's cow and spoiled butter, and they did catch crabs by the seashore at Benbecula; but their diet brought on bleeding gums and dysentery, described by O'Sullivan as the "bloody flux."

From Benbecula a messenger was sent to Clanranald, who came with food, spirits, and changes of clothing, for the garments they wore were stiff as buckram from the salt water. When a company of independent militia arrived on the island in the first week in June, the fugitives took refuge at Glen Corradale in South

Uist, but they had to keep away from the coast because ships looking for the Prince came to several nearby lochs. The local inhabitants, however, did nothing to assist these search parties.

For a while Charles was safe at Corradale. He diverted himself with fishing and shooting muircocks and hens found all over the island. It was here that Charles heard about the landing of the caskets of gold. He sent Donald to the mainland with a letter for Murray of Broughton requesting money, current news, and, of course, brandy. Murray had not yet been arrested, and he had already disbursed a considerable amount of the gold to the chiefs and to those trying to escape to France, reserving a hefty amount for himself and his wife. The rest had been placed in the care of Lochiel and Cluny.

Donald returned to Corradale with no money, but because he knew that the Prince could not exist from day to day without liquor, he brought back two ankers of brandy (about five gallons), which he had purchased for a guinea each. It was here that Charles heard from MacDonald of Boisdale that Sheridan had managed to get away to France. He appeared to utterly disbelieve that the ships had left without looking for him and that Sir Thomas had seemingly deserted him.

The Prince received visitors at Corradale. One was Hugh MacDonald of Baleshare in North Uist (Campbell of Scalpa's brother-in-law). His account describes a drinking session with the Prince and others that lasted for three days and three nights. Baleshare was staggered by the amount of liquor Charles consumed. He had always reckoned MacDonald of Boisdale to be the most able "bowlman," or drinker, in Scotland, but Baleshare said the Prince got the better even of the champion toper.

Lady Margaret MacDonald of Sleat, who was also in communication with the Prince, sent gifts of clothing, newspapers, and fifty guineas from Skye, and Lady Clanranald sent several shirts and a silver cup from her home in Benbecula. MacDonald of Baleshare tells us Charles's new Highland clothes consisted of a tartan shortcoat and vest, a short kilt, tartan hose, Highland brogues, and a night cape. All his vestments, including his shirt, and his hands and face were covered with sooty stains, possibly from gunpowder burns. As Baleshare said, the Prince shot literally dozens of birds on the wing each day, "scarce ever making a miss."

The relatively pleasant days of "skulking," as Highlanders called roaming around the countryside, were marred by Charles's bloody flux, "which kept him pretty busie while it lasted." Although sick himself, O'Sullivan became "frightened out of his witts" when the Prince's dysentery persisted. Charles gave up drinking milk, saying it was causing his dysentery; but nothing helped the ulcerous sores that were beginning to form chiefly on the legs and thighs. The scurvy symptom of bleeding gums appeared, and it is highly likely that the Prince lost some teeth. He began to use the sailors' old remedy of tobacco, according to a report from Dr. John Burton, who saw the Prince two months later: "Having been so much afflicted with the Toothach in his wanderings, he was oblidged to smoke, to obtain some Mitigation of his Pain."

The authorities were well aware of the general vicinity of the fugitive's whereabouts; the cordon of soldiers around the fifty-mile stretch taking in the islands of Barra, South Uist, Benbecula, and North Uist was growing tighter and tighter. MacLeods and MacDonalds who had not come out for the Prince had formed independent companies for the government, and there were already several encampments in the neighborhood as well as warships patrolling the waters. The *Baltimore* and *Raven* had sailed into Loch Boisdale, and the *Tryal* was lying off Barra. The prison ship *Furnace*, commanded by the Jacobite-hating Captain John Ferguson, a naval officer from Aberdeen, was also in the vicinity.

The plan was to disembark troops under the command of the notoriously cruel Lowlander Captain Caroline Scott, who had been merciless in his hounding of Highlanders. He and Ferguson had lain waste entire islands lying off the mainland, burning homes and driving cattle away. Overall command of the hunt for Prince Charles in the islands was given to Major General John Campbell of Mamore. He was a humane man, but Scott and Ferguson committed several atrocities before Mamore put a stop to their rampages.

Boisdale was one of the first to be arrested in South Uist and taken aboard the *Furnace* for questioning. Lady Boisdale was confined to her house; she had been sending food and clothing to the Prince. Captain Scott sent her a note that he would call on her the next day, and she passed the word to Charles, saying that she would inform him of everything that took place. When nothing was heard from Lady Boisdale, a messenger was dispatched to find out what had happened. He found Lady Boisdale, her daughters, and all the members of the household bound hand and foot, and he was told that Scott's men had carried off every valuable in the house.

As a result of this outrage, some members of the independent companies of militia, many of whose relatives had suffered house burnings by Scott and Ferguson, now decided to hamper the government troops by any means possible. Hugh MacDonald of Armadale, a fiercely proud captain of one of the independent companies, had already quietly determined to do everything he could to see that the Prince escaped, and there is evidence that he met secretly with Charles.

From somewhere Charles's party acquired a tent. It had just been taken down at Corradale on the morning of June 20 when a man came running down the hill with the news that all the rowboats from seven men o' war anchored at the mouth of Loch Boisdale were making toward land laden with soldiers. Scott's men were said to number seven hundred; he had dispatched 150 of them to kill all the cattle on the island. Some were searching houses for arms and the Prince, while others were looking for the Spanish gold they had heard was hidden near Boisdale's home.

According to O'Sullivan, everyone panicked except the Prince (but then, the Irishman made Charles out to be the hero at all times in his written report for James). The boatmen immediately wanted to make a frantic dash west to the far end of Loch Boisdale ahead of the oncoming soldiers and from there escape across the hills to the west side of the island. But Charles would not rush: " 'A Gad,' says the Prince, 'they shall never say yt we abandoned our meat,' & goes him self & takes a quarter of mutton & a boul of meal yt was left, & wch was by the by, all we had left of the meal."

The messenger's warning gave them enough time to reach the top of Loch Boisdale and cross over the mountains before they could be surrounded. There Charles took leave of everyone except Felix O'Neill and a guide. The smaller the party, the faster they could move, and the Prince and O'Neill were the only ones wearing Highland clothes. When Charles took O'Sullivan aside to bid him farewell, unabashed tears streamed down the Irishman's face. Giving him one hundred guineas, Charles told O'Sullivan to stay close to the boatmen to prevent them from dispersing in case he should need them to get across to Skye. Pointing to a hill named Sheaval, the Prince told O'Sullivan the guide would take him and O'Neill to a place where he could hide safely for a while. This had been arranged beforehand with Hugh MacDonald of Armadale. Charles's plan was to have Lady Clanranald make women's clothing for him so that he could escape in disguise from South Uist across to the Isle of Skye, where he hoped to be sheltered by Lady Margaret MacDonald of Sleat. Before leaving, Charles gave Donald MacLeod an order to draw sixty pistoles from Hay of Restalrig, but the latter was already in France along with the others, and Donald never did see his money.

Because the Hebrides are so far north, night does not fall for two weeks in June. There is a perpetual twilight, sometimes called the "summer dim," when the luminous northern lights of the aurora borealis can be seen in the sky. Friday, June 20, was such a night. On Sheaval, high above the village of Milton, overlooking the Atlantic on South Uist's west coast, a young lady was alone in a small shieling. Her name was Flora MacDonald, and although she had been born at Milton twenty-four years before, her home was now at Armadale, across the water in the Isle of Skye. Her mother was the daughter of a minister from South Uist, and her father, a cousin of the Chieftain Clanranald, had died when Flora was two years old. Her mother later married Hugh MacDonald of Arma- dale, the captain of the independent company who had vowed to help Charles escape. It was Flora's cousin, Neil MacEachain, who was acting as the Prince's guide.*

Flora's brother Angus had inherited the farm at Milton after his marriage. She was staying with the couple that summer, helping to take their sheep to different grazing grounds. She was by no means a simple herdsgirl, since she was considered to be "gentlefolk." She spoke both Gaelic and English and had also studied Latin and French, as did all clan hierarchy. Flora had finished her education while living with wealthy cousins on the mainland; she had a poised ladylike manner and an easy famil- iarity with the social graces. She also had strength of character and was far from shy when it came to asserting herself. Flora had escaped to Milton when Skye was thick with militia, but now that they had come to South Uist looking for Prince Charles, she was anxious to return home again.

As Flora tells the story in her journal, written some years afterward, she had taken the sheep to graze on Sheaval and was

---

Both Flora and MacEachain were descendants of Somerled, King of the South Isles from the year 1156. King Somerled was killed in 1164.

asleep. Shortly before midnight on June 20, her cousin Mac-Eachain came to the shieling door and woke her up to tell her that the Prince and O'Neill were outside and wanted to speak with her. Writing in the third person, Flora continues: "She was surprised and wanted to know what they had to say to her but went out fast as she could throw on some of her cloaths and met the collonel at the door, leaving the prince behind the hutt." (What Flora meant to say was that O'Neill had stationed Charles behind the shieling out of sight.) O'Neill asked when troops were due to pass by that way, and Flora told him it would be on Sunday—in less than forty-eight hours. O'Neill then launched into a description of Hugh MacDonald's plan for the Prince's escape to Skye. Since Flora wished to return to that island, Hugh would issue a pass for his stepdaughter to show to any guards she encountered on the way. Naturally, he would not want her to travel alone, so the pass would make provision for an accompanying maid and manservant. Mac-Eachain would fill the latter requirement. The maid was to be Charles dressed in women's clothing.

Flora was stunned. This was the first she had heard of any such plan, and she refused outright to be party to such a dangerous plot. When O'Neill, a blustering, badgering man, persisted, Flora protested that if such a dangerous cargo were conveyed to Skye, she would bring ruination to her chieftain, Sir Alexander Mac-Donald (who was then at Fort Augustus). O'Neill then told her that MacDonald's wife, Lady Margaret, had been sending brandy, shirts, and money from Skye for the past two weeks and had promised to give them protection. But still, as Flora wrote, she had "many qualms and objections." One concern was for her reputation, since she would be the only woman involved in the escapade. But O'Neill had an answer for that: He said he would marry Flora himself if she felt her honor and good name were at stake.

Flora, who had heard of Boisdale's arrest and confinement on board a prison ship, stood her ground. At this point O'Neill gave a low whistle, signaling the hidden Charles to show himself. He told Flora that even if she would not help on his account, she could hardly refuse the Prince himself. "Don't think, sir," she retorted, "that I am quite so fainthearted as that comes to."

The sight of the royal personage was hardly awe-inspiring. Charles was ragged, dirty, sunburned, and dissipated from bouts with diarrhea (and doubtless too much drinking), and his feet and legs were contused and bleeding. Ridiculously, he still clutched the periwig he had brought from France, which now housed a colony of lice. Speaking in Italian (he had seen service in Italy for the King of Spain), Colonel O'Neill related what had transpired between him and Flora. Charles turned to Flora and said he had met her stepfather when he first arrived in Scotland and thought very highly of him. He was sure that Hugh wished him well since he had promised passes for his escape, and he impressed upon the girl, who was only two years younger than himself, "the sense he would always retain of so conspicuous a service." O'Neill also assured Flora of "the honour and immortality that would redound to her by such a glorious action." Perhaps the Prince's physical distress touched Flora MacDonald, for by the time the men left her that night, she had agreed at least to speak to her stepfather on the matter.

The next day Flora journeyed northward to Benbecula, where Hugh's company was stationed, but while making the crossing from South Uist, she was promptly arrested. The soldiers happened to be in her stepfather's command, but since he was temporarily absent from the post and her identity could not be verified without a pass, Flora was placed in detention for the night. The matter was cleared up when Hugh MacDonald appeared the next morning, but the incident made Flora more reluctant than ever to be mixed up in taking the Prince to Skye. Even before the plan had gone into operation, she had been arrested by vigilant soldiers who were questioning everyone who passed from island to island. She failed to see how a tall figure sporting a few days' growth of red beard could pass for a female under close scrutiny. Rather than return to South Uist, Flora stayed in Benbecula and took refuge at Lady Clanranald's home in Nunton.

Assuming Flora MacDonald was falling in with their plans (Neil MacEachain hinted more than once that O'Neill fancied himself a ladies' man but that Flora was unimpressed), MacEachain brought Charles and O'Neill across to Benbecula on Monday, June 23, to hide in a crofter's cottage near Rossinish. By Wednesday, when they had neither eaten anything for thirty-six hours nor heard from Flora, Charles sent O'Neill to Nunton seven miles away to ask about the disguise and to see what was keeping the ladies. It would have been better to send Neil MacEachain to Nunton, but the Prince was taking no chances and was beginning to be distrustful of the Highlanders. Felix O'Neill was expendable, but Neil MacEachain knew the language and country and was the only guide Charles would have at his side should soldiers be waiting at Nunton. When Colonel O'Neill arrived at Lady Clanranald's house, he was dismayed to find that Flora had decided not to take the Prince to Skye. Instead, she suggested that the men go to MacDonald of Baleshare's house in North Uist to see if he would help them.

It was now Thursday, June 26, and Charles's physical condition was worsening. Weeping sores were opening up all over his body and face, attracting tiny black midge flies, which bite fiercely in the summer months. He was, noted MacEachain, also drinking an entire bottle of brandy each day. Vastly accelerated by the brandy, his scurvy had reached the stage where the connective tissue between the bones was so impaired that he could hardly walk. On their way to Baleshare's house on Thursday, Charles had to be supported by MacEachain and O'Neill because he "fell at almost every step in some ditch or mire." When they finally arrived, Baleshare refused to admit them, saying that there was a company of fifty government soldiers not half a mile from his house. There was nothing to do but tramp back to Benbecula.

Charles now became deeply melancholic, alternating his despondency with sudden outbursts of extreme anger. MacEachain prevailed upon him to drink milk for his condition, and the Prince agreed, provided that it was first boiled to a froth. Returning to the cottage near Rossinish, the crofter's wife obliged them by heating milk in a pot, but Charles scalded himself when he tried to drink it. Jumping up, he railed furiously at the woman, cursing her in several languages and screaming that "she contrived it a purpose that we might burn ourelves." Neil MacEachain was appalled at this and other displays of violent temper on the Prince's part.

The crofter's wife, who believed the men to be shipwrecked Irishmen, told them they would have to leave her house because the militia were in the habit of stopping by daily for milk. So they were turned out of doors in a "vehement wind" and pelting rain with no shelter in sight but granite rocks by the shore. Intermittent bursts of sunshine sometimes broke through the leaden clouds, bringing swarms of midges that were as voracious as piranhas. They were drawn to the Prince's open sores and wrung from him "hideous cries and complaints."

While MacEachain stayed with Charles, O'Neill stormed off

to Nunton, bearing a terse message for Flora "to hasten and get her affairs in readiness for going off." This time he was taking no chances. He intended to stay at Nunton until all preparations were complete. "The ladies were busy night and day making a dress for the Prince and other things," wrote MacEachain in his account, but there was no time to be lost.

On Saturday morning word came to Nunton that General Campbell of Mamore had landed with an additional fifteen hundred men, which, when added to the seven hundred commanded by Captain Scott and one hundred from the independent companies, made up a force of 2,300 soldiers to comb the 250-square-mile area of South Uist and Benbecula. Most of the troops were in Benbecula, since it was believed that the Prince had already departed South Uist. Perhaps this was how the long-awaited ship from France plucked O'Sullivan from South Uist that very day. He was near death, suffering from extreme exposure and deficiency disease. Since he had not seen Charles in eight days, he assumed the Prince was already in Skye or on the mainland. The French ship's officers, Captains Lynch and Warren, did look for Charles but could not afford to stay too long in those waters. They sailed back to France, to return to Scotland several weeks later.

On the news of Mamore's arrival, Lady Clanranald and Flora hastily put together the clothes Charles was to wear and packed a dinner of roasted bullock, heart, and liver with a few bottles of wine and set off on Saturday evening for Rossinish. The party also included Lady Clanranald's seven-year-old daughter Peggy, Flora's brother Angus, and his wife, Penelope. O'Neill had gone on ahead. Flora also carried a letter from Hugh for her mother, Marion. This was subsequently destroyed, but later Flora approved this version of what its contents had been:

My dear Marion:
I have sent your daughter from this country lest she should be in any way frightened with the troops lying here. She has got one, Betty Burke, an Irish girl, who, she tells me, is a good spinster. If her spinning please you, you can keep her till she spin all your lint, or if you have any wool to spin, you may employ her. I have sent Neil MacEachain along with your daughter and Betty Burke to take care of them.
I am, Your dutiful husband,
Hugh MacDonald.

"Betty Burke" put on a long white linen dress sprigged with lilac, a cap and apron, a quilted petticoat, and a hooded cape. A bonnet was also made for the Prince, "but he could not keep his hands from adjusting his headdress," said MacEachain, "which he cursed a thousand times." Charles tried to hide a brace of pistols under his petticoat, but Flora insisted he give them to Angus and Penelope, saying they would give him away if he were searched. The Prince retorted that if he were to be examined that closely he would be discovered anyway, but he armed himself instead with a short stout cudgel concealed under his cloak. MacLeod of Gualtergill and his boatmen had already been detained for questioning and were aboard the prison ship *Furnace*, but Flora had been able to obtain another boat, described as "a shallop of nine cubits," and four MacDonald boatmen for the crossing to Skye. Charles wanted Felix O'Neill to accompany them, but Flora, who disliked O'Neill intensely, refused to take him, saying that the colonel had no pass if they were stopped and that "she could more easily undertake the preservation of one than of two or more."

The crossing to Skye was made famous by the beautiful "Skye Boat Song":

> "Speed Bonnie Boat like a bird on the wing,
>   Onward," the sailors cry,
> "Carry the lad that's born to be king
>   Over the sea to Skye."
>
> Loud the winds howl, loud the waves roar,
>   Thunder clouds rend the air;
> Baffled our foes stand on the shore,
>   Follow they would not dare.
>
> (First verse repeated as chorus)
>
> Though the waves leap, soft shall ye sleep,
>   Ocean's a royal bed,
> Rocked in the deep, Flora will keep
>   Watch by your weary head.

It was actually the Prince who kept watch by Flora's weary head during their storm-tossed crossing of the Sea of the Hebrides. Having been up the last two nights sewing, she fell asleep while Charles sang Jacobite songs, such as "The Twenty-ninth of May" from the rising of 1715 and "The King Shall Enjoy His Own Again":

> *For who better may our high sceptre sway*
> *Than he whose right it is to reign*
> *Then look for no peace for the wars will never cease*
> *Till the King shall enjoy his own again.*

According to Flora's testimony, her cousin Neil MacEachain had been with Charles for some weeks before she first met him. His valuable account has also been preserved. Because it was not written for James, MacEachain could afford to be objective, and he was a skillful observer. Although Felix O'Neill referred to MacEachain as a "herdsboy," he was far from that. He was a talented linguist (French, English, Gaelic, Latin, and Greek) and had once studied for the priesthood but never took his vows. He eventually went to live in France, where he dropped the name MacEachain and took the name MacDonald. Neil married a French woman and fathered a boy who became Napoleon's famous Marshal MacDonald, the Duc de Tarentum.

Both Charles and Felix O'Neill underestimated MacEachain and treated him disdainfully. Charles once ordered him to swim out to sea and bring back a whale that he was sure he had shot and killed. "Neil, in obedience to his orders, and to humour him, began to strip very slowly till he saw the whale, which had received no hurt, out of sight." Another time, just before he brought Charles over from South Uist to Benbecula, high tide filled the stretch of sands between the two islands, which at low tide could be negotiated on foot. Neil tells us:

> The Prince started up like a mad man and walked to the end of the island at such a rate as if he had a mind to fly over to the other side, but his career soon stopped; whereupon he fell a scoulding Neil as if it had been his fault and the cursed rascals [Donald's boatmen] who land'd them upon that desert island designedly that he might starve with hunger and cold. In short, there was no pacifying him, till, at last, Neil told him to comfort himself, that he would sweem over to the other side and would bring a boat in half-an-hours time. From that moment he never gave Neil one minute's rest, till, to please him, he began to strip, notwithstanding that it rained most prodigiously.

In recording Charles's deteriorating physical condition, Mac-Eachain noted several of the perplexing symptoms that were described by Dr. Lind as typical of scurvy patients. Lind said that black melancholy would suddenly give way to extraordinary euphoria, and extreme lassitude would give way to amazing bursts of energy. Throughout it victims often showed no appreciable loss of weight because fluid collected in the body's cavities gave them a bloated appearance. And their appetite was unimpaired. The victims complained of hunger constantly and could eat vast amounts of food at one sitting. MacEachain said of the Prince that "Notwithstanding his melancholy fits, yet at other times he was so hearty and merry that he danced for a whole hour . . ." He also attested to Charles's voracious appetite and incessant complaints of hunger. Certainly they were often short of food, but on one occasion when brandy, bread, and cheese were brought, the Prince ate "more than ever he was seen to eat at three ordinary meals." One day he was not able to walk, but after a decent meal his energy was quickly restored.

However, the scurvy sores on Charles's legs and thighs grew worse; Felix O'Neill had certainly recognized what ailed his master by the time he parted from him at Benbecula. O'Neill was captured a few days later and was taken to the Earl of Albemarle at Fort Augustus for questioning before being eventually released and sent back to France. During that meeting O'Neill said that Charles's body had been covered with a "scorbutic humor" when he last saw him. Since that had been at the end of June and O'Neill's questioning did not take place until late August, Albemarle conjectured that the Prince had already "died of misery in one of his hidden places." At the beginning of September, Albemarle was sufficiently convinced that Charles was dead to call off the hunt in the Highlands. Then and only then was the Prince able to make his escape from Scotland on September 20.

In the meantime the Prince's sojourn in Skye was very brief. When the boat landed near Lady Margaret MacDonald's house at Mugstot (now Monkstadt), Flora and MacEachain went on ahead and found Lieutenant MacLeod of the Skye militia there and his men camped a short distance from the house. Flora drew Lady Margaret into another room to tell her that the Prince was only a stone's throw away and was looking to her for help. Far from agreeing to assist Charles, Lady Margaret was horrified at the news. She turned for advice to her trusted factor, Alexander

MacDonald of Kingsburgh, who was visiting Mugstot at the time. He instantly agreed to take charge of everything.

Kingsburgh sent MacEachain back to the shore to take "Betty Burke" behind a hill near the house, out of sight of MacLeod's militia. The factor promised to meet them there shortly and then take them to his own house, where Charles could spend the night. Kingsburgh also sent for Donald Roy MacDonald—the man who had pleaded with Keppoch not to throw away his life at Culloden; he was seeing a surgeon nearby for treatment of a severe foot wound suffered during the battle. Donald Roy offered to take Charles to Portree the next day. His aim was to get the Prince off to the Isle of Raasay between Skye and the mainland. He went immediately to Portree to look for MacLeod of Raasay, who had also taken the field for Charles at Culloden. Understandably, with Ferguson, Scott, and Mamore hunting Jacobites as well as the Prince, Raasay had not been seen in quite a while.

As Kingsburgh and "Betty Burke" set out across the moors, Flora and Lady Margaret "kept a close chit-chat" with Lieutenant MacLeod to detain him a little longer. Although nobody knew it yet, at that very moment across the water Lady Clanranald was undergoing stringent questioning by both Captain Ferguson and General Campbell of Mamore, who demanded to know why she had left her home the evening before. (In fact, Ferguson had taken advantage of her absence and had slept in Lady Clanranald's bed.) They were unable to shake her story that she had gone to visit a sick child on the other side of Benbecula. They also wanted to know where her husband was. Clanranald had already escaped to the mainland several days before to avoid arrest; it is interesting that he did not take the Prince with him.

Lieutenant MacLeod's presence at Mugstot can only mean that soldiers were now anticipating Charles's movements rather than following one or two steps behind him. Nevertheless, MacLeod did not appear to be in the least suspicious of Flora, although he asked her many questions about news from the Outer Isles. They talked pleasantly; then Flora and MacEachain left for Kingsburgh's house by coach. They were halfway there when they caught up with Kingsburgh and "Betty Burke" striding across the moor. It was early evening, and people walking home from church gaped openmouthed at the spectacle. Whether Charles was drunk or in the throes of scorbutic euphoria is hard to say, but he was making no attempt to behave in character with his female disguise. He seemed to be thoroughly enjoying himself; he talked animatedly to Kingsburgh and raised his skirts to an indecent height when fording a stream. The people of Skye were shocked, and when Flora stopped the coach so that MacEachain could plead with the Prince to tone down his display, a lady commented that the figure looked like a man dressed as a woman. Flora hastily assured her that the maid was an Irish girl she had known before, which seemed to satisfy the woman. To a Highlander, Irish nationality was sufficient explanation for a multitude of oddities!

This was the first time Charles had ever been in the hands solely of Highlanders, without Sir Thomas or Franco-Irish sycophants breathing in his ear at every opportunity. Yet he seemed perfectly at ease, and if he still believed the Highlanders would betray him for the 30,000-pound reward, it was no longer apparent. But he seemed to be oblivious to the fact that his behavior was endangering everyone, including himself.

Kingsburgh's wife had already gone to bed when the group arrived near eleven o'clock. Her husband sent a servant to bid her rise and prepare supper, while her daughter confided that her father had brought home Flora MacDonald and "a very odd, muckle, ill-shapen-up wife as ever I saw!" Mrs. MacDonald of Kingsburgh dressed and went downstairs to find a strange figure in a lilac-sprigged dress sporting red chin whiskers striding up and down the hall. When Kingsburgh confessed that it was the Prince, his wife was alarmed to a great degree. "O Lord, we are a'ruin'd and undone for ever! We will a' be hang'd now!" But yet the good woman brought eggs, butter, and cheese for supper. The Prince called for tobacco and a dram afterward, artfully saying, "I have learn'd in my skulking to take a hearty dram." He and Kingsburgh smoked and drank convivially for most of the night.

It was hard to awaken Charles the next morning; Flora agitatedly paced the floor at Kingsburgh House, wanting the man to be off her hands. It was now the last day of June—ten days since she had first met Charles, although she had barely spent that many hours in his company. At length the Prince arose and dressed as "Betty Burke" for the last time. Although everyone agreed that the disguise was disastrous because Charles could not carry it off with his masculine walk, airs, and manner, it had been decided that he should leave the house as "Betty Burke" since this was the way the servants had seen him enter. He was to change into a philibeg and other Highland clothes given him by Kingsburgh when he reached the edge of a wood before proceeding to Portree.

Flora meanwhile went to Portree on horseback. There she and the Prince took leave of each other once she was satisfied that Donald Roy had been able to procure a boat to take the fugitive to Raasay. As he stepped into the boat, Charles turned to Flora and said, "For all that has happened, I hope, Madame, we shall meet at St. James's yet and I will reward you there for what you have done." Flora never saw or communicated with the Prince again, and if he remembered her services at all in later life, it is not evident. There was no romance between Flora and Charles, as earlier writers would have us suppose. In fact, she greatly resented his intrusion upon her life.

Flora MacDonald was arrested ten days later, as were Kingsburgh and his wife and daughter. Kingsburgh was first placed in irons at Fort Augustus and then taken to Edinburgh Castle; Flora was transported by ship to London and imprisoned. She was put on board the *Furnace* (where MacLeod of Gualtergill, Father Allan MacDonald, and Boisdale were also confined) and came face to face with yet another prisoner—Colonel Felix O'Neill. Believing that she was to be put on trial for her life, Flora confronted him and soundly slapped his face, saying, "To that black face do I owe my misfortune!" As it happened, her fortitude and calm manner under questioning in London won her much respect and admiration, so that by the time she was released under the general amnesty a year later, Flora MacDonald had become a heroine.

Flora married Allan MacDonald of Kingsburgh, son of Alexander, in 1750. The family, including her stepfather Hugh, who was never caught by the Redcoats, emigrated to North Carolina in 1774. In the American war of independence, Allan fought for King George III and was taken captive at the Battle of Moore's Creek Bridge. After his release in 1779, Flora and her husband returned to Skye, where she died in March 1790 at the age of sixty-eight. Hugh stayed in North Carolina, dying there in 1780.

Alexander MacDonald of Kingsburgh and all the other prisoners were also released in 1747 following the general amnesty. It was said that he suffered one year's imprisonment for one night's hospitality. He apparently told Sir Alexander MacDonald of Sleat that he felt sorry for Charles, who was rain-soaked, pestered by flies, "maigre, ill-colored and eat up by the scab," and bleeding from the nose when he last saw him. Kingsburgh died at home in Skye in 1772 at the age of eighty-three.

The Prince had been passed from hand to hand quickly in the last days of June and the first days of July, but the tempo became even more rapid when those he sought for assistance could not be found. MacLeod of Raasay was one such person, so his cousin, Captain Malcolm MacLeod, was prevailed upon to take the Prince to Raasay Island. But they stayed only two days because it was a desolate, burned-out strip of land and offered no hiding place or source of food. Government troops led by Captain Ferguson had torched three hundred homes there, including the Laird's mansion and thirty-two boats; they also slaughtered 280 cows and 700 sheep—stark evidence of what Charles's actions cost Scotland.

The Prince and MacLeod went back to Skye and took refuge in a cow byre near Camastianavaig. Charles, however, wanted to walk south to Strathaird, which was Mackinnon country, because the Laird of Mackinnon had supported the recent rebellion. Malcolm learned that the Laird of Raasay wanted nothing to do with Charles, and he was very reluctant to bring trouble to the Mackinnons by conducting the Prince into their territory. He suggested instead that they take to sea again and make for the Isle of Rona. But Charles ignored the danger he was visiting upon these people, and insisted on being taken to Strathaird.

From the moment he had ill-advisedly left the mainland at the end of April, the decisions as to where to go, how to go, when to leave, and when to stay had been Charles's. He felt he had to be the leader and in charge at all times, even when it was not in his best interest. This attitude caused him to miss at least three French rescue attempts. (Between Sheridan and O'Sullivan's rescues, the *Hardi Mendiant* had come looking for Charles.) He had to dictate events and appear to know best. O'Sullivan fatuously tells us, for example, that Donald MacLeod of Gualtergill and his eight boatmen would never have made the first landing at Rossinish from the mainland had the Prince not whispered encouragement in his ear. Actually, Donald had been sailing those tortuous seas all his life, and the Prince sat crouched between his feet. Malcolm of Raasay, too, was treated to the royal expertise and assertive tactics when on the way back from Raasay to Skye, Charles jumped into the water and ordered the oarsmen to haul the boat ashore—as if they had to be told.

One now gains a fuller appreciation of the problems Lord George Murray faced in dealing with Charles. It made the situation difficult that the Prince was adept at making people feel sorry for him while at the same time he insisted on being in command. Did he learn to do this early in life when walking was painful and Mrs.

Sheldon protected him? When MacDonald of Sleat was bargaining for Kingsburgh's freedom, he said that Charles had played on the factor's feelings and sympathies. The Prince did the same with Gualtergill, Flora, and MacEachain and had admittedly left France hoping to tyrannize Louis XV with shame. Manipulation was the Prince's very long suit; he would have his own way no matter what it cost others.

In some interesting letters written by James at this time the Stuarts' imperious attitude toward those whom they considered their subjects is partially explained. The first news of Culloden had arrived in Rome on May 30 (N.S.; May 19 in Scotland). In contrast to his son, who still seemed to believe he would one day grace the portals of St. James's, the exiled monarch knew there was no hope. In fact, he was again busily angling the Governorship of Navarre for Charles. With regard to handling the Scots, James wrote the following advice to his son in July:

> . . . [t]o keep our own people in a due subordination without allow-
> ing them to break your head with accusations & invectives against
> one another, but showing them that you are Master, & will act your
> own way, without being unkind much less unjust to any; and after
> all, with all our misfortunes, we may if we please be more Master of
> our own people on this side of the sea than most other Princes,
> because where we do not transgress the rules of justice & prudence,
> we have no politick considerations to constrain us in such matters,
> for except a very few who have really sufferd for us, & may be
> hereafter of use to us, the gros are people who owe us a great deal,
> while we owe them little & who expect a great deal from us, while
> we can expect little from them.

This sounds like something James II might have written, for its philosophy is reminiscent of an earlier age, when exiles were literally dependent on the Stuarts for pensions or commissions. But for this new breed of Scottish exiles, the American colonies provided opportunities for an independent life, and neither James—for the remaining twenty years of his life—nor Charles was ever to be "Master of our own people on this side of the sea than most other Princes." One also might wonder why the Stuarts felt the Scots owed them "a great deal." The unfeeling sentiments expressed in that one paragraph of James's is precisely the philosophy his son had been fed all his life—and Charles believed it totally.

Strathaird was about twenty miles away; since they were to walk rather than go by boat, as Malcolm MacLeod preferred, the Prince suggested he pose as the Captain's servant. But he was not capable of "dissemblimg his air." Even dressed in dirty rags, his body crawling with many-legged creatures, he still had the manner of a prince. Malcolm grew irritated at Charles's constant squirming and scratching, which he attributed to "the coarse odd way he behoved to live in, both as to sustenance and sleep." Many Highlanders found the Prince's carelessness about personal hygiene particularly offensive. His habit of throwing himself in bed night after night fully clothed had been noted from the moment he arrived in Scotland. It may have been a lifelong habit, which would account for his extraordinary wardrobe expenditure in Italy. Others noticed this peccadillo during his wanderings, when there was no need for him to sleep in the same garments he had worn during the day because of the great amount of clothing given to him everywhere he went.

In his third-person account, Malcolm said he took the Prince behind a hill "and opening his breast, saw him troubled with lice for want of clean linen . . . he believed he took fourscore off him . . ." Charles still held on to the flea-infested peruke that, a few nights before, Kingsburgh had tipped off his head while Lady Kingsburgh went to fetch a clean nightcap. Now Malcolm watched Charles stuff the offensive peruke into his coat pocket and tie a dirty white napkin around his head.

When the men reached Strathaird, Charles was immediately recognized by the Mackinnons, who "wept bitterly to see him in such a pickle." Malcolm took Charles to the house of his brother-in-law, Captain John Mackinnon, who agreed to take the fugitive back to the mainland, where he would be far safer than on the islands.

On the morning of July 5, eleven and a half weeks after Culloden, Charles, the Laird of Mackinnon, and Captain John Mackinnon reached the shores of Loch Nevis on the mainland. They slept several nights in the open and rowed along the coast by day hoping to find a French ship. But this proved to be too dangerous. A party of soldiers spotted their boat from the shore and called for them to beach immediately; when they refused the order, five of the militia gave chase, but without catching them.

The three men next went to Mallaig and made for MacDonald of Morar's home (Lochiel's son-in-law). They found the family living in a hut because Ferguson had burned down their house. Clanranald was also hiding in this area, and when he heard that Mackinnon had brought Charles back to the mainland, he exclaimed in exasperation, "What muckle devil has brought him to this country again?" He refused to meet with the Prince, telling the Mackinnons to take him off to Rona before he brought a second destruction upon them all.

After talking with Clanranald, Morar also became distant in manner toward the Prince, but he did show him a cave in which to hide. Charles became indignant that he was being treated so coolly, and he wailed in despair, begging Old Mackinnon not to desert him. However, Mackinnon had left his wife alone to face reprisals, so he started back for Skye, leaving the Prince with Captain John. As it happened, his wife had already been arrested, and Old Mackinnon was captured before he left the mainland. He was held for three years—two years longer than any other prisoner—before being released. Tradition has it that the Prince gave him the secret recipe for the world-famous Drambuie liqueur, which is still made by the Mackinnons of Skye today. They call it Prince Charles Edward's Liqueur.

Charles now decided to make his way to Borrodale again— the site of his first arrival on the mainland and his destination after the Battle of Culloden. He found that Ferguson had also put the torch to Borrodale's home, but Angus MacDonald was living in a nearby shieling with two other men. To Captain John's relief, Angus agreed to take the Prince off his hands, and the younger Mackinnon set off for home. He was arrested shortly before landing on Skye.

By July 18, General Campbell of Mamore and his troops had sailed to Loch Nevis with six men o' war, and Captain Scott was in Arisaig. This part of the mainland as far inland as Glenfinnan was still Clanranald's domain, where the royal standard had been raised a year before. Therefore, the entire territory was now ringed by government troops, whose orders were to move slowly inward, searching every conceivable hiding place. Charles and his companions were surrounded.

In his usual imperious way, Charles tried to dictate where they should go for safety. First he wanted to be taken to Lochiel, then to Glenfinnan; but neither was possible because of troop movements, and he was forced to rely on the common sense of Glenaladale men, into whose hands he had now been committed, and on a guide named Cameron. Moving northward and traveling only at night, the challenge was to break through the cordon of soldiers and negotiate mountains fraught with sudden precipices and stones that were made slippery by gushing springs. From one mountaintop they could see Glenaladale tacksmen driving their herds from the oncoming soldiers; at night the lights from enemy fires were all around in the glens below. Sometimes they passed so close that they could hear the conversations of soldiers as they sat by their campfires. Finally, on the night of July 21, they passed between two fires at the base of a hill, and they knew they had broken through the net. Climbing up the hill with Cameron in the lead, the Prince behind him and Major MacDonald of Glenaladale following closely, Charles missed his footing on a slippery ledge that dropped down to a sheer precipice. But as the major wrote, "I caught hold of one arm and Donald Cameron of the other and recovered him in a tryce."

They moved on northward to Glen Shiel, territory belonging to Lord Seaforth of the Isle-of-Lewis. Like Clanranald, Seaforth's holdings extended to the mainland, and since the men of Lewis had been so hostile toward Charles, it was doubtful that the government soldiers would look for him there. Here they came upon a Glengarry man who had escaped to Glen Shiel after Redcoats had killed his father the day before. Since Cameron had to return home to take care of his wife and children, the Glengarry took over as guide.

Charles wanted to go to Poolewe, a port several miles to the north, because he heard a French ship had come there looking for him. But no French ship could linger for long in the waters of the Minch, and indeed, later reports came that the ship, the *Bien Trouvé*, had surrendered to the *Tryal*. Unknown to anyone yet, two of its officers, the Chevalier de Lancize and one other, had been put on land to search for Charles.

The Prince then suggested once again that they should go southward to find Lochiel, but the major and Borrodale's son, John MacDonald, vetoed the notion. Why Charles persistently suggested going into areas that were bound to be patrolled by Redcoats was beyond their comprehension.

It was time to hand over the Prince to someone else. Charles was taken eastward along the shores of Loch Cluanie toward Invermoriston to a cave in a high pass between two mountains. There he was introduced to the famous Glenmoriston men—a band of eight outlawed Jacobites, each with a price on his head, who had existed since Culloden by making lightning raids on the militia and taking off with everything they could plunder. One of them, yet another named Alexander MacDonald, wrote lyrically about Charles's reception. After making a bed for him "his royal highness was lulled asleep with the sweet murmurs of the finest purling stream that could be, running by his bedside within the grotto, in which romantic habitation his royal highness pass'd three days." At the end of that period, July 27, Charles said he felt refreshed enough to face any hardship. It may have been here that he picked up the empirical Highland intelligence that of all the sustenance available thereabouts, wild blackberries and milk would help to cure what ailed him. Dr. John Burton recorded that this diet made a startling improvement in the Prince's condition.

Leaving on the twenty-eighth, the Glenmoriston men took Charles along the north shore of Loch Affric through to Strath Glass, where they climbed the craggy heights of Beinn Acharain. They were now on the other side of the mainland near the eastern coast; perhaps their design was to look for French ships on that side of Scotland. If so, they were disappointed, although they stayed in the area for more than a week. Charles again pressed to be taken to Lochiel, so they came back again through Glen Affric, reaching Glenmoriston on August 12. The weather had been kind for a while, but now it began to rain ceaselessly again. The Prince and the Glenmoriston men crossed the swollen River Garry on August 14 on their way to Loch Arkaig, where they had arranged to meet the messengers Charles had sent to Lochiel.

Like all the others, Lochiel could not—dared not—receive the Prince or come to him. He still had not recovered from the two broken ankles suffered at Culloden, and he was also skulking following the burning of his seat, Achnacarry House. Lochiel's hiding place was ringed by soldiers; Charles's dogged persistence in trying to meet with him placed him in great danger. Lochiel sent his brother Archibald and another relative, John Cameron, to see what they could do. They found Charles in a small hut near Loch Arkaig. "He was then bare-footed, had an old black kilt coat on, a plaid, philabeg and waistcoat, a dirty shirt and a long red beard, a gun in his hand, a pistol and durk by his side. He was very cheerful and in good health, and, in my opinion, fatter than when he was at Inverness." The Camerons had run into the Chevalier de Lancize and his companion, whom they brought with them. At first

Charles was suspicious of the Frenchmen and thought they might be spies, but after two days of talking with de Lancize he was convinced that the man was genuine. There was, however, no ship to carry them away.

Charles stayed in the vicinity of Loch Arkaig for about ten days. The Glenmoriston men left him after a memorable night when they had killed a large stag and feasted "most deliciously" on venison roasted over an open fire. He was now in the hands of the Camerons and MacDonald of Lochgarry, whom he had sent for. On August 27—about the time the Earl of Albemarle received Felix O'Neill's report that Charles had scurvy—the Prince received a message from Lochiel that the vigilance around him had been relaxed and that it was now safe for him to come to Badenoch, where he was hiding.

With Dr. Archibald, John Cameron, and Lochgarry, traveling only at night, they passed south of Loch Lochy and over Corrieyairack Pass and continued south to Ben Alder Forest. On or about September 3 the Prince and Lochiel met again after almost five months. Outside the door of his poor habitation Lochiel attempted a crippled kneel on his shattered ankles. "Oh! no, my dear Lochiel," said the Prince; one might have thought he had the Cameron chieftain's infirmities at heart. But he continued, "You don't know who may be looking from the tops of yonder hills, and if they see any such motions they'll immediately conclude that I am here, which may prove of bad consequence."

From somewhere—and it must have taken days and the tireless effort of many to produce—came a feast. That night there was plenty of fresh mutton, which is preferred by many Highlanders over lamb, aged beef sausages, well-cured ham, collops (sliced meat in a butter sauce), cheese, freshly baked bread, and an anker of whisky (two and a half gallons). Cluny MacPherson's younger brother Donald was at the gathering and wrote about it.

> Upon his entry he took a hearty dram, which he pretty often called for thereafter to drink his friends healths; and when there were some minch'd collops dress'd with butter for him in a large sawce pan that Locheil and Cluny carried always about 'em, which was all the fire vessels they had, he eat heartily, and said with a very chearful and lively countenance, "Now, gentlemen, I live like a Prince," tho' at the same time he was no otherwise served than by eating his collops out of the sawce pan, only that he had a silver spoon.

After two days with Lochiel, Charles was passed on again—this time to Cluny MacPherson, keeper of the Loch Arkaig Treasure. Cluny took him to his own unique abode on Ben Alder, which he had built after his eighteen-room mansion was burned in June. Called The Cage, it was constructed in a wood high up in the part of the mountain called Letternilichk by the locals. Trunks of trees were laid down to serve as a floor; the downhill end was raised by earth and gravel to make a level platform. Stripling trees grew in between the logs, and the top branches were interwoven with heath and birch twigs, then covered with moss to form a roof. The whole structure appeared to be suspended from the limb of a large tree that spanned the entire roof section, hence its name. The Cage was oval in shape and large enough to hold six or seven men comfortably, "four of which number were frequently employed in playing at cards, one idle looking on, one becking, [a servant] and another firing bread and cooking." A steep precipice was on one side of Cluny's Cage, and the outside fireplace was sheltered by two enormous boulders fronting a slate rock face that was the same color as smoke from the fire; so even on the clearest day it was impossible to detect the presence of habitation. It was so cunningly constructed that Cluny was able to hide here for the next eight years before he went to the Continent.

No outsider was admitted to see Cluny except Lochiel and Cluny's brother Donald. When business had to be transacted—such as the distribution of the Loch Arkaig Treasure to needy families—Cluny would leave The Cage and travel to Loch Arkaig. Charles and the MacPherson chieftain became bitter enemies a decade later when the destitute Prince demanded the money back and, when he learned it had all disappeared, accused Cluny of "imbiseling."

The amount could not even begin to compensate for all the burned homes lost by Charles's lies, or to finance escapes, or to recompense innocent people for the loss of their livestock, or to hire ships to buy meal from Ireland and Holland to keep the Highlanders from starving in the coming winter and the next. Added to the toll of lives taken at Culloden and the reprisals of that summer were many stillbirths and deaths from starvation in the winter of 1746. It was the beginning of the decimation of the Highland population, from which they never recovered.

The refugees in Badenoch and Ben Alder were deeply grieved by the recent executions of Lords Kilmarnock and Balmerino in London. The latter had been particularly popular and close to many of the chieftains; his blood was still fresh on the block as Charles was lying back in The Cage hoisting bowl after bowl of whisky in toasts to the raven-haired Princess Henrietta of France, whom he had never met. It is usually said that dipsomania caused him to lose touch with reality in the winter of his life, but it is clear that he had lost it before he ever set foot on Scottish soil.

Several accounts relate that the Prince often insisted that his brother had landed in England with ten thousand men and that he would fly into a rage if anyone dared to contradict him. There was his usual braggadocio about taking over at St. James's Palace, as well as talk of using the Loch Arkaig Treasure to form the clans for another attempt. One can imagine the occupants of Cluny's Cage looking sideways at each other; all anyone could do when the Prince was in his cups was humor him. It is small wonder that Cluny MacPherson kept a very tight rein on the treasure buried near Loch Arkaig. We are not sure that even Charles was made aware of its exact location.

From time to time Charles would wail about the "poor Highlanders" and what they had suffered, but an element of self-pity was always connected with these outbursts. Even when bemoaning hardships, he would follow up with a remark calculated to bring praise—which he craved in any form—for his own stoicism.

Charles could be generous when he had money. He once left a pile of gold coins on a rock to compensate fishermen for the haddock left to be dried by the wind that they had taken. His attitude toward money was that it should come to him by right in a never-ending supply. But when there were limitations on that supply, his generosity turned into meanness.

If Bonnie Prince Charlie had been caught by the Redcoats, there is no doubt that he would have been killed immediately. A public beheading would not have been his lot because the last thing the intertwined histories of Scotland and England needed was another Stuart martyr. The fate of a young Jacobite named Roderick Mackenzie bears this out. When Charles was with Cluny on Ben Alder, government troops triumphantly brought Roderick's severed head to Kingsburgh's prison cell, believing it was the head of the Prince. Roderick had been cornered in a barn by soldiers who had been killing every Jacobite they could find. He was trying to make his escape to France, but he was outnumbered and knew his end had come. When the soldiers demanded to know if he was Prince Charles Edward Stuart—he was handsomely dressed and of the same age, height, and coloring as the Prince—he confessed that he was, and then he was slaughtered.

In Cluny's Cage, eleven wearying days of the Prince's rambling talk were interspersed with periods when he would disappear to eliminate his bloody flux, which had returned again. Then came word that two French ships were at anchor in Loch nan Uamh and that the Prince should immediately make ready for his escape to France. It was not a rescue for the Prince as much as it was a welcome respite for Cluny and his men. Nobody could tolerate Charles's company for very long; this held true all his life.

John William O'Sullivan had reached France via Bergen, recovering his health en route. Working with Daniel O'Brien in Paris, he created a creditable ruckus at the Court of France until finally Captains Lynch and Warren were given permission to sail in two ships hired with papal money. Although the few ships sent to Scotland had French names, they were Antoine Walsh's privateers sailing out of St. Malo; it was the Pope who actually financed the rescue by raising money from the Spanish bishoprics of Cordova and Legovia. More French ships and soldiers had been sent to Ireland as decoys than were ever sent to Scotland because Louis was trying to make George believe that Ireland was now his objective. Actually, the cream of the French fleet was sailing to India and the West Indies in hope of usurping British strength in those regions.

England's naval power had been diverted from Scotland to cope with French and Spanish threats elsewhere. This was how the ships were able to wait for Charles at Loch nan Uamh and enable him to escape, but by this time, also, Albemarle believed that the Prince was dead. Warren, now promoted to colonel and in overall command of the rescue mission, was aboard *L'Heureux*, and Lynch captained *Le Prince de Conti*. Also with them was young Michael Sheridan, to whom James had given the commission of captain. They had first put in at Loch Boisdale, only to find desolation all around, and at the island of South Uist, which was almost devoid of its population. They then sailed the route now familiar to us across the Sea of the Hebrides to Loch nan Uamh. Flying British colors to deceive any remaining militia, they anchored and made contact with Glenaladale at Borrodale. It took nine days to get a message to Charles in Cluny's hideaway, which he received at one o'clock on the morning of September 13.

That same day the Prince and his companions set out on his last trek over Scottish soil toward the shores of Loch nan Uamh, arriving on the evening of September 19. Early the next morning, Charles went aboard *L'Heureux* with Lochiel, his brother Archibald, Lochgarry, de Lancize, and John Roy Stuart, who had recently made contact with the party. The ships slipped out of Loch nan Uamh in the small hours of the morning of September 20. Romanticists give us a vision of Bonnie Prince Charlie taking a long last look at the purple-clad mountains of the land of his ancestors as he bade a sad farewell. But whatever his own feelings actually were, all Scotland sighed with relief.

Chapter 12

The Treaty of Aix-la-Chapelle

It took nine days for *L'Heureux* and *Le Prince de Conti* to reach the northern coast of France, at Roscoff in Brittany. The date in Britain was September 29, but it was October 10 (N.S.) on the Continent, the dating system we will use hereafter.

In Rome, James had been perturbed for several weeks about the general climate that Charles would find upon his return. He was particularly concerned about the Prince's tendency to be hotheaded and arrogant when it came to dealing with the Court of France. He had written his son earlier cautioning to tread carefully; he still hoped that there was a chance, however slim, that King Louis would maintain the Stuarts out of gratitude for the Scottish diversion. He was also worried about Charles's reaction to Henry and had written O'Brien in July saying that he hoped "there will be no more disharmony between my children." At the same time he urged the Prince always to love his brother and his father.

A further concern was that although Sir Thomas Sheridan had been in Paris for two months, he had not communicated with James and was avoiding contact with Daniel O'Brien and Henry. The Duke of York had returned to Paris from Navarre, having found that the climate was disagreeable to his delicate constitution and also that the Stuart bid to rule that territory had met with no enthusiasm whatsoever. Even before it became known that Charles had landed in France, James claimed in letters to O'Brien that Sheridan, Lord Dunbar, and Strickland had been part of a clique trying to alienate the Prince from him and that Strickland had been the prime motivator.

On July 25, the King finally sent a sharply worded order to Sir

Thomas to travel to Rome immediately. He had several questions to which he demanded answers. Sir Thomas went to see O'Brien and paid a visit to Henry as well, but it was three weeks before he obeyed James's command to start for Rome. He told everybody that he would stay in the Papal City no more than twelve days before returning to Paris to wait for the Prince. At the meetings with O'Brien and Henry, Sir Thomas was closed-mouthed on the subject of Strickland and what had led to the Prince's decision to go to Scotland. He was also extremely hurt because it was being said that he had abandoned the Prince in Scotland; apparently O'Brien and Henry believed the rumors without checking with Sir Thomas himself.

Before departing from Paris, Sheridan wrote to James explaining why it had been impossible for him to wait for Charles when he boarded the *Mars* at Loch nan Uamh. He stated that he would bring the original copy of the letter the Prince had written him on April 23, in which he had said, "Follow me as soon as you think it Convenient. Adieu." But in the same letter Charles had also enclosed a copy of the Address to the Chiefs, which said he was going to France. Sir Thomas explained that he had not seen the Prince since eight days before that communication—the day of the Battle of Culloden—and that he fully expected that his master had preceded him to France.

Sheridan was reluctant to leave for Rome before he got word of the Prince's safe arrival in France; he delayed his journey at Avignon en route hoping to hear good news. But he could procrastinate no longer without risking James's further wrath. He arrived in Rome on September 23 "very fit and in excellent health," as the King reported to O'Brien. But O'Brien had already warned that if there were to be unity in the Royal Family—particularly between the brothers—it would not be a good idea for Sheridan to return to France; he had been stiff and cold with Henry, and none of those who had arrived from Scotland had come to pay their respects to the duke, except for O'Sullivan.

Of the Scottish refugees, Lord Ogilvy and several of his clan had been rescued in Norway; Lord George Murray had gone to Holland; and his brother, Old Tullibardine, had expired in an Edinburgh prison on July 9. According to O'Brien, Lord Elcho was in the Flanders area writing letters to try to obtain a government pardon (which was never granted). O'Brien was furious at Elcho because his actions bespoke a lack of loyalty to the Prince; Lord

Traquair, who had not been involved in the "Forty-five," fled England for fear that Elcho might implicate him in the early planning stages of the rebellion.

The person spreading rumors that Sheridan had abandoned Charles was O'Sullivan, who wished to replace the old man as the Prince's minister at the Court of France. O'Sullivan told Daniel O'Brien that Charles and Sheridan did nothing but quarrel all the time they were in Scotland. When James was finally able to question Sir Thomas in Rome, he confirmed the rumors he had heard at the time when Charles first landed in Scotland: that there was a movement afoot to support the Prince as king rather than himself. James also said that he was afraid the men behind the scheme—Sheridan, Strickland, and Dunbar—had poisoned the Prince's mind against the Duke. He had heard that Charles had been persuaded to distance himself from Henry's Romanism to avoid offending those who were prejudiced against that religion. The King talked of recalling Henry to Rome or of sending him to Spain before Charles arrived from Scotland to prevent an open rift between the brothers.

Another Stuart family secret began to unfold at this time. On October 10, 1746—the day Charles disembarked in Brittany, unknown to Henry until a few days later—the Duke of York wrote a highly secret and heavily coded letter to his father. He had met with Cardinal Tencin on that day to discuss the very sensitive issue of where he and his brother would go if Louis did not allow them to live in France. Tencin suggested that James negotiate with the government of Switzerland "underhand." He explained that he dared not communicate on such an issue in writing to Rome but impressed upon Henry that he should repeat in cipher to his father exactly what he had said. Henry did, and in the same letter he stated, as if it were a fact long known by the Stuarts, that the underlying cause of their present predicament was that the Pope was not willing to recognize Charles as the legitimate King of England upon James's death.

This tends to support the earlier assertion that Charles *already* knew the Vatican would not recognize him as King after his father's death. This would explain many things, such as James's frantic bid to have the crowns of France and Spain commit themselves to the maintenance of his sons. It would also explain the Prince's rash, now-or-never, do-or-die actions, and why he vowed several times never to return to Rome. As it was, the decision to stop recognizing the Stuarts was taken by the Sacred College of Cardinals—not by the Pope—because lack of diplomatic relations with Britain was economically disadvantageous to Rome. The date of the secret decision has not been discovered, but everything points to the resolution being adopted around 1740. The decision may explain the division between the men of Charles's household and those surrounding Henry, particularly the widespread aversion to the Duke of York's plans to enter the Church. Strickland, Dunbar, and undoubtedly Sheridan obviously believed the Prince could pull some irons out of the fire by appearing before the people of Great Britain, but neither man had set foot in that country for more than thirty years, and all were hopelessly out of touch with the changes that had rapidly occurred under the most enlightened rulership system in Europe.

For this reason even the rigidly Catholic Sheridan opposed Henry's plans to enter the Church as a profession. He knew that that step would be anathema to the English. Sheridan, the first-born son of James II, was a dreamer and had inculcated his visions upon Charles; but the Prince was now left to resurrect what he could from the wreckage of those broken dreams alone. Knowing Charles's penchant for blaming everyone else when things went wrong, James was anxious to remove Henry from the Paris area before the Prince returned. However, Spain would not take Henry; nor did he want to go. He really wanted to return to Rome, but he chose to stay and await his brother's arrival from Scotland. Why, we do not know, except that Charles was returning as a failure, and Henry, who had suffered much at his brother's hands, may have wanted to gloat a little.

On July 9, 1746, three months before the Prince returned to France, Philip of Spain died of apoplexy after a long illness. He was followed in death less than two weeks later by his daughter, who had married the King of France's son just before Charles left for Scotland. She died at eleven o'clock on the morning of July 22 after giving birth to a princess, who survived. But since a female could not inherit the crown, Louis XV was absorbed in finding a replacement wife for the Dauphin as soon as possible.

These matters were weighing heavily on the French King's mind when news came that Charles had landed. Anglo-French conflicts in Canada and India had become a sore drain on his purse. The French had taken Madras in India, but the British had captured Louisbourg in Nova Scotia, and Louis was looking for a way to make peace. His nation was also not faring well in the War of the Austrian Succession, which continued until 1748. The reason for Henry's meeting with Cardinal Tencin was to discuss the likelihood that during the inevitable peace talks Louis would be required to expel the Stuarts from France. Tencin, in fact, gave Henry advance warning by divulging this information, which was why he dared not write to Rome himself.

Henry thoroughly understood the tenuous position the family was in and strove not to ruffle feathers, but Charles came back fully expecting to be treated like a hero. It is said that at first he did not recognize Henry, who had grown from an awkward youth to manhood in the two years and ten months since they had seen each other. Henry found the Prince "somewhat broader and fatter than before," which is surprising in view of the hardships he had suffered in his wanderings. But his girth—which, as Sheridan noticed, had begun to expand in the summer of 1744—was probably due to his great fondness for the bottle, or perhaps the bloating associated with scurvy had not yet subsided. He was, however, now in much better health.

Anonymous tracts penned by some of the Prince's followers in Paris stated that the brothers were overjoyed to see each other again, but the reunion was cool, and matters went from bad to worse. Charles criticized Henry's lifestyle and ordered him about, telling him he should marry a daughter of the Polish Prince Radziwill "becose one of that cuntry would be more agreable to our nation than any other." As for his own possibilities of marriage, Charles told his father, "I cannot as yet Marry unless I got ye Kings Dauter," but the chances of that were very slim. Louix XV found the Prince as much of a nuisance as he had been before.

An anonymous pamphleteer wrote a glowing description of the Prince's triumphant procession into Paris. He sent it to "friends in Great Britain" in an attempt to persuade lingering followers that the King of France backed Charles to the hilt. The writer described Charles resplendent in a rose-colored velvet coat, embroidered with silver and lined with silver tissue: ". . . his waistcoat was a rich gold brocade, with a spangled fringe set on in scollops. The cockade in his hat, and the buckle of his shoes were diamonds; the George Cross which he wore at his bosom, and the order of St. Andrew which he wore also tied by a piece of green ribbon to one of the buttons of his waistcoat, were prodigiously illustrated with large brilliants; in short he glittered all over like the star which they tell you appeared at his nativity." The writer would have us believe that Louis XV put the Castle of St. Antoine at the Prince's disposal and interrupted a meeting of the Council at Versailles to greet the Prince and smother him in a warm embrace. This fanciful account, which Charles's biographers have relied upon, goes on to say that Louis declared to his cousin, "You have shown me that all the great qualities of Heroes and Philosophers are united in you . . . ," and so on.

Actually, the meeting between Charles and Louis—their first ever—was a very brief affair arranged by Cardinal Tencin. It took place not at Versailles but at Fontainebleau on the evening of October 21. Charles did not have a private audience with the King, nor did he appear as a prince. He was presented incognito as Baron Renfrew, with Henry, who had always been addressed as the Count of Albany during his stay in France. Court etiquette demanded that those presented to the King of France were to respond only if His Majesty addressed them; under no circumstances was anyone to initiate a conversation on his or her own. Charles could barely contain his fury at the imposition of the incognito, but he managed to get through the presentation without making his feelings obvious. According to the French chronicler the Duc de Luynes, Charles asked Tencin to thank those who had received him (the princes had earlier that evening been presented to the Queen and her ladies) and to excuse any shortcomings. "He said he was just a highlander and not used to the ways of this country and that besides he didn't know French well and that the inflammation he had caught in the mountains stopped him understanding as easily as usual." This foot-shuffling humility seems out of character, but Charles's hauteur was back in force the following day.

George Kelly now rejoined the Prince as secretary. They were living not at the Castle of St. Antoine but at the Hôtel d'Hollande in Clichy. Nor did the brothers share the same residence, as is often reported. Henry was living elsewhere in Paris "in a little house loaned to him by a nobleman"—so said Michel Vezzozi, who had reappeared on the scene and was sending bulletins to James. On October 22, Kelly penned a memorandum from Charles to Louis addressed to "Monsieur mon frère et cousin," which was signed "Sa bon frère et cousin, Charles P." That in itself was a slap in the face of the French King, who had insisted upon an incognito. He said that he regretted having had no opportunity the previous evening to discuss his affairs at length, and he urged a private audience with Louis "at the first opportunity"—without his brother present, "because I wish to avoid making him jealous." Louis made no response to this, but Charles followed up with a memorandum setting out precisely what he wished to discuss with His Most Christian Majesty.

Charles had tricked his way into France and then had tried to shame Louis into supporting him, so it was ill advised for him to have mentioned that the gold from France (actually, it was Spanish gold) was a little late arriving in Scotland. Charles gave the impression that this was the sole reason for his presence in France. He avoided the use of words such as *defeat* and *failure*, saying that with a little help from France he would soon be master of Scotland "and undoubtedly of all England." At the beginning of this epistle Charles claimed that discontent was widespread in Britain and that all he needed would be a "handful" of men. By the conclusion of the document, the "handful" had escalated to a request for eighteen to twenty thousand soldiers, plus money and supplies. Louis, who was still fighting a losing battle against the British on the Flanders front as well as in India and Canada, must have thought his cousin deranged.

Charles took a very high tone with Louis, whom he considered "such a weke man." The knowledge that his bloodline was closer to the great Henry IV than Louis's was may have been the source of his misguided inspiration. He pressed on in the memorandum, describing the events of the previous eighteen months with little regard for the truth:

> With three thousand regular soldiers I penetrated England immediately after having defeated Mr. Cope, and none opposed it till my arrival in London . . . I was in a position to pursue General Hawley at the Battle of Falkirk and destroyed his troops which were the flower of the English force . . .

Then he mentioned the lack of money, hinting it was France's fault, and continued: "I fought the Duke of Cumberland with an equal number of soldiers and could have certainly beaten them with 4,000 men against 12,000."

That last sentence alone—never mind his lies about reaching London—bespeaks a man who could not distinguish between truth and falsehood, nor separate fact from fiction. *Denial* is the best word to describe what Charles was doing. After so many years of being paraded as the "heir to the throne" and not understanding much of the politics that brought his family to the position it was in, he was not equipped to deal with anything less than what he had come to expect. Henry and James coped with their shift in fortune and status very well, but for some reason Charles could not. His father and brother spent the rest of their lives trying to protect the Prince from himself and combating adverse reactions to his manner and conduct.

No reply or acknowledgment came from Versailles to this memorandum, so continuing to ride recklessly on his tidal wave of hauteur, the Prince apparently demanded that the royal palace of Vincennes on the Seine (not to be confused with the prison of Vincennes) be made available to him as a residence. Through Daniel O'Brien, Cardinal Tencin relayed the short, tart message that His Most Christian Majesty absolutely rejected the request of the Vincennes palace as out of the question. It would be necessary to locate a residence "either in Paris or elsewhere" that would be mutually convenient.

In addition, Louis was prepared to offer 10,000 francs a month, 4,000 of which had already been apportioned to Henry. Six thousand francs (*franc* was synonymous with *livre*) was a pittance; even the frugal Henry had to be supplemented by James because his share had not even halfway met the bare essentials in the very expensive city of Paris. The offer was an insult, and the Prince refused it outright. O'Brien was a very hesitant go-between in these negotiations and was most reluctant to write the "very dry" responses Charles ordered him to make to Cardinal Tencin. The Prince's anger was fueled by the discovery that his father— who was only too familiar with his son's spendthrift ways—had recently commandeered all the funds on deposit with banker Waters and was controlling the money in Rome. It was a small fortune—450,000 livres—some of which the King used to redeem Charles's pawned jewels. The remainder he kept to ration to the Prince as the occasion demanded. It was a shrewd and necessary move.

Charles continued to bluster and protest to the French Court, claiming that many Scots were dependent on him for their subsistence. Actually, he himself owed many of them money that they had loaned him at various stages throughout the campaign. The most well known of these loans is probably the 1,500 guineas advanced by Lord Elcho on the day Charles marched into Edinburgh. The son of Lord Wemyss spent the next several years trying to retrieve that sum but to no avail. Charles claimed it was not a personal loan but money advanced for the public cause, to be repaid upon his family's restoration. Elcho was not the only one he used thus. All the Lords at Perth had also given money, and on the night of the Battle of Culloden, when Charles fled to Gortuleg, he had borrowed 150 guineas from Captain Shea of FitzJames Horse. Twenty years later, impoverished, Shea tried to retrieve it, though "he blushed to be forced to this extremity."

Charles had no thought for what others had done for him or suffered in his name, said Lord Elcho. Although in later years that young man was often accused of being bitter on account of the 1,500 guineas, what he said contained more than a grain of truth. O'Brien, who almost never outstepped the boundaries of his role as a factual reporter or mixed in personal politics, broke the rule when it came to Charles. He obviously disapproved of the Prince and told James that in his view Charles needed excessive amounts of money because he was in the habit of entertaining thirty-five men at lunch and twenty men for supper, complete with a vast array of expensive wines and liqueurs at the table.

James did send 8,000 livres to tide his son over, and Cluny or Lochiel must have released money from the Loch Arkaig hoard, because in the year-end financial report to Rome, Waters said he had 1,236 guineas on hand belonging to the Prince. From this amount Charles ordered Waters to pay 300 livres each to a Colonel Mackintosh, Captains Byers and Johnson, Richard Thomson, and a Mr. Fotheringham—presumably men who had accompanied him back to France. But in only three months the Prince had run up almost 46,000 livres in household expenses, and a further 120,000 was owing to the banker. Another note said that Charles had ordered payments in amounts ranging from 300 to 1,000 livres to Duncan Buchanan, Archibald Cameron, a Rory MacDonald, a Captain MacKenzie, and Andrew Lumisden, who eventually became undersecretary to the arthritic James Edgar in Rome. Several other gentlemen, such as Lord Ogilvy, were advanced sums up to 3,000 livres by Waters after promising to reimburse him at a later date.

It should be remembered that nobody in Paris knew that James had contrived Charles's initial entry into France. Louis himself never could put his finger on exactly what had happened, and to his credit he did not publicly voice his suspicions of the Stuarts because he had no proof of their mendacity. The French also believed that their government had been behind Charles's venture to Scotland, so in many quarters he was regarded as a hero. The Prince was counting on this, and he continued to play upon public sympathy to push Louis to give him more money. Even the Dauphin wondered why his father was being so harsh, but he was told not to meddle in affairs about which he knew nothing. Charles was hoping to edge Louis into a tight corner, and so he continued to flaunt the monarch's authority by appearing publicly at the opera, concerts, and salons without observing the incognito.

George Lockhart of Carnwath, who had been involved in the rebellion, fled with others on the *Mars* and *Bellona* and was now in Paris. He put together two volumes of *Memoirs on the Affairs of Scotland*, which unfortunately contain many accounts that may be apocryphal. However, one contains a ring of truth and hearkens back to concessions France tried to gain from James II and the exiled James III. During one meeting with the Prince after he returned from Scotland, Cardinal Tencin said it would be difficult for France to make any contributions for another expedition in view of the government's present difficulties but that aid would be considered to put Charles on the throne of England if he agreed to give up Ireland to France as payment for the expense of doing so. According to Lockhart, the Prince shook with rage and flew into a temper. Jumping up from his seat, he cried, "*Non, Monsieur le Cardinal, tout ou rien! Point de partage!*" ("All or nothing! There will be no division!"). After this Charles had little to do with Tencin, branding him a "Roge and a rascal," although Henry continued to keep in close touch with the Cardinal.

In trying to find a way to deal with Prince Charles Edward Stuart, Louis XV briefly engaged the services of his mistress, Madame de Pompadour. She was no mere sexual plaything, although her beauty and sensual allure kept the King captivated; she was a sharp-minded woman of Charles's age and a very shrewd judge of character. A few evenings after the Prince's first presentation at Fontainebleau, he was invited to sup with La Pompadour. We do not know the substance of their conversation except that afterward Madame had no time for the Prince at all. Messages came from Versailles that the French had no intention of increasing the pension and that perhaps the Prince should remove himself to Fribourg, in Switzerland. But he refused to leave until the King of France gave him soldiers so that he could return to Scotland. Henry, Tencin, and O'Brien pleaded with him to be reasonable, but the Prince was not a reasonable person.

His demands were ridiculous in view of the fact that he would have been hard pressed to find anyone in Scotland willing to join him, and the Scots in Paris were against another attempt as well. In fact, most of them were trying to obtain commissions in the French army or pardons from the British government, and Charles's behavior was affecting their chances. Furthermore, news of the executions in London, which continued throughout November and December, was widely reported in Paris, and gradually the French learned that most of the supporters Charles claimed were waiting for him had died on the scaffold. The most damaging news of all was that Murray of Broughton was in custody in London and was telling the government everything he knew.

Throughout all this, the Prince was reaping heavy criticism from his own people, for he nightly caroused at the opera house, where the citizenry stood and applauded the young man they believed was a fine hero indeed. His drinking continued, and he foolishly made remarks in public criticizing the relationship between Louis and Madame de Pompadour. Perhaps this was done to curry favor with the Polish Queen in the hope that she would use her influence to support him, but Queen Maria had no power whatsoever at Court. He then took to broadcasting far and wide that after risking his life for France, he was being treated shamefully. He may have believed his inital crest of popularity would win the day, but by the end of November the novelty had worn off. Charles was too often drunk, and when literary ladies invited him to their salons to meet the *philosophes*, his lack of formal education was an embarrassment.

Charles felt the need for a person of stature to represent his interests, so he wrote James to send Sheridan back to him as soon as possible. As for O'Sullivan's bid to take his place, Charles found that "Mr. O has all the appearence of not being a rite man," although he later changed his mind and used O'Sullivan for a few more years. Then at the end of November, word came that Sir Thomas had died on the twenty-third of that month, after dining with James only three days before. Apparently he was seized with "an apoplexy & lethargy" that lasted two days and slipped away before he could make confession. His proposed twelve-day stay in Rome had lasted two months. The King related the death of the man who had served the Prince for twenty-two years in a curiously dispassionate manner. He launched immediately into a tirade about Charles's keeping information from him and about his lack of response to a letter in which he had specifically requested that he open up his heart on the subject of Henry.

Weekly bulletins followed from James. He again told Charles to get rid of Kelly, and he revealed that the secretary had sent him "scurrilous' information about the Prince. (He must have been referring to the time when Kelly had complained to O'Brien that Charles was drinking with Glengarry in the *ginguettes* of Paris.) James also attacked Sheridan—a man he had always urged his son to heed—as a person who had given wrong counsel. He went on to tell Charles that he should accept the money France offered and stop acting in a "dry and haughty manner."

At the same time, unknown to Charles, James was secretly corresponding with Henry, plotting to separate the brothers from each other before their differences became any more public. Henry was utterly miserable. Charles attacked his younger brother's "lifestyle" in front of an audience of hangers-on at the Hôtel d'Hollande. Henry, miserable, wanted to return to Rome to tell his father things he could not put even in a ciphered letter. The Royal House of Stuart, which had never been healthy, was now beginning to seem rotten to many, despite all of James's pathetic efforts over the years to present a different view to the world.

The old warming-pan baby was now fifty-eight. The "defluxions" on his gums and face seemed to have disappeared; it was now a defluxion of the eyes. James appeared to be a clear thinker and in control of most situations, but there was always trouble in his household. He demanded loyalty from everyone, including his sons, but he himself was incapable of returning it. Even as his favorite, Henry, was writing, James was asking O'Brien for confidential information about the Duke's possible shortcomings. He said he knew Henry was not perfect, but he asked the Irishman to write at length on what it was about the Duke that drew criticism. If the Irishman responded, the letter was not kept; but it is very doubtful that he did. He knew James of old. The King would often solicit the free opinion of others, then use it against them when the occasion demanded. Perhaps that was why Charles would not open up on the subject of Henry. When he did finally respond, he falsely said that he would always love his brother.

It was as if James could not exist without dissension in his life, some brouhaha that he with all his kingly wisdom could put right. He had, after all, no other useful way to exercise his God-given royal prerogative. An anonymous letter signed by "J"* that he had received when Charles was in Scotland may have inflamed him against the Prince at this point. It said that Kelly was a drunkard (several reports suggest the same) and had circulated a paper, supposedly at the Prince's instigation, asserting that King James was troubled with "vapours" that affected his judgment and that he was governed despotically by Dunbar. It was said, the letter reported, that the King was a fool and Dunbar was a knave. Henry also wrote that "Mr. Kelly does everything and meddles in all things. I am much mistaken if he will not grow in a short time very troublesome."

Nobody governed James despotically. He himself was too much of a despot. Even Henry admitted this some years later to O'Brien, when they were all living in Rome after Dunbar had finally left for Avignon. According to the private letters of Pope Benedict XIV, the Duke of York told O'Brien—then Lord Lismore—that "his father, having by his manners put his wife underground, was disposed to doing the same to his son."

Although Charles had criticized the French King's liaison with Madame de Pompadour, he began to look for a paramour of his own. As if emulating Louis, Charles decided that a woman could best represent his interests at the Court of France. He came to this conclusion after falling out with one Lord Clancarty, an Irishman in French service whom Charles had picked to replace Sheridan. That relationship came to an abrupt end when Clancarty discovered that the Prince "lied just as well drunk as sober."

Charles's sights alighted on a cousin of Queen Maria Leczinska, the Princess Marie-Louise Jablonowski. She was at least ten years older than the Prince and since 1730 had been married to the French Prince de Talmond. But she decided to cast her lot with Charles and appears to have been in love with him. Madame Talmond became the mistress of Bonnie Prince Charlie and is the first woman of record with whom he had a sexual relationship. It was a stormy association. She liked to drink, too, apparently, and there are reports of loud arguments and quarrels and even of Madame Talmond being beaten by Charles.

By now, so many people—including the Scots—were willing

---

*"J" may have been John Stuart, who trailed Balhaldy to Siena at the end of 1743.

to repeat any unsavory gossip about the Prince that not much can be relied upon. The Princesse de Talmond stayed with her lover for approximately four years. Perhaps the quality of their relationship—and Charles's attitude toward women—can be summed up by his letter of March 1750, when they were nearing the end of their association:

> I see with chagrin that you torment yourself and me as well quite uselessly and in everything without sense. Either you wish to serve me or you do not wish to serve me; either you wish to protect me or you do not; there is no possible alternative. If you wish to serve me, you must not always be arguing that white is black in the most obvious matters and never admit you are wrong even when you feel you are. If you do not wish to serve me, it is useless to talk to you about my business. If you wish to protect me, you really must not make my life more unhappy than it is. If you wish to abandon me you must tell me so in good French or Latin Visus Solum.

It is said that when lovers quarrel they often accuse each other of the things of which they themselves are guilty. Arguing that white was black "in the most obvious of matters" and never admitting he was wrong was Charles's forte. The English diplomat Horace Walpole noted the Prince's stubborn mien and announced, "What a mercy that we had not him here! With a temper so impetuous and obstinate as to provoke a French government when in their power, what would he have done with an English government in his power?" And Marischal's view was that Charles possessed "an intrepidity which never lets him doubt where he desires."

He was making no progress in France. His suggestion that Henry marry brought a sharp letter from James, again reminding him that "You are his brother not his father." Charles was afraid Henry would become an ecclesiastic in the Church of Rome, which he said would ruin all his hopes forever. One wonders what hopes he had at all. Here the denial issue comes up again—as if he had a great fear of readjusting to a new life. The fear of having to change must have been very real indeed.

One gets the distinct impression from the letters of James and Henry that they both bent over backward for a number of years to accommodate Charles's delusions. They had allowed him time to try to realize his dreams, and he had failed. Yet his actions and utterances since his arrival in France showed that he was unwilling to admit that. Henry tried to reason with him, which infuriated Charles, who saw himself as the one to dispense advice, and he complained to his father that Henry contradicted him in everything. James despaired that his son would ever give up the lost cause and told Cardinal Tencin in confidence that he felt Charles was "on the edge of a precipice."

Henry suffered greatly. There is every indication that his desire to become an ecclesiastic was a true calling, felt from the heart. When James finally came to the realization that Henry's interests and happiness had been subordinated to Charles's hotheaded, passionate dreams for too long, he immediately put plans into motion to recall his younger son to Rome to be named a Cardinal. Of this Charles knew nothing.

Before these plans were executed, Charles surprised everyone by leaving for Avignon at the end of January 1748. He stayed only a short time, then set out on horseback with Archibald Cameron for Madrid. He sent O'Sullivan to Rome with a letter of explanation to his father. Before leaving Paris, Charles had heard that Lord George Murray was to come through the city, and he left orders with Henry to exert all efforts to have him "clapped up" in prison. Naturally, the Duke of York ignored his brother; it was clear to him—and later to James—that the Prince was scapegoating Lord George for his own failure.

Murray was accompanied by Lord Elcho, and from Paris they went on to Venice, where they met up with Lord Marischal for the carnival season. Charles was obviously keeping track of Lord George, for he wrote to James that from Venice Lord George ". . . proceeded to Room [Rome]. If it be so it is of ye Laste importance he shou'd be well secured there untill He can justifie himself to me for his past Conduct of which, putting it in ye Best light, one will finde severall demonstrative acts of disobedience, insolency and Creating dissention. Enfin besides for what he deserves, I humbly represent your Majesty it wou'd be of ye Moste dangeross Consequence if such a Divill was not secured immediatly in sum Castle where he might be at his ease, but without being able to escape, or have ye Liberty of Pen or paper." James wisely ignored this medieval request and later urged Charles to make his peace with Lord George, but he never did.

The Prince's reception at Madrid in March 1748 was ice-cold. He had not sought permission to enter Spain, and Chief Minister Caravajal urged him to leave immediately. As Charles told his father, he had gone to offer himself in marriage to the new King's half-sister, daughter of Elizabeth Farnese; for this act Spain was to give as her dowry twenty thousand men to go with Charles to Scotland. Given short shrift and told to leave, he arrived back in Paris on March 26, believing that nobody knew about his movements. In fact, everyone knew what he had been up to, and he became the laughingstock of Europe. Even James wrote: ". . . it would be a jest to think that you could have either a Daughter of France or Spain, and I should think that during our misfortunes we may be very well satisfied if you can marry a Princess of the same family as my Mother." He went on to suggest the daughter of the Duke d'Este of Modena and urged Charles to make his suit now "in which the court of France may be willing to do all in their power to soften the turning you out of France. After this, my dear Child, I cannot but say that without you put your affairs on another footing than they now are, I take it to be next to impossible that any thing you go about can succeed." Charles refused to follow his father's advice.

When he returned to Paris, another shock awaited the Prince. On the evening of April 29 he made his way to Henry's house, where he was expected for dinner. He arrived to find servants there and the house lit up with candles, but Henry was missing. Three days later, Charles received an undated note from his brother telling him he had left for Rome and that he regretted concealing his plans, but he desired to see their father again after an absence of two years. He gave the impression that his absence would be temporary and that he would return to France if that was what James decided. One wonders if he felt this secrecy was necessary because he feared Charles would stop him. His exit was in many ways reminiscent of Charles's flight from Rome, when Henry had not been told beforehand. Perhaps it was a question of tit for tat. The Prince was reportedly bewildered and even believed Henry may have been assassinated.

In June, Charles received a letter from James telling him that his brother was to become a Cardinal in the Church of Rome. The Prince was utterly stunned, both by the announcement and by the realization that Henry and James must have been planning this behind his back for a long time. He reacted to the news as if "I had got a Dager throw at my heart," and from that moment onward his decline was rapid. For the next three months he spent his time sulking and drinking.

In October 1748 the countries involved in peace talks for the previous seven months met to ratify the Treaty of Aix-la-Chapelle, which ended the War of the Austrian Succession. Eight powers were represented: Britain, France, Spain, Holland, Sardinia, Genoa, Modena, and Hungary and Bohemia as one state headed by Maria Theresa. The first article stipulated that in the Christian, universal, and perpetual peace to be agreed between them, no "assistance or protection, indirectly or directly, [was to be given] to those who would injure or prejudice any of the contracting parties." Article 19 of the Treaty of Aix-la-Chapelle was the death knell for Charles:

> The 5th article of the treaty of the Quadruple Alliance, concluded at London the 2d of August, 1718; containing the guarantee of the succession to the Kingdom of Great Britain in the house of His Britannick Majesty now reigning, and by which every thing has been provided for, that can relate to the person who had taken the title of King of Great Britain, and to his descendants of both sexes, is expressly confirmed and renewed by the present article, as if it were here inserted in its full extent.

The British succession in the House of Hanover was reaffirmed once again. Louis XV was glad to sign the treaty because that summer he had lost fully eighteen thousand men in battles against the British and Dutch led by the Duke of Cumberland in Flanders and the Austro-Hungarians in the Alps.

France did not fare well in the Treaty of Aix-la-Chapelle. She had to give up the potentially wealthy Madras in India and the enormous concession of the Austrian Netherlands (Belgium), for which she had fought so hard. Louis was also forced to recognize the Pragmatic Sanction, guaranteeing Maria Theresa's right to the Habsburg dominions. Although England relinquished Louisbourg in Nova Scotia, the French had no assurance that they could hold on to their North American holdings in the future.

At the conclusion of the meetings at Aix-la-Chapelle, there was no one in Europe with any use for Charles Edward Stuart. In fact, the terms of the treaty expressly forbade the signators to allow him into their territory. Charles was told to leave France forthwith for the Swiss city of Fribourg, a retreat Louis had arranged for him; but he refused to be dictated to and paraded around Paris as if he owned the city and all of France. He was warned that he would be arrested and bodily thrown out if necessary, but he still believed he could bluff out an existence in France by putting Louis to shame.

On the night of December 8, Charles arrived by coach at the opera house. The footmen who opened the doors were swiftly brushed aside by armed guards. Upon orders from His Most Christian Majesty, the Prince was arrested, trussed hand and foot, and carried off to the prison of Vincennes, where he was to remain until his senses were restored. On December 12, Charles finally made his submission to the King of France by letter. After a groveling preamble about his undying devotion to Louis's sacred person, the Prince said he was ready to leave France as commanded. He was released with money and an escort and ordered to Avignon. There on December 31, he spent his twenty-eighth birthday and saw in the year 1749. He was given a residence by the Pope, with Michael Sheridan and John Stafford of old days to care for him.

Two months later he disappeared, and for the next seventeen years, until his father's death in 1766, his whereabouts were shrouded in mystery. He would write sporadically to Rome, but the letters were never dated, nor did they give an account of where he was.

From the pen of Sir Horace Mann in Florence, who seemed to have spies everywhere, we get some accounts of Charles's tawdry life; and also from Glengarry's accounts to England's secretary of state. The secretary of state was hoping to find a breach of the Treaty of Aix-la-Chapelle on the part of Louis, because England had not yet finished with France. Many wandering Scots, too, ran into him and gave reports; and some information comes from the fragmented and distracted letters that Charles wrote himself. They were barely coherent and were covered with ink-blots and scratched-out sentences in a hand that rambled all over the page. One pathetic note to himself read: "What can a bird do that has not found a right nest? He must flit from bough to bough." There is evidence that he tried his hand at emulating the great poets and came up with "To speke to ete/To think to Drink," which he changed thus: "To ete to think/To Speke to drink."

He was accompanied by Henry Goring, an old friend from Rome, and had the temerity to try to gain acceptance at Maria Theresa's Court. Rebuffed, they went next to Strasbourg and then to Lunéville in Lorraine, home of the former King of Poland, Stanislas Leczinski. He was the father of the Queen of France and a relation of Charles's mother. There was talk of a scheme whereby Charles would marry a daughter of Prince Radziwill and be a candidate for the Polish throne, but nothing came of that.

Posing as "Mr. John Douglas," Charles was back in Paris in the summer of 1749. There he was sheltered by Madame Talmond and other ladies who lived in the Convent of St. Joseph on the rue Dominique. From each of them he borrowed money until one, Madame de Vassé, grew tired of his incessant demands. Another lady, Mademoiselle Ferrand, told Talmond she wanted Charles gone because she was sick of their constant loud bickering. James sent his son another 15,000 livres via Waters—who served as the central point for letters—but the Prince's clothes had become threadbare. He sent Goring to Britain to retrieve some of the money at Loch Arkaig.

Still bent on an uprising in Britain, Charles commissioned (probably with the Loch Arkaig money) a silver medal to be struck with his bust on one side and an old tree shooting forth a vigorous branch on the other and the word *Revirescet* ("it will flourish again"). Then in September 1750, Charles walked the streets of London for the first time in his life.

In company with Colonel Bret, an old-time crony of Lord Sempill, Charles sought out Lady Primrose, the widow of the third viscount Hugh Primrose. Her home on Essex Street had been a haven for Jacobites in the old days. In fact, it was Lady Primrose who had taken pity on Flora MacDonald when she was imprisoned in London and had raised 1,500 pounds as a parting gift when Flora was released. Charles always seemed to gravitate toward women when he wanted something. Lady Primrose called in Dr. William King, Principal of St. Mary Hall of Oxford University; King had publicly espoused the Jacobite cause to his students in a speech delivered in Latin. Dr. King's meeting with the Prince cured him of Jacobitism forever because he found Charles devoid of any learning or intellect and because he had "formed a scheme with was impracticable . . . no preparation had been made, nor was anything ready to carry into execution. He was soon convinced that he had been deceived; and therefore, after a stay in London of five days only he returned to the place from whence he came." Dr. King also observed of Charles that "the most odious part of his character is his love of money . . . the certain index of a base and little mind. His most faithful servants, who had closely attended him in all his difficulties, went unrewarded."

Charles did not leave London, however, without abjuring the

Roman faith and formally embracing the Church of England. It is believed he did this at St. Martin-in-the-Fields. His own account describes the place as being "the new church in the Strand."

> I went to London in the year 1750; and in that capital did then make a solemn abjuration of the Romish religion, and did embrace that of the Church of England as by Law established in the 39 Articles in which I hope to live and die.

The Prince was not sincere. He later reverted to the Church of Rome when he realized which side his bread was buttered on and whence his income would most likely come in the future. But for the moment he made a great show of hating papists, including his father and brother, and for two years he did not write to Rome. Even when he did his letters were addressed to Edgar, never to his father, whom he could not forgive for arranging Henry's ecclesiastic appointment.

There followed desperate schemes to attack St. James and assassinate George II and all the Royal Family at one time. It was to be carried out by one Murray of Elibank, whose courage failed him at the last moment. Archibald Cameron was sent to Scotland in connection with the plot and to obtain money from Loch Arkaig, but he was betrayed by one of his own who had no wish to witness another coming of Charles. Cameron was caught and executed. By this time Charles was buoying up the hopes of his adherents by saying that Frederick the Great would stand solidly behind him. Lord Marischal was now Frederick's ambassador to France, but as always, though he couched his sentiments in diplomatic terms, he had no qualms whatsoever about telling the Prince that he wished he would go away forever. The more Charles was boxed into a corner, the more he lied about his connections; but after Cameron's death (his brother Lochiel had passed away in 1748), no one adhered to the Prince except O'Sullivan—who had been knighted by James in 1747—and Henry Goring. But the latter did not last for very long.

The rupture came in the summer of 1752 over Clementina Walkinshaw, or "Miss Clemi," as Charles referred to her. He had met her at Bannockburn before the Battle of Falkirk. According to Henry Goring, Clementina was "a bad woman," and when the Prince learned she was at Dunkirk in financial troubles and sent her 50 louis d'or, he objected. Charles was then in Ghent. He used both Goring and O'Sullivan as messengers to entreat Clementina to come and live with him as his mistress. Goring objected to being used thus, telling Charles:

> When the desire of the thing you now wish for is over, you will despise me for having consented to dishonour myself to procure you a momentary pleasure, the consequence of which may end in ruin to yourself and all the honest men engaged in your affairs. The man who keeps a mistress is indeed not so much liable to censure, but surely he that procures her for him or bears the name of it is no better than a pimp which title no other can cover and a blue ribbon would not so much serve to cover as to expose his infamy.

Two other letters written by Goring to Charles in June 1752 make it plain that he was dismissed. "I am not come of a race of Spaniel dogs who the more they are beat the more they flatter and fawn," he wrote. "My honour will not suffer me to act a low part in your pleasures." Apparently, Goring was worthy enough that Lord Marischal procured him a commission in Prussian service, but he died less than two years later.

By November 1752, Clementina Walkinshaw and Charles were living together. They moved to Liège, where a daughter was born to them on October 29, 1753. She was given the name Charlotte and was the only child the Prince ever sired. Clementina received no better treatment than her predecessor, the Princess de Talmond. In one of Talmond's last letters to Charles she had said that she loved him but that "I won't let myself be killed." The women seemed to be similar; each claimed to love the Prince desperately yet suffered his physical and verbal abuse at the same time. But Clementina had no financial resource other than the Prince, and now she also had a young daughter to raise.

One month after Charlotte's birth, the ugliness that Charles seemed to be filled with manifested itself yet again. He had apparently made up with Goring, possibly because his Prussian connection might be useful, and he wrote him a letter saying that he was dismissing all the papist servants from his household in Avignon. He added, "My mistress had behaved so unworthily that she has put me out of patience and she is a Papist too, I discard her also! P.S. She told me she had friends that would maintain her, so that after such a declaration, and other impertinences, makes me abandon her. I hereby desire you to find out who her friends are that she may be delivered into their hands. Daniel [a servant] is charged to conduct her to Paris."

Charles may have been heated with alcohol when he wrote this; he did not abandon Clementina. She was too useful as a submissive whipping post, and few around him would allow that to be their fate. Kelly had gone, and so had Goring. The sycophantic O'Sullivan—now Sir John William O'Sullivan—was still in the background, but he was not part of Charles's household. The inept former quartermaster general was last heard from around 1760; it is believed he finally took his vows as a priest and reverted to his old occupation of tutor.

There is no evidence that Charles, now thirty-three, was much of a father. If he referred to the little girl at all, it was to "ye cheild"; and he was often gone on "jaunts," as he called his periodic disappearances. He is said to have made another secret journey to England in 1754 under the alias "John Douglas" or "Dr. Thompson," two of the assumed names that he used most frequently. Money was a constant problem, although James foolishly sent amounts to Waters for Charles's use periodically. But no amount of money was ever enough for the Prince.

He even tried through an agent in Holland to claim funds from the British government owed to the estate of his grandmother, Mary of Modena. An agreement had been made between James II and William of Orange that 100,000 pounds a year be paid to Mary when she became a widow, but the agreement was never honored. The debt, with accrued interest, now amounted to millions, but Charles was never able to lay his hands on it. In any event it really belonged to James, who was also trying to claim it.

This may have been why Charles, Clementina, and the baby temporarily moved to Paris; perhaps Clementina believed the Prince would change once he came into his fortune. But his alcoholism only grew worse, until more than one person claimed he had quite lost his senses. Banker Waters saw the couple in a café on the Bois de Boulogne engaged in a particularly ugly argument that was witnessed by all the other patrons as well. As he wrote O'Sullivan, no doubt with the intention that James should be informed, everyone was talking about the Prince's drunkenness, and his reputation was suffering. Charles was beyond caring about his image or about controlling his temper. He could always justify his actions, feelings, and rage because what happened in life was always someone else's fault. The Prince himself was the only person who could have reversed the trend, had he been able to recognize what his affliction was; but there was no chance of his doing that as long as James continued to send money and implore his "dearest Carluccio" to come home.

From Paris the trio went to Basel, where "Dr. Thompson" was noted to be a very bad husband because he constantly beat his wife. Finally after eight years her gypsy life with the constantly intoxicated Prince became too much for Clementina. She contacted James, saying that she desired a Catholic education for her daughter and that she herself wanted to retreat into a convent. Perhaps believing that a separation might bring Charles back to Rome, James agreed to pay Clementina 10,000 livres a year for the support of herself and her child. There is evidence that he even employed agents to help her escape from the ever-watchful Charles. According to Lord Elcho, who was living not far away in Neufchâtel, where Marischal was governor, Charles was so jealous that he surrounded their bed with chairs placed on tables. On top of the chairs were little bells, so that if anyone stole in during the night the bells would ring. This primitive alarm system may not have had as much to do with the Prince's jealousy as it did to his unreasonable fear that he was a target of assassination by the British government.

In March 1760, James tried to woo his son to Rome and sent him 12,000 livres for the journey, but Charles refused to go. Then in the third week of July, Clementina stole away with seven-year-old Charlotte in a coach that was waiting to take them to the Paris convent of the Nuns of the Visitation, one of several habitations she was to adopt to elude the Prince. She left a letter:

> Sir: Your Royale Highness cannot be surprised at my having taken my partty when you consider the repeated bad treatment I have matte with these eight years past, and the Dealy risque of loossing my life, not being able to bear any longer such hardships my health being altered by them has obliged me at last to take the Desperate Step of removing from your Royalle Highness with my child which nothing but the fear of my life would ever have made me undertake any thing without your knowledge. Your Royalle Highnesse is to great and just when you refflect not to think that you have push'd me to the greatest extremeti and that there is no one woman in the world that would have suffer'd so long as what I have done. However it shall never hinder me from having for your Royalle person all the attachment and respect and I hope in time coming by

my conduct to merit your protection and friendship for me and my child. I put myself under the care of providence which I hope wont abandone me as my intentions are honest and that I will never doe a dirty action for the whole world. I quite my Dearest prince with the greatest regreat and shalle always be miserable if I dont hear of his welfair and happiness. May God Almighty bless and preserve him and prospere all his undertakings which is the ernest wish of one how will be till Death my dearest Prince.

Your most faithfull and most obedient Humble Servant

Clementine Walkinshaw

There is one thing I must assur your R.H. that you may not put the Blame on innocent people that there is not one soul, ether in the house or out of it that knew or has given me the smalest help in this undertaking nor anybody that ever you knew or saw.

In her postscript Clementina may have been trying to protect the servants—who were indeed guiltless—from one of Charles's sudden rages, during one of which, it was reported, he chased his retainers around with a drawn sword. His fury that Clementina had escaped him could barely be contained, and he circulated descriptions of both. The mother was described as fair, about forty, of average height, and thin-faced with a complexion marred by crimson blemishes. Little Charlotte was described as being about seven with white-blonde hair (which turned darker as she grew older), having large eyes like her father, and being rather well built for her age. The descriptions were of no use. Clementina and her daughter had disappeared, and if anyone knew their whereabouts, they did not inform Charles.

James, of course, knew, and he even confessed to Charles in a letter that he had known for "many months" of Clementina's desire to leave. He also admitted that he had financially assisted her and Charlotte. He urged Charles that, if he had any feelings of tenderness toward his daughter, he should prefer her good education above all other considerations.

"O my Dear Child," James wrote to the forty-year-old Charles, "could I but once have the satisfaction of seeing you before I dy." His wish was not granted. Further letters were written in more harsh terms, one exhorting, "If you are in a lethargy, rise out of it, if you are not show it by your actions." Another in 1762 said, "I shall take it for granted that in your present situation you are not only buried alive, as you really are, but in effect you are dead and insensible to everything."

James was right. Charles's retreat into alcohol obliterated days, months, and years without his being aware of what was happening in the world and in Great Britain in particular. George III ascended the throne after the death of his grandfather, George II, in October 1760. The King had suffered a burst right ventricle of the heart at the age of seventy-seven. His eldest son, Frederick, had expired in 1751, which was how his grandson came to rule. Between 1757 and 1760 England wrested Quebec, India, and African territories from the French, and in November 1758 Admiral Sir Edward Hawke wiped out what remained of Louis's naval power at the Battle of Quiberon Bay.

Rome did not give up on Charles. When both James and Edgar became too ill to write, Edgar's undersecretary, Andrew Lumisden, urged Charles to come home and see his father before he died. But the faithful Edgar, the peacemaker and pinnacle of quiet strength in the stormy Palazzo Muti, died first, in 1764. Charles had nowhere near the same rapport with Lumisden as he had had with Edgar.

Henry took it upon himself to break the silence that had existed between the brothers for seventeen years. Cardinal York, as he was now known, had become highly influential and enormously wealthy, with a seat at Frascati delivering up healthy benefices. He had long ceased to live with James, finding his constant instructions, his regal advice, his love of intrigue, and his meddling with his choice of advisers and confessors too oppressive to bear.

In February 1765, Henry tried to bury the hatchet in a letter to Charles by speaking of the "disunion between two brothers that has render'd them for so many years past so useless to one another. This is indeed a very great misfortune but of such a nature that it depends in reality on us two to put a speedy remedy to it." It took another letter from Henry before Charles condescended to reply in October of that year. James, Charles knew, was by now merely clinging to life, hoping for one last chance to embrace his son. But the Prince's October letter contained a request, as if it were a command, that Henry do all in his power to make sure the Pope (now Clement XIII; Benedict XIV died in 1758) recognize him as King Charles III of Great Britain after his father's death.

It was a callous request and a stupid one. The Sacred College had made its decision long ago, and Clement had every intention of abiding by it. But as Marischal rightly pointed out, the Prince was incapable of believing that a measure he strongly desired could fail. Past failures had not made him deviate from this pattern because in his mind they had not been failures as much as transgressions or treachery on the part of someone else. Even when he received an urgent express from Lumisden that his father was near the end, Charles steadfastly refused to set foot in Rome unless the Pope agreed to recognize him as a monarch.

On January 1, 1766, the day after his "dearest Carluccio" celebrated his forty-fifth birthday, the titular King James III of Great Britain passed peacefully away in his sleep at 9:15 in the evening. James died, wrote Lumisden, "with his usual mild serenity in his countenance."

Chapter 13

The Queen of Hearts

Charles was living at Bouillon, on Belgium's border with France, and had set out for Italy on December 30. But it was not until January 23 that he reached the outskirts of Rome. On the way he had been met by a messenger with the news of his father's death. He was too late for the lying-in-state and burial at St. Peter's. "The Romans were vastly impatient to bury him," said Sir Horace Mann, "that their theaters might be opened." It was a spiteful remark to make, but it was probably true.

Charles had sent the messenger back with an order that Henry make preparations for his royal welcome in the Papal City after an absence of twenty-two years. One longs to know his thoughts as the coach navigated the ice-bound roads over the route he had taken on horseback with Vivier, Buchanan, and Godinet so long ago. And one wonders if he thought of the father he had not seen in all that time. All reports tell us that Charles showed no remorse whatsoever when he received the news that James was dead. His dogged determination to be received as King was uppermost in his mind. Despite what Henry had told him, he persisted in his belief that what he desired most would come true.

Outside the walls of Rome he halted the coach at a small inn on the Flaminian Way with the intention of driving triumphantly down the Corso via the Porto del Popolo. At the inn he was met by Henry, who broke the news that there would be no official reception, no heralds, trumpets, gilt coaches, processions, or cheering throngs.

The brother who met Henry's eyes after nineteen years was a stooped-over man with a bloated red face, dead eyes, and a

275

drooping mouth. His nose was slumped down to meet his upper lip, and fatty jowls melded with a fleshy neck to spill over his cravat. Charles's girth was enormous, and he had to be assisted by a valet as he hobbled unsteadily on two bad legs, which had been injured, he said, in a coaching accident. But as we shall see, the weeping ulcers had started up again, and he had to keep them constantly bandaged in the winter months. It is not recorded who accompanied him, but undoubtedly Lord Caryll—Sempill's brother-in-law, who had been with him at Gravelines—was one of them. John Hay of Restalrig (now Sir John) was possibly another since we find him among Charles's early staff at the Palazzo Muti, and a Captain Urquhart may have been a third.

Waiting at the Muti was Andrew Lumisden (O'Brien had passed away in 1759), whose letter notifying Charles about the death was addressed to "Your Majesty" and congratulated him on his accession to the throne! Including Henry, Charles could count on only four people to pay him regal respect. When the two rectors of the English and Scots Catholic Colleges also decided to recognize him, they were immediately dismissed by the Pope.

Henry unwisely drove around in his opulent coach with Charles seated on his right side. Since this was the position that Cardinals were permitted to grant only to reigning monarchs, Clement III was highly displeased. It was at this point, many writers say, that the English royal arms were removed from above the doorway of the Palazzo Muti. If so, it was the second time, because the late Benedict XIV noticed the disappearance in the early 1740s. Perhaps they had been reinstalled and were removed again.

Charles sulked and swore he would not leave the Muti as long as he was not recognized by the Pope. Of course he resumed his love affair with the "nasty Bottle," as Henry called it. At length, Cardinal York prevailed upon his brother to agree to a papal audience in which Charles, as the Count of Albany, was to kneel at the feet of His Holiness, while Henry's exalted position as a senior Cardinal and Bishop of Frascati permitted him to take a chair by the Pope's side. In Rome, the younger brother was now the more exalted by rank and title; the shoe was on the other foot.

Forty-one-year-old Cardinal York had become a very wealthy man since he left France, and he reaped enormous sums from his bishopric at Frascati. Eventually he became Dean of the Sacred College in Rome, but his elevated status was due solely to his birth, for he possessed no extraordinary talents except a shrewd head for business. Since Charles had almost bankrupted the family in 1745 and could not be trusted to handle money matters or even his own jewels, James had arranged that Henry be custodian of the Sobieski-Stuart fortunes. The Cardinal had been managing funds for years before James's death with the assistance of Abbé Lercari, who was schooled in law. Lercari eventually brought about a settlement of the litigation involving the 400,000 Polish florins left by Prince James Sobieski in 1737. But his close friendship with Henry caused many scenes with James. As the old King slid into his dotage, he tried to cling to the only son he had left and to some semblance of power, but Lercari and Henry had taken over financial affairs, and the latter preferred to stay at Frascati. Henry, too, was absent when his father expired.

Because of his hawklike hold on family matters, it was up to Henry to make his brother a monthly allowance of 10,000 Roman crowns, which came through the Pope via the Spanish benefices. Since Charles was living at the Muti, this was a sufficient amount to live on, but Henry was repeatedly called in to settle squabbles because Charles refused to pay his retainers. His stinginess was by no means a new trait; it had always been part of his makeup. Sir Thomas Sheridan, for instance, was not paid in all the time he was in Scotland, and it was James who had to make up arrears. Michael Sheridan and John Stafford, in charge of Charles's household at Avignon, were constantly dunning him for their pay. Henry Goring also complained that he had never been given "one farthing" for his services, and Dr. King in London observed that those who served the Prince went unrewarded.

In Sir Horace Mann's opinion Charles was a rich man and had the means to live a contented life at last if he chose to do so. Instead, he quarreled incessantly with his retainers and verbally and physically abused them in private and in public. Cardinal York was humiliated beyond measure by his brother's drunken displays. The bouts with the bottle went on from morning till night; his physical condition had deteriorated to an appalling degree; and alcohol had destroyed many of his brain cells. Charles found it hard to concentrate, his conversation was distracted, and he let his mind wander. His complexion was blotchy, and he looked far older than his years. When he was a young man, companions had commended his ability to hold his liquor, but now he was regarded as a disgusting old drunk and was shunned by everybody. An often-quoted description of his morose life was given by an English lady visiting Rome in 1767:

> As for his person it is rather handsome, his face ruddy and full of pimples. He looks good-natured, and was overjoyed to see me; nothing could be more affectionately gracious. I cannot answer for his cleverness, for he appeared to be absorbed in melancholy thoughts, a good deal of distraction in his conversation, and frequent brown studies. I had time to examine him for he kept me hours and hours. He has all the reason in the world to be melancholy, for there is not a soul goes near him, not knowing what to call him. He told me time lay heavy upon him. I said I supposed he read a good deal. He made no answer. He depends entirely for his subsistence upon his brother whom he never loved, much less now, he having brought him into the scrape.

One day in 1748 Charles became hopelessly drunk at the dining table. He proposed to Lumisden, Hay, and Urquhart that they go to an oratorio that evening. The men protested that he was in no condition to show himself, and they refused to accompany him. Charles staggered out to the coach, commanding them to follow, but still they resisted. With that he marched back to the Muti and dismissed them all.

Two days later he commanded them to return to duty, but Lumisden, Hay, and Urquhart had had more than enough and would serve him no further. Caryll stayed on as his secretary, and Charles appointed Italians "more fit for his purposes and designs." One was Count Spada, who had been brought up in the Court of Modena. The "purposes and designs" mentioned by the anonymous writer who sent this account to Scotland were that His titular Majesty needed people with whom he could carouse who would not dare to criticize him. One thing Lumisden and the others had objected to was cleaning up after Charles, who frequently had diarrhea when he was out. This unpleasant chore was performed by the Italians; Count Spada was often seen supporting his tipsy master when he cavorted idiotically on the dance floor.

For a while after the departure of Lumisden and the others, Charles seemed to tone down his drinking, now principally of wine from Cyprus. He was generally referred to as "the brother of Cardinal York." Perhaps Henry's tight control of the purse-strings was instrumental in Charles's reformed behavior over the next few years. But he was bored and took to consulting Tarot cards at

Princess Palestrina's palazzo for amusement. That Tarot cards existed in the Papal City, where reading them was viewed as evil necromancy, seems strange. One English visitor, who had grown up with the saying that the unholy trinity was made up of the Pope, the Devil, and the Pretender, struck up a conversation with Charles one evening at Princess Palestrina's. She had never before seen Tarot cards, and he displayed them for her, saying, " 'There is everything in the world to be found in these cards—the sun, the moon, the stars; and here,' says he throwing me a card, 'is the Pope; here is the devil; there is but one of the trio wanting, and you know who that should be!' " The lady was "so amazed, so astonished, though he spoke this last in a laughing good humoured manner, that I did not know which way to look; and as to a reply I made none."

In the summer of 1770, Charles journeyed to Pisa to take the mineral baths. Then he presented himself in Florence, where the Grand Duke of Tuscany, Maria Theresa's second son, ruled. He was by no means welcome, but nevertheless, to the acute embarrassment of the Grand Duke, he stayed on until a letter from Henry told him to withdraw and return to Pisa. Surprisingly enough, Charles did as he was bidden. The next year at the same time he again went to Pisa—supposedly to take the waters—and then vanished. Nobody, least of all archspy Sir Horace Mann, who was on the scene, knew where he had gone.

Late in the summer of 1771 it was discovered that Charles was in Paris once more. This time it was at the request of the French. Using the Duc de FitzJames as liaison, the French government was now trying to persuade Charles to marry and produce heirs. Exactly what was behind it is anyone's guess, but the Boston "massacre" of 1770 and rumbles from the American colonies may have been part of it. Perhaps Louis XV, now sixty-one years old, sought to take advantage of this and make use of Charles or one of Charles's heirs to set up the standard in the North American continent in the hope of uniting Canadian territories with Louisiana.

When Sir Walter Scott rummaged through the Stuart Papers after they were discovered in Italy in the nineteenth century, he said he had found evidence that France was plotting at this time to use Charles Stuart to accomplish her ambitions on the North American continent. It is more likely that France wanted another Stuart heir to use as a scarecrow against England, the way she had always used the exiled family. Charles may have been aware of this, but the prospect of a young wife and the solid promise of a French pension of 40,000 livres a year caught his attention. This promise turned out to be as empty as all the other French pledges of pensions to the Stuarts, but for the moment Charles was content to allow them to search for a suitable mate.

The bride selected for Charles was Princess Louise of Stolberg-Gedern. She was born at Mons in Belgium on September 20, 1752—the same time he began to live with Clementina Walkinshaw and one year and one month before Charles's own daughter was born at Liège, about eighty miles away. Her father was Gustave Adolphe, Prince of Stolberg-Gedern; he was killed while fighting for the Empress Maria Theresa when Louise was five years old. Her mother, Lady Charlotte Bruce, a daughter of Prince Maximilien Emmanuel of Hornes and granddaughter of the Scottish Earl of Elgin, had been left with four daughters to provide for on her own. Louise, the eldest, was placed in a Mons convent at the age of six, a year after her father's death.

Ten years later she emerged, a very pretty and accomplished young lady, to look for a husband with the assistance of her mother. Louise's mother tongue was German, but she was also proficient in French, had studied Latin, and spoke English. She loved to play stringed instruments such as the guitar, harp, and mandolin and had a strong leaning toward the then very fashionable study of philosophy. Her younger sister had already married into the FitzJames family; this is how she came to be considered as a bride for the titular King of England in Rome who was more than thirty-one years her senior. At the time the nuptial arrangements were concluded, with haste that could scarcely be credited, Princess Louise was just nineteen and a half years old. Her husband, who for a long time had been rumored to be impotent, may have had the French pension uppermost in his mind.

Charles was now back in Italy, but a proxy marriage took place in Paris on March 28, 1772, and Louise was conducted to Venice. From Venice she sailed to Ancona, then traveled on southward by coach to Macerata. There Charles and Lord Caryll awaited the bride for a formal ceremony to be conducted by the Bishop of Macerata. On Good Friday, April 17, the pair set eyes on each other for the first time.

Years later Louise told a friend that her mother, to get rid of her, "married me to the most insupportable man that ever existed, a man who combined the defects and failings of all classes, as well as the vice common to lackeys—that of drink." That was said in hindsight. But who knows what thoughts raced through Louise's mind when she first saw the stooped-over, bloated wreck of a man with a hobbled gait an hour before the evening ceremony. She was tough, physically, emotionally, and mentally; perhaps the thought crossed her mind then, as it often did during the marriage, that this man could not possibly last long. She decided to grit her strong white teeth (a description given to Charles of her dental condition beforehand) and brave it out for the duration. A few days later their coach rolled to a halt in front of the Muti. Another Stuart exile had brought home a wife to the dingy palazzo.

Bonnie Prince Charlie had always loved the adulation of crowds and adored to play to the gallery; but for some years nothing startling had happened in his life with which to hold the public's attention. Even he was sensitive enough to recognize that as a curiosity he had become a bore except to travelers from England who strove for a glimpse of the man who called himself their King. With his bloated frame, uncertain walk, and lamentable health he had long since ceased to be a figure of admiration, awe, and attention. But now that he had a pretty consort, Roman society began to take notice once again. A medal was struck to commemorate the marriage and, attracted by having the titular Queen of England in their midst, the aristocracy left their calling cards at the Palazzo Muti.

From the very beginning Louise was determined to insist on some royal prerogatives. One of these was not to return visits made to her by ladies of noble birth. Rome allowed her a few such airs, as if in recompense for the Pope's direction that they could not be addressed as "Your Majesty." Charles and Louise were frequently invited to dinners and grand balls, or they attended concerts and theaters. They entertained lavishly at the palace. Everywhere they went it was noted that Charles danced attendance on his pretty wife. Long bored by his own melancholy company, he delighted in this vibrant young woman and the gaiety she brought into his life. He even wrote his old flame, Madame Talmond, and told her how fortunate a bridegroom he was.

Charles temporarily halted his excessive drinking, and because of Louise's inborn leaning toward cultural pursuits, the palace became a center where aspiring young writers, painters, musicians, and philosophers would congregate. One of these was

Charles Victor Bonstetten, the Swiss philosopher and writer from Berne, who found Louise so captivating that he called her "the Queen of Hearts." He described her as "of medium height, she had dark blue eyes, a slightly turned-up nose, and the complexion of an English girl. Her expression was bright and piquant, and at the same time so sympathetic, that she turned all heads." From her portraits in middle age, the features would not seem to warrant such accolades when she was in repose, but from various descriptions her beauty shone through when she was gay and animated. Her looks were Germanic, but by her demeanor and bearing she was thought of as "more French than German."

Louise was also a magnetic flirt. Bonstetten remarked that when she was in high spirits, she would often make malicious comments disguised as raillery. During the philosopher's visits, Charles spoke in English, using his unique phraseology. He told stories of his flight through the Hebrides, and Louise laughed heartily to hear that a man of his mien and stature had escaped disguised as "Betty Burke." Bonstetten admitted that during those evenings of bright, happy talk, he became very attracted to Louise, although he said that at the time, "I did not admit it to myself." Louise was definitely a man's woman, and when she later offended the ladies of Florence, it mattered little to her, since she far preferred the company and intellectual conversation of men.

On the other side of the Alps the French watched and waited to see if Charles and Louise would produce an heir. The English government contemplated the possibility with distaste. And the thought that Charles might produce a child was viewed with distracted panic by Clementina Walkinshaw and her daughter, Charlotte.

Ever since Clementina fled from Charles's house twelve years before, she and Charlotte had been living quietly at various convents in France. Following his futile efforts to get his daughter back in 1760, Charles's heart had hardened toward Charlotte, as if she had been responsible for her mother's actions at the age of seven. He never forgave Clementina (now styled the Countess Alberstroff) for depriving him of "ye cheild," and he had consistently refused to pay anything toward their support throughout the years. When James died, the annual pension of 10,000 livres that he had sent Clementina stopped. Henry took it upon himself to meet his brother's obligation and made them an allowance, but he cut the amount of the pension in half and extracted a statement from Clementina that she had never been married to Charles—a statement that she afterward tried to retract.

Now reduced to living on 5,000 livres a year, the two women could hardly be called affluent. When they heard that Charles had married, they pressured him to legitimize Charlotte before the birth of an heir put her beyond all hope. Before his marriage was a month old, Charles received this plaintive letter from his daughter.

> Sire,
>
> It is with the most profound respect, Mon Auguste Papa, that I take the liberty of sending you my compliments to your household, and I beseech Your Majesty to be convinced that notwithstanding your forgetfulness, and the terrible emptiness in which you have left me, that will never prevent me from expressing all the most sincere wishes for everything affecting your happiness and prosperity; I cannot add anything since I exhausted all the feelings of my heart in the infinite number of letters that I have had the honour to write to you of which none has left any impression on you, Mon Auguste Papa, which is very clear proof to me of your total neglect, which I have never deserved. But I see that I must resign myself because nobody even dares to speak to you about me nor even to mention my name to you.
>
> I spoke with M. le Principal Gordon,* who appeared to me to be very touched by my situation of neglect. But he said that he could not undertake to write to you because of fear of displeasing Your Majesty, and many others have told me the same thing. So, Mon Auguste Papa, all that is left of the honour of being your daughter is despair, because I am without any future and without any status and consequently I am condemned to lead the most unfortunate and miserable life than to implore Heaven most earnestly to shorten my sad days, which already are too filled with bitterness, and I have the honour to finish, Mon Auguste Papa, with the deepest respect,
>
> Your most humble and most obedient servant and most unfortunate daughter,
>
> Charlotte
>
> From the Abbey of Notre Dame de Meaux en Brie
>
> 27th April 1772.

Pitiful entreaties had never before touched Charles, but this was the most touching letter he had ever received from his daughter.

*Gordon was the rector of the Scots College in Paris who acted as the channel of communications between Rome and Clementina.

He began to contemplate bringing Charlotte to Rome. Perhaps he believed that since there was only a year's difference in the ages of his wife and daughter, they could be good companions. However, this change of heart was not without qualifications and conditions. Lord Caryll responded through Principal Gordon and said it would be impossible to help Charlotte unless she could be persuaded to leave her mother behind.

> If the mother should ever determine to come on this side of the hills, all we could possibly do would be rendered ineffectual. You are sensible I should not speak this strongly, but on proper grounds and will therefore, I am persuaded, use every argument against such a step if you perceive it is thought of. . . . Be pleased to give me a quick decision on this, but observe also that a delay might be of prejudice to the young lady, as the vacancy there is in Mr. D's* family may soon be filled up, in which case there is no more remedy.

In the following August, Charlotte replied to the effect that although she would do anything for her father, she could not be expected to abandon her mother. Tactlessly she reminded him that Clementina was, after all, her other parent. The letter was long, woeful, and depressing and ended with a begging plea that Clementina be allowed to accompany her to Rome to hand her over to those who would be responsible for her welfare.

It is hard to understand why Charlotte pressed this point, except that the suggestion probably came from her mother. For the first time in twelve years there was hope that Charles would legitimize her. She should have realized that to bring her mother to Rome would not only be an embarrassment to him and his consort, but would also be disastrous to her own claims. When her letter arrived, Lord Caryll wrote a short and curt letter to Gordon saying that he had been unable to speak further on the matter with Charles because the latter was ill, and from the Rome end of this sad correspondence, the matter was considered closed.

Toward the end of the year—suddenly, unannounced, and ill-advisedly—Clementina Walkinshaw and her daughter arrived in Rome to make their supplications in person. Predictably, Charles was furious. Seething with outrage at the affront, he refused to see them and gave orders that they were not allowed near the palazzo.

---

*With overseas correspondents, Charles often used the old alias of "Mr. Douglas."

The distraught Clementina, who had gone into debt to make the journey, turned in every direction, appealing in vain for help to gain access to the man to whom she had devoted eight years of her life. Her protests fell on deaf ears.

It must have been a sad scene indeed: the aging ex-mistress, then fifty-three years old, pleading to see the man she had once loved so that he would give their daughter a place in the world. Disillusioned and heartsick, the women could do nothing but return to their convent in France, from where Charlotte began another series of long, sad, but unavailing letters.

For a year or more Sir Horace Mann had very little to report to London, except that the Prince had ceased to drink to excess and that he was constantly at Louise's side in their frequent public appearances. Then, at the end of 1773, he reported: "For a time after his marriage, he abstained from any great excess in wine, but of late he had given in to it again as much as ever, so that he is seldom quite sober, and frequently commits the greatest disorders in his family." Charles's retainers had been too sanguine in their hope that he had put aside drink forever. The pattern of his life had been to resort to this vice when thwarted, and nothing would change it. It was an aspect of her husband that Louise had yet to witness; in coming years she witnessed it often.

The occasion in 1773 that plunged Charles back to the bottle was the old queston of royal honors. Pope Clement XIV had now replaced the late Clement XIII, and celebrations for his Jubilee were drawing near. Once more Charles tried to demand the place of honor accorded to a sovereign, but the Pope refused to go back on the resolution of the Sacred College never to recognize the Stuarts again. Charles therefore declared that he would leave the Papal City forever and never return.

In 1774, Charles and Louise left Rome and lived temporarily at Leghorn, where he was seen by Casanova. The famous lover referred to him as "the Pretender-in-vain." They also went to Siena for a short period before finally making their home in Florence. A palace was put at their disposal by Prince Corsini, an old friend of the Stuarts. There they set up house while they looked for a permanent residence in the Tuscan capital.

Needless to say, the Grand Duke of Tuscany was not happy that Charles had bestowed the dubious honor of his presence upon his state. As the son of the Empress Maria Theresa, he had no wish to offend Britain by harboring the man who called himself King

Charles III of England. Accordingly, he gave orders that no official receptions were to be held for Charles, and he declined to recognize or even acknowledge his presence. The Prince was piqued by the Grand Duke's stand and held himself aloof from the Tuscan Court. Circumventing the inevitable, he announced that henceforth he and Louise would be known as the Count and Countess of Albany and would answer to no other name.

Sir Horace Mann must have been delighted that the couple had come to his city of residence, for now he could send first-hand accounts of their movements to London rather than rely on his spies in Rome. He recorded almost with relish many of the incidents that marred the later years of Charles's life. There was the night Charles insulted a French officer at the theater. Having hated all Frenchmen since his arrest at the opera in Paris, he engaged the officer in a heated exchange, during which he delivered some "injurious language." When the Frenchman haughtily supposed that the Count of Albany did not know whom he was addressing, Charles replied, "*Je sais que vous êtes français, et cela suffit!*" ["I know you are French, and that's enough!"]

Seventy-three-year-old Mann had now spent forty years dogging the footsteps of the Stuart family. The British government had confined him to this lifetime post because of his knowledge of Italy and the nature of its inhabitants. He had no family in Italy and was often lonely and homesick. His disposition was soured by the gout, from which he suffered, but he attached himself to the Stuarts like a limpet and now declared, "I have the most authentic means of being informed of everything that goes on in the Pretender's house."

Clement XIV did not long survive his Jubilee, and after his death in 1774 the Conclave of Cardinals met in Rome for the long process of electing his successor. Mann learned that Charles was entertaining the hopeful notion that Henry would be the new Pope and was telling everyone that now he would be recognized as Charles III of Great Britain: ". . . but what will make your Lordship smile," Mann wrote to the secretary of state, "is that the Pretender has said here that he will not return to Rome till his brother is made Pope, and that he is daily in expectation of receiving a courier with the notice of it. He probably was heated with wine (which is very often the case) when he said this, as he was remarkably noisy that evening at the public Casino, which he and his Consort always frequent." Cardinal Braschi was elected and assumed the title of Pope Pius VI. Charles stayed on in Florence.

As in Rome, Louise insisted that her station exempted her from returning visits made to her by the ladies of Florence. But unlike their counterparts in Rome, they did not let this pass without protest. To have the titular Queen of England in their midst was an honor of a sort, but a display of royal pomp in any form was quite a different matter. The result of Louise's airs and graces, according to Mann, was that society ladies stopped calling. However, the Marchesa Nobili-Vitelleschi* tells us that society was as polite to the Count and Countess of Albany as it had been at Rome. Prominent nobles and even ministers of the Grand Duke came to pay their respects and granted the couple all courtesies and attentions—but no royal homage.

When they came near the Grand Duke and his wife at any of the lavish balls that Charles loved to frequent, the two couples would steer away from one another to avoid a direct confrontation. The situation calls to mind the Prince's behavior in Paris and his overlong stay in South Uist. He certainly had no scruples about embarrassing his host, but as he wrote all those years ago, "What can a bird do that has not found a right nest? He must flit from bough to bough."

Almost three years after her ill-fated journey to Rome, Charlotte Stuart was heard from again. Now in her twenty-second year and despairing of recognition or maintenance from Charles, she decided the only avenue left to her was to marry. Principal Gordon presented her case, saying that she was "inclined to marry the first person who will seek her and has enuff to make her live." He went on to hint that at her age she should wed now before it was too late. "I am heartily sorry for her misfortunate situation and think she deserves better, being esteemed by all who know her as being one of the most accomplished women in this town . . . her spirits are entirely brock and the Doctor says that her grief has given her an obstruction on the Liver." As early as 1768 this liver complaint (from which her grandmother Mary of Modena also suffered) was mentioned by Clementina, who attributed it to her daughter's grief at not being recognized by her father.

The sympathetic Gordon obviously did not relish his role as intermediary in this affair. The message he was required to relay to Charlotte from her father was that if she married, he would have nothing further to do with her. After this, Gordon begged to be given no more errands of such nature, explaining that "Her health

*A Court in Exile, vol. 2.

at the present is not in a good way and I believe my conference with her will make it worse. I beg therefore you will give me no more such commissions, as it hurts me to be anyways, tho' innocently, the occasion of the death of a person I esteem and respect much." With very good reason Charlotte believed that her father was heartless and that he was punishing her for her mother's actions. He would not contribute a penny toward their welfare and yet denied her the right to marry. Once again she found herself awaiting—she did not know for how long—her father's royal pleasure.

By the summer of 1775, after three years of marriage, there was no sign of an heir. It was said that Charles had taken a young bride to perpetuate the line, but there is no reason to suppose that this is what he desired and even less to believe it possible; impotency appears to have been a feature of his life at this time and perhaps had been for several years past. Charles had once deeply wounded his father by calling him "unpatriotic" for having brought children into the world without being able to regain the throne—a statement that speaks volumes about the way the Prince perceived himself and his relationship to the rest of the world. We can only assume that he married Louise for companionship and to gain a French pension.

As for the young Countess of Albany, she was bored with her husband. She took to writing long amatory letters to Bonstetten when he returned to Switzerland. During the sweltering Florentine summer of 1775, her frustration and malice surfaced in a spiteful letter she wrote to Charles on June 5. He loved to display himself and be taken note of, but she was thoroughly tired of being asked to ride through the boulevards with him during the heat of the day.

The subject must have been a running battle between them for some time, for apparently Charles told her that if she arose earlier in the morning, she could accompany him while it was still cool. How was it possible to arise at seven in the morning when the entertainments of the previous evening had kept them up until two hours after midnight? Louise protested. She could only suppose that he must be joking to make such a suggestion; otherwise she must think that he was talking nonsense. "But this cannot be so," Louise continued, "because Your Majesty has not yet reached the age when one babbles senselessly." As if on a different subject but with deliberate intent to wound, she continued in French:

It would be to your shame if the world knew that you, who always had the reputation of a *gaillard**, have now degenerated to the point of not wanting to stay with a young and pretty woman who loves you, even for just a little while. But if Your Majesty continues to sulk the way he is doing now, I think I should justify myself publicly considering that I am the innocent cause of the fact that your Royal Face is not as radiant as it was before and that your beautiful eyes are dull.

Louise concluded this malicious letter with a threat to send all her friends a copy of a separate memorandum outlining Charles's treatment of her.

The letter speaks for itself. At the same time, Mann reported that Charles was "jealous to such a degree of his wife that she is never out of his sight; all the avenues to her room, excepting through his own, are barricaded: The reason he gives for this is that the succession may never be dubious." The couple was becoming irreconcilably estranged. The malice that even Bonstetten admitted Louise was capable of was no longer masked with humor. The retreat into the bottle again became a means to blot out the futility of Charles's life, and he cared little that his behavior humiliated and disgusted his wife.

On September 5, 1775, Sir Horace Mann sent the following letter to the secretary of state:

The Pretender's health continues still to be in a declining state; the habitual discharge from one of his legs is still stopped, and of late he has been troubled with violent pains in his stomach after eating (though very moderately). Nevertheless he goes out constantly to take the air in his coach, and to the Theatre, where for the most part of the time he remains in the corner of his box in a drowsy posture . . . though the sickness at his stomach very commonly obliges him to retire in a hurry into the public passage, where two of his servants attend to give him assistance. His physician is using all the means proper to procure the return of the discharge from his leg, which may relieve him.

Charles did nothing to heed nature's warning. Giving in to his constant need for gaiety, attention, and diversion, he let no impor-

---

*Gaillard as used by Louise has been variously translated. The term means a vigorous, robust, lusty man. It is also the French word for the buck deer, and she could have meant "young buck."

tant social event pass without making an appearance. The couple was seen at all the grand balls, he in mask and costume, she undisguised. Frequently they crossed the path of the Grand Duke and his lady, but Mann assured London that "no civilities have passed between him or his wife and the Great Duke and Duchess." In response to this particular bulletin of Sir Horace's, the Earl of Rochford wrote a reply from London demonstrating that the British government was still interested in Charles's connections and "authentick Intelligence where he resides, how he continues to be treated in the Country where he lives, and with whom he is chiefly connected; you will therefore do well not to lose sight of these objects."

Charles and Louise continued to live in a succession of borrowed homes, which made Mann's spying difficult. But early in 1776, we learn from him, Charles was seized by an epileptic fit. His entire household was alarmed to the extent that they believed him on the verge of death. But his iron constitution prevailed, and although he suffered many of these attacks during the year, he insisted upon going regularly to the theater. "These frequent Epileptick fits . . . must end in an Apoplexy," opined Mann. "The couch has been placed in his box that he can lie at full length and Sleep with greater ease." Sir Horace also confided that he had seen Charles sip from a bottle of Cyprus wine while he dozed during the performance, and Louise was forced to endure the humiliation of it all.

Louise had once told Bonstetten that she did not believe she could love any man seriously but that "if I found a man full of originality I should love him always." In the summer of 1776, a poet and dramatist by the name of Count Vittorio Alfieri visited Florence, where he noticed "a beautiful, amiable, and very distinguished foreigner. It was impossible not to meet and remark this lady, and still more impossible not to seek to please when once in her company." The "beautiful foreigner" was, of course, the Countess of Albany, and in the following year, when Alfieri returned to Florence the two met again, beginning a long association that scandalized the whole Continent.

Count Vittorio Alfieri, who was three years older than Louise, was born in 1749 to a rich and noble family with estates at Asti in the Piedmont region of Italy. He was tall, with a fair complexion crowned by an unruly shock of red hair, and he was so thin that his schoolmates had called him *"Carcase."* Nonetheless, Alfieri was generally considered a handsome man, and when he met Louise he was beginning to be spoken of as if he were a genius. He was fully convinced himself that this was the case, and in his autobiography* he candidly informs us: "I have regarded myself as an individual whose actions could not fail to prove interesting to posterity." So fascinating and lively were his actions and writings that barely anyone today recognizes his name.

Alfieri was vain, shallow, and arrogant; the main object of his adult life was to find a woman to love him. In the years before he met Louse, he had tried very hard to find that woman. At the age of nineteen he visited all the European capitals and in London fell in love with the notorious young wife of Lord Ligonier, who was related to the general who had commanded one arm of the forces against the Jacobites. Unknown to Alfieri, the lady was also having an affair with her husband's groom; the groom tipped his Lordship off about Alfieri.

A duel was scheduled to take place in Green Park. Alfieri arrived on the scene with his arm in a sling, saying he said he had fallen from his horse. "I was never a proficient in the use of the sword," Alfieri confessed. "I rushed on him contrary to all the rules of the art, like a mad man as I was, for in fact I wished to meet death at his hands." This was typical of the Italian's dramatism. Ligonier solicitously inquired if Alfieri's injury would disable him from fighting, and there was no real duel at all. Ultimately both of them looked like fools, for when his Lordship returned home, he found his wife had run off with the groom.

Alfieri continued his journeys through Holland, Sweden, Spain, and back to Italy, falling in love several times over, usually with married women. He seemed to derive fuel for his writings from each tormented relationship. But his goal was to find the one love who would appreciate his talents and inspire him to greater heights. He found her in the wife of Bonnie Prince Charlie.

In contrast to Bonstetten's statement that Louise had dark blue eyes, Alfieri described her thus: "Large black eyes, full of fire and gentleness, joined to a fair complexion and flaxen hair, gave to her beauty a brilliancy it was difficult to withstand." He admired her "taste for letters and the fine arts, an amiable character, an immense fortune, and placed in domestic circumstances of a very painful nature. How was it possible to escape when so many reasons existed for loving?"

By the end of 1777, Charles had decided to purchase the

Vita di Vittorio Alfieri di Asti.

Palazzo Guadagni, a Renaissance building with balconies over-looking the hills of Fiesole. Situated near the Church of the Annunziata on what is now Florence's via Gino Capponi, Charles erected a weather vane shaped like a flying standard atop the central tower. Bearing the initials C.R. (for "Carolus Rex"), the weather vane could still be seen until very recent years, as could an inscription over the broad stairway proclaiming Charles King of Great Britain, Defender of the Faith, and the date of his "accession," 1766.

To the Guadagni Alfieri came as often as he deemed wise. Having enjoyed success at Turin with his production of *Cleopatra*, at Louise's suggestion he began work on the tragedy *Maria Stuarda*. Perhaps Charles was flattered that this star on the rise should devote so much time to the life of his great-great-great-grand-mother. He seemed to like the young man and invited him often to dinner, talking with him afterward until he fell asleep by the fire. Charles was taking laudanum to relieve pain in his legs and the great discomfort caused by an anal fistula; the drug, combined with wine, obliterated most of his evenings.

We cannot say that Louise's relationship with Alfieri was adulterous while she was living under her husband's roof. The playwright complained that Charles was constantly present, or at best in the next room. "In the nine years or more that the Count and Countess lived together, never, no never, did he once go out without her, nor she without being accompanied by him; such a bondage would have wearied even the most devoted lovers." And from the inveterate Mann we learn that Charles insisted Louise share his bed. This must have placed a great strain on her, for many nights her husband was seized with coughing fits or he would have to rush from his bed to perform emergency ablutions. After six years of marriage Louise began to look pale and drawn. "His wife's beauty has faded of late," said Mann. "She has paid dear for the dregs of Royalty!"

Florentine society became aware of Louise's increasing re-liance upon her *cavaliere servente*, and she had their sympathy. Sir Horace Mann also heard the gossip, but Charles seemed to be impervious to the romance blossoming under his nose and contin-ued to invite Alfieri to dinner. For his part, the young writer took great care not to arouse suspicion in the older man, limiting his visits and contenting himself with seeing Louise briefly. During the rest of the time he threw himself into a round of prolific writing. From this period come many amatory poems inspired by the Countess of Albany. In 1778 he penned these lines:

> *O Lady is my fear for thee displeasing,*
> *When my warm love is half compact of fear?*
> *Since I behold thee forced with grief unceasing*
> *The harsh yoke of an aged spouse to bear,*
> *Like some trapped dove in vain for mercy pleading*
> *From hands so impious and from home so drear*
> *I mean to snatch thee, my alarm increasing*
> *With each foul act, with every falling tear.*

Alfieri spent a great deal of time wondering just how to snatch his dove away from her aged spouse, but it was no easy matter. Because the Piedmontese were prohibited by law from removing their assets from the region, Alfieri's funds were limited, although his sister was allowed to send him a small income. This is, at least, the way Alfieri explained his penury. In the meantime, Louise occupied herself by reading, studying mathematics, and taking Italian lessons from Alfieri. She now hated her husband and earnestly hoped that each new bout with illness would be his last.

Charles, however, confounded everyone by his extraordinary ability to rally from each seizure. Twice in 1779, both Mann and Louise (for separate reasons) were ready to bury the man, but he had a tenacious hold on life. As he had done with James, Sir Horace was predicting Charles's death to London years before it happened, and the government was tired of hearing about it. One chastening letter from Viscount Weymouth at Westminster told Mann: "It is not necessary to send an Express with the account of the Death of the Pretender if that should happen, as the early notice is not of importance." Two months later the exasperated Mann had to confess that Charles had been seen at a masked ball, the neck of a wine bottle peeping out of his pocket. "He was so heated with it . . . that he would dance a minuet with a young lady, though he was obliged to be supported through it by Count Spada his gentleman, which exposed him to the ridicule of the crowd that surrounded him."

Louise must have wondered just how many more times this man would return from the edge of the grave. "Her afflictions augmented every day," wrote Alfieri, "and the barbarous treatment which she suffered from her unrelenting husband induced her at length, in order to save her health and life, to consider by what means she might emancipate herself from the dominion of her cruel persecutor." She wrote to Henry to sound him out on the possibility of his moral and financial support if she separated from Charles. But the Cardinal was no help at all. As a man of the Church he could only look upon his brother's union with Louise as indissoluble, and he counseled her to endure her circumstances with prayer and patience.

On the evening of November 30, 1780, Saint Andrew's Day, Charles was drinking more heavily than usual in honor of Scotland's patron saint. Late that evening, after he and Louise had retired, shouts and screams came from their bedroom. The household arrived on the scene—according to Mann, who was not there—just in time to save Louise from being choked by her husband. Charles was also "committing the greatest indecencies upon her, in bed."

Whatever happened that night, Louise determined to leave the Guadagni Palace forever within the week. A plan was formed after a hurried conference with Alfieri. He was to take no obvious active part in effecting Louise's escape, but he secured the protection and approval of the Grand Duke of Tuscany for what followed. He also enlisted the aid of a Mr. Geohagan and a Madame Orlandini, both friends of Louise.

One morning in the first week of December, Louise invited Madame Orlandini to breakfast with her and Charles. During the course of the meal, the ladies suggested that a visit to the Convent Bianchette to examine the embroidery of the nuns would be a pleasant day's outing. As anticipated, Charles agreed, and the party set off by coach. When they arrived at the convent, Mr. Geohagan happened on the ladies and Charles as if by chance. As the two men exchanged pleasantries, Louise and her friend ran up the steps leading to the main entrance of the convent. They were hurriedly let in; then the heavy door was shut and bolted.

At length Charles began to wonder what was keeping his wife, so he took leave of Mr. Geohagan and hobbled up the steps. At first there was no response to his knocks at the door, so he banged louder. Presently a small grating in the doorway was opened, and the abbess appeared to notify Charles that his wife had sought and would receive sanctuary at the convent. He was stunned, but as the truth slowly began to dawn, he began to bluster and demand that his wife be brought immediately to him. But the grating was firmly closed. The abbess, under orders from the Grand Duke of Tuscany, refused to discuss the matter further. Enraged, humiliated, and defeated, there was nothing the Count of Albany could do but return to the Guadagni and seek solitary solace in a wine bottle.

Chapter 14

Epilogue: The Count of Albany

Either Henry had not taken the trouble to become fully acquainted with the temperament of his vivacious sister-in-law, or he was ill-equipped to assess her character. When she wrote to him on December 9 asking for his help, he immediately made arrangements for Louise to retire to the Ursuline Convent of Santa Cecilia in Rome, where his mother had once sought sanctuary. With no prior discussion with Charles, Henry instantly took Louise's part in the dispute, telling her he was convinced of "the integrity of your motives" because the Tuscan Court had approved of her flight from the Palazzo Guadagni. He also imagined that she would be content to spend the rest of her days in convent seclusion, but all she really wanted was to be with Alfieri. Louise was not one to kick over all the traces in the name of love, particularly before a separation and financial settlement had been arranged. It was going to take some artful scheming and manipulation of the Cardinal, therefore, before she could get what she wanted.

In the meantime Charles fussed, fumed, and got drunk, publicly denouncing Alfieri as a seducer and threatening to have Geohagan shot for his part in Louise's flight. Sir Horace Mann enjoyed the squalid gossip along with the rest of Florence. By this time the Count of Albany had become a laughingstock and the butt of cruel jokes, for he was still fond of prophesying that his people would call him to Westminster one day. With tongue in cheek, Mann reported to London, "The mould for any more casts of Royal Stuarts has been broke, or what is equivalent to it has been shut up in a Convent of Nuns under the double lock and key of the Pope and Cardinal York, out of the reach of any dabbler who might foister in any spurious copy. Historians may now close the lives of that family, unless the Cardinal should become Pope, and that would only produce a scene short of ridicule."

Alfieri took himself off to Naples in hope of quelling the scandal, while Louise schemed ways to extricate herself from her pious prison without giving offense to Henry, who held the purse-strings. The Cardinal invited her often to dine with him at his home in Frascati, where she provided gay and intelligent company. She complimented him on his enormous collection of exquisitely bound books encased in Morocco leather and hand tooled with gold. Henry was a collector of gem-encrusted trinkets as well as of rare books. Louise shrewdly took note of every foible and facet of her brother-in-law's character, the better to entrench herself in his favor.

Henry was completely taken in by Louise. When she complained after four months in the convent that the restricted life brought on daily blinding headaches, he promptly offered her the use of the second floor of the Palazzo Cancelleria, his official residence in Rome. He saw himself as the protector of this amiable and cultured lady who, like Talmond and Walkinshaw, had suffered barbarous physical abuse at the hands of his besotted brother. Henry also arranged with the Pope to have Charles's income divided so that half of it was paid directly to Louise.

Henry was a total innocent when it came to affairs of the heart between men and women. Although all Rome knew and relished the gossip surrounding Alfieri and his sister-in-law, the Cardinal seemed to be unaware of it. He appeared only too glad to have this opportunity to punish Charles for all his sins by depriving him of half his income. He also assisted in arranging a 20,000-livre pension for Louise from the Court of France and was delighted to find himself occasionally drawn into her circle of artistic friends. Louise noticed that Henry's library lacked a copy of Virgil, and she cunningly arranged for Alfieri to come to Rome to meet the Cardinal, bearing as a gift a handsome volume of Virgil.

Duping Henry was all too easy. Usually he resided in the bishopric of his beloved Frascati, where he was deeply engrossed in the lavish restoration of many churches. But even if he had lived in Rome, it is doubtful that common gossip would have been relayed to him as he was often the subject of talk himself. The handsome Lercari had been replaced by one youthful seminarian after another; it was said that Henry kept a young catamite for his pederastic pleasures. Pederasty was commonplace among higher ecclesiastics and even bore a mantle of respectability when cata-mite youths frequently rose to high positions in the Church. But for the most part Romans were tired of the power, social domina-tion, and indulgences exercised by churchmen. Bishops and Cardinals were now left out of the mainstream of social happen-ings, particularly Henry, who annoyed many by his preference for being addressed as "highness" rather than "Eminence." His social isolation explains his initial pleasure when his sister-in-law intro-duced him to Alfieri and other artists. As for his homosexuality and the claim that he kept a young boy—which was whispered but never proved—he was as circumspect in his private life as he was in all other matters and took great care that his public actions were beyond reproach. Nevertheless, talk persisted, its usual source being English visitors traveling in Italy, who were sur-prised to find that Romans also derided the Stuarts and held them in contempt.

Henry lived a strange life, caught between the asceticism of his profession, in which personal adornment meant little, and his fervent dedication to upholding the name of the Royal House of Stuart, of which he and Charles were the last representatives. His brother was a wife-beating drunkard in Florence, afflicted with an obese and putrifying carcass borne on legs no longer able to support his weight. It remained for Henry to bring a semblance of respectability to the name of Stuart, and he left his mark every-where. The English royal coat of arms was painted over the doorways and stairwells of his many residences and was stamped in gold on the leather covers of his books. His greatest indulgence was to spend money on beautiful objects, and his homes were richly furnished; but while his guests dined from the finest hand-painted porcelain and china, he ate from a plain earthenware plate. He was not known for his intelligence, although he attained the position of Vice Chancellor to the Holy See before becoming Dean of the Sacred College; he appeared too anxious to be liked to have many friends. But the friendships he did form with other ecclesiastics usually lasted for several years—which is more than can be said of his brother's associations.

Although Louise flattered and danced attendance on the Cardinal of York when he was in residence at the Cancelleria, she did not like him. She thought him an insipid bore and stupid as well. Years later in letters to friends, she called Henry a "jailer" and said he was even more despicable than Charles. She also accused "this comical figure, my brother-in-law," of absurd and wanton extravagance in his manner of living. To demonstrate his simple-mindedness, Louise related that once when Henry was aboard a ship with all sails unfurled, he ordered the vessel to halt in the middle of the ocean. "Can you believe such a thing possible?" she asked. Nevertheless, Louise took everything she could from Henry and deceived him by stealing away to meet with Alfieri, who had now taken an apartment in Rome.

Matters began to come to a head with the public performance of Alfieri's tragedy *Antigone* at the Spanish Embassy in November 1782. For two years the couple had been meeting in secret, but this evening Louise could not resist appearing publicly at Alfieri's side. She wore the magnificent Sobieski rubies flanked by the Stuart diamonds, and the titular Queen of England looked stunning. At the reception afterward the evening was a success because Roman society had more fuel for gossip than ever before.

Four months later, Henry received an urgent message that his brother was dangerously ill and dying in Florence. Although he and Charles had not been communicating for some time due to financial squabbles and his sheltering of Louise, Henry made arrangements to leave for Florence immediately.

Whether Charles contrived to bring Henry to his bedside is hard to say, for when the Cardinal reached Florence he found that his brother had indeed been dangerously ill but was far from death's portal. He was not ambulatory and never would be again. He had to be carried from room to room. His mind wandered to the point that he repeated himself every quarter of an hour, and of his own admission he was "bothered in the head." But Charles had not lost his ability to persuade, particularly when he was incensed that his wife was getting away with so much at his expense. Henry listened intently, and doubtless Charles had a parade of Florentine witnesses attesting to his wife's flirtatious ways. Some said they could never tell when Charles Edward Stuart was lying, but Henry did not doubt that he was hearing the truth.

The Cardinal had always been slow to anger, but when he did anger he could be volatile and vindictive. Without even confronting Louise about her indiscretions, Henry had an audience with Pope Pius VI as soon as he returned to Rome, and he told everyone he knew that he now had a bad opinion of his sister-in-law and Count Alfieri. Perhaps it was less embarrassing to have a brother who was cuckolded by his spouse than one who was a known wife-beater. The self-satisfied Horace Mann wrote smugly, "The cat is at last out of the bag."

Louise was furious at Henry, denied any wrongdoing, and went so far as to rebuke him for "most unnecessarily" informing the Pope. He began to wonder if Louise was innocent after all. Hating to be disliked, he made her a peace offering of the Stuart diamonds. She responded tartly that since she was his brother's wife, she had a right to the diamonds anyway and then wrote nastily: "I only ask for your affection. In any event everybody will hear you wanted to give them to me, for I shall tell this to all my friends."

Was she referring to the diamonds or to Henry's affections? There is room for conjecture on that point, but there is no doubt that the Princess of Stolberg-Gedern was not above using black-mail to keep the Stuart brothers in line. This was neither the first nor the last time she threatened to tell all about her treatment at their hands. It was an effective ploy because both Henry, who was deeply affected by unsavory talk, and Charles knew that Roman society was only too eager to believe the worst of them.

Before the Pope ordered Count Alfieri to depart, he left the capital of the ancient world discreetly and quietly. He retired to Siena and stayed with his friend Francesco Gori, a wealthy silk merchant. He next went to Paris, from where he wrote to Louise describing the "majestic and noble spectacle" of hot-air balloons, which were the current rage in France. Traveling on to England—a country for which he had a deep affection—he indulged his passion for buying Thoroughbred horses. During his long absence, Louise was distraught and poured out the "utter torment" of life without Alfieri in long, soulful letters to Gori. "If only you knew how miserable and depressed I am!" she wrote in French. "It appears to me that my burden of wretchedness increases daily. I do not know how I am to exist without the Friend . . . I do nothing but weep . . ."

Although Louise believed herself deeply in love with Alfieri, she was probably dependent upon him for emotional support more than anything else. Almost every eighteenth-century con-vent-bred woman of genteel birth had to depend on a man for her passport out of convent life, but all too often she exchanged one prison for another, as Louise had by marrying Charles. If she had truly loved Alfieri, Louise would have quit Rome to be with him if he had asked her. (However, we know nothing about his thoughts on the matter when he left the Papal City.)

The Princess of Stolberg-Gedern, however, was something of an opportunist. She enjoyed being recognized as the Queen of England by those who flattered her as such, and she did not want to give up the pensions, allowances, and jewels that would be hers when her aged spouse died. Her letters to Gori clearly show that foremost among her desires was the death of her husband. She wrote of Charles, "Who knows what will be the end of this Man? This man in Florence who has been ill such a long time? He seems to me to be made of iron to destroy us. You will tell me in order to reassure me that he cannot last long; . . . but I think he can hold out very easily for a year or two longer. Of course he may at any moment succumb to the gout in his chest. What a brutal thing it is to expect one's happiness through another's death! O God, it degrades the soul! Yet none the less I cannot refrain from this desire."

Almost a year after the lovers parted, King Gustavus III of Sweden came to Italy to tour the major cities. The Swedish crown had earlier been engaged in Jacobite plots against the Hanoverians, who had wrested territory from the Swedes. When the Jacobites had to flee their native land in 1746, hundreds sailed northward to Sweden and several became distinguished officers of the Swedish army. Gustavus, therefore, made a point of paying his respects to Charles when he arrived in Florence. He was deeply shocked by Charles's appallingly decrepit condition; the former adventurer had recently celebrated his sixty-third birthday. The air was foul with the stench of his putrid flesh rotting under bandages, and his repetitive conversation dwelt morosely on the past and on the injustices he had suffered in the name of his family. He was pitiful, reduced to near-beggary from having to manage his household on 5,000 crowns a year. He wrote to Gustavus's equerry in March 1784, "at the moment of writing to you I haven't got a sou . . ." He also complained that Henry was a tyrant about money.

Historians have said that Gustavus persuaded Charles to obtain a legal separation from his wife, but Louise's correspondence with Baron Carl Sparre of the Swedish Court makes it clear that it was she who wanted to be free. She had spent an agonizing year apart from Alfieri and was worried that he might seek a love to replace her. Louise indicated that she was willing to relinquish the "pin-money" that had been granted to her under the terms of the marriage contract and that she would make over to Charles the 5,000 crowns she was receiving from the papal pension—a move that infuriated Henry later when he learned about it. But to compensate for what she gave up to her husband, she got the French pension increased to 60,000 livres a year and asked that 6,000 Roman crowns be given to her upon Charles's death.

The kindly Swedish King (who was assassinated eight years later) became a mediator between the couple, and it was through his influence that Charles also received pensions from both France and Spain. Gustavus went about this in a far different manner from Charles. Signing himself "Charles R," he had written to Louis XVI that now was the time for a strike on England and that he would be willing to march at the head of his people and so forth.

Gustavus finally persuaded him to put away his demands to be recognized internationally as a king. Charles had never before availed himself of advice from a respected source. He had always dictated to "advisers" to do as they were told and when matters went awry suffer the blame. A counsel as wise and revered as Gustavus was entirely different.

Charles had been so blinded by ambition to succeed where his father had failed—as if to repay James for his heavy-handed and highly intrusive manner at parenting—that he was oblivious to the threat his claims represented to the sovereign laws of France and Spain. They could never recognize him, just as they could never have recognized his father. It would have had complicated legal ramifications, particularly since James II had fathered several illegitimate children and nobody knew for sure just how many Stuart scions existed.

James had been aware of the legal entanglements but had played the game anyway to extract an income upon which the family could survive. He had arranged ecclesiastic preferment for Henry, and Charles might have been Governor of Navarre if he had not rashly sailed for Scotland to best the father he had come to hate. King Gustavus knew the family history, but more important, he recognized the Stuarts for what they were—victims of a worldwide movement to exterminate the privileges of kings and clergymen. The King of Sweden was being plagued by similar troubles in his own country, although he was considered an enlightened monarch; perhaps he imagined himself in Charles's position and wondered if he might one day suffer the same fate. Gustavus asked the Kings of France and Spain to provide an income for Charles Stuart, on grounds of simple humanity toward a fallen monarchical house. His request was granted because the letters were not signed by the man claiming to be King Charles III.

In Florence, however, the Count of Albany still kept up appearances. By the end of March he had consented "absolutely to a separation from my wife and that she no longer bears my name"; but Louise held on to the Stuart diamonds until he put it in writing. On April 3, 1784, "We, Charles, legitimate King of Great Britain" set his hand and seal "in Our Palace at Florence" to an order granting his wife a legal separation.

Although Louise was now free to travel and live wherever she chose, she still had to be careful about her behavior; the couple was not divorced and Charles was still alive. In the middle of August she journeyed secretly to Alsace and met Alfieri at the Inn of the Two Keys in Colmar, where the poet was "speechless from plentitude of my joy." They spent two idyllic months together, then returned separately to Italy, she to winter in Bologna, Alfieri in Pisa.

Even after Charles died three winters later, the couple never married, although they lived together in Paris and Italy and traveled extensively throughout Europe. Louise was even presented at the Court of George III in 1791 through a relative of her mother, and she tried unsuccessfully to wrest a pension from that quarter. She and Alfieri returned to Florence and became close friends of French artist Francois Xavier Fabre, who painted portraits of the middle-aged couple. The pert and pretty Princess of Stolberg-Gedern had either grown careless about her appearance or else was one of the growing number of women who rebelled against spending hours in front of a mirror braiding and teasing their hair into impossible styles. Fabre depicted Louise with unkempt graying hair and simple clothes, unadorned by any jewelry. Her frame was comfortably ample, and her face was strong and handsome rather than pretty. Fabre saw her as an intelligent, self-possessed woman with no time or use for the fripperies of artificial adornment. Peace was on her face, and there is no doubt she was one of the few female survivors of an age when married women usually ended up victims of their husbands. Alfieri died in 1803, by which time Fabre had come to love the widow of Bonnie Prince Charlie. The two remained together until Louise's death at Florence in 1824.

Charles had fallen seriously ill in 1783, after Louise left him. He legitimized his daughter and revised his will to include her. He still had not seen Charlotte since she was seven; her futile journey to Rome was now almost a dozen years in the past. In July 1784, three months after he had granted a legal separation to Louise, Charles decided to send for his daughter and install her in the Palazzo Guadagni as the Duchess of Albany. She was now thirty-one years old, and although Charles had forbidden her to marry, she had done just what Principal Gordon had hinted was her only avenue: she had sought a protector with the wherewithal to provide a reasonably comfortable life. Charlotte was the mistress of Prince Ferdinand Rohan, the Archbishop of Bordeaux. She had three children by him, two girls named Algae and Marie, born in 1780 and 1782, and a boy named Charles Edward, from whose birth she was recovering when she received the summons from her father in Florence.

If Charles was aware of the existence of these grandchildren, there is no evidence of it. Moreover, Charles's brain had degenerated to the point that he was beyond comprehending anything more intricate than how to get through the physical motions of each day, so it is safe to assume that he was totally ignorant of the matter. Even if he had known about them, he would not have considered them legitimate; each was born out of wedlock. Charlotte arrived in Florence at the end of 1784, leaving the children in the care of her mother. She would write coded letters home asking about her "*ami*" (Rohan) and the children, to whom she referred as "the flowers in my garden." There would have been no need for such subterfuge if her father and uncle had been aware of the children.

Charlotte was a fairly good-looking woman. She had inherited the large eyes of her Sobieski grandmother, the generous mouth of her father, and the nut-brown curly hair of her Walkinshaw progenitors. Her upbringing and life also shaped Charlotte, but her physical resemblance to the Sobieski-Stuarts—and to her father in particular— was unmistakable.

They had only three years together before Charles succumbed to his extreme infirmities. They were not pleasant years for Charlotte. She loathed his disgusting physical condition and was embarrassed that in his lighter moods of senile whimsy (a condition undoubtedly heightened by opiates, which were commonly prescribed at the time) he insisted upon being carried to public places in a litter. As Charlotte wrote to her mother, "It is cruel that in his condition he has the rage to see and be seen. . . . What a pitiful figure he cuts and how miserable I am that he will show himself to the public." But show himself he did, every evening at the theaters with Charlotte on his arm decked out in the Sobieski jewels, which—possibly through the intervention of King Gustavus—Henry had grudgingly sent from Rome.

However, Henry would not part with two large rubies that Poland had pawned to his Sobieski grandfather for one hundred years in return for a large sum of money. The time was drawing near for the redemption of the jewels. Sir Horace Mann opined that the impoverished Republic of Poland was not in a position to redeem them. According to Mann, Henry's stated reason for not giving his brother the rubies was that he intended to sell or pawn them to some court to provide an annuity for Charles and his daughter. He probably kept the jewels to himself because he was afraid that Charles in his dotage might make an outright gift of them to Charlotte.

Rich as he was, in his declining years Henry grew inordinately covetous of the family's assets. This might well have been understandable if he had had progeny of his own whose inheritance he desired to protect, but that was not the case. When James died, Henry had cut in half the allowance that his father had given Clementina Walkinshaw, although there was enough money left to continue the full pension of 10,000 livres. But now Charles assumed the responsibility of paying Clementina's 5,000 livres a year, and it appears that Henry was forced to turn over the funds to meet that obligation.

Again, this arrangement may have come about at the intervention of the Swedish King, but whatever the financial adjustments were between Charles and Henry, the latter bitterly resented the appearance of the new Duchess of Albany and did nothing to welcome her into their sad little family. Henry has often been depicted as a benign and near-saintly soul, but we cannot forget that he had extracted a statement from Clementina Walkinshaw that she and Charles had never been married. Why should he do this unless he were seeking to reduce the number of heirs of the brother he would surely outlive? Why also should he have taken such an active role in the separation of Charles and Louise unless it were to eliminate the possibility of more heirs?

Like James and Charles, who for the past quarter-century have enjoyed a reputation more flattering than they deserve, Henry's life also bears closer scrutiny. At least two of the many disparaging remarks made about him are impressed in our minds. One was the Marquis d'Argenson's observation in 1745—when it was hard to believe of the ascetic young man in black—that Henry was "Italian, superstitious, a rogue, avaricious, fond of ease, and jealous of the Prince." The other was Louise's indictment that the Cardinal of York was even more despicable than her husband.

Charles's health was declining daily, but Charlotte's arrival brought new vigor to him. People had grown tired and bored with him, so that he had not been invited to any dinners or balls in a long age. Now he began to send out announcements of his daughter's arrival with invitations to receptions at the Palazzo Guadagni in her honor. But he counted on Charlotte's presence to court from society a renewed interest in himself; he displayed little genuine concern for her welfare. The pair received "great civilities" for as long as it took the citizens of Florence to satisfy their curiosity about the new Duchess of Albany.

Charles so craved adulation, respect, and homage that he attempted to use what he perceived as an advantage to ask leave to canopy his two theater boxes in a Cloth of State embroidered with the royal coat of arms. His request was denied by the Grand Duke of Tuscany, although he was allowed to ornament the inside of the boxes any way he chose. "One is hung with red damask," described Mann, "and another of yellow, with velvet cushions to each, laced with gold, but of the common size with those of all the other boxes. All the ladies and gentlemen of the country leave tickets of their visits at her door, which she is to return." This was written in October 1784. Charles always celebrated November 30, St. Andrew's Day, by giving a grand dinner. This year, he decided Charlotte should be invested with the Order of St. Andrew at a special ceremony. Mann described the event to England's secretary of state:

> He performed the mock ceremony of investing his daughter with the order of St. Andrew, though she had worn that badge some days before. For that purpose he was seated in a chair with a sword in his hand, she kneeling before him, with which he touched her shoulder declaring her to be a Knight of that Order. She then rose and made her obeisance of thanks and went round to the company, repeatedly saying *Je suis Chevalier*; at the same time favours made

up to represent a thistle were distributed to the company, who wore them for that day.

Your Lordship will perceive by mentioning the above trifling circumstances that nothing of a serious nature is passing here worthy of your notice, though they serve to show how weak the understanding of the Pretender is grown.

This was one of Sir Horace Mann's last reports on Prince Charles; the old diplomat preceded his quarry in death by one year. If he meant to convey that Charlotte was foolishly flattered and pleased by the attentions lavished upon her, her letters to her mother tell a different story. Unfortunately, none exist that describe this particular St. Andrew's Day gathering, but many survive that tell of her tiredness and exhaustion from having to perform scrivener tasks for her father. She was hoping (in vain) that he would make her presents of money and/or jewels, but Charles was as close-fisted as ever. There was obviously no love between father and daughter at this time, and that was no more and no less than he deserved. Charlotte has been criticized by historians for her self-seeking behavior toward her father, but her reason for dying to get money from him was mainly her desire to relieve the abject penury in which the aging Countess Alberstroff was living.

Charlotte Stuart's preoccupation with providing for her mother's welfare may have been heightened by a sense of her own mortality. She died less than two years after Charles, probably of cancer. The "obstruction in the liver" that Principal Gordon and Clementina Walkinshaw had many years before said Charlotte was suffering from was a genuine complaint; earlier mention of it had not been a ploy to win sympathy from Charles. Soon after her arrival in Florence, the growth inside Charlotte's body began to increase and protrude, causing her to send for additional fabric from Paris to adjust the dresses she had brought to Italy. She complained little to her mother except of not being able to breathe deeply or lie on her side without pain; but she did ask Clementina to send an "*opiate pour les dents*" and some tobacco.

If the opiate was for a toothache, the tobacco could also have been, for sailors were accustomed to so using it. It also may have been for her father. His condition was deteriorating badly, and hers went into a steep decline from the moment she arrived in Italy. Alcoholism was an obvious reason for Charles's dysfunction, but he also had bad dietary habits; and this regimen also affected his daughter. A different diet might have saved him from the dreadful ulcers all over his body. Charlotte also developed ulcers on her ankles and feet. Household accounts for this period still exist and show that their food supplies consisted of fish, poultry, meats, dairy products such as eggs and cheese, and enormous quantities of Cyprus wine. But never was the purchase of fruits or vegetables recorded, not even during the summer months, when these were in abundance. It is hard to resist the conclusion that extreme malnutrition, coupled with an addiction to the "nasty bottle," shortened Charles's life by at least a decade.

Letters from the last years of his life are very rare. Like his legs, which were so grossly swollen that they "resembled columns," his arms and hands also became useless. He relied on his daughter to pen all correspondence. Charlotte had virtually no help in tending her father, who was now almost daily subject to fainting fits and seizures. She struggled to cope with his needs, at the same time running the household and acting as secretary. Lord Caryll had left for Boulogne a long time before, having tired of earning "dogs' wages" for all his years of trouble and for being treated, as he said, "like a common cur." There were servants at the Guadagni, of course, and a spineless, shadowy man by the name of John Stuart who had been on the fringes of the family since the early forties if not before. But there was nobody of substance to head the household. It is hardly surprising that resentment toward Henry crept into Charlotte's letters to her mother; he allowed her to shoulder the awesome responsibility. Yet when the end came for his brother, the Cardinal would be in a position to turn Charlotte away penniless if he chose. Indications were that he might.

Despite Charlotte's own physical discomfort and the pain of being separated from her loved ones, she grew sympathetic and even protective toward her father.

One evening Charles was visited by an Englishman named Mr. Greathead. The conversation turned to the events of 1745 and 1746, which evoked dark memories of the bloody fate of Jacobites butchered at Kennington Common and Tower Hill. While those executions were carried out, the Prince had nightly attended the opera in Paris and people had said he did not care. But the killing of humans had always shocked and revolted him, and he spent the rest of his life vainly trying to blot out memories and denying any responsibility for the misery he had brought upon Scotland.

On this evening Charles, who was alone with Mr. Greathead,

began to talk of the Highlanders. His eyes suddenly filled with tears. He choked on his words as he struggled to control his emotions; then he collapsed onto the floor in the grip of a seizure. Hearing the commotion, Charlotte rushed in from an adjoining chamber. "Oh Sir, what is this?" she cried to Mr. Greathead. "You must have been speaking to my father about Scotland and the Highlanders. No one dares to mention those subjects in his presence!"

The "iron man" survived the fit, but Charlotte knew his end was near, and her overriding concern was now to reconcile her father and uncle as soon as possible. She needed Henry's help with her burden, but she also desired to win the favor of the man who would control the finances when Charles died. Her motives were not entirely self-serving, however. (But who could blame her if they had been?)

We do not know what Charles talked about during the nights when he was unable to sleep; rambling words fell from his lips. His defenses were down; he had none left. During the long hours of bedside vigil, his daughter seemed to come to a deeper understanding of why her father was so tormented. It was not Scotland; his torment, like his drinking, had begun long before that. Charlotte ceased to refer to her father in derogatory terms when writing to Clementina, and she was also unwilling to discuss the details of his illness. It was as if she wanted to preserve his privacy and what dignity he had in the last days. These last days, she felt, should be spent at the Palazzo Muti in Rome.

Charlotte learned that the Cardinal of York was to visit Perugia at the end of October 1785 on official church business. Since Perugia is midway between Rome and Florence, she decided to journey there publicly as the Duchess of Albany and present her calling card at the Cardinal's lodgings to force him into meeting with her.

Henry could hardly refuse to receive his own niece when all Perugia knew that both Stuarts were in the same city. So he reluctantly consented to a meeting, although he was extremely annoyed at being manipulated in this manner. We do not know what transpired between Henry and Charlotte, except that he appeared to be captivated by her simple charm. He could plainly see that, unlike Louise, she earnestly cared about her father's welfare. The Cardinal benevolently consented to recognize the Duchess of Albany as his legitimate niece, and he decided that the time had now come to be reconciled with his brother. He also agreed to assist Charlotte in bringing the sick man back to Rome.

It was no easy matter to persuade the truculent old Count of Albany to return to the city that had refused to honor him the way it had honored his father. But winter was upon them, and Charlotte persuaded her father that the milder temperatures of Rome would be far better for his health. She also placated him with promises that they would return to Florence in the spring. But he never saw Florence again.

They arrived at the Palazzo Muti in Rome during the first week of December 1785, having been met by Henry at Viterbo. Charlotte almost worked herself to the bone catering to her demanding father's nursing needs and his constant desire to be entertained. At the dinners and concerts she arranged at the Muti, Charles lolled lazily back on cushions fondling a lapdog. His affection for the dog calls to mind his beloved Stellina, who had died giving birth to a second litter a year after he left Italy as a young man. His relationship with Stellina all those many years ago was the only one of record in which he exhibited genuine affection; now this lapdog took her place. His daughter was dying before his eyes, but he did not notice. He had always had ambivalent feelings toward her, for it was never a wish of his to sire children. To him she was only someone who would fetch and carry.

Charlotte sorely missed her mother. She slavishly catered to Charles's every whim in the fruitless hope that he could be persuaded to allow Clementina to come to Rome. Her dispirited letters became filled with details about stomach pains and thoughts that "her little flowers" would grow and she would never see them again. She feared that Rohan would seek solace with someone else; the thought of never seeing her children again dragged Charlotte down. All she could do was bide her time with the man who was taking a long time to die.

In the summers of 1786 and 1787, Charles saw the Palazzo Savelli again. The Stuart estate at Albano had been the scene of his early hunting. On that terrain Father Vinceguerra had trained and hardened the young Prince's body; and there he had practiced the marksmanship for which he was justly renowned.

Soon after his return from Albano in the autumn of 1787, Charles lapsed into semiconsciousness and stayed that way for several weeks. He was barely aware of the passing of his sixty-seventh birthday on December 31. A week later he suffered a stroke from which he never recovered. Lord Hervey, who had replaced the late Sir Horace Mann as Britain's envoy in Italy, sent an account to the secretary of state in England:

> I think it also my duty to acquaint Your Lordship that some days ago the Pretender was seized with a paralytic stroke, which deprived him of the use of one half of the body and he has continued dangerously ill ever since, notwithstanding the application of eleven blisters. His death is expected every moment, and I am assured he cannot outlive the night. His brother the Cardinal applied strongly to the Pope for leave to inter his remains in the Church of St. Peter's with every Regal dignity but was refused by him, saying he had never been acknowledged a Sovereign and therefore could not have the honours. He will be interred at Frascati where the Cardinal has a villa. His natural daughter who is here at present, will at her father's death receive an income of near three thousand pounds sterling a year; partly granted by the Court of France, partly by this government, and partly arising from his personal property left to her. I mention this circumstance because it has been insinuated here, with some pains, that she would be left in a distressed situation.

This was written on January 29, 1788. Indeed, Bonnie Prince Charlie just barely outlived the night. Life slipped away from him at nine o'clock on the morning of January 30. Official records give the date of his death as January 31 because Henry wished to avoid any superstitious association with their great-grandfather Charles I's execution at Whitehall on January 30 almost a century and a half before.

Henry's meticulous diary (which still exists) provides no details of his brother's last days or hours. The pages chronicling that period were torn away by someone and have never come to light. Charlotte's letter to Clementina announcing the death of her father was very brief. It mentioned only the date and time. Henry's friend Hercules Consalvi, who later become chief minister to Pope Pius VII, was also on the scene. His silence on the matter speaks louder than words. All his life Consalvi had been deeply dedicated to medicine, and his memoirs give long, drawn-out details about the illnesses of friends, relatives, and prominent citizens. But he wrote nothing about Bonnie Prince Charlie's passing, although he devoted considerable attention to Charlotte's illness and death later on. It was as if everyone had been waiting too long for the end; the man of iron had outstayed his welcome. None of them was really sorry to see him go.

Unlike his father and mother, whose final resting place was St. Peter's Church in Rome, Charles was buried at his brother's Cathedral in Frascati. Henry conducted the funeral service of King Charles III of England, France, Ireland, and Scotland and then later struck a medal announcing himself as Henry IX, King of Great Britain, France, and Ireland, Defender of the Faith, Cardinal Bishop of Frascati. On the reverse side were the Latin words *Non desideriis hominum, sed voluntate Dei*—"Not by the desire of men but by the will of God."

Charlotte never saw her children again. Death claimed her in November 1789, only twenty-two months after her father. She was staying at Bologna with her friend the Marchesa Giula Lambertini-Bovio when the end came. By her own request she was buried at Bologna in the Church of San Biagio, which was unfortunately destroyed in World War II. We do not know what happened to the daughters, Algae and Marie, except that they were cared for by Clementina Walkinshaw until her death in Switzerland in 1802, where she was living in very reduced circumstances.

In her will Charlotte left her mother a lump sum of 50,000 livres, and 15,000 livres were also to be paid annually to provide for Clementina and her grandchildren. But it was two years before Henry would allow the money to be released. Even then, Clementina was required to sign a "quittance" document in settlement of the terms of her daughter's will stating "that no other claim can be made in my name by any heir whatsoever."

It is assumed that Algae and Marie were later placed in the care of Thomas Coutts, the London banker who had distant ties of blood and marriage to the Walkinshaws and an old line of the Stuarts. The girls chose anonymity for themselves and were most likely absorbed into the mainstream of English society by marriage. Their younger brother, Charles Edward, however, did not choose anonymity. He came to England and Scotland in his midtwenties after travels through Germany, Austria, Russia, India, America, and the West Indies. Calling himself Count Roehenstart (from Rohan and Stuart), he related impossible stories about his background and kept changing the salient points of his history, so not many believed that he was really the grandson of Prince Charles Edward Stuart. He told a friend that he had been captured by Turkish pirates in the Gulf of Mexico and taken to the Barbary Coast, whence he escaped to England. This sounds like an adventure worthy of the grandson of Bonnie Prince Charlie, but he told so many lies about his past, including the date and place of birth, that very few took Count Roehenstart seriously at all.

However, the late American historian Professor George Sherburn established thirty years ago that Roehenstart was indeed who he said he was. He never made any pretentious claims to rulership, but he revealed his identity because he sought a continuance of the pension that had been paid by the British government to Henry Stuart until his death in July 1807. Unsuccessful in that endeavor, Roehenstart twice married older women for money and outlived them both without having fathered any children.

He came to his end in Scotland on October 28, 1854. He was traveling near Stirling Castle by stagecoach when the vehicle overturned and he suffered fatal injuries. He was carried to the cottage of an old woman, and in a sad and lonely final gesture he gave her some money so that she would buy a black mourning ribbon to wear for him. He was buried in nearby Dunkeld Cathedral, where the inscription on his tombstone lists his age as seventy-three. But if he had been born in 1784, as all accounts state, he would have been seventy at the time of his death.

Henry was the longest-lived Stuart of all. He became known as the Cardinal King after Charles's death, but he quickly dropped his pretentions—not that they were suffered by his fellow ecclesiastics anyway—when bulletins from France brought one shattering report after another that the populace was violently tearing away the corrupt privilege that had suffocated their nation's growth for so long. When Henry received news of the executions of Louis XVI and Marie Antoinette in 1793, he conducted a solemn requiem Mass in their honor at the Cathedral of Frascati. Three years later Napoleon Buonaparte's French revolutionary army occupied the Papal States. In 1798, they menaced the gates of Rome, bent on exterminating Pope Pius VI, who represented yet another symbol of corrupt authority.

Six years before, in 1792, the Pope had deeply offended Henry by formally recognizing King George III and receiving his envoy, Sir John Coxe-Hippisley, in Rome. But that offense was swept aside when, leaving all their valuable treasures behind, Henry, the Pope, and all other prominent ecclesiastics fled southward to Naples and then to Sicily, where they hired a Greek merchant ship to take them to Venice. There they were granted protection by the Austrians. Pope Pius VI expired a broken man in August 1799.

In due course, Napoleon's marshals and generals (among them the son of Neil MacEachain of South Uist) proclaimed the Roman Republic. Many palazzos, including Henry's, were looted by French soldiers, who auctioned all the valuables they could not carry off. A French directive declared that there would never be another Pope or papal election, but the destitute Henry worked tirelessly in Venice to organize the secret conclave that elected Cardinal Chiaramonti as Pope Pius VII in November 1799. A few weeks later came the year 1800.

It was a new era, and it was time for old men like seventy-five-year-old Henry to reflect on their past and on what the future might bring. Things looked very bleak for the Cardinal King. He had lost almost everything to Buonaparte's soldiers, and he could barely buy himself a dinner. He had had the presence of mind, however, to hang on to the family jewels. One of them was the lustrous Sobieski sapphire (which is now set in the crown of Queen Elizabeth II).

Since the current keeper of the crown jewels can shed no light on how this gem was acquired, we must suppose that Henry parted with it and others in return for a pension from the British government, which he was receiving at the time of his death at Frascati in 1807 at the age of eighty-two. He had returned to Italy when the political situation grew calmer; in the meantime he had secured the offices of Cardinal Borgia to act as a middle-man in liquidating his jewels, which now only the English government could afford to purchase. Borgia contacted Sir John Coxe-Hippisley, saying that it was greatly afflicting for him "to see so great a personage, the last descendant of his Royal House, reduced to such distressed circumstances, having been barbarously stripped by the French of all his property."

In February 1800, a sympathetic article in *The Times* of London described the plight of Cardinal York, who had been driven from his residence, "his house sacked, his property confiscated, and [he] constrained to seek his personal safety in flight, upon the seas, under every aggravated circumstance that could affect his health and fortunes." It was tear-jerking material. No voices were raised against George III's decision to award Henry an annual pension of 5,000 pounds sterling. This may have been charity, but we can be reasonably sure that the jewels Henry Stuart parted with were of value far in excess of the 35,000 pounds paid him for the remaining seven years of his life. But perhaps the arrangement was poetic justice. Bonnie Prince Charlie's actions in his heyday had cost the British government far more than they could possibly recoup from the jewels they received from Henry.

The "Cardinal King" was financially responsible for the present memorial to the Stuarts in Rome. He commissioned the sculptor Canova to create the graceful monument depicting James and his sons that now stands in St. Peter's Church. The present Stuart heirs are traced through Henrietta Stuart, a daughter of Charles I who married Philip, Duc d'Orléans, the younger brother of Louis XIV. Their daughter married Victor Amadeus of Sardinia, and from that line we come to the present Albert of Bavaria.

Countless royal outcasts like Charles were produced by the centuries-old system of royal intermarriage. Too few thrones existed to satisfy the number of hopeful princelings, pitting royal families against each other in disputes frequently settled with the blood of their less privileged countrymen. By the middle of the eighteenth century, most of the displaced princes had come to terms with their circumstances, as James Stuart had been on the verge of doing before his son went to Scotland.

Out of all the displaced royalty in Europe, why did Charles alone persist with impossible claims? Part of the answer is in the manner King James II lost his throne; this was considered by his son and many powerful figures of the period to be a gross violation of the law. It was the illegality of the maneuver—and the belief that fellow monarchs would assist him in overturning a precedent that might one day befall them all unless they took a stand—that kept James fighting for so long. By the time he realized that it was in no monarch's interest to uphold his claims, Charles was already full of expectations—and his unyielding personality would never take no for an answer. For precisely this same trait English politicians had removed his grandfather. The Prince often wailed about the injustice that had been inflicted upon him; yet when his own daughter pleaded for his recognition, he heartlessly ignored her until it suited his purpose to send for her.

The loss of life and ruined fortunes among the Scots were never compensated for. They had made a mistake in trusting Bonnie Prince Charlie and paid dearly for it. But there were many success stories among the Scottish exiles who flocked to Canada and America to rebuild their lives. There they were immediately faced with a new stand to take against the authority of George III.

As history records, they and other inhabitants of the New

World broke away from the governmental system headed by a monarch and became "we the people." George III, who was suffering from the blood disease porphyria, did not suffer the fate of the French monarchy because Parliament had curbed the power of the Crown long ago, and he was no threat to their supremacy. Actually, the New World rebels were not fighting George as much as they were fighting their older brothers in Europe, who by law claimed superiority and precedence and expected their younger siblings to toil for their enrichment. It was one more system of privilege that had to be broken down—as eventually it was. If the Stuarts had been allowed to return to rule, they could have set that process back many years.

Bibliography and Notes

A wealth of material has been published on the last Stuarts, much of it in the last century and some in the eighteenth century. The material is predominantly concerned with events in Scotland. I have made use of those sources, and I have also included a list of modern publications that contain narratives of the Prince's contemporaries and some of his letters.

Notes on the Stuart Papers appear at the end of the bibliography for each chapter. In instances where too many documents can be listed by volume and folio number, I cite only volume numbers where the material can be found. (There are 547 volumes each, comprising an average of 130 documents, although some contain 200.) In other instances where sources need to be more precisely identified, I cite both volume and folio number. Volume numbers do not necessarily denote the year in which a document was written, since many papers were bound out of date order.

Abbreviations
HMC—Historical Manuscripts Commission (Great Britain)
MAE—Ministère des Affaires Étrangères, quai d'Orsay, Paris
PRO—Public Record Office, London

Chapter I: The Warming-Pan Baby

Berwick, James FitzJames, duc de. *Mémoires*, 2 vols. (Paris, 1778).
Bolingbroke, Henry St. John, Viscount. *A Letter to Sir William Windham*. (London: Carey & Hart, 1841).
Brown, Beatrice Curtis. *The Letters of Queen Anne*. (London, 1935).

Clarke, J.S., ed. *Life of James II.* 2 vols. (London, 1816).

Dangeau, Philippe de Courcillon, marquis de. *Journal, 1684–1720.* (Paris: Firmin Didot, 1704).

Haile, Martin. *James Francis Edward, the Old Chevalier.* (London, 1907).

HMC. Calendar of Stuart Papers, 9th and 10th Reports.

Mahon, Philip Henry Stanhope, Lord. *History of England from the Peace of Utrecht to the Peace of Aix-la-Chapelle.* (London, 1836).

Macaulay, Thomas Babington. *History of England, 1849–61.*

Miller, Peggy. *James Edward Stuart.* (London, 1971).

Oman, Carola. *Mary of Modena.* (London, 1971).

Petrie, Sir Charles. *The Jacobite Movement: The First Phase.* (London, 1948).

Petrie, Sir Charles. *The Marshal Duke of Berwick.* (London, 1953).

Stuart MSS: Vols. 5–45; James's letter to Queen Anne, vol. 132/fo. 33; judgment of French bishops that it would be heresy for James to maintain Church of England, vol. 275/fo. 5.

Chapter II: Beyond the Alps

Doran, J. *Mann and Manners at Florence 1740–86.* (1876).

Heeckeren, Emile de, ed. *Correspondance de Benoît XIV.* 2 vols. (Paris, 1912).

Lang, Andrew. *Prince Charles Edward.* (London, 1900); reprinted by AMS Press of New York, 1967.

Lewis, Lesley. *Connoisseurs and Secret Agents.* (London, 1961).

Lind, James. *Treatise on Scurvy.* Reprint of his 1753 edition, edited by C.P. Stewart and Douglas Guthrie. (Edinburgh University Press, 1953).

Miller, Peggy. *A Wife for the Pretender.* (London, 1965).

Tayler, Henrietta. *The Jacobite Court at Rome in 1719.* (Edinburgh: Scottish History Society, 1938).

Stuart MSS: Life in Muti Palace and Charles's early childhood, vols. 60–88; breakdown of marriage and Clementina's health, vols. 89–125; Charles as a youth, vols. 129–99; Hamilton, "selling your Bible . . .," vol. 256/fo. 73. Financial information: misc. vol. 39, vols. 246–75; James's pension, vol. 249/fo. 24.

Chapter III: The Twilight of Princes
Anderson, M.S. *18th Century Europe 1713–1789*. (Oxford University Press, 1966).
Elcho, David, Lord. Unpublished *Journal*.
HMC. 10th Report, Lord Braye's Manuscripts.
Murray, John of Broughton. *Memorials*. Robert Fitzroy Bell, ed., (Edinburgh, Scottish History Society, 1898).
Sareil, Jean. *Les Tencin*. (Geneva: Librairie Droz, 1969).
Tencin, Pierre Guérin de. *Cardinal Tencin's Plan, Presented to the French King, for Settling the Pretender's Family upon the British Throne and Compleating the Long-concerted Scheme of Universal Monarchy in the House of Bourbon.* Pamphlet, (London: M. Cooper, 1745). The only known copy exists in the MacBean Collection, Aberdeen University Library.
Stuart MSS: Vols. 234–54; "Great Britain is sufficient unto herself," vol. 280/fo. 17; "As long as Cardinal Fleury governs. . .," vol. 246/fo. 31; Balhaldy's memo about Marischal having no powers, vol. 254/fo. 151B; James's memo forbidding Highlanders to emigrate to New World and Commissions for Lords Lieutenants, etc., Misc. Box 1/fo. 185, box 2/fo. 54, misc. vol. 20/fos. 238–54; Balhaldy's letter about deceiving French Court, vol. 247/fo. 80; Dunbar's report on Henry's schedule, vol. 246/fo. 139.

Chapter IV: Charles Goes to Paris
Casanova, Giacoma. *History of My Life*. vol. 7. (New York, 1966).
Ducros, Louis. *French Society in the Eighteenth Century*. (New York, 1927).
MAE. *Memories et Documents Angleterre*, 76–80, unpublished correspondence between Louis XV and Philip V.
Perkins, James Breck. *France Under Louis XV*. (1897).
PRO. State Papers 98, for letters of Sir Horace Mann.
PRO. British Admiralty Records, 1743–44.
Voltaire, François Marie Arouet. *The Complete Works of Voltaire*. 93 Correspondence IX, 1743—46. (Geneva, Institut et Musée Voltaire, 1970).
Walpole, Horace. *Correspondence with Sir Horace Mann*. W.S. Lewis, Warren Hunting Smith, and George L. Lam, eds. (Yale University Press, 1954).

Wilkinson, Spenser. *Defence of Piedmont*. (Oxford, 1927).
Stuart MSS: Vols. 251–55; visit of Lord Wemyss, vol. 251/fo. 124;
Balhaldy's statements concerning the Prince's journey to
France, vol. 254/fos. 112, 123, 124, 125, and 151, vol. 279/fo.
126, and box 1/fo. 188; James's letter to Louis, vol. 254/fo.
108; J. Stuart's damaged letter, vol. 254/fo. 113

Chapter V: The Expectant Heir
Broglie, Albert, duc de. *Frédéric II et Louis XV*. (Paris, 1885).
Colin, J. *Louis XV et Les Jacobites*. (Paris: Librairie Militaire R.
Chapelot, 1901).
Elcho, David, Lord. *A Short Account of the Affairs of Scotland*.
The Hon. Evan Charteris, ed. (Edinburgh, 1907).
Engel, Claire E. *Knights of Malta*. (New York, 1963).
Lacour-Gayet, Georges. *La Marine Militaire Sous Louis XV*.
(Paris, 1902).
Lang, Andrew. *Pickle the Spy*. (London, 1897). Reprinted by
AMS Press of New York, 1970.
Luynes, Albert, Duc de. *Mémoires sur la cour de Louis XV*.
(Paris: Didot, 1861).
Richmond, H.W. *The Navy in the War of 1739–48*. (Cambridge,
1920).
Sareil, op. cit.
Vulliamy, C.E. *Voltaire*. (Kennikat Press, 1970).
White, Jon Manchip. *Marshal of France; The Life and Times of
Maurice de Saxe*. (Rand McNally & Co., 1962).
Stuart MSS; Vols. 256–65; "ye melancholy prospect," vol. 258/
fo. 139; Marischal to James complaining about Ormonde's
treatment, vol. 259/fo. 42; Marischal's letters to Charles, vol.
256/fos. 74, 92, 94, 97, 126, and 134. James's warning about
"wine and play," vol. 256/fo. 201; letters about Charles
frequenting *ginguettes*, vol. 258/fos. 16, 17; "Your going into
France without any authentick invitation," vol. 258/fo. 117;
"To be particularly inform'd," misc. box 1/fo. 199; "The
Princes resolution of going to Scotland," vol. 265/fo. 72;
letters to Scottish chiefs, misc. box 1/fo. 200; petition of Sir
Hector Maclean, vol. 260/fo. 88; "I am going in to or three
days," vol. 262/fo. 1.

Chapter VI: The Road to the Isles

Blaikie, Walter Biggar. *Itinerary of Prince Charles Edward Stuart.* (Edinburgh: Scottish History Society, 1897).

Blaikie, Walter Biggar, ed. *Origins of the Forty-Five.* (Edinburgh: Scottish History Society, 1916).

Browne, James. *A History of the Highlands and of the Highland Clans.* 4 vols. (Glasgow, 1838).

Chambers, Robert. *History of the Rebellion In Scotland in 1745, 1746.* 2 vols. New edition. (1828).

Chambers, Robert. *Jacobite Memoirs of the Rebellion of 1745.* (1834). Containing Lord George Murray's "Marches of the Highland Army" and narratives of Aeneas MacDonald and Duncan Cameron.

Forbes, the Rev. Robert. *The Lyon in Mourning.* Henry Paton, ed. 3 vols. (Edinburgh: Scottish History Society, 1895–96).

Tayler, Alistair and Henrietta Tayler. *1745 and After.* (London, 1938). Contains O'Sullivan's Narrative.

Tayler, Henrietta. *A Jacobite Miscellany.* (Roxburghe Club, 1948). Contains Sir John MacDonald's narrative and portions of Lord Elcho's *Journal.*

A Full and True Collection of All the Proclamations and Orders published by the Authority of Charles, Prince of Wales. 2 vols. (Glasgow, 1745–46).

Stuart MSS: Vols. 265 and 266; the Prince's letters from Navarre in June 1745, vol. 265/fos. 129, 135; seasickness at Belle Île, vol. 266/fo. 102.

Chapter VII: The Battle of Prestonpans

Cadell, General Sir Robert. *Sir John Cope and the Rebellion of 1745.* (Edinburgh, 1898).

Carlyle, Alexander. *Autobiography of the Reverend Dr. Alexander Carlyle Containing the Memorials of the Men and Events of his Time.* (Edinburgh, 1861).

Crichton, Patrick. *Woodhousele Manuscripts. A Narrative of Events in Edinburgh and District During the Jacobite Occupation, September to November 1745.* (Edinburgh, 1907).

Doddridge, Dr. Philip. *Some Remarkable Passages in the Life of the Honourable Col. James Gardiner.* (Edinburgh, 1747).

Elcho, David, Lord. *Journal* and *Affairs of Scotland.*

Gray, M., ed. *Memoirs of the Life of Sir John Clerk of Penicuick.*
(Edinburgh: Scottish History Society, 1892).

Home, John. *The History of the Rebellion in the Year 1745.*
(London, 1802).

Johnstone, Chevalier de. *Memoirs of the Rebellion in 1745 and
1746.* (1821).

Maxwell, James of Kirkconnell. *Narrative of Charles Prince of
Wales' Expedition to Scotland in the Year 1745.* (Maitland
Club, 1841).

Murray, John of Broughton, op. cit.

Scott, Sir Walter. *Tales of a Grandfather,* 1827–29.

Tayler, Alistair and Henrietta, op. cit.

*The Report of the Proceeding and Opinions of the Board of
Officers in the Examination into the Conduct, Behaviour
and Proceedings of Lieut-General Sir John Cope.* (London,
1749).

Stuart MSS: Vol. 267.

Chapter VIII: To England and Back Again

Atholl, John, 7th Duke of. *Chronicles of the Atholl and
Tullibardine Families.* (1908).

Duke, Winifred. *Lord George Murray and the Forty-Five.* (1927).

Elcho, David, Lord, op. cit.

Forbes, Duncan, ed. *The Culloden Papers.* (1815).

HMC.Vol. 8, MSS. of the Hon. Frederick Lindley Wood, M.L.S.
Clements, and S. Philip Unwin.

Jarvis, Rupert C. *Collected Papers on the Jacobite Risings.* vol. 1,
(University of Manchester Press, 1971).

Locke, Miriam Austin. *Henry Fielding the True Patriot, and the
History of our Own Times.* (University of Alabama Press,
1964).

Mounsey, George G. *Authentic Account of the Occupation of
Carlisle in 1745.* (1846).

Thomson, K.B. *Memoirs of the Jacobites.* (London, 1846).

Tomasson, Katherine. *The Jacobite General.* (London, 1958).

Stuart MSS: Vol. 267–71; Edgar's remarks on Walsh's title, vol.
269/fo. 181; "I would not make haste to wear them," vol.
267/fo. 182.

Chapters IX and X: Master of His Own House; Culloden

Blaikie. *Itinerary*, for letters between the Prince and Lord George Murray.

Charteris, the Hon. Evan. *William Augustus, Duke of Cumberland, His Early Life and Times.* (1913).

Cunningham, Audrey. *The Loyal Clans.* (Cambridge University Press, 1932).

Forbes, op. cit.

Johnstone, op. cit.

Mackenzie, Compton. *Prince Charlie and His Ladies.* (New York, 1935).

Maxwell, op. cit.

Murray, op. cit.

Prebble, John. *Culloden.* (1961).

Seton, Sir Bruce, and J.G. Arnot, eds. *The Prisoners of the '45.* (Scottish History Society, 1938–39).

Tayler and Tayler, op cit. (O'Sullivan's narrative).

Terry, Charles Sanford. *The Forty-Five.* (London, 1900).

Tomasson, op. cit.

Tomasson, Katherine, and Francis Buist. *Battles of the '45.* (1962).

Stuart MSS: Vol. 271–73; Sheridan's letter to O'Brien of December 31, vol. 271/fo. 121; Lord George Murray's letter dated April 17, 1746, vol. 273/fo. 96 (a copy of this also exists at Blair Castle); Charles to Sheridan, April 23, and Address to the Chiefs, vol. 273/fos. 116 and 117.

Chapter XI: Over the Sea to Skye

Albemarle, William Anne Keppel, 2nd Earl of. *The Albemarle Papers.* 2 vols. Charles Sanford Terry, ed. (New Spalding Club, 1902).

Blaikie, op. cit., for Neil MacEachain's account.

Boswell, James. *Journal of a Tour to the Hebrides with Samuel Johnson.* Frederick A. Pottle and Charles H. Bennett, eds. (New York, 1936).

Cameron, Dr. Archibald. *Two Accounts of the Escape of Prince Charles Edward.* H. Tayler, ed. (Oxford University Press, 1951).

Forbes. *Lyon*, vols. 1 and 2 for various accounts, including those of Felix O'Neill, Donald MacLeod of Gualtergill, and Flora MacDonald.

Gibson, John S. *Ships of the '45.* (London, 1967).

Hamilton, Marion. *The Loch Arkaig Treasure.* (Edinburgh: Scottish History Society, Miscellany, 1941).

Macphail, J.R.N., ed. *Letters of Anne Grant.* (Edinburgh: Scottish History Society, 1896).

PRO. State Papers, Domestic 87, Examination of Aeneas MacDonald, September 17, 1746.

PRO. State Papers, Scotland 54:32 and 33, Statements made by Flora MacDonald.

Vining, Elizabeth Gray. *Flora MacDonald: Her Life in the Highlands and America.* (London, 1967).

Stuart MSS: Vol. 274.

Chapter XII: The Treaty of Aix-la-Chapelle

Argenson, René, Marquis de. *Journal et Mémoires.* E.J.B. Rathery, ed. (Paris, 1859).

Jenkinson, Charles. *A Collection of All the Treaties of Peace, Alliance, and Commerce, Between Great Britain and Other Powers.* vol. 2. (London, 1885).

King, Dr. W. *Political and Literary Anecdotes of His Own Times.* (London, 1819).

Lang, Andrew. *Pickle the Spy.*

Lang, Andrew. *Companions of Pickle.* (London, 1898).

Lockhart, George of Carnwath. *The Lockhart Papers.* 2 vols. (London, 1817).

Luynes, op. cit.

Mackenzie, op. cit.

Polnay, Peter de. *Death of a Legend.* (1952).

Stuart MSS: Vols. 275–409; Henry's letter of October 10, 1746, vol. 277/fo. 129; Charles to Louis, October 22, 1746, vol. 278/fo. 3; "With three thousand regular soldiers," vol. 278/fo. 153; Charles about Lord George Murray's journey to Rome in 1747, vol. 282/fo. 128.

Chapters XIII and XIV: The Queen of Hearts; Epilogue

Bonstetten, Charles Victor de. *Souvenirs.* (1831).

Consalvi, Hercules. *Mémoires.* J. Crétineau-Joly, ed. (Paris, 1866).

Crosland, Margaret. *Louise of Stolberg.* (1962).

Fothergill, Brian. *The Cardinal King.* (London, 1958).

Howells, William D., ed. *Life of Vittorio Alfieri.* (Boston, 1877).

Lee, Vernon. *The Countess of Albany.* (London, 1909).

Mahon, Philip Henry Stanhope, Lord, ed. *The Decline of the Last Stuarts; Extracts from the Despatches of British Envoys to the Secretary of State.* (London: Roxburghe Club, 1843).

Nobili-Vitteleschi, Marchesa. *A Court in Exile.* 2 vols. (London, 1903).

Sherburn, George. *Roehenstart, A Late Stuart Pretender.* (1960).

Sieveking, Isabel Giberne. *Memoir of Sir Horace Mann.* (London, 1912).

Skeet, F.A.J. *The Life and Letters of H.R.H. Charlotte Stuart, Duchess of Albany.* (London, 1932).

Tayler, Henrietta. *Prince Charlie's Daughter.* (London, 1950).

Walpole, Horace. *Letters to the Countess of Ossory.* (London, 1903).

Walpole, Horace. *The Letters of Horace Walpole.* Paget Toynbee, ed. vol. 9. (Oxford, 1904).

Stuart MSS: Vols. 480–540.

Index

A

Act of Settlement, 12
Albermarle, William Keppel, 2nd
  Earl of, 217, 234, 244, 247
Alberoni, Cardinal, 55
Albert of Bavaria, 315
Alembert, Jean d', 43
Alfieri, Count Vittorio, 290–97,
  299–301, 303
Amelot, M., 82, 85, 98; and
  French plot to use Jacobites, 88,
  90, 94; as scapegoat in French
  government, 62–63, 66–68,
  71–72
Ancrum, Lord, 208
Anderson of Whitburgh, Robert,
  146–49
Anne, Queen of England, 3–4,
  9–13, 31
Aquaviva, Cardinal, 51, 55, 62,
  76, 78–79, 88
Argenson, Marquis d', 164, 184,
  306; and Cardinal Tencin, 62;
  and Stuart cause, 83, 85, 92,
  109–10, 112

Argyll, John Campbell, 2nd Duke
  of, 105, 160
Atholl, James Murray, 2nd Duke
  of, 114, 127–30

B

Balhaldy (William MacGregor or
  Drummond of Balhaldies),
  55–58, 158, 261n; with Charles
  in France, 90, 94, 102; and
  Charles's first journey to Paris,
  74, 79, 82; James's interests as
  represented by, 65–67, 70–75,
  84–85
Balmerino, Lord, 158, 206, 209;
  execution of, 245–46
Bandini, 75–76, 84
Batoni, Pompeo, 36, 94
Battle of Bannockburn, 147
Battle of Culloden, 179, 201,
  203–10, 217, 245, 257
Battle of Dettingen, 69–70
Battle of Falkirk, 188–90